Well-Being of Academic Staff in Rapidly Changing Higher Education

HIGHER EDUCATION RESEARCH AND POLICY

VOL. 11

The *Higher Education Research and Policy* (HERP) series is intended to present both research-oriented studies of higher education systems in transition, especially for comparative international perspectives. Higher education systems worldwide are currently under multi-layered pressures to transform their funding and governance structures in rapidly changing environments. The series intends to explore the impact of such wider social and economic processes as globalization, internationalization and Europeanization on higher education institutions, and is focused on such issues as the changing relationships between the university and the state, the changing academic profession, changes in public funding and university governance, the emergent public/private dynamics in higher education, the consequences of educational expansion, education as public/private goods, and the impact of changing demographics on national systems. Its audience includes higher education researchers and higher education policy analysts, university managers and administrators, as well as national policymakers and the staff of international organizations involved in higher education policymaking.

Gabriella Pusztai / Klára Kovács (eds.)

Well-Being of Academic Staff in Rapidly Changing Higher Education

A Focus on Central and Eastern Europe

PETER LANG
Berlin · Bruxelles · Chennai · Lausanne · New York · Oxford

Bibliographic Information published by the Deutsche Nationalbibliothek
The Deutsche Nationalbibliothek lists this publication in the Deutsche Nationalbibliografie; detailed bibliographic data is available online at http://dnb.d-nb.de.

Library of Congress Cataloging-in-Publication Data
Names: Pusztai, Gabriella editor | Kovács, Klára editor
Title: Well-being of academic staff in rapidly changing higher education : a focus on Central and Eastern Europe / Editors: Gabriella Pusztai & Klára Kovács.
Description: New York : Peter Lang, 2026. | Series: Higher education research and policy, 2193-7613 | Includes bibliographical references.
Identifiers: LCCN 2025019772 (print) | LCCN 2025019773 (ebook) | ISBN 9783631939680 hardback | ISBN 9783631939710 pdf | ISBN 9783631940273 epub
Subjects: LCSH: College teachers--Job satisfaction--Europe, Central | College teachers--Job satisfaction--Europe, Eastern | Well-being--Europe, Central | Well-being--Europe, Eastern | Educational change--Europe, Central | Educational change--Europe, Eastern | Higher education and state--Europe, Central | Higher education and state--Europe, Eastern | Universities and colleges--Europe, Central--Sociological aspects | Universities and colleges--Europe, Eastern--Sociological aspects
Classification: LCC LB2331.74.E8515 W45 2025 (print) | LCC LB2331.74.E8515 (ebook) | DDC 378.1/20943--dc23/eng/20250605
LC record available at https://lccn.loc.gov/2025019772
LC ebook record available at https://lccn.loc.gov/2025019773

This publication was financially supported by the University of Debrecen. This research was supported by the project 'Investigating the role of sport and physical activity for a healthy and safe society in the individual and social sustainability of work ability and quality of work and life (multidisciplinary research umbrella program)' and by the János Bolyai Research Scholarship of the Hungarian Academy of Sciences. Project no. TKP2021-EGA-20 has been implemented with the support provided by the Ministry of Culture and Innovation of Hungary from the National Research, Development and Innovation Fund, financed under the TKP2021-EGA funding scheme.

ISSN 2193-7613
ISBN 978-3-631-93968-0 (Print)
ISBN 978-3-631-93971-0 (ePDF)
ISBN 978-3-631-94027-3 (ePUB)
DOI 10.3726/b23030

Published by Peter Lang GmbH, Berlin (Germany)

info@peterlang.com

This publication has been peer reviewed.

www.peterlang.com

Reviewers
Irén Gábrity Molnár, Tamás Kozma and Silvia Matúšová

English Proofreader
Johnathan Dabney

Table of Contents

List of Figures ... 9

List of Tables ... 13

1. Challenges and Well-Being of Academics on the Eastern Border of the European Union. The Background and Rationale for the Book ... 17
   Gabriella Pusztai & Klára Kovács

PART I

Higher Education Systems as the Working Environment of Academic Staff in Central and Eastern Europe: Country Studies

2. Changes in Higher Education and Academic Staff in Hungary ... 45
   István Polónyi
3. Higher Education Academics in Slovakia ... 71
   Dana Hanesová, Lenka Rovňanová & Patrícia Zólyomiová
4. Academics in the Romanian Higher Education Context ... 105
   Imre Tódor
5. Characteristics of the Higher Education System and Academic Staff in Serbia ... 145
   Elvira Kovács & Zoltán Papp
6. Challenges in Higher Education and for Academics in Ukraine ... 177
   Katalin Pallay

PART II
Well-Being of Academics in Central and Eastern Europe

7. Performance Assessment: A New Dimension of Institutional Culture 207
Gabriella Pusztai, Zsuzsanna Demeter-Karászi & Katalin Pallay

8. (Inclusive) Teaching Practice and Well-Being Among Higher Education Academics in Central and Eastern Europe 231
Anett Hrabéczy & Zsófia Kocsis

9. International Mobility and Its Impediments for Academics 263
Ilona Dóra Dabney-Fekete, Ágnes Réka Dusa & Katalin Pallay

10. Research Productivity and Workplace Stress Among Academics 287
Klára Kovács, Marianna Moravecz & Gabriella Hideg

11. Work-Life Conflicts: A Dual Functionality Approach on Career of Academics 305
Emese Beáta Berei, Ágnes Engler & Klára Kovács

12. The Cultural Involvement Patterns of Academics 327
Edina Márkus, Judit Herczegh & Márta Miklósi

13. What Have We Learned About the Well-Being and Performance of Academics in EU Border Region Countries? 347
Klára Kovács & Ilona Dabney-Fekete

Notes on Contributors 361

Index 363

List of Figures

Figure 2.1 The population aged 18–22 and the number of students and academic staff in Hungarian higher education from the regime change until today 50
Figure 2.2 Gross enrollment rate of higher education in Hungary and the EU and OECD average 51
Figure 2.3 Graduates as a percentage of the population 25–34 years of age 51
Figure 2.4 Development of academic staff and student-academic staff ratio in Hungarian higher education, 1990–2022 53
Figure 2.5 Percentage of women among academic staff in Hungary 54
Figure 2.6 Changes in the number of academic posts in higher education 2000–2020 61
Figure 2.7 Average total monthly earnings of university graduates and academic staff by age (HUF/month) in 2016 63
Figure 2.8 Cumulative lifetime earnings based on 2016 data with a discount rate of 2 percent (million HUF) 64
Figure 3.1 Numbers of HEIs and their faculties in Slovakia 75
Figure 3.2 HE students as % of 20–24 years old in the Visegrád Four countries 76
Figure 3.3 Gross enrollment rate of HE students in Slovakia 77
Figure 3.4 The proportion of HE graduates aged 25–34 (%)—international comparison 78
Figure 3.5 HE students-academic staff ratio 2000–2017 (Slovakia, Hungary, Poland) 81

Figure 3.6 Comparison of the % ratio of enrolled HE students (within 18–34-years-old) in 2000 and in 2017 as well as the % change in the number of academics between 2000 and 2017 (Visegrád Four countries) 82
Figure 3.7 Proportion of females among Academics in HE in the EU/OECD and in Slovakia 85
Figure 3.8 Net flow ratio of internationally mobile students (inbound–outbound), both sexes (%) 92
Figure 3.9 Government expenditure on HE as a percentage of GDP (%)—Visegrád Four and Finland 94
Figure 3.10 International comparison of public expenditure on HE (% of government expenditure on education) 2004–2021 95
Figure 3.11 Academics' compensation as a percentage of total expenditure in public HEIs (%) 96
Figure 4.1 The evolution of the total number and types of Romanian higher education institutions (1990–2023) 110
Figure 4.2 The evolution of the faculties of Romanian higher education institutions (1990–2023) 113
Figure 4.3 Government expenditure on education (% of GDP)—Romania, Hungary, Slovakia 114
Figure 4.4 The evolution of the number of students enrolled in Romanian higher education institutions (1990–2023) 117
Figure 4.5 Ratio of students-to-academic staff, by type of institution (1990–2023) 118
Figure 4.6 Academic staff in higher education institutions, by academic year (1990–2023) 120
Figure 4.7 Academic staff in higher education institutions by macro-regions, development regions, and counties (2022–2023 academic year) 121
Figure 4.8 Female and male academic staff in the Romanian higher education (1990–2023; in percentages) 124
Figure 4.9 Distribution of academic staff in Romania by age groups (2022/2023 academic year) 125
Figure 4.10 Distribution of academic staff in Romania by age groups (2012–2023; in percentage) 126
Figure 4.11 Academic staff in Romanian higher education institutions, by academic rank (2000–2022; in numbers) 127
Figure 4.12 Academic staff in Romanian higher education institutions, by academic rank (2021–2022 academic year; in percentage) 129

Figure 5.1 Serbian higher education system 152
Figure 5.2 Number of academics and associates 155
Figure 5.3 Distribution of academics and associates 155
Figure 5.4 Distribution of male and female academic staff 156
Figure 5.5 Distribution of academic staff by gender and title 157
Figure 5.6 Number of enrolled students vs. the number of academic staff 161
Figure 5.7 Number of students per academic staff/lecturer 162
Figure 5.8 Number of enrolled and graduated students 163
Figure 5.9 Distribution of newly enrolled male and female students 164
Figure 5.10 Distribution of newly enrolled students across Serbia's statistical regions 165
Figure 5.11 The trend of net salary bases in higher education 169
Figure 5.12 Salary comparison of public professionals in Serbia 170
Figure 6.1 Share of population aged 15 and over with tertiary education, by country 180
Figure 6.2 Number of students by field for the academic year 2022/23 186
Figure 6.3 Growth in the number of male students by age group over the past four years 187
Figure 6.4 Number of Ph.D. students in Ukraine from the regime change to the present 189
Figure 6.5 Ph.D. students in Ukraine by age group 189
Figure 6.6 Change in the number of Ukrainian academic staff over the last five years (N) 196
Figure 6.7 Distribution of academic degrees and titles among Ukrainian academics (%) 197
Figure 6.8 Share of women of academic staff in Ukraine and the Visegrád countries 197
Figure 6.9 Average salary of academic staff in Ukraine and Visegrád countries in Euro 198
Figure 10.1 Research productivity of academics over the past four years based on self-report 294
Figure 11.1 The dual functionality of humans at the personal and professional levels (Authors' design) 308
Figure 11.2 Different social environments implication on work-life imbalance (Authors' design) 317
Figure 12.1 Attitudes toward culture by average of responses to attitude questions (N=757–764) 340

List of Tables

Table 2.1 Institutions, faculties, number of students (short-term, tertiary, bachelor, master and undivided, and doctoral) and number of academics 48
Table 2.2 Distribution of academic staff working in higher education by age 53
Table 2.3 Structure of academic staff in Hungarian higher education 61
Table 2.4 Salary ratios of academics' degrees in higher education (Data around 2015–16) 64
Table 2.5 Ranking of countries by world share of doctoral students and number per 100,000 inhabitants 66
Table 3.1 The number of HE students per academic staff in 2020 81
Table 3.2 The changes in numbers of HEIs, their students, and academics in Slovakia (2015–2023) 83
Table 3.3 Age distribution of academic staff/senior staff (OECD and Slovakia) 84
Table 3.4 The age structure of HEI staff in Slovakia—% (2024) 84
Table 3.5 Distribution of academic staff by seniority (% in 2020) 86
Table 3.6 Distribution of academics in HE due to their academic degrees (Between 2003 and 2023, Slovakia) 87
Table 3.7 The salary ratios of academics rank in HE in Slovakia (2022) 97
Table 4.1 Higher educational institutions by macro-regions, development regions, and counties, types (2022/2023 academic year) 112
Table 4.2 The largest higher education centers (2022/2023 academic year) 112

Table 4.3 The largest higher education centers, by academic staff numbers (2022/2023 academic year) 122
Table 4.4 The largest private higher education centers, by academic staff numbers (2022/2023 academic year) 123
Table 5.1 Number of higher education institutions 159
Table 5.2 Distribution of enrolled students in public and private higher institutions 160
Table 5.3 Distribution of academic staff in public and private higher institutions 160
Table 5.4 Descriptive statistics of students-to-academic staff and students-to-lecturer 162
Table 5.5 The transition from vocational colleges to academies of applied studies 166
Table 5.6 Distribution of higher education institutions 167
Table 5.7 Complexity coefficients for financing the salaries 168
Table 6.1 Higher education institutions and student numbers (Undergraduate, bachelor, master, and postgraduate) 182
Table 7.1 Types of institutional culture and its characteristics 219
Table 7.2 Types of effectiveness and their characteristics 223
Table 7.3 Evaluation of the academic effectiveness of each type of institutional culture 225
Table 8.1 The teaching approach (N=818) 242
Table 8.2 The existence of teacher competencies (N=812) 242
Table 8.3 Types of inclusive teaching activity 244
Table 8.4 The teaching approaches of the academic clusters (N=770, average points) 245
Table 8.5 Types of inclusive teaching activities by academic clusters (N=758, average points) 246
Table 8.6 Interrelations between educational activity and well-being (N=720) 248
Table 9.1 The ratios of academic staff mobility by country (N= 804) 270
Table 9.2 Ratios of teaching and research mobility by academic field (N=800) 271
Table 9.3 Ratios of academic staff mobility by position (N=800) 271
Table 9.4 Ratios of academic staff mobility according to position—the Hungarian and Romanian subsample (N=615) 272

Table 9.5 Ratio of academic staff mobility according to academic degree (N=803) 272
Table 9.6 Ratio of academic staff mobility according to types of academics (N=806) 273
Table 9.7 The connection between education of foreign students and academic staff mobility. p=0.012 (N=772) 277
Table 10.1 Correlations of workplace stressors with research productivity (means, SD) 295
Table 11.1 The statistical values of the main components of work-related factors 310
Table 11.2 Perception of the work-life conflict (%) and the principal component factor scores 311
Table 11.3 Differences in the WLC factor by the demographic, family, and professional factors (means on 0–100 points scale) 312
Table 11.4 Multiple stepwise regression analyses. Prediction of WLC 314
Table 12.1 Cultural consumer/leisure types in Hungary from the mid-1980s to the mid-2010s 332
Table 12.2 Frequency of academics' use of cultural and leisure activities by cluster 334
Table 12.3 Frequency of use of cultural and leisure activities (%) 335
Table 12.4 Cluster groups (cluster weights 1–7) and averages of visits to cultural and leisure activities (N=679) based on the frequency of cultural and leisure activities of the academics 337
Table 12.5 Respondents by age group and cultural cluster (N=660) 338
Table 12.6 Distribution of academics by number of books read in the last year (%, persons) 339
Table 12.7 Comparison of cultural clusters with the number of non- or light readers 340
Table 12.8 Means of attitude statements on attitudes toward culture by cultural cluster (1–5 scale) 341

1. Challenges and Well-Being of Academics on the Eastern Border of the European Union. The Background and Rationale for the Book

Gabriella Pusztai & Klára Kovács

1. The World of Academics: Research Foundations and Insights

There is a long and distinguished tradition of international research on the academic professions in higher education. The literature draws attention to its changing character over time and space (Altbach, 2005; de Wert et al., 2006; Höhle & Teichler, 2013). Our research takes as a model the excellent analyses and summaries of the Carnegie Study on the Academic Profession from the 1990s (Enders & Teichler, 1995; Altbach, 2005; Teichler, 1999). We also take as an inescapable predecessor the study "The Changing Academic Profession" conducted in the 2000s (Teichler et al., 2013) and its follow-up, the 2009–2012 study "The Academic Profession in Europe: Responses to Societal Challenges" (EUROAC), which has provided insights into the marked changes in this professional group. Among the most important of these are the composition of academics, the diversity and inequality of careers, their working conditions, their job satisfaction, the internationalization of the academic career, and issues of hierarchization and competition within this vocation (Kehm & Teichler, 2013; Höhle & Teichler, 2013; Fumasoli, et al., 2015; Kwiek, 2022).

These analyses have attempted to capture external challenges and the responses to them. These, in the form of structural changes in higher education systems, have contributed to changes in the emphasis on academic professionals and to changes in the everyday life of the profession. Researchers have also raised the question of the extent to which changes in external circumstances affect the socialization of academics and influence their academic identity, their values and their identity (Teichler & Kehm, 2013). This latter question was also of interest to our research team, and, continuing the line of thought of our predecessors, we sought to answer how these processes influence the working and living styles and well-being of academics in a region on the periphery of the European Union.

A quick review of the main trends identified by the above-mentioned large-scale international research is important here because they have also emerged in the region we are studying and have had an impact on the lives of academics. There is no doubt that the changing role of higher education in society, in particular the expansion and increasing diversity of the student population, has had a direct effect on the everyday life of academics worldwide. At first sight, this seemed to be an expansion of the tasks of higher education pedagogy, teaching methods, mentoring and catching up, but, already during the first wave of expansion, researchers noticed the widening cultural gap between the world of students and that of academics. Later on, keeping those at risk of dropping out engaged became one of their tasks (Jencks & Riesman, 2002; Tinto, 1993; Pusztai, 2015; Bocsi et al., 2022; Pusztai et al., 2022). As an indirect effect, early research recorded that academics were affected by scarce resources and dissatisfaction with the quality of their own teaching work as a result of the increase in student numbers (Höhle & Teichler, 2013). Research has also revealed a number of indirect effects of the systemic and institutional transformation triggered by the expansion on the living and working conditions of academics. One of these is the increase in the functional diversity of higher education as a result of the expansion of student numbers, which has led to an increase in the size and diversification of academics themselves. In addition to institutions with a mixed profile, institutions with a purely educational profile have emerged, with only an ostensible research function or no whatsoever (Höhle & Teichler, 2013; Kwiek, 2022). The role and tasks of academics in these institutions have begun to resemble more closely the role of a teacher in public education. The shift in the division of roles between institutions has also had significant ramifications on professional identity and working conditions. The unity of teaching and research was broken, and serious fault lines emerged between types of institutions and types of teachers in terms of the nature of work, working conditions and working hours (Höhle & Teichler, 2013). A major development was the recognition of the lack of career prospects and the dissatisfaction of academics who were only concerned with teaching (Höhle & Teichler, 2013). At the same time, at the other pole, it was a completely different world to belong to the top ten who produce half of the most successful academic outputs (Kwiek, 2016). Kwiek points out that although the careers and expectations of academics seem to be very similar internationally, the stratification within the profession has become so great that it is increasingly difficult to speak of a single profession (Kehm & Teichler, 2013; Kwiek, 2022). While academic careers require a very long-term investment and persistent work, the high institutional context-dependence makes the returns very uncertain, and there are significant inequalities in terms of gender, age, national and ethnic origin, disciplinary and territorial differences (Enders & Teichler, 1995; Goastellec et al., 2013; Kwiek & Roszka, 2022a; Kwiek & Roszka, 2022b). Another empirical finding relevant to our research is the suggestion that academics may be internally stratified in terms of working habits, lifestyles, rules, norms, and values and social networks (Enders & Teichler, 1995; Kwiek & Antonovicz, 2015; Kwiek, 2015; Teichler & Höhle, 2013)

The academic profession has perhaps been even more significantly moved by the transformation of higher education governance, the decline in state funding and the emergence of an evaluative role for the state (Enders, 2004). Despite national differences, there has been a unidirectional change in the way governments approach mass higher education (Boer et al., 2008). In the 1990s, governments began to view higher education as a knowledge economy, expecting a return on budgetary expenditure and interpreting higher education as a productive sector. This led to the proliferation of market-oriented institutional practices, which the literature calls entrepreneurialism (Clark, 1988; Kwiek, 2012). The functional transformation of higher education also weighed on expectations about the content of the knowledge produced and transmitted, with managers demanding applied research and the transfer of knowledge almost exclusively for practical application, rather than disciplinary knowledge based on academic interest (Höhle & Teichler, 2013). This required academics to re-learn what they had known about research and education, to revise their research designs, in which development and innovation, and even impact assessment of innovations, became really emphasized, and to expect the involvement of economic and industrial resources (van der Kaap & Weert 2016). The introduction of practice-oriented training has meant that they have had to adapt the content and methodology of their courses, develop their links with the labor market and develop ways of working with them. In addition, new tasks and roles such as organizing, planning, networking, quality management, student recruitment, writing applications, and finding funding have emerged anew or have been strengthened (Musselin, 2007; Hyde et al., 2013)

In higher education institutions with an entrepreneurial attitude, not only the activities and funding have changed, but also the governance, which has led to the rise of managerialism (Enders, 2004). If we focus only on the phenomena that have the most important impact on academics, we must mention the increasing bureaucratization, the growing number and power of the administration. A recurrent experience in research is that the process of administrative staff taking up space in academic buildings and having a decisive voice in academics' deliberations has created a sense of loss of control and power over academics' academic work (Clarke et al., 2013).

After organizational and planning issues, the assessment and promotion of individual performance moved from the hands of the collegiate bodies of the academic profession to the hands of management, and this fundamentally changed the nature of teaching and research, as academics now focused on meeting measurable and measured performance indicators (Hyde et al., 2013; Enders, 2013). Researchers have drawn attention to the fact that the state does not directly control higher education, but through complex referrals (Neave, 1998). Research has observed that academics have gradually internalized the new value system of higher education through the mediation of intermediary organizations and institutional leadership. Often still contesting the validity of the new values, they have become involved in peer reviews based on the new ideology, and as a result they themselves are beginning to strive to improve performance and acquire new competences (Musselin, 2013). Traditional, collegial values were replaced by the new values when members of the academics profession themselves began to identify with these managerial values and to adopt the corporate way of speaking (Clarke et al., 2013; Hyde et al., 2013). Hyde et al. 2013 have done an excellent job of summarizing the further points at which the internalization of the audit approach impacts on the everyday work of academics, right down to the choice of teaching and research methods, such as the preference for standardized tests and randomized controlled trials. This process has also affected an important element of academic identity, the understanding of the professional community, which is divided on how it relates to managerial values.

Professional community recognition seems to have been devalued, and individualized career paths have been framed by competition according to external assessment criteria (Clarke et al., 2013; Kwiek & Antonowitz, 2015). Examples of the classic incubators around the professor are few and far between, from which a regular and predictable career can be launched. Professional socialization is therefore not straightforward and goal-oriented. Rather it is fragmented, and under the influence of changing institutional environments, multiple, fluid reinterpretations and the rebuilding of academic identity become commonplace (Drennan et al., 2020). The struggle for limited research resources intensifies growing fierce due to the influence of financial resources on research productivity (Daizen, 2015; Kwiek, 2022). Moreover, the reinterpretation of the community is the emergence of grant, publication and peer review networks. It is unclear whether the access to research funding through invisible networks makes someone successful, or the groundbreaking results are responsible.

One of the trends affecting academics is the internationalization of education and research. This is reflected in the massive mobility of students and academics. However, a new element is that, instead of the previous mainly individualized collegiate internationalization, internationalization is also an indicator of excellence of countries and institutions and is therefore also an area of institutional governance. In education, the comparability of training content means that it is necessary to ensure that it is internationally valid and in line with standards. Nor does it depend on the individual excellence of academics to produce internationally renowned publications; institutions themselves are beginning to organize and encourage this, and to sanction progress. Academics have thus found themselves in an internationalized arena, where institutions compete with each other for students and research performance for funding (Probst & Goastellec, 2013). This means that the field of competition and network building within the occupational group has expanded for academics. What is more, the opportunities for them have increased, along with the workload. The result: stratification within the academic society becomes even more significant (Kwiek, 2022).

Research on the academic profession clearly demonstrates that academics have responded to systemic changes in higher education by essentially adapting, despite grumblings (Teichler, 2013; Hyde et al., 2013). Research on academics reports changing working conditions, job dissatisfaction, overwork, deteriorating opportunities and job insecurity, but has not shown strong criticism (Kogan & Teichler, 2007). In addition to a reduced sense of teaching effectiveness, a reduction in researcher autonomy and rights to make research decisions tends to result in a sense of malaise (van der Kaap & Weert, 2016). While an important facet of professional identity is the traditionally high social prestige of the profession, research reports perceptions of declining social and material esteem alongside decreasing power within the institution (Höhle & Teichler, 2013). Increasing control and loss of a sense of autonomy have been reported to affect an important element of academic identity (Moraru et al., 2013). According to several researchers, a sense of well-being has emerged that can be described as the proletarianization of academics, their becoming knowledge workers and commodities (Gould, 2006; Musselin, 2007; Hyde et al., 2013; Goastellec et al., 2013). This sense of well-being affects their performance in the workplace and ultimately gives a competitive advantage to those higher education systems and institutions that, according to their capabilities, are best able to support academics' well-being.

The theoretical thesis of our research is based on the assumption gathered from previous research findings, that the changed institutional context of higher education determines professional identity. This is due to the fact that the institutional environment has such a significant impact on career models, employment and working conditions, division of labor and cooperation that it can eventually influence individual values, attitudes, lifestyle and well-being at work and in life. This thesis is best explored in a higher education region where global, general challenges are intertwined with additional regional and local challenges. These specific challenges arise from the post-socialist existence, the political legacy of the party-state that has eroded the traditional ideal of academic excellence, and the often-dead-end path of recovery from the economic crisis. The underfunding of higher education institutions is a major determinant (Moraru et al., 2013), but in this area it has emerged in combination with other factors. Our research focuses on how the academic profession perceives and interprets its situation in institutions in a specific region.

2. Why Are Academics in the Post-Socialist Region Special?

The region is linked by common historical roots. For centuries they were part of a more or less united political entity, more or less unified in terms of government, but also very diverse in terms of culture and religion. This formation reached its heyday in the early twentieth century, when the Austro-Hungarian Empire was established. The region is characterized by internal migration for historical reasons, and therefore cultures have learned to live side by side, to which many attribute the flow of international academic excellence (Hargittai, 2008; Janik & Toulmin, 2023). What binds this region together is its critical geopolitical location in the twentieth century and today, the border between East and West. It was this geopolitical situation that led to its being condemned to belong to the Soviet sphere of interest during the negotiations that ended the Second World War. The shared experience of the post-communist transition, the attraction of Western welfare capitalism in the same period, and the experience of not attaining the latter, is also a common heritage. After the political regime change, while striving to integrate with the West, the region became a hunting ground for the market expansion of the Western European economy. The successive economic difficulties that followed the political regime change, the debt crisis inherited from state socialism and the austerity-laden ups and downs of the search for economic paths have led to greater social disparities than in the West. Though there is a constant drive to unite with Western ways of life and institutions, the region's nations still lag behind. Traditional values such as respect for family ties, religious diversity (Catholic, Orthodox and Protestant) and a stronger social presence thereof are other common features. Furthermore, territorial and developmental differences within the region and between countries, and greater urban-rural inequalities are found more here than in the West. Civil society, which was abolished under state socialism, is relatively weak and the level of trust in public institutions is below that of Western Europe. Education is state-supported, access to primary and secondary education is free, and higher education is predominantly free or at low cost. There is also a decades-long struggle for educational integration of marginalized groups. The region under our study is in the eastern part of the Central European area. It is distinct from the parts of the post-socialist countries that started from a less disadvantaged position, that had been more successful in correcting their socio-economic backwardness and that are generally more prosperous today.

Another common feature is the significant number of Hungarian minorities living in the countries under study, who have institutions of higher education with Hungarian as the language of instruction. The Czech Republic and Slovenia are not included in the study because of the aforementioned factors, though other and previously mentioned features of the historical past would place them in this category.

The specialty of higher education in the examined region is that two major strands of change have over the last three decades simultaneously influenced this level of education. One of the major processes of change is the impact of the political regime changes in the post-socialist region, and the other is the trends of change that have affected higher education throughout the modern world. The two major waves of transformation have influenced changes in higher education, partly by following each other in rapid succession and partly by modifying one another's impact.

The evolution of education systems is characterized by *path dependency*, and the regional emergence of global trends affecting higher education is also fundamentally determined by historically evolved structures and norms (Trow, 2007; Teichler, 2004). The higher education of the region today cannot be understood without understanding the profile of higher education before the political regime changes. One of the most significant socio-economic changes in the CEE region in the last half century, even by global standards, has taken place following the collapse of the state socialist political experiment. This is also seen as the starting point of a three-decade process of transformation in higher education.

Some of the main features of the socialist system that influenced higher education can be highlighted. The most important is the centralized control of the CEE region, which ignored the educational history, traditions, social development, educational indicators and the development of the higher education network in each country. In the CEE countries, the educational and cultural policy guidelines issued by the Moscow headquarters were applied for almost half a century after the Second World War. At the beginning of the period, this Soviet model was copied slavishly, later, especially after the revolutions in some countries, local authorities imitated the center somewhat more cautiously, but it was not possible to deviate substantially from the educational policies issued from the center (Gyuris, 2014). The communist parties in power everywhere were responsible for the disciplined copying. Their functionaries controlled the work of government. Higher education policy was guided by a few priorities, listed below:

On the one hand, higher education was subordinated to the socialist planned economy, which saw education as a supply factory for socialist large-scale production. This planned economy sought to calculate precisely how many higher education specialists were needed, afterwards giving higher education institutions the set target number of graduates to produce. Individual interest and social demand did not override these calculations.

On the other hand, strict ideological and socio-political considerations demanded that the new class structure that had emerged as a result of the communist takeover be preserved. To this end, higher education was subject to strict ideological control, and complex bureaucratic management and control was built into higher education. The selection of lecturers was based on the control and approval of the Communist parties. Undercover informers among the lecturers reported on their colleagues and on the mood of the students, while trying to recruit agents. In the higher education institutions of the Central and Eastern European countries, the communist secret police were active in observing, controlling and manipulating teachers and students. Ideological education was included in the curricula of the courses, in the teaching materials and in the textbooks and notes. Every student had to pass an examination in scientific socialism and Marxist political economy. Applicants to higher education were screened to ensure that only children of trustworthy parents were admitted to university, and students and graduates were required to write a "development" profile of their beliefs and worldview for prospective employers. They also did not allow the graduate class to grow in numbers, with a maximum of one-tenth of each age group allowed to continue their studies, because the creation of a graduate mass was identified as a quantitative threat.

Research in higher education was also subject to ideological and political control, with disciplines and research topics arranged in a hierarchy according to their ability to serve the political goals set by the party.

Like the Communist Party's takeover in the second half of the 1940s, the collapse of state socialist regimes in the CEE region occurred almost simultaneously between 1989 and 1991. In the first period after the political regime changes that took place, the first breakthroughs were freedom of political expression, the public emergence of previously illegal civil society organizations, the emergence of a multi-party system and the organization of democratic elections. Even before that, it had become apparent in higher education institutions that dissent and dissenting opinions could no longer be banned. In several countries, discontent and criticism of the system also emerged within the ruling party elites. Intellectuals opposed to the regime, whether they emigrated or stayed at home, were more visible in academic societies than spokespersons for the ideology and policies of the state party. Secret, samizdat studies were circulated among lecturers and students, radio broadcasts from abroad were listened to, and where possible, critical thinkers were invited to give lectures in a restricted circle. So, it can be said that although the socialist regimes guarded the universities jealously against reformist and anti-establishment thinking, these institutions became catalysts for political change. In Romania, during the revolution of December 1989, students and faculty at the universities of Timişoara played a key role in organizing the resistance, the 1989 'Velvet Revolution' began with a student demonstration and faculty played a major role in the political transformation. In the regions of the former Yugoslavia, university youth supported both autonomy efforts and reforms. In Hungary, the faculty and students of the voluntary extracurricular study groups that were being set up at universities were the leaders of the new political formations. The moment of political regime change found academics in the countries studied as a relatively prestigious and influential occupational group.

The first governments that came to power after the change of government were the first to face the dilemma in higher education policy of whether removing controls on the number of applicants and graduates would be the right thing to do. Would it not lead to an overproduction of labor and a dilution of the intellectual elite? And, above all, the question was whether the bankrupt CEE economies would be able to cope with the additional costs of increased public higher education. Whether to open the doors of higher education to the masses of students was widely debated by political parties, governments and the general public (Kozma 1990, Kozma 1998). After some hesitation, the increased social demand for higher education in each country was finally met, and enrollment and completion rates increased. The dilemma of whether all this growth should be financed by the state or whether students should cover their costs has been with us for the last three decades. Various solutions have been sought and found in the region and there have been several changes of direction in this respect. Each of these attempts has placed a heavy burden on academics, as widening participation implies a pedagogical challenge and extra work, narrowing participation and strengthening selection rather a greater evaluation administration and the mental burden of whether the selection decision is indeed made on a fair and meritocratic basis.

Many of the manifest institutions of ideological control in higher education were abolished in the first stage of the political transformation (party leadership, Marxist departments and political indoctrination courses). Several university professors with a history of agents were exposed, but there was no consistent public screening in the region under study as in East Germany or even in Poland and the Czech Republic (David, 2011). Political and public debates led to the decision not to publish the names of agents on the grounds that many had been recruited by force or blackmail. On the other hand, the mechanisms of state socialism made it almost impossible to unravel the role played by unethical service and political connections to the ruling party in the development of individual academic careers. Thus, in these countries, the last representatives of academics/academics with a history of agency or who have been brought in through ideological selection will only be out of the system in the generational transitions in the 2020s.

In addition to struggling with the legacy of the past, higher education in the region was very quickly confronted with global challenges that also had a significant impact on the world of CEE academics (Kozma, 2008). One of the main trends was global expansion. This expansion was not only caused by the release of social demands that had been suppressed in the CEE region, but it coincided with the second wave of expansion in the modern world, the challenges of which were already being addressed by the Bologna Process. As social participation rates in the region under study were very low, the mass of people wishing to continue their studies suddenly came upon the higher education systems with great force in the mid-1990s. In the space of a few years, this fundamentally changed the internal world of the institutions, the teaching methods and the workload. Neither the institutional capacities (buildings, classrooms, teaching equipment) nor the pedagogical competences of the higher education staff were ready to cater for them. The composition of the student body is highly diversified. Despite the large social differences that characterize the region, in the past, teachers encountered a relatively homogeneous student population and found it difficult to cope with students from diverse cultural backgrounds and with a wide range of motivations. The typical response to this diversity in the countries of the region has been the expansion of supply, the diversification of courses, privatization and the emergence of new providers (Levy, 2014). These phenomena have been accompanied by a moderate increase in the number of academics, but also by an internal stratification of the student population, as those working in different segments of higher education have found themselves with very different student populations, workloads, development and career prospects. The increase in the number of young people and women in academics was significant.

The challenges facing higher education in the western half of Europe had become common in the eastern part of the CEE region by the end of the 1990s. Despite demographic stagnation, enrollment rates increased, and graduates were not only a labor market asset but also a symbolic social asset. The introduction of multi-cycle education as a result of the Bologna Process was a response to both expansionary pressures and the labor market redeemability of diplomas. In the Central and Eastern Europe (CEE) region, the transition to multi-cycle education has generally been rapid (Pusztai & Szabó, 2008; Kozma et al., 2014). Academics have been given the task of revising the structure and curricula of education and research, a task that requires expertise, thoughtful decision-making and a very time-consuming process. From then on, training design became an almost permanent task, as demand for training and the constantly changing needs of the labor market meant that courses had to be adapted to frequent closures and new courses that were added. For academics, this was an unexpected and demanding task.

Another aspect of the global transformation of higher education was internationalization, which the region's higher education sector encountered as an important initiative as regarded European integration, pointing toward the creation of a European Higher Education Area. This was achieved through the promotion of student and teacher mobility, the introduction of a credit system to ensure comparability and interoperability, quality assurance and the introduction of the diploma supplement. Academics have found themselves in an increasingly competitive situation as academics and researchers in the wake of internationalization. As students progressed through the multi-cycle training pathway, it became easy for them to switch to a transfer route, and the fight to retain them began. In CEE countries, this has led to a huge Western brain drain. Young people from these countries were looking for a richer, more modern environment, Western European universities, and in many cases were not content with semester-long mobility but left their home countries after secondary school. The internationalization of the higher education arena has therefore posed a greater challenge to this region (Dabney-Fekete, 2020).

After the political transition, funding autonomy, maintenance pluralism and entrepreneurism have emerged in higher education in the context of the drive toward more decentralized models. For various reasons, private and foundation-based institutions are of great importance in higher education in the countries under study, most notably in Romania, where privatization was very intense during the expansionary wave and later curtailed. Minority Hungarian language institutions are maintained by foundations, and the share of non-state-maintained institutions has increased in Hungary after 2020. Regardless of the sponsor, institutions everywhere were looking for professionals who could steer higher education with a business approach. Kwiek's studies have shown how higher education in CEE countries adopted entrepreneurial practices in the post-communist transitions in response to globalization, Europeanization and reduced state funding (Kwiek, 2013). In the region under study, entrepreneurialism and managerialism arrived in the region under study not on the theoretical arguments of 'value state' ideologies, not with a focus on rewarding quality work, but with a reference to decreasing state funding (Kwiek, 2013). The positive returns of the entrepreneurial approach were a greater emphasis on development and innovation in higher education research, and closer cooperation with economic actors, whether in research or training. However, managerial leadership in these countries has also brought an increase in the proportion of administrative staff. Soon after the shackles of state socialist bureaucracy were removed, this new type of bureaucracy began to emerge. Moreover, it was often created by those who had been running the old state socialist bureaucracy (Kozma & Polónyi, 2022).

The democratization and liberation from ideological control for those working in higher education has clearly led to a boom in research activity. In different ways and rates, institutional structures for research funding, mediating between governments and the scientific community, have begun to emerge in the countries of the region. As the level of national income available for research funding in these countries is very low compared to Western European countries. Thus, the competition for these resources is very intense. What is new, however, is that it is no longer only the government that decides who gets the funds, but academics judge each other's proposals, and the public funder decides on the basis of this. Non-governmental, but also foundation and international research grants have become available, but these are very limited. On a positive note, the role of scientific excellence in the career prospects of academics has slowly started to increase as a result of the policy change, but the limited resources available have created inequalities in access to research funding and scientific excellence and innovation are not fully reflected.

For the vast majority of academics working in the region, there was no well-trodden path to international academia, as under socialism there was a strict bureaucratic process before crossing national borders, and not everyone had a world passport. From this point of view, participation in the European mobility programs, which symbolized the examined countries' rapprochement with and symbolic acceptance of European integration, was a major turning point. Although mobility once a year was generally modestly subsidized by European funds, the ever-increasing cost of attending international conferences and publishing in refereed journals in prestigious databases remained beyond the reach of many for financial reasons. They found themselves in the vicious circle of internationalization drop-outs. This explains why the proportion of academics involved in internationalization is relatively low in the countries of the region. In the 2020 decade, the broad swathes of academics who dropped out of internationalization at a young age were no longer able to win grants and therefore could not finance publications and conferences, leaving them at a severe cumulative disadvantage. Science and medicine academics were able to develop international research links somewhat sooner. They were able to study abroad even before the political regime change, because their field was not ideologically risky and the development of these disciplines was already a priority under state socialism because of industrial links. At the same time, it is precisely in these fields that a significant migration of academics has occurred. The increased value of individual achievement, limited research funding and local shortcomings in underdeveloped research infrastructure, as well as the opening up of mobility opportunities after the fall of the Iron Curtain and European Union (EU) accession, have allowed a significant brain drain from the countries of the region. This has also made the question of going or staying in certain disciplines a commonplace one for cutting-edge academics.

A recent development in higher education in the region is that governments have moved toward performance-based funding, which emphasizes productivity in research, publications and winning proposals. This has increased the pressure on academics to perform, and the changes have also led to job insecurity, especially for academics who do not belong to a narrow group of elite researchers. Regional differences in the composition of students in higher education institutions also create serious inequalities in the internally stratified academic occupational group but also create new inequalities in performance-based funding, which affect life and job satisfaction (Kovács et al., 2024).

In summary, the examined region's recovery of academic freedom after state socialism was followed so quickly by waves of expansion, managerialism and internationalization that it missed out on the golden age of abundant resources and high social prestige in the western world. The golden age described by Altbach and Enders (Altbach, 2005; Enders, 2007) ended before it had even begun in this region. Higher education in the region moved from a strictly state-controlled, centrally planned, socialist higher education policy, first to a fleeting moment of freer, more autonomous educational governance, and then to a market-oriented and performance-based model, which resulted in a radical transformation of governance, funding and accountability mechanisms within higher education institutions.

From the academics' point of view, after the political transition, the hope was that academics here could achieve a similar status to academic professionals in Western Europe, becoming an occupational group with full research, policy and time-allocation freedom, generously supported by the welfare state. Their hopes of this were soon dashed, and they became employees of an impoverished and plundered state instead of the welfare state, facing increased workloads, fierce competition and job insecurity caused by the extremely rapid, overlapping changes in expansion and education policy. The age stratification of academics in this region is a special segmentation, as the age gap is further blurred by the fact that some of today's professors were socialized under socialism, the middle generation remained in the financially miserable but hopeful circumstances after the change of regime, while for the 30-year-old generation, being a university teacher is no longer prestigious, the career then needing to offer some substitute value.

Our research is one of those studies focusing on a post-socialist region that in recent decades has faced two interrelated challenges. On the one hand, it dealt with the serious legacy of the past and, on the other hand, with building newly developed systems that had to be adapted to more advanced European higher education systems. This was done while they themselves were in a state of searching for a new path (Kwiek, 2012; Höhle & Teichler, 2013; Brankovicz et al., 2014; Pavlin & Sušanj, 2020).

3. New Challenge: The Well-Being of Academics

The novelty and significance of our research is that we are at a critical moment, facing new challenges, unlike before. With the emergence of managerialism, the audit approach has exploded and become dominant in higher education in the region over the last half decade. The bureaucratic management that higher education in the region had under state socialism it was accustomed to, and the power of administrators was not an unknown phenomenon. But in the 2020s, serious performance evaluation, with implications for pay, was introduced in the region's institutions. This has caught most academics in the region off guard. The direct consequence of applying performance measures to teaching and academia is acceleration. Of course, flexibility and the capacity to evolve are almost a fundamental requirement in this occupational group, but the persistence of time pressures and the acceleration of work can fundamentally disrupt the 'peace of human life and work' (Vostal, 2015, p. 296).

Even the more gradual transformation of the academic profession has in some respects made academics the victims of their own careers, as early studies have indicated (Enders & Teichler, 1995). However, coming in congested waves, this rapid transformation is likely to create entirely new selection breakpoints among academics. Our research is timely in observing the impact of the incursion of managerial values and practices on organizational commitment and various dimensions of employee well-being. The effects have been widely studied elsewhere (Bryson, 2004; Findlow, 2008; Hyde et al., 2013; Loveday, 2018), but little research has addressed this area. We hypothesize that our research with a regional focus is also necessary because research shows that there is no uniform response from academics to the growing managerialism. The differences are first felt in the area of well-being.

The issue of public perception is also interesting because the changes in higher education in the region under study were not gradual, but rather a very rapid process, which is difficult to work through. In the post-socialist countries, the academic community, freed and reorganized after ideological pressure, became proletarianized again only a few years after gaining freedom. Therefore, a large part of academics see themselves as victims of the worst decisions made by their governments, rather than as participants in a process that is following international trends everywhere.

Mood is a subjective perception of the current physical, mental and spiritual state of an individual and his or her general well-being. In the case of academics, well-being is also a diffuse concept, involving specific dimensions, the most important of which we have tried to examine in our research. These sub-domains are the perception of workplace culture, the evaluation of academic development, two key areas of professional self-actualization, international mobility and publication productivity, work-life conflicts, physical activity in support of physical and mental health, and cultural involvement as a source of intellectual pleasure and recreation. Of course, there are many other dimensions of well-being in academia, but in this paper we have only addressed the most fundamental ones.

The precursors of scientific research on the well-being of academics date back to the period following the first big wave of mass enrollment in higher education. In the 1980s, the problem of burnout and career dropout among academics due to long-term stress was already a fact (Melendez & De Guzman, 1983). In the 1990s, systematic research on workload, job security and anxiety due to increasing demands began (Allen, 1996). It has become apparent that for this occupational group, a workplace environment that supports mental and emotional well-being is of paramount importance, with the potential to reduce the significant work challenges, increased workload and feelings of insecurity. On the other hand, physical fitness and the perception of opportunities for physical activity were also considered to be included, as well as intellectual satisfaction, meaningful intellectual activities related to career and leisure, and work-life balance. We believe that the well-being of academics is not a private matter, but a prerequisite for creative, efficient, productive higher education that is able to retain and develop human resources. Since the 2000s it has integrated aspects such as mental, emotional and social well-being (Seligman & Csíkszentmihályi, 2000). The study of some dimensions of well-being has become increasingly common in higher education. Some are associated with higher-than-average job risks, others directly deal with crises, and there is ever-growing discussion of the related responsibilities of higher education institutions leaders and administrators (Jayman et al., 2022; Nicholls et al., 2022; Hammoudi Halat et al., 2023). Research has highlighted the impact of a supportive work environment and the need for institutional policies to improve work-life balance and reduce workplace stress. More recently, research has begun to examine the well-being of academics and has found that the most important dimensions are the culture of the work environment, career and development opportunities, work-life balance, workload and personal leisure balance (Gibbs & Miller, 2014; Pace et al., 2021; Buda & Kovács, 2024). Qualitative and mainly psychological studies exist but rarely interpret the phenomenon embedded in the changes in higher education, and no large-scale, multi-country study has been conducted in our region.

This raises several research questions. The question is whether the academics of the region under study, located on the eastern periphery of the European Higher Education Area, are close to the types described in international research or show new characteristics in comparison to them. As previous research has mainly focused on the conflict within the role of academics (Fukudome, 2015) rather than its compatibility with private life and well-being, it is questionable how the examination of academics from new perspectives nuances the picture of academics in the early twenty-first century. The question that remains to be answered is: will there be significant differences between countries or between academic strata according to the aspects studied, or will European developments have different effects in different countries?

The study of this region is also of political importance, as it has historically been a region struggling to balance between East and West under constant external influence. Our research can provide information, through the various higher education policy initiatives, on the state of the academic staff, without whose involvement the vision of a new model of higher education could not be realized. Education policy actors and institutional leaders can build on research findings to develop better practices, training, supportive policies and services. Our research is also of great importance beyond the region under study, as the aspects examined bring new approaches and perspectives to the international discourse from the already rich body of academic research. Although some of the issues examined are not unprecedented, and the members of the research team are following in the footsteps of renowned researchers, together we gain a complex picture of higher education in several countries from a new dimension. In this approach, there is no empirical evidence base for policy development at national or regional level. Our research also aims to initiate the development of an academics well-being evidence-based knowledge base.

From a theoretical point of view, the examined countries constitute a natural laboratory for comparative studies, allowing us to examine how developments in managerialism may affect the well-being of academics. The book is intended to provide a reliable contribution of higher education research to ongoing reform processes in the policy area.

4. The Research Design of the Studies

Changes in higher education in recent decades—such as expansion, the Bologna reform, internationalization, competition for students, managerialism and the emergence of a service-oriented approach—have fundamentally changed the work of academics. Whereas research and teaching used to be the backbone of their work, academics now have a much wider range of responsibilities: they are expected to act as tutors, researchers, mentors and sometimes counselors. The expectations (or demands) associated with these roles and activities place great pressure on them and are a major source of stress, which negatively affects health and well-being, as well as determines their job satisfaction and performance. Thus, it has important implications for institutional effectiveness. The aim of our research, which forms the basis of this volume and is essential in the region, was to examine the well-being, working conditions and performance of academics in five Central and Eastern European countries (Hungary, Slovakia, Ukraine, Romania and Serbia).

In the first part of our research, we conducted focus group interviews with academics from Hungary and in Hungarian minority higher education institutions in Romania, Slovakia, Serbia and Ukraine. Seven focus group interviews were conducted online with academics from nine higher education institutions in the five countries (N=41). The interviews covered a wide range of topics, including the work and situation of academics. After analyzing and processing the interviews, the questionnaire on which this volume is based was compiled. Our detailed questionnaire survey examined the factors that characterize academics' teaching and research work, working conditions, workplace outcomes, health, lifestyle, institutional, family, and social backgrounds (over 300 items).

The questionnaire being translated into Serbian, Slovakian, Ukrainian and Romanian, and being sent, with the permission of the head of the institution, 2 or 3 times over the internet to all academics of the institutions surveyed in the spring of 2023, ensured a probability sample (all academics had a chance to be included in the sample). We examined the higher education establishments of two disadvantaged regions in Hungary, the Northern Great Plains Region (the University of Debrecen, the Debrecen Reformed Theological University, and the University of Nyíregyháza), and the Southern Transdanubia Region (the University of Pécs). When scrutinizing institutions in the other countries, we targeted minority Hungarian institutions. The examined universities were as follows: the University of Novi Sad in Serbia, the J. Selye University, the University of Prešov and the University of Trnava in Slovakia, the Partium Christian University, the Oradea State University, the Emanuel University, the Sapienta Hungarian University of Transylvania, and the Babeş-Bolyai University and their satellite branches in Romania, the Ferenc Rákóczi II Transcarpathian Hungarian College and Uzhhorod National University in Ukraine.

Though we looked into Hungarian minority institutions, we still sent out the survey in the language of the majority population. Academics from these regions filled out the survey, those working in institutions from inner Ukraine (non-Transcarpathian Region) did as well (n=62). Regarding academics in Ukraine, most of the respondents in the Ukrainian subsample live and work in the Transcarpathian region, though several academics from the other regions of the country moved there because of the war. Based on their answers, we could collect a lot of valuable information about the special situation of academic work during the war. It has a significant impact on their working conditions and well-being, which is the most important question in our research. We therefore decided to keep the respondents from inside Ukraine for further analysis.

To reach representativity we strove for a 10 percent sample for each institution devoid of faculties, and for each faculty in larger universities. We reached much larger samples with the smaller universities and colleges, where fewer than 100 were employed. In the interest of reaching probability sample, we sent the survey on two or three occasions to all academics who work in the institution via the registrar or correspondence offices. From there, where the number of teachers per department and the total number of academics on campus were known, we compared the data with the ratio of respondents from the given institutions and faculties. Following this, we sent the letter of request only to the places where the level of academics was less than 10 percent. Thus, the Hungarian sample is representative per faculty, while the sub-samples from other countries are mainly representative of Hungarian minorities and the majority academics working with them, mostly in the same institution. In total, 853 filled out the survey and following data cleansing, that number dwindled to 821. We gave the database the name, Central and Eastern European Teachers in Higher Education (CEETHE 2023).

Among the respondents, 514 were Hungarian (61.8%), 115 Ukrainian (14.1%), 113 Romanian (13.8%), 40 Serbian (4.9%) and 36 Slovakian (4.4%). For three of them, we could not identify their institutions of employment or countries of origin. A total of 43.7% were men and 56.3% were women, with an average age of 46 years (SD=10.7). The average number of years worked in higher education was 17 (SD=11 years). The fields of study in which they activate were medical (16.1%), teacher training (13.6%) and humanities and social sciences (12.9 and 8.2%, respectively). The smallest ratios were for theology (1.1%), art mediation (1.9%), and law (1.5%). The ratio of other areas is 2.6–6.7%. 21.1 of the respondents did not have any degree, 46.8% had a Ph.D./DLA, 17.1% were habilitated doctors, and 9.2% had DSc degrees. Of the traditional academic positions, 29.6% were senior lecturers and 26.8% were associate professors. Additionally, 11.3% were college and university teachers and almost the same proportion (11.2%) were assistant lecturers. Smaller percentages worked as senior teachers (2.6%), language teachers, physical education teachers, or professional subjects (4%). Far less work as a research assistant (2.3%), 1.8% as a research fellow, 1% as a senior research fellow, and 1.2% as a research professor. 6% marked the "other" category. Of the respondents, 69.3% did not fulfill the leader's function.

We listed academic jobs, based on the experiences received from the focus group interviews conducted before the quantitative research, asking respondents to rate on a 1 to 4 scale to what extent they hold the given tasks to be part of their jobs. Based on the answers, we did first factor, then cluster analysis, separating four different academic types: *teaching-focused academics* (33.4%), *academics with an administrative focus* (19.7%), *research-focused academics* (20.3%), and *academic leaders* (26.6%). The teaching-focused academics are those who boast the largest group in our database, they consider activities connected to teaching; course material development; formation and development of an online teaching environment; professional teaching of academics, specialty area and new results; cooperation with external partners while in the field / during practice; trial of new teaching methods, and also academic research all equally important.

Within the latter, publishing research is obligatory, academics must be the utmost effective to meet that requirement, what is more, publication must be in their mother tongue. The other types attempt to teach and do academic research at the highest possible quality. Among other things, those in this group must deal with international grant writing and publishing articles in high prestige journals in English.

The second group, the academics with an administrative focus, received the worst average value in the most examined dimensions. Teaching is less important to them than to the other groups, but it is more characteristic of their work than academic work, particularly belonging to a research group, publishing, and writing international grants. Meanwhile, they value cooperation with colleagues in teaching, and carrying out administrative tasks is more characteristic of them.

The third type, the research-focused academics gave similarly high values for academic research activities, especially international publishing and academic research as the teaching-focused academics, but the teaching activities were less important to them than the academic activities. Like the first group of academics, they considered leader-administrative tasks more characteristic of their jobs, which most likely refer to leading and doing the administration for grants won. Likewise, the academic researcher activities carry greater weight in their circle, while publishing in their mother tongue is least important to their work, which might be explained by the fact that, in high-level researcher work and grants, success is measured by how many publications appear in Q-level English language journals registered in the international database. All the while, they still teach classes, considering it part of their job, putting great emphasis on increasing the academic re-supply. However, the professional teaching of new and specialty area results was of less interest to them, just like course material development.

The last group, academics leaders, gave high marks to teaching and academic researcher activities equally, but carrying out the tasks of a leader were of utmost importance (namely within the university), these tasks defining their work the most, and thus winning them their name.

Our volume consists of two main chapters, which present empirical findings using qualitative and quantitative survey data from our research and national and international statistical databases. The main comparative criteria used in the analyses were country, the types of academics described above, and their main job characteristics (title, discipline, academic degree, etc.).

In the first chapter, the authors analyzed the main higher education statistics of the five countries studied (Hungary, Slovakia, Romania, Serbia and Ukraine) and described the educational policy environment that determines the work of their academics. The second chapter examines the background and effectiveness of academics' work. It analyses data from our empirical studies to show the background factors of academics' well-being, productivity, work-life conflicts and the characteristics of their teaching methods, participation in international mobility and cultural consumption.

The first paper in this chapter, based on interview research, shows the types of institutions that have been distinguished in terms of the impact of the introduction of a performance appraisal system on the institutional climate. The next study examines the factors that encourage and discourage participation in international mobility, and moving on to the issue of workplace outcomes, the third study looks at two specific dimensions of this, namely the background factors of well-being and productivity of academics. The fourth study in the chapter presents the characteristics of work-life conflict among academics, while the fifth study compares teaching methods with the characteristics of academics. The last study examines the characteristics of academics' cultural consumption.

We recommend the studies of our volume to the leaders of all higher education institutions in the region, to policymakers responsible for higher education, and to researchers familiar with the topic. Moreover, it is for those who wish to understand the opinions, experiences, and underlying factors that shape the work, well-being, and effectiveness of the human resources within the institutions they lead and coordinate. These insights are essential for improving organizational efficiency and development, and we have also formulated recommendations in our writings to support this process.

Primarily, however, we dedicate our work to our academics, who can gain a deeper understanding of the background factors behind the experiences and challenges they encounter daily—sometimes struggling with them—and possibly find suggestions for overcoming and resolving these difficulties.

Finally, we would like to express our gratitude to all institutional and department leaders who permitted data collection, participated in the process, and encouraged their colleagues to complete the survey. Most importantly, we thank the academics who sincerely shared their opinions and patiently answered every question in our detailed, rather lengthy questionnaire. Without their contributions, this research could not have been successfully conducted, and this volume would not have come to life.

References

Allen, H. L. (1996). Faculty workload and productivity in the 1990s: preliminary findings. *Instructor, 246*(100), 32–6.

Altbach, P. (2005). Academic challenges: The American professoriate in comparative perspective. In A. Welch (Ed.), *The professoriate: Profile of a profession* (pp. 147–165). Springer Netherlands.

Bocsi, V., Fényes, H., & Pusztai, G. (2022). First-generation students at universities from the aspect of achievement, motivation and integration. Revija za sociologiju, 52(1), 61–85. <https://doi.org/10.5613/rzs.52.1.0315>

de Boer, H. F., Enders, J., & Schimank, U. (2008). Comparing Higher Education Governance Systems in Four European Countries. In N. C. Soguel, & P. Jaccard (Eds.), *Governance and Performance of Education Systems* (pp. 35–54.). Springer. <https://doi.org/10.1007/978-1-4020-6446-3_3>

Branković, J., Kovačević, M., Maassen, P., Stensaker, B., & Vukasović, M. (2014). *The Re-Institutionalization of Higher Education in the Western Balkans. The Interplay between European Ideas, Domestic Policies, and Institutional Practices*. Peter Lang Verlag. <https://doi.org/10.3726/978-3-653-03179-9>

Bryson, C. (2004). What about the workers? The expansion of higher education and the transformation of academic work. *Industrial Relations Journal, 35*(1), 38–57. <https://doi.org/10.1111/j.1468-2338.2004.00299.x>

Buda, A., & Kovács, K. (2024). The digital aspects of the wellbeing of university teachers. Frontiers in Education, 9, 1406141. <https://doi.org/10.3389/feduc.2024.1406141>

Clark, B. R. (1998). The entrepreneurial university: Demand and response. *Tertiary Education and management*, *4*(1), 5–16.

Clarke, M., Hyde, A., & Drennan, J. (2013). Professional Identity in Higher Education. In B. M. Kehm, & U. Teichler (Eds.), *The Academic Profession in Europe: New Tasks and New Challenges. The Changing Academy—The Changing Academic Profession in International Comparative Perspective*, vol 5. (pp. 7–21). Springer. <https://doi.org/10.1007/978-94-007-4614-5_2>

Dabney-Fekete, I. D. (2020). International Academic Mobility as a Capacity Building Factor in Higher Education. *Central European Journal of Educational Research, 2*(1), 82–91. <https://doi.org/10.37441/CEJER/2020/2/1/5761>

Daizen, T. (2015). Research Productivity. In A. Arimoto, W. Cummings, F. Huang, & J. Shin (Eds.), *The Changing Academic Profession in Japan. The Changing Academy—The Changing Academic Profession in International Comparative Perspective*, vol 11. (pp. 149–167). Springer. <https://doi.org/10.1007/978-3-319-09468-7_10>

David, R. (2011). *Lustration and transitional justice: Personnel systems in the Czech Republic, Hungary, and Poland*. University of Pennsylvania Press.

Drennan, J., Clarke, M., Hyde, A., & Politis, Y. (2020). Academic identity in higher education. In P. N. Teixeira, & J. C. Shin (Eds.), *The international encyclopedia of higher education systems and institutions* (pp. 35–40). Springer Netherlands.

Enders, J. (2004). Higher education, internationalisation, and the nation-state: Recent developments and challenges to governance theory. *Higher Education*, 47, 361–382. <https://doi.org/10.1023/B:HIGH.0000016461.98676.30>

Enders, J. (2007). The Academic Profession. In J. J. F. Forest, & P. G. Altbach (Eds.), *International Handbook of Higher Education. Springer International Handbooks of Education*, vol 18. (pp. 5–21). Springer. <https://doi.org/10.1007/978-1-4020-4012-2_2>

Enders, J. (2013). The university in the audit society: on accountability, trust and markets. In L. Engwall, & P. Scott (Eds.), *Trust in Universities* (pp. 53–62). Portland Press.

Enders, J., & Teichler, U. (1997) A victim of their own success? Employment and working conditions of academic staff in comparative perspective. *Higher Education, 34*, 347–372. <https://doi.org/10.1023/A:1003023923056>

Findlow, S. (2008). Accountability and innovation in higher education: a disabling tension? *Studies in Higher Education, 33*(3), 313–329. DOI: 10.1080/03075070802049285,

Fukudome, H. (2014). Teaching and research in the academic profession: Nexus and conflict. In A. Arimoto, W. Cummings, F. Huang, & J. Shin (Eds.), *The Changing Academic Profession in Japan. The Changing Academy—The Changing Academic*

Profession in International Comparative Perspective, vol 11. (pp. 169–183). Springer International Publishing. <https://doi.org/10.1007/978-3-031-04439-7_5>

Fumasoli, T., Goastellec, G., & Kehm B. (2015). *Academic Work and Careers in Europe: Trends, Challenges, Perspectives*. Springer. <https://doi.org/10.1007/978-3-319-10720-2>

Gibbs, S., & Miller, A. (2014). Professors' resilience and well-being: A role for educational psychology. *Professors and Teaching, 20*, 609–621. <http://dx.doi.org/10.1080/13540602.2013.844408>

Goastellec, G., Park, E., Ates, G., & Toffel, K. (2013). Academic Markets, Academic Careers: Where Do We Stand?. In B. M. Kehm, & U. Teichler (Eds.), *The Academic Profession in Europe: New Tasks and New Challenges. The Changing Academy—The Changing Academic Profession in International Comparative Perspective*, vol 5 (pp 93–120.). Springer. <https://doi.org/10.1007/978-94-007-4614-5_6>

Gould, E. (2006). Professor or Knowledge Worker? The Politics of Defining Faculty Work. *Higher Education in Europe*, *31*(3), 241–249. <https://doi.org/10.1080/03797720601058690>

Gyuris, F. (2014). Basic education in communist Hungary. A commons approach. *International Journal of the Commons*, *8*(2), 531–553.

Hammoudi Halat, D., Soltani, A., Dalli, R., Alsarraj, L., & Malki, A. (2023). Understanding and fostering mental health and well-being among university faculty: A narrative review. *Journal of Clinical Medicine*, *12*(13), 4425.

Hargittai, I. (2008). *Martians of science: Five physicists who changed the twentieth century*. Oxford University Press.

Höhle, E. A., & Teichler, U. (2013). The Teaching Function of the Academic Profession. In U. Teichler, & E. Höhle (Eds.), *The Work Situation of the Academic Profession in Europe: Findings of a Survey in Twelve Countries. The Changing Academy—The Changing Academic Profession in International Comparative Perspective*, vol 8. (pp 79–108). Springer. <https://doi.org/10.1007/978-94-007-5977-0_5>

Hyde, A., Clarke, M., & Drennan, J. (2013). The changing role of academics and the rise of managerialism. In B. M. Kehm & U. Teichler (Eds.), *The academic profession in Europe: New tasks and new challenges* (pp. 39–52). Springer.

Janik, A., & Toulmin, S. (2023). *Wittgenstein's Vienna*. Rowman & Littlefield.

Jayman, M., Glazzard, J., & Rose, A. (2022). Tipping point: The staff wellbeing crisis in higher education. *Frontiers in Education 7*, 929335. <https://doi.org/10.3389/feduc.2022.929335>

Jencks, C., & Riesman, D. (2002 [1968]). *The Academic Revolution*. Doubleday.

Kehm, B. M., & Teichler, U. (2013). *The academic profession in Europe: New tasks and new challenges* (Vol. 5). Springer. DOI 10.1007/978-94-007-4614-5

Kogan, M., & Teichler, U. (2007). *Key challenges to the academic profession*. UNESCO Forum on Higher Education. Retrieved from <https://unesdoc.unesco.org/ark:/48223/pf00001>

Kovács, K., Dobay, B., Halasi, S., Pinczés, T., & Tódor, I. (2024). Demands, resources and institutional factors in the work of academic staff in Central and Eastern Europe: results of a qualitative research among university teachers in five countries. *Frontiers in Education*, 8, 1326515. <https://doi.org/10.3389/feduc.2023.1326515>

Kozma, T. (1990). Higher education in Hungary: Facing the political transition. *European Journal of Education, 25*(4), 379–390. <https://doi.org/10.2307/1502624>

Kozma, T. (1998) New challenges of tertiary education in East-Central Europe. In E. Leitner (Ed.), *Educational Research and Higher Education Reform in Eastern and Central Europe* (pp. 131–143). Peter Lang.

Kozma, T. (2008). Political transformations and higher education reforms. *European Education, 40*(2), 29–45. <https://doi.org/10.2753/EUE1056-4934400202>

Kozma, T., Rébay, M., Óhidy, A., & Szolár, É. (2014). *The Bologna Process in Central and Eastern Europe*. Springer Fachmedien Wiesbaden.

Kwiek, M. (2012). *Knowledge production in European universities: States, markets, and academic entrepreneurialism* (Vol. 3). Peter Lang.

Kwiek, M. (2015). The unfading power of collegiality? University governance in Poland in a European comparative and quantitative perspective. International Journal of Educational Development, 43, 77–89. <https://doi.org/10.1016/j.ijedudev.2015.05.002>

Kwiek, M. (2016). The European research elite: A cross-national study of highly productive academics in 11 countries. Higher Education, 71, 379–397.

Kwiek, M. (2022). Global Vertical Stratification of Institutions and the Academic Profession: The Role of Research in Future High Participation Environments. In M. Klemenčič (Ed.), *From Actors to Reforms in European Higher Education. Higher Education Dynamics*, vol 58 (pp. 299–312). Springer. <https://doi.org/10.1007/978-3-031-09400-2_21>

Kwiek, M., & Antonowicz, D. (2015). The changing paths in academic careers in European universities: Minor steps and major milestones. In T. Fumasoli, G. Goastellec, & B. M. Kehm (Eds.), Academic work and careers in Europe: Trends, challenges, perspectives (pp. 41–68). Springer <https://doi.org/10.1007/978-3-319-10720-2_3>

Kwiek, M., & Roszka, W. (2022a). Are female scientists less inclined to publish alone? The gender solo research gap. *Scientometrics*, 127, 1697–1735 <https://doi.org/10.1007/s11192-022-04308-7>

Kwiek, M., & Roszka, W. (2002b). Academic vs. biological age in research on academic careers: a large-scale study with implications for scientifically developing systems. *Scientometrics*, 127, 3543–3575. <https://doi.org/10.1007/s11192-022-04363-0>

Lee, J. J., Cheslock, J., Maldonado-Maldonado, A., & Rhoades, G. (2005). Professors as Knowledge Workers in the New, Global Economy. In J. C. Smart (Eds), *Higher Education: Handbook of Theory and Research*, vol 20 (pp. 55–132). Springer. <https://doi.org/10.1007/1-4020-3279-X_2_>

Levy, D. (2014). Evolving Privatization in Eastern and Central European Higher Education. *European Education*, 46(3), 7–30. <https://doi.org/10.2753/EUE1056-4934460301>

Loveday, V. (2018). The neurotic academic: anxiety, casualisation, and governance in the neoliberalising university. *Journal of Cultural Economy, 11*(2), 154–166. <https://doi.org/10.1080/17530350.2018.1426032>

Melendez, W. A., & De Guzman, R. M. (1983). *Burnout: The New Academic Disease. ASHE-ERIC Higher Education Research Report No. 9.* Publications Department, Association for the Study of Higher Education.

Moraru, L., Praisler, M., Marin, S. A., & Bentea, C. C. (2013). The Academic Profession: Quality Assurance, Governance, Relevance, and Satisfaction. In B. M. Kehm, & U. Teichler (Eds.), *The Academic Profession in Europe: New Tasks and New Challenges. The Changing Academy—The Changing Academic Profession in International Comparative Perspective*, vol 5 (pp. 141–162). Springer. <https://doi.org/10.1007/978-94-007-4614-5_8>

Musselin, C. (2007). *The transformation of academic work: Facts and analysis.* Research & Occasional Paper Series: CSHE.4.07. Center for Studies in Higher Education.

Musselin, C. (2013). How peer review empowers the academic profession and university managers: Changes in relationships between the state, universities and the professoriate. *Research Policy, 42*(5), 1165–1173. <https://doi.org/10.1016/j.respol.2013.02.002>

Neave, G. (1998). The evaluative state reconsidered. *European Journal of Education, 33*(3), 265–284.

Nicholls, H., Nicholls, M., Tekin, S., Lamb, D., & Billings, J. (2022). The impact of working in academia on researchers' mental health and well-being: A systematic review and qualitative meta-synthesis. *PloS one*, *17*(5), e0268890. <https://doi.org/10.1371/journal.pone.0268890>

Pace, F., D'Urso, G., Zappulla, C., & Pace, U. (2021). The relation between workload and personal well-being among university professors. *Current Psychology, 40*(7), 3417–3424. <https://doi.org/10.1007/s12144-019-00294-x>

Pavlin, S., & Sušanj, Z. (2020). The academic profession in the Western Balkans: Time for a turning point?. *European Journal of Education*, *55*(4), 471–475.

Polónyi, I., & Kozma, T. (2022). From the bureaucratic model to the bureaucratic model: The post-socialist development of the Hungarian higher education. *Hungarian Educational Research Journal*, *12*(1), 80–90.

Pusztai, G. (2015). Pathways to Success in Higher Education. Rethinking the Social Capital Theory in the Light of Institutional Diversity. Peter Lang Edition.

Pusztai, G., & Szabó, P. C. (2008). The Bologna Process as a Trojan Horse: restructuring higher education in Hungary. *European Education*, *40*(2), 85–103. <https://doi.org/10.2753/EUE1056-4934400205>

Pusztai, G., Fényes, H., & Kovács, K. (2022). Factors influencing the chance of dropout or being at risk of dropout in higher education. *Education Sciences*, *12*(11), 804. <https://doi.org/10.3390/educsci12110804>

Probst, C., & Goastellec, G. (2013). Internationalisation and the academic labour market. In B. M. Kehm, & U. Teichler (Eds.), *The academic profession in Europe: New tasks and new challenges* (pp. 121–139). Springer.

Seligman, M. E., & Csíkszentmihályi, M. (2000). *Positive psychology: An introduction*. American Psychological Association.

Teichler, U. (1999). Higher education policy and the world of work: changing conditions and challenges. *Higher Education Policy*, *12*(4), 285–312.

Teichler, U. (2004). The Changing Debate on Internationalisation of Higher Education. *Higher Education, 48(1)*, 5–26.

Teichler, U., Arimoto, A., & Cummings, W. K. (2013). *The changing academic profession*. Springer.

Teichler, U., & Höhle, E. A. (2013). *The work situation of the academic profession in Europe: Findings of a survey in twelve countries*. Springer Science & Business Media.

Tinto, V. (1993). *Leaving college. Rethinking the Causes ad Cures of Student Attrition*. The University of Chicago Press.

Trow, M. (2007). Reflections on the transition from elite to mass to universal access: Forms and phases of higher education in modern societies since WWII. In J. J. F. Forest, & P. G. Altbach (Eds.), *International handbook of higher education* (pp. 243–280). Springer Netherlands.

van der Kaap, H., & de Weert, E. (2016). A portrait of the changing academic profession in the Netherlands. In J. F. Galaz-Fontes, A. Arimoto, U. Teichler, & J. Brennan (Eds.), *Biographies and Careers throughout Academic Life* (pp. 143–163). Springer International Publishing.

Vostal, F. (2015). Speed kills, speed thrills: Constraining and enabling accelerations in academic work-life. *Globalisation, Societies and Education*, *13*(3), 295–314.

PART I

Higher Education Systems as the Working Environment of Academic Staff in Central and Eastern Europe: Country Studies

2. Changes in Higher Education and Academic Staff in Hungary

István Polónyi

ABSTRACT
This study examines the characteristics and employment patterns of Hungarian higher education academics. It briefly outlines the development of Hungarian higher education after the change of the socialist regime (post-1990) and describes the force field in which academics work. It then presents some of the academics' characteristics (age, gender, ratio) in an international comparison and studies the rules governing their appointment and employment under the Hungarian Higher Education Act. The paper investigates the structure of university teaching staff by their function and evolution. It also analyses the lifetime earnings of doctoral graduates in the Hungarian context, including the rise in the number of doctoral students. Finally, the paper briefly describes a critical piece of instructive research that surveys the situation of young Hungarian academics in higher education.

Keywords: Hungarian higher education, academic staff, academic staff wages

Introduction: Topics, Data, and Methods

This study examines the characteristics and employment patterns of Hungarian higher education academic staff. The first part of the paper briefly outlines the development of Hungarian higher education following the post-socialist transition (after 1990). The analysis addresses trends in student enrollment and compares participation rates internationally. The investigation is based on higher education statistics from the Hungarian Educational Authority and the Central Statistical Office, as well as databases from the World Bank and Eurostat. Subsequently, the study reviews several characteristics of academics in higher education (age, gender ratio) in an international comparison. The analysis utilizes data from the Educational Authority and the Central Statistical Office, along with databases from the World Bank and the OECD. The investigations are presented using simple tables and figures.

Next, the study reviews the main regulations regarding the appointment and employment of academic staff. In terms of methodology, this review is carried out through a documentary analysis of Hungarian higher education legislation.

Following this, the paper examines the structure and evolution of academic positions and monthly and lifetime earnings on academic career paths, both internationally and domestically. The data sources for this analysis are the National Employment Service and the Central Statistical Office. The analysis is conducted using simple comparative charts and tables.

Finally, the study addresses the international comparison of the number of doctoral students who represent the future supply of higher education academics, using the UNESCO database. This examination is based on a simple tabular analysis.

1. Some Characteristics of the Development of Hungarian Higher Education After the Change of Regime

First, we review the most important features of the development of Hungarian higher education following the system change. Several studies analyze the development of the period (Berács et al., 2014; 2017), and a Polish analysis (Donina & Jaworska, 2024) is worth mentioning among the studies of Hungarian higher education. But several international comparative studies can be mentioned, of which we highlight only two here: Scott, 2007, Keczer, 2014.

Hungary entered the democratic social order after the change of regime with a somewhat fragmented and low-capacity higher education system. In 1990, there were less than 1,000 students per 100,000 inhabitants (see Table 2.1), compared with 5,500 in North America. This figure may have almost doubled in the five years up to 1995—not coincidentally the year in which Hungary's first Higher Education Act set the goal of achieving[1] the participation rate in higher education of advanced democratic societies—but it was still only three-quarters or half that of the developed European countries taken as examples (e.g., Austria 2970, Germany 2628, France 3600, U.K. 3125, Finland 4190).[2]

Table 2.1 shows the changes in Hungarian higher education policy and the contradictions of thirty years of development. This educational policy environment constitutes the force field for the employment of academic staff, and it is worth briefly reviewing the most significant changes of the period that (also) affect them.

One of the critical elements of this environment is the introduction of pluralism in the establishment and maintenance of institutions in 1990, which led to the creation of many non-state institutions (Church-run and foundation-based universities and colleges). As a result, by 2020, almost a third of all academic staff

---

1 According to the preamble of Act LXXX of 1993 (on Higher Education), "Parliament feels a special responsibility for higher education as a sector of special importance, and in this spirit, it shall do its utmost to ensure that the number of students of the appropriate age group entering higher education can be raised to the level achieved in developed democratic societies."

2 Source of data: (UNESCO 1998).

were employed in non-state higher education (11% in Church-run and 20% in foundation-based institutions).[3] The privatization (outsourcing) of most public universities reduced the number of academics employed in public higher education to 25%, in Church-run higher education to 13%, and in foundation-based higher education to 62% by 2023.

The other such element includes higher education admission policies and the development of student numbers. Several factors have influenced the development of student numbers.

One that is most crucial is the demographic trend, that is, the change in the number of people seeking higher education. After the third-generation effect of the demographic wave of the 1950s (which was the result of the government's demographic intervention, the abortion ban), the population aged 18–22 began to decline after peaking in the mid-1990s, resulting in a decline in the number of applicants to higher education. (See Figure 2.1 for the number of 18–22-year-olds.) Moreover, the exhaustion of the demand for further education, which was postponed due to the low enrollment in higher education, was an influencing factor affective right up until the change of the regime.

Another impacting element was the introduction of two-cycle education. The two-cycle system was introduced in 2005 in the framework of the Bologna reform (creation of the European Higher Education Area). The two-cycle education radically reshaped the system of higher education, (the introduction of bachelor's education makes the degree process faster, while the introduction of a master's degree shortens the second-degree process, which accounts for an increasing share of adult education). Moreover, perhaps the higher education admissions policy had the most sizable effect.

At the end of the 1990s—until 1998, when the conservative government abolished tuition fees—a reimbursement system was introduced for some of the admitted students (those who did not meet the ministry's state funding threshold in the entrance exam) instead of the state support previously available to everyone. In other words, most of the students paid tuition fees, and those who got in under one point limit paid an expense reimbursement fee. (This was 2.2% for students in 1998). This system had a significant deterrent effect on applications. It should be added that the abolition of the tuition fee did not mean the abolition of the cost reimbursement, so those students who did not

---

3 Source of data: Higher education statistics of the Oktatási Hivatal (Office of Education): <https://dari.oktatas.hu/firstat.index>.

reach the funding threshold score continued to pay cost reimbursement (in 2000, 6.4% belonged to this category).[4]

Then, in 2013, the conservative government significantly reduced state support for higher education and increased tuition fees for paying students, reducing the number of state-funded students and, in the longer term, pursuing an elitist policy of reducing enrollment.[5] In 2020, conditions were further tightened by making the advanced final exams compulsory for access to higher education.[6] The high requirement for the advanced final exam led to a radical drop in enrollments in some crucial courses (STEM[7] and teacher training), which attracted students from weaker secondary schools. The decline in enrollments and admissions resulted in an immediate change in higher education policy.[8] From 2021, admissions requirements were radically relaxed.

All these effects are visible in the evolution of the specific number of students (per 100,000 inhabitants) and the overall participation rate (Figures 2.1 and 2.2).

Table 2.1: Institutions, faculties, number of students (short-term, tertiary, bachelor, master and undivided, and doctoral) and number of academics

	Institutions	Faculties	Total tertiary education students	Academics	Higher education students per 100 thousand inhabitants
1990/91.	77	117	102 387	17 302	986.9
1991/90.	77	118	107 079	17 477	1032.3
1992/93.	91	132	117 463	17 743	1132.3
1993/94.	91	137	135 483	18 687	1307.1
1994/95.	91	137	157 137	19 103	1518.2

4 Source of data: Statisztikai Tájékoztató Felsőoktatás 2000/2001.

5 The allowed number of state-funded students was reduced in the case of some programs (scientific fields), and the highest amount was increased. Since the HEIs received less funding, they were pressed to require the higher or the highest tuition fee.

6 Until 2020, the higher-level baccalaureate—that is, centrally organized with higher-level tasks—was only compulsory for specific subjects and certain specializations, while for most specializations, the baccalaureate organized by the secondary school was sufficient

7 STEM: summary abbreviation of higher education study fields in science, technology, engineering and mathematicsn.

8 Source of data: Oktatási Hivatal <https://www.felvi.hu/felveteli/ponthatarok_statisztikak>.

	Institutions	Faculties	Total tertiary education students	Academics	Higher education students per 100 thousand inhabitants
1995/96.	90	138	183 021	18 098	1770.5
1996/97.	89	139	202 762	19 329	1964.6
1997/98.	90	140	237 662	19 716	2307.2
1998./99.	89	141	263 398	21 323	2562.2
1999/00.	89	143	285 452	21 249	2784.1
2000/01.	62	155	305 256	22 873	2986.3
2001/02.	65	156	324 743	22 863	3183.8
2002/03.	66	157	354 745	23 151	3486.4
2003/04.	68	169	382 001	23 288	3766.5
2004/05.	69	170	395 529	23 787	3909.5
2005/06.	71	172	399 095	23 188	3952.2
2006/07.	71	172	394 445	22 076	3914.3
2007/08.	71	173	378 942	22 376	3764.6
2008/09.	70	172	363 439	22 475	3618.1
2009/10.	69	171	353 403	21 934	3523.1
2010/11.	69	184	345 627	21 495	3451.4
2011/12.	68	183	344 754	21 357	3452.4
2012/13.	66	181	323 413	20 555	3256.3
2013/14.	66	185	300 412	21 137	3031.7
2014/15.	67	184	289 154	21 080	2927.5
2015/16.	66	185	278 829	21 668	2829.0
2016/17.	65	186	271 382	22 436	2760.8
2017/18.	64	187	266 920	23 110	2724.2
2018/19.	64	190	264 511	22 519	2705.2
2019/20.	64	191	269 315	23 383	2755.7
2020/21.	62	189	271 149	23 511	2775.3
2021/22.	63	..	276 402	24 903	2840.4
2022/23.	63	..	273 755	26 357	2825.4

Source: Higher education statistics of the Education Office and data from the Central Statistical Office.

Note: Number of students without further education.

Analyses show (Polónyi, 2023a) that the impact of conservative education policies over the last decade and a half reduced the opportunities of certain groups (women, young people from disadvantaged areas, and those in vocational education and training with a final exam, vocational secondary school/technical high school) to enter higher education—i.e., increased inequality in access to higher education.

Finally, the higher education policy slowed down the development of tertiary education over the last fifteen years. It missed a historic opportunity to increase the proportion of graduates, offered by the decline in the number of the age group. As a result, social mobility slowly froze; the share of young graduates fell in 2014 and has since stagnated at a low level, well below the 40% proposed by the EU 2020 strategy (Figure 2.3).

These changes in the higher education policy and, consequently, in higher education have formed and continue to impact the force field in which Hungarian higher education academics work.

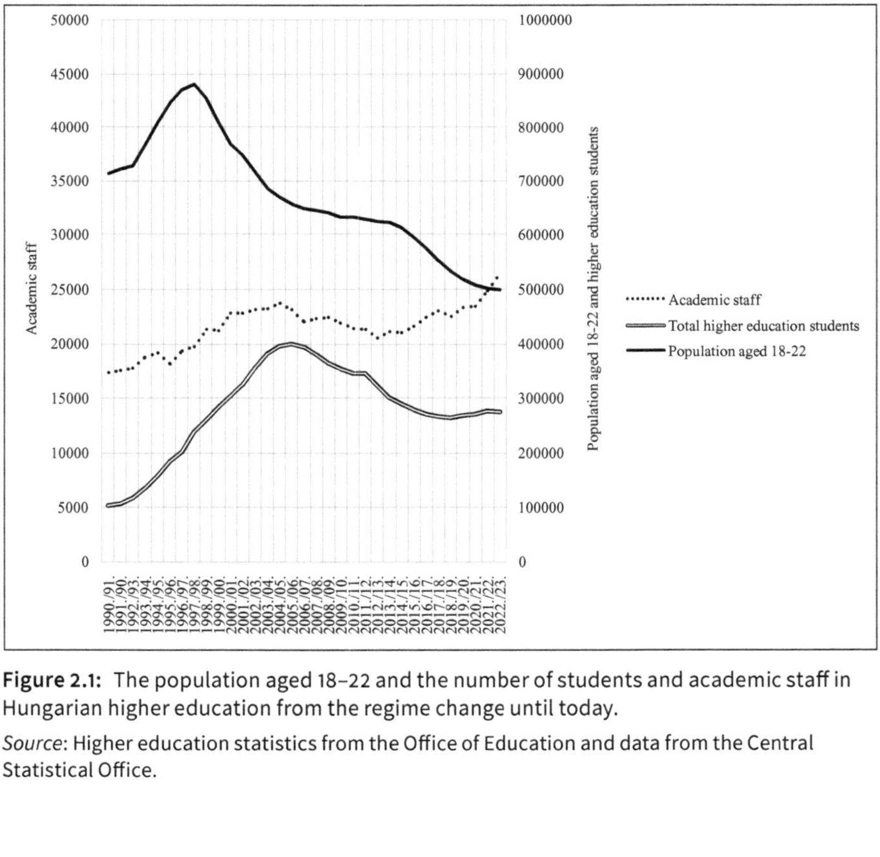

Figure 2.1: The population aged 18–22 and the number of students and academic staff in Hungarian higher education from the regime change until today.

Source: Higher education statistics from the Office of Education and data from the Central Statistical Office.

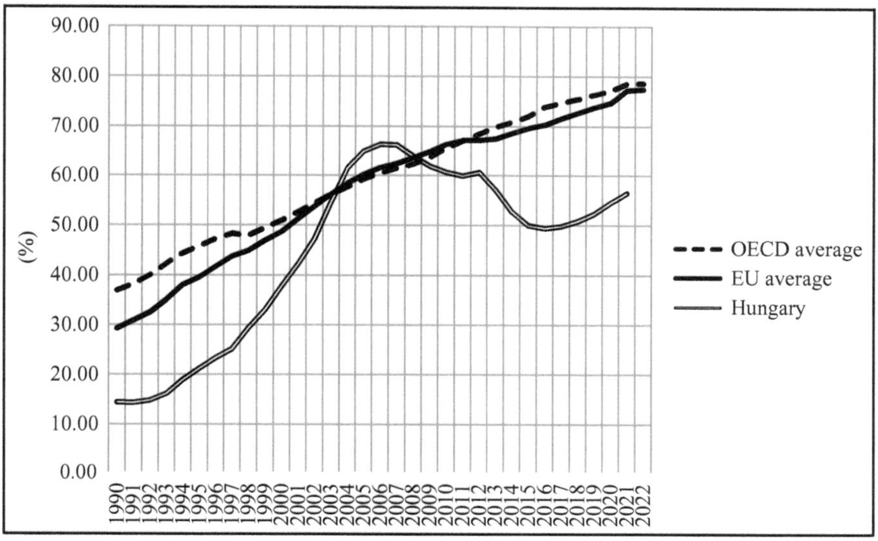

Figure 2.2: Gross enrollment rate of higher education in Hungary and the EU and OECD average.

Source: Author's editing based on the World Bank database.

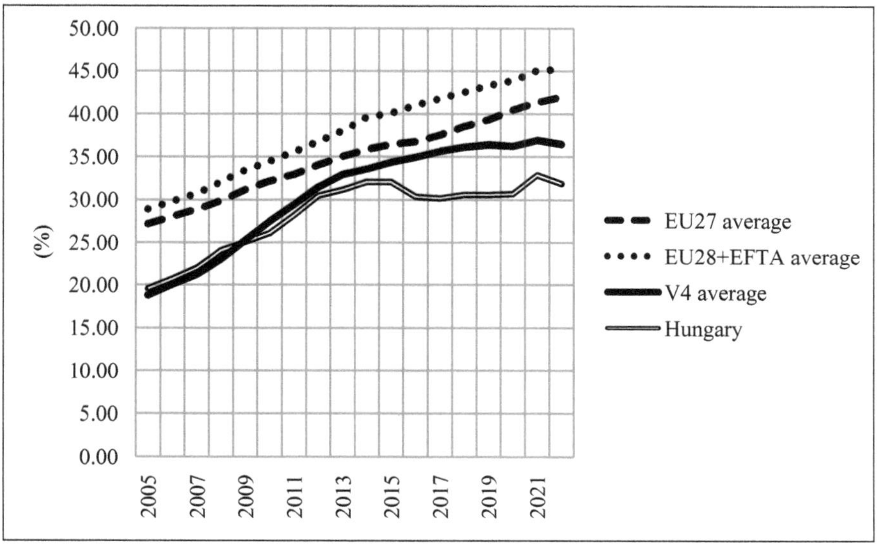

Figure 2.3: Graduates as a percentage of the population 25–34 years of age.

Source: Author's calculation and editing based on Eurostat data.

2. The Characteristics of Academics in Hungarian Higher Education

From the data presented earlier (Table 2.1 and Figure 2.1), we can see that the number of academics has not moved in line with the student population since 2005 (while between 1990 and 2004, there was a robust positive correlation of (+0.9752) between the number of students and academics. The period of 2005 and 2022, however, saw a weak negative correlation of (–0.3135). Between 1997 and 2004, the number of academics increased by just over a third (6.5 thousand), followed by a decrease of around 15% (3 thousand). Between 2012 and 2022, there was an increase of almost 28% (6 thousand people). The student-academic staff ratio increased from 5.9 in 1990 to 17.9 in 2006 and then decreased to 10.4 in 2022 (Figure 2.4).

Looking at the trend in the number of academics more closely, we can see that it correlates with three main factors. There is a relatively strong negative correlation with the number of institutions (–0.7338) and a similarly significant positive correlation with the number of faculties (+0.7700) and the student population (+0.7221). The increase in the number of academics until the early 2000s was quite clearly related to the increase in the number of students. The subsequent decline in the number of academics is understandable as it coincided with a decline in the student population and a significant integration into state institutions in 2000, leading to a cutback in the number of universities. The reduction in budget support following the government change in 2010 further exacerbated the downward trend. Since 2015, however, the number of academics has increased again, probably due to the higher education strategy formulated at that time, which aimed to develop higher education in certain areas (teacher training and STEM), and the budgetary conditions have also improved somewhat.

Assuming that the teaching load can be compared over the period, we can conclude that the teaching load tripled by 2006, and, despite the increase in teaching staff, it was still about twice the level of 1990, even in 2022.

Looking at the international data on student-academic staff ratios for OECD and EU countries between 1990 and 2017, we see that the average of the 39 reporting countries[9] is just over 14. Hungary's data for the last decade was more favorable than this—thanks to the policy limiting the number of students in higher education during this period.

---

9 Data calculated based on World Development Indicators from the World Bank.

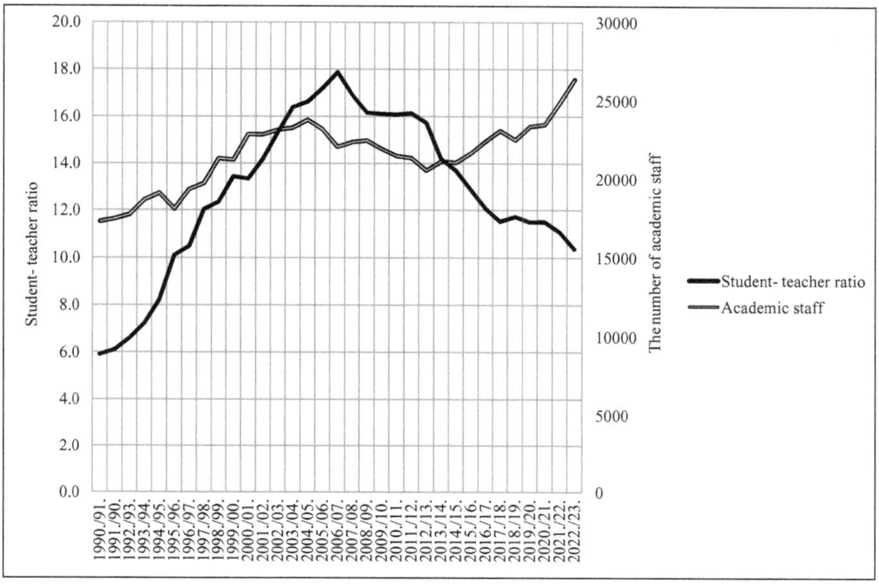

Figure 2.4: Development of academic staff and student-academic staff ratio in Hungarian higher education, 1990–2022.

Source: Higher education statistics of the Education Office and data from the Central Statistical Office.

The analysis of the age distribution of academics in higher education (Table 2.2) shows that the Hungarian teaching staff in higher education is older than the average in developed countries. Nevertheless, Hungary is in the middle range in terms of age composition. In 2021, Hungary ranked 21st among the 30 OECD reporting countries for those aged 30–49 and 16th for 30–39 years. In the same year, Hungary ranked 16th out of the 30 reporting countries for those under 30 and 15th out of 30 for 50 years and over.

Table 2.2: Distribution of academic staff working in higher education by age

	Less than 30 years old		Between 30 and 49 years old		Over 50 years old		Total	
	Hungary	OECD average	Hungary	OECD average	Hungary	OECD average	Hungary	OECD average
2013	5.6	9.0	53.7	51.0	40.7	40.0	100	100
2015	4.5	8.9	54.0	50.7	41.5	40.4	100	100
2017	6.1	8.9	53.5	51.1	40.4	40.0	100	100
2019	5.7	8.6	54.5	51.6	39.8	39.8	100	100
2021	5.6	8.3	53.7	51.2	40.7	40.4	100	100

Source: OECD.

In higher education, the proportion of women among academics is increasing in parallel with massification. In terms of national data, we see a similar trend in Hungary (with a correlation of (+0.5778) between the number of students and the proportion of women in the case of Hungarian data). However, there is a non-insignificant fluctuation[10] (Figure 2.5). In 2020, Hungary ranked 80th among 144 reporting countries with a share of 41.5% of female academics in higher education, which was significantly lower than in the case of the leading countries.

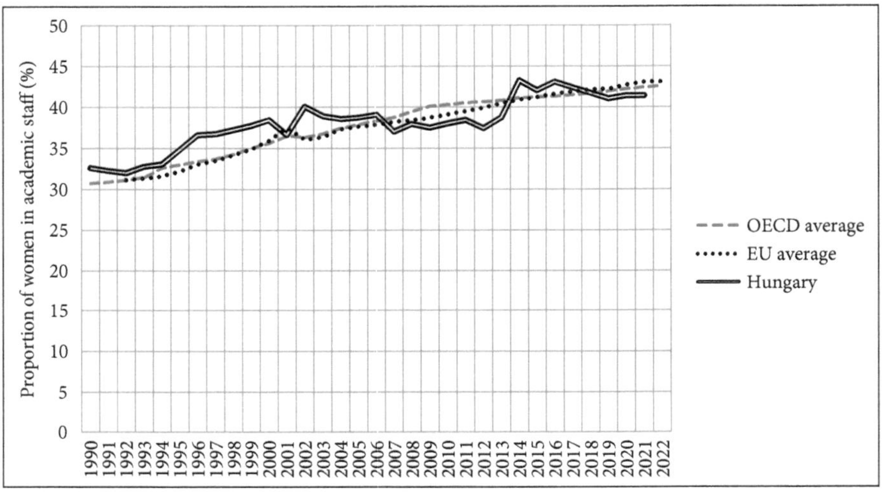

Figure 2.5: Percentage of women among academic staff in Hungary.
Source: World Bank database.

3. Employment Rules for Academics Working in Higher Education

Before the Second World War, academic qualifications were a privilege of universities. One consequence of the Soviet-style transformation of universities was the separation of research and academic qualifications from universities. In 1951, a decree with the force of law[11] stipulated that "as a first step in systematically ensuring scientific succession following the example of the training of the leading scientific cadre in the Soviet Union," the academic title of the Candidate of

[10] The reason for the increase after 2016 is probably that family-friendly measures were strengthened in the government's higher education strategy (Polónyi & Kozma, 2020).
[11] Decree-Law No 26 of 1951 and Ministerial Council Decree No 184/1951 (X. 16).

Sciences should be introduced for novice researchers, since "the previous degrees (old-style doctorate, private academic) do not adequately contribute to raising the general level of our scientific life." The decree set out that the Hungarian Academy of Sciences would award the degrees of Doctor of Sciences and Candidate of Sciences through a Scientific Qualification Committee. The legislation also stated that the committee would review the scientific work of former title-holders at their request to determine whether they were eligible for the Doctor of Sciences or Candidate of Sciences degrees. Thus, in 1951, the scientific qualification became centralized and at the same time it was used as a tool for cadre selection, serving the establishment and selection of a scientific elite loyal to the "the party and the government" (Polónyi, 2018).

The Scientific Qualification Committee and the Hungarian Academy of Sciences played this role until the fall of communism. Moreover, even after that, at least to a small extent, since the 1993 Higher Education Act, which restored the right of universities to award Ph.Ds. and degrees, it allowed the Academy to retain the rights associated with the Soviet system of awarding doctorates ("senior professorship"). It was indeed renamed the "Doctor of Sciences" (but its holders also retained their lifelong, non-performance-related honorary degrees),—and this is still the case today, in the first quarter of the twenty-first century (which, except for one or two post-socialist countries, is very different from international practice). It should be added that one of the reasons why it took three years for the first law on higher education to be introduced into Parliament after the change of regime was the veto of the Academy, which had long wanted to keep the academic qualification for itself and would have insisted on the exclusive right to award doctorates.

The first law on higher education after the change of regime (Act LXXX of 1993) stipulated that universities had the right to provide doctoral education and to award doctoral degrees (Ph.D.), to develop and implement the habilitation[12] procedure.[13] The law established the National Accreditation Committee,[14] which had the right to decide which disciplines and fields of study a university could provide doctoral education and award doctoral degrees (Ph.D.). The law also stated that universities and colleges might establish academic researcher

[12] Habilitation is the highest post-Ph.D. (doctorate) degree awarded by the university, recognizing that the lecturer is ready to teach at university level (habil for short) <https://jelentese.hu/idegen-szavak-szotara/habilitacio>

According to the Higher Education Act: habilitation is an institutional recognition of teaching and lecturing ability and academic achievement.

[13] Act LXXX of 1993, § 3.

[14] Act LXXX of 1993, § 80.

statuses for university and college professors, associate professors, assistant professors, assistant lecturer, language, sports, art and college teachers, and other teaching and scientific research posts.[15]

The law also stipulated that university professors had to hold a doctorate (Ph.D.), a master's degree and a habilitation and that associate professors have a doctorate (Ph.D.) and a master's degree. University professors and associate professors must also have demonstrated through their teaching, scientific, and artistic activities that they could supervise the academic, scientific, and artistic work of students, doctoral candidates, and teaching assistants and that they could give lectures in a foreign language.[16] University professors were appointed or dismissed by the Hungarian President of the Republic on the recommendation of the Minister of Education, who acted on a proposal from the institutional council (senate) (or, in the case of a non-state university, the maintenance body).[17]

According to the 2000 and 2003 amendments to the law, before suggesting a professor, the university was required to obtain the opinion of the Accreditation Committee on the candidate and, taking this into account, submit it to the Minister.[18] The appointment of an associate professor was made by the rector after the senate gave its opinion. University and college assistant professor and assistant lecturers were appointed for a fixed term of up to four years. Appointments of university and college assistant professors could be renewed twice, while those of assistant lecturers could be extended once. Although the law did not explicitly require it, it was generally the case that teaching assistants were required to start their doctoral studies by the end of the four years, and assistant professors had to pursue their ongoing doctoral studies.[19] Employees of state institutions were considered civil servants. A salary scale determined their remuneration compared to the basic salary of a university professor. The salary scale was determined by

---

15 Act LXXX of 1993, § 13.

16 Act LXXX of 1993, §§ 17–19.

17 In the case of a college professor, the requirements are similar—except habilitation—and the appointment authority rests with the Prime Minister.

18 According to the amendment, the following point j) shall be added to paragraph (2) of Article 81 of the Higher Education Act: [(2) The MAB shall issue an opinion at the request of the Minister of Education, the FTT or a higher education institution] "j) on the appointment of university or college teachers pursuant to paragraph (4) of Article 17 or paragraph (2) of Article 18."

19 Section 6 of Act XXXVIII of 2003 amended Section 14 (2) of the Higher Education Act of 1993 in the sense described above.

the country's annual central budget law.[20] The 2003 amendment introduces a mandatory retirement age of 70 for university professors.[21]

The Higher Education Act of 2005 (Act CXXXIX of 2005) essentially failed to make much difference. In the case of university professors, it added the requirement of international recognition to the previous requirements. The law extended the requirement of public competition to the positions of assistant professors and teaching assistants. It consolidated the above-mentioned practice that the commencement of doctoral studies was a prerequisite for employment as a teaching assistant, and the establishment of a doctoral relationship was a prerequisite for employment as an assistant professor. It also tightened their employment conditions by stipulating that academics who had not obtained an academic degree within twelve years of their employment could not be further employed.[22]

The effective Higher Education Act of 2011 (Act CCIV of 2011), which entered into force, introduced a number of innovations. Among other things, it stipulated that granting the right to use the title of university professor did not have the effect of establishing or terminating an employment relationship. The employment relationship of a college or university professor could be established or terminated by the rector, who exercised the authority of an employer in the higher education institution.[23] In other words, the Hungarian President's appointment of a university professor essentially became an (academic) title. It did not automatically entail the employment relationship of a university professor.[24] The conditions for appointment as a university professor now included a stronger emphasis on international recognition requirements and the obligation to publish in a foreign language. The regulation allowed for the dismissal of academics who failed to fulfill the requirements of the position.

---

20 Act XXXV of 2004 defined the term "university professor I." which is also the salary base for university staff. At that time, a table was added to Annex 2 to the Public Servants Act (Act XXXIII of 1992), which sets the salaries of university teachers in relation to the salary of "university teacher I."

21 Article 7 (1) of Act XXXVIII of 2003 amended Article 17 of the Higher Education Act of 1993 so that the President of the Republic shall exonerate a university professor if he or she has reached the age of seventy.

22 Act CXXXIX of 2005 § 91.

23 Act CCIV of 2011, § 27.

24 Therefore, a university lecturer employed under a contract at one university, does not automatically become a university professor when he or she moves to another university. It is at the discretion of the universities to decide whether a university professor appointed by the President will be employed as a university professor.

In line with the aims of the Hungarian higher education policy, the Act and its 2014 amendment significantly reduced the financial autonomy of higher education institutions. It introduced the chancellor system, which meant that the Prime Minister appointed a 'chief manager' to oversee the economic decisions of key institutions. The appointed official had exclusive authority over all economic, financial, and personnel policy decisions, radically reducing the powers of the senate and the rector (Kováts, 2023, Kováts & Zsátku, 2023).[25] The composition of the accreditation committee was also radically changed to ensure that the government appointed the majority of delegates.[26] The law diminished the powers of the committee by making it possible to bypass the opinion of both the university senate and, consequently, the accreditation committee. This was achieved by allowing proposals for the appointment of university professors to be made by the Hungarian Academy of Sciences in the case of academic appointments, the Hungarian Academy of Arts in the field of the arts, and the Hungarian Olympic Committee in the field of sport.[27] (It should be added that the intervention of the Minister of Education was also quite common.)

It is essential to mention that considering or ignoring the opinion of the Accreditation Commission has been a critical point in the procedure almost since the introduction of the Accreditation Commission's power to qualify university professors was introduced in 2000. In the case of the Minister of Education, we find more than one case in which the Accreditation Commission, despite its negative recommendation, referred a candidate for a university professorship to the President of the Republic. It is noteworthy that the decisions of the Accreditation Commission were subject to pressure from various institutional, professional, and political lobbies, which the Commission had never really been able to resist since its creation. The extent to which university autonomy was violated by the Accreditation Commission's interference in personnel matters was still a matter

---

[25] Section 19 of Act XXXVI of 2014 adds a new section to the Higher Education Act of 2011, which reads as follows: "Section 13/A (1) In a public higher education institution, the Chancellor shall be responsible for the operation of the institution." The Chancellor, appointed by the Prime Minister, does not have to consult the Senate or the Rector. Then, Act CXXXI of 2015 clearly delimits the powers of the rector, the senate and the chancellor, resulting in a significant reduction of autonomy in institutional self-governance.

[26] Act CCIV of 2011, § 71.

[27] The 2014 amendment of the Higher Education Act (Act XXXVI of 2014) introduced the possibility for the Hungarian Academy of Sciences, the Hungarian Academy of Arts and the Hungarian Olympic Committee to propose to the President of the Republic of Hungary the appointment of a university professor, bypassing the Senate of the higher education institutions.

of debate, as was the extent to which the Minister's similar interference, or overstepping his role as a mere postman, was also unlawful.

A crucial innovation of the 2011 Act was the regulation of working hours.[28] According to this law, academics were obliged to devote the following time (averaged over two consecutive academic semesters) to lectures, seminars, exercises, and consultations for the preparation of students, depending on their classification.

- at least eight hours per week for university or college professors,
- at least 10 hours per week for associate professors,
- at least 12 hours per week for assistant professors and teaching assistants.

Academics were required to devote at least twenty percent of their working time to academic research and perform all duties related to the operation of the higher education institution, which required the expertise of the academic, as determined by the employer.

The latest development is that in 2020, the conservative government reorganized the vast majority of state higher education, 22 institutions (excluding five universities, all state institutions) into a public foundation (officially known as a "public trust for the performance of public tasks").[29] The government appointed separate five-member boards of trustees for each university, known as "model changers," above the senates and rectors, thereby eliminating their autonomy. These boards of trustees (loyal to the government) were empowered to make decisions on all matters relating to assets, finances, management, human resources, research organization, and educational content. The government privatized and brought the major part of public higher education under political control. Consequently, the civil service status of those employed in these universities was abolished and replaced by employment in the labor market. The employees of the reorganized universities lost the advantages of civil service employment (the stability and predictability of employment, the legally guaranteed—albeit relatively low—salary) and were placed in labor market employment that is more vulnerable to the will of the employer.[30]

However, as a result, academics at the "model-changing" universities received a relatively substantial pay rise. However, their pay was linked to a detailed

---

[28] Act CCIV of 2011, §26.

[29] First, Act XIX of 2019 placed Corvinus University in public foundation status, followed by Act LXXV of 2020 and Act LXXXV of 2023, which placed all but five (22 in total) universities and universities of applied sciences in public foundation status.

[30] For a comparison of public employee and labor market employment, see: (Jakab et al., 2020).

performance evaluation system, including standardized requirements and measurements of teaching, educational organization, research and publication activities. Meanwhile, staff at the remaining state universities remained employed as civil servants.

4. Some Characteristics of the Structure of the Academic Staff in Higher Education

Before turning to the situation of the academic staff in Hungary, it is worth pointing out that there is a relatively modest literature on this issue in Hungary. However, there is a relatively large number of international publications. To mention just a few, the work of the renowned labor economist Ehrenberg (Ehrenberg & Zhan, 2005) should be highlighted. A similar analysis is provided by (Bettinger & Long, 2004). A relatively recent work is an analysis by the Higher Education Policy Institute (Odgen, 2023).

Turning to the situation of Hungarian higher education academics, the number of academics in Hungarian higher education has shown a pronounced fluctuation trend since the change of regime (Figure 2.1). Looking at the different job categories, we can find that the oscillation trend is also reflected here. It is striking that while the total number of academics employed in higher education has more or less stagnated since 2005, the proportion of academics in each category—especially university and college professors—has fallen, while the proportion of academics in other categories[31] has risen. Notably, the number of university and college professors fell by two-thirds between 2005 and 2020 (Table 2.3, Figure 2.6).

There has been no analysis of the decline in the number of university and college professors, but the drop is likely due to several factors. One is the consequence of demographic processes, as those born at the demographic peak in the 1950s reached retirement age in the 2020s. Another factor is the cut mentioned above in higher education funding in 2011, which meant that universities hired fewer new professors at universities due to a lack of resources rather than replacing retiring professors. The stricter requirements for university professors mentioned in the law (international recognition, high-level foreign language publications) also played a noticeable role.

---

31 The increase is due to the reclassification in 2011 of teachers from university-based training schools as employees of higher education institutions.

Table 2.3: Structure of academic staff in Hungarian higher education

	University and college professor	University and college associate professor	Assistant professor	Assistant lecturer and teaching assistant	Other lecturer and teacher	Total
2000	2999	5196	5387	3517	5775	22874
2005	3224	5870	5506	3756	4832	23188
2008	3239	5892	4933	3638	4773	22475
2012	2851	5604	4305	3229	4566	20555
2016	2320	5266	4176	2935	7721	22418
2020	2100	5335	4301	2781	8994	23511
2020/2005	65%	91%	78%	74%	186%	101%

Source: Author's calculation and editing based on data from the National Employment Service and the Central Statistical Office.

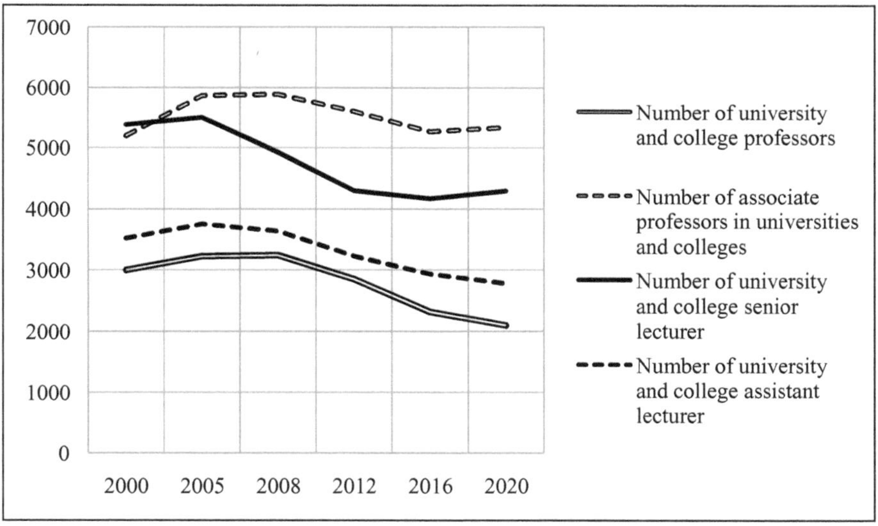

Figure 2.6: Changes in the number of academic posts in higher education 2000–2020.
Source: Education Office statistics on higher education, and Statistical Information on Higher Education 2000/2001 and 2005/2006 based on own editing.

Another probably fundamental factor is the salary. The guaranteed salaries of civil servant academics in higher education are determined based on the ratios projected onto the salary base of university professors at grade 1 as defined in the Budget Act. The salary base of university professors at grade 1 in the Budget Act was

437,300 HUF/month from 2009 to 2016, then 528,000 HUF/month in 2017, and 554,400 HUF/month in 2018, which remained the same in 2023 (despite an inflation rate of over 30 percent between 2018 and 2022). It is about half the monthly income of a 40–49-year-old unit manager in industry or public administration and a third of the monthly income of a unit manager in a financial institution. The salaries of assistant professors and assistant lecturers are even lower than those available in the non-university labor market. (This situation has changed in the case of "model-changing" privatized universities, where salaries have been increased by around 70–80 percent as an incentive to compensate for the loss of institutional autonomy).

5. The Living Wage of Academic Staff With Scientific Qualifications

The situation of Hungarian academics raises the question of how profitable an academic career is and whether it is worthwhile to obtain a doctorate. International research indicates a favorable return on investment in doctoral education, especially in developed Western countries. An analysis of 2009 data in the United States found that individuals with a doctorate earned about 22 percent more than those with a master's degree (Carnevale et al., 2011). A similar study conducted in the U.K. (Britton et al., 2020) found similar results. It revealed that the pay advantage of doctorate holders over master's graduates (taking into account average salaries) was evident for men in their late thirties and women in their early thirties compared to master's graduates (taking into account average salaries) (Britton et al., 2020, p. 27, Figure 2.6).

Hungarian analyses (Polónyi, 2022) of the careers of doctoral graduates in higher education teaching and research show that the highest salaries in academic employment are at the end of the career, similar to the public sector, where earnings tend to increase with the age of the employee. According to Hungarian data, the earnings of graduates working in the business sector are characterized by a peak in earnings at the end of their 30s—in the mid-2010s. (Figure 2.7.) It can also be seen that the earnings of graduates working in the academic sector are the lowest in this period—under the age of 37—compared to all graduates in the education sector. Essential to note that the monthly earnings of academic graduates in the academic sector remain below those of university graduates in both the public and business sectors until around their late twenties and early thirties. Those with a doctorate working in the academic sphere roughly reach the average salary of all graduates in the national economy at the end of their forties, and in their early to mid-fifties they catch up with university graduates working in the business sphere. This situation is not conducive to attracting the best people into academia.

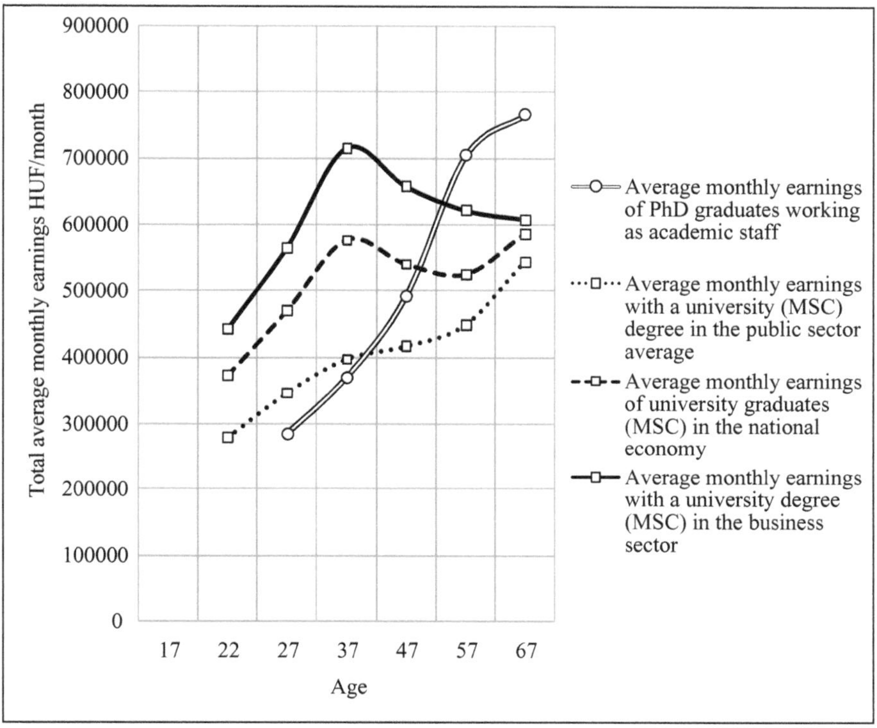

Figure 2.7: Average total monthly earnings of university graduates and academic staff by age (HUF/month) in 2016.

Source: Author's editing based on data from the National Employment Service and the Central Statistical Office.

International comparisons (Table 2.4) of the earnings ratios between different categories of academics show that the domestic ratios between full professors and associate professors were broadly in line with international practice, while the earnings ratios between assistant professors and assistant academics were below the international practice.

The financial situation of university graduates was much more clearly reflected in the development of lifetime earnings than in monthly earnings. We examined lifetime earnings using discounted cumulative earnings with Hungarian wage data. The data showed that the lifetime earnings of young people entering academia after a doctorate were below the average lifetime earnings of all university graduates in the national economy and only slightly above the average lifetime earnings of public sector graduates (Figure 2.8).

Table 2.4: Salary ratios of academics' degrees in higher education (Data around 2015–16)

	Professor	Associate professor	Assistant professor	Assistant lecturer
United Kingdom	1			0.5
Germany	1	0.8	0.71	
Sweden	1	0.73	0.61	
Switzerland	1	0.93		
Denmark	1	0.76	0.66	
Netherlands	1	0.8	0.53	
France	1	0.73		
Belgium (Fl)	1	0.68	0.6	
Finland	1	0.69		
U.S.A.	1	0.78	0.69	
Canada	1	0.78	0.62	
Hungary 2016 (according to legal classification)	1	0.76	0.52	0.38
Hungary 2016 (according to total earnings)	1	0.7	0.5	0.4

Source: Author's calculation based on international data <https://academicpositions.com/career-advice/professor-salaries-from-around-the-world>.

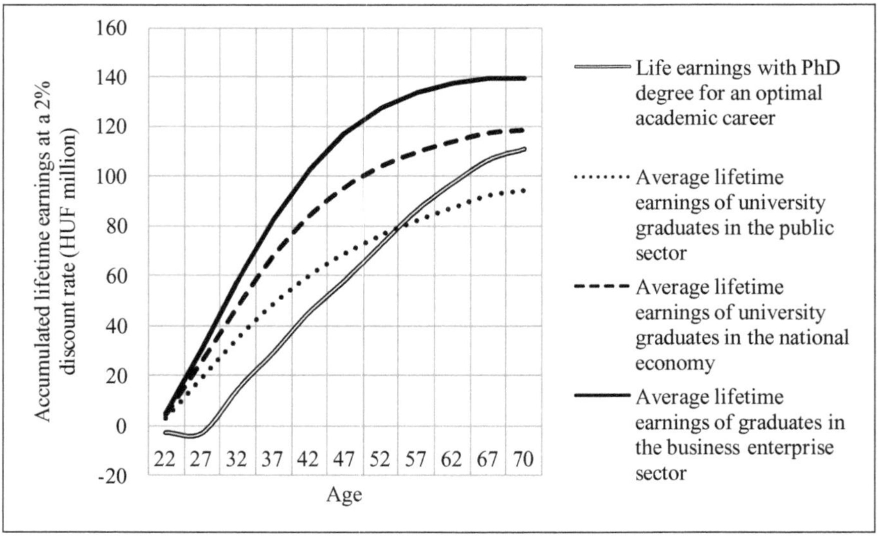

Figure 2.8: Cumulative lifetime earnings based on 2016 data with a discount rate of 2 percent (million HUF).

Note: During the five years of doctoral studies, the statutory scholarship is deducted from the loss of earnings calculated on the basis of the average total earnings of graduates in the national economy for the age group.

These data make it clear that, in the Hungarian earnings context, the loss of earnings associated with obtaining an academic qualification and the financial opportunities related to starting an academic career were significant disadvantages in the development of lifetime earnings. In terms of education economics, therefore, obtaining a Ph.D. in Hungary seemed to pay off only for those university graduates who, without the academic qualification, would have found a job in the budgetary sector. It was far from rewarding for those who would have found a career in the competitive sector (business sector). It is noteworthy that these analyses referred to doctorate holders working in public higher education institutions, whereas higher salaries in private or privatized higher education and research institutions might have been more favorable for those concerned.

6. The Shortage of Scientific Researchers—Doctoral Students

The number of young researchers, that is, doctoral students, is crucial for future scientific and innovative results. According to UNESCO 2015 data, there were 2.9 million doctoral students worldwide in 2015, and this number was expected to increase by 14 percent to 3.3 million by 2020. Almost a quarter of this total is concentrated in the United States and China. However, the ranking of the top 20 countries with the highest number of doctoral students has changed since 2000. The US dropped to second place behind China, and India moved up to third place. It can also be seen that while eight European countries (including five EU member states) were in the top twenty in 2015, only six European countries (including three EU member states) remained in there. Two European countries (Poland and Italy) and one African country (Egypt) dropped out of the top 20 and were replaced by one Asian country (Malaysia), one South American country (Mexico), and one African country (Morocco) (Table 2.5).

A radically different position is obtained when the countries are ranked according to the number of doctoral students per 100,000 inhabitants (right-hand side of Table 2.5). In this ranking, the US was only 28th in 2015 and 38th in 2020, while China was 76th and 78th, respectively. It is also striking that 15 of the top 20 countries in 2015 and 2020 were European (and within them, 11, i.e., 10 EU member states). Hungary is in a worse position than 40th in both rankings.

However, the number of doctoral students per 100,000 inhabitants seems to be a co-variable with scientific performance. If we examine the relationship between the number of doctoral students per 100,000 inhabitants and the number of international publications per 1,000 inhabitants (taking into account all internationally published documents between 1996 and 2018) for the fifty most developed countries[32] we observe a relatively close correlation. We find a reasonably strong (+0.7257) and significant correlation between the specific number of Ph.Ds. and the specific number[33] of international publications. (See Polónyi, 2023b) for more details).

Evidently, doctoral students form the foundation of future academics and researchers in higher education. If this foundation is weak, the human resources for the country's higher education and research may be at risk. It is feared that Hungary may be facing this danger.

Table 2.5: Ranking of countries by world share of doctoral students and number per 100,000 inhabitants

Share of all doctoral students worldwide						Ph.D. students per 100,000 inhabitants					
	2015			2020			2015			2020	
1	U.S.A.	13.6%	1	China	13.4%	1	Finland	362.6	1	Liechtenstein	492.8
2	China	11.1%	2	U.S.A.	10.1%	2	Liechtenstein	305.2	2	Macao	446.6
3	Germany	6.8%	3	India	6.1%	3	Switzerland	286.1	3	Finland	333.7
4	Russian Fed	4.2%	4	Germany	5.5%	4	Austria	278.4	4	Switzerland	300.4
5	India	4.1%	5	Iran	4.4%	5	Greece	264.9	5	Greece	291.3
6	U.K.	3.9%	6	Türkiye	4.1%	6	Australia	241.4	6	Germany	219.8
7	Brazil	3.5%	7	Brazil	3.7%	7	Germany	240.2	7	Austria	213.2
8	Iran	3.2%	8	U.K.	3.3%	8	Czechia	233.1	8	Australia	212.1
9	Türkiye	2.7%	9	Spain	2.8%	9	Estonia	220.7	9	Portugal	209.8
10	Japan	2.5%	10	Russian Fed	2.7%	10	Sweden	218.0	10	Czechia	197.8
11	Korea Rep	2.5%	11	Japan	2.4%	11	Macao	202.8	11	Spain	195.6
12	France	2.4%	12	Korea Rep	2.4%	12	New Zeal.	191.4	12	New Z.	192.1
13	Algeria	2.3%	13	Algeria	2.2%	13	Portugal	186.4	13	Sweden	181.9
14	Australia	2.0%	14	France	2.0%	14	Denmark	174.9	14	Ireland	178.4
15	Canada	1.8%	15	Canada	1.7%	15	Ireland	174.5	15	Estonia	173.2
16	Poland	1.5%	16	Australia	1.6%	16	U.K.	173.2	16	Norway	171.7
17	Egypt	1.5%	17	**Mexico**	1.5%	17	Algeria	169.7	17	Algeria	171.4
18	Malaysia	1.3%	18	**Indonesia**	1.5%	18	Slovak R.	167.2	18	Iran	168.9

32 Number of OECD, EU27 and G20 countries combined until 2018.

33 Author's calculation based on data from Elsevier's reference search database Author's calculation based on data from Elsevier's reference search database.

Share of all doctoral students worldwide				Ph.D. students per 100,000 inhabitants			
	2015		2020		2015		2020
19 Italy	1.1%	19 Malaysia	1.4%	19 Iceland	156.9	19 U.K.	164.2
20 Spain	1.1%	**20 Morocco**	1.1%	20 Canada	147.2	20 Türkiye	163.0
53 Hungary	0.2%	49 Hungary	0.3%	28 U.S.A.	123.1	38 U.S.A.	102.1
				47 Hungary	73.4	42 Hungary	96.6
World	2.9 mill.	World	3.3 mill	76 China	23.4	78 China	31.7

Source: Author's calculation based on UNESCO database.

Summary

Hungary's higher education system has undergone a period of intense development in an attempt to move away from the constraints of state socialism and toward mass education. However, this massification was halted in the 2010s, and was replaced by an elitist, recruitment-restrictive higher education policy that has led to one of the lowest rates of young graduates in the EU. These changes in higher education policy and higher education in its wake have created and continue to create the force field in which Hungarian academic staff works. As a result of the decline in the student population due to the cutbacks in higher education, which has not been accompanied by a similar decline in the number of academics (although their number has declined), the student-academic staff ratio in Hungarian higher education has remained relatively low over the past decade. The age distribution of teaching staff in higher education is in the international middle range.

The traces of the post-war communist reorganization of the Hungarian scientific qualification system are still visible today. They are manifested in the Hungarian system of scientific qualification in that the Academy has retained some elements of the Soviet system of scientific qualification and has sought to position its doctoral degree above the doctoral degree awarded by universities. Although this hierarchical positioning is not explicitly stated in the laws, it can be observed in the practices of particular institutions.

The Hungarian Higher Education Act regulates the academic qualification and performance requirements for teaching posts in detail (university professor, associate professor, assistant professor, assistant lecturer), and these requirements have become more stringent over the past decade and a half, in line with the elitism of higher education policy. As a result, the number of university professors has fallen significantly. Nevertheless, there are other factors behind this decline, in particular, low levels of funding.

In the context of Hungarian earnings, the lifetime earnings of doctoral graduates entering higher education teaching and research are significantly lower than those of graduates working in the business sector. Our data analysis shows that the loss of earnings suffered during doctoral studies, the modest starting salaries and the low early earnings of those who choose a career in higher education teaching and research are significant disadvantages in terms of lifetime earnings. This situation is not conducive to attracting the best people into teaching and research careers in higher education. The data also show that Hungary does not perform well in the international comparisons of the number of doctoral students.

Further analysis of the employment and earnings of academics in higher education is also essential in the domestic context because, as (Ehrenbeg & Zhang, 2005) point out, academics' employment conditions affect both graduation rates and doctoral training.

Finally, it is worth mentioning the findings of another analysis. A 2018 study conducted among young researchers and academics at universities and research institutes highlighted several factors that could prevent higher education and research and development in Hungary from serving the country in the best possible way regarding intellectual and material capacities (Alpár et al., 2018). Some of these factors include low incomes, career abandonment, emigration, rigid and hierarchical institutions, lack of transparency in grant applications, disadvantages for women and those with families, limited access to foreign connections and exchange experiences, infrastructure problems, and the lack of advocacy for young academics and researchers (Alpár et al., 2018).

For the future of Hungarian higher education, it would be essential for higher education policymakers to reconsider the position of academics and address the factors that hinder progress.

References

Alpár, D., Barnaföldi, G. G., Dékány É., Kubinyi E., Máté, Á., Munkácsy, B., Neumann, E., Solymosi, K., & Toldi, G. (2018). Fiatal kutatók Magyarországon. Felmérés a 45 év alatti kutatók helyzetéről, karrierterveiről, nehézségeiről. Kutatási jelentés [Young researchers in Hungary. Survey on the situation, career plans and difficulties of researchers under 45. Research report] Retrived from <https://mta.hu/data/dokumentumok/fiatal_kutatok_helyzete_felmeres_eredmeny.pdf> (Download date 2023. 12. 05)

Berács, J., Derényi, A., Kováts, G., Polónyi, I., & Temesi, J. (2015). Hungarian Higher Education 2014: Strategic Progress Report. Corvinus University of Budapest.

Berács, J., Derényi, A., Kádár-Cobot, P., Kováts, G., Polónyi, I., & Temesi, J. (2017). Hungarian Higher Education 2016 Strategic Progress Report. Corvinus University of Budapest.

Bettinger, E., & Long B. T. (2004). Do college instructors matter? The effects of adjuncts and graduate assistants on students' interest and success, National Bureau of Economic Research working paper no W10370. National Bureau of Economic Research. Retrived from <https://www.nber.org/system/files/working_papers/w10370/w10370.pdf> (Download date: 2021.01.15)

Britton, J., Buscha, F., Dickson, M., van der Erve, L., Vignoles, A., Walker, I., Waltmann, B., & Zhu, Y. (2020). The earnings return to postgraduate degrees in the U.K. Research report. GDR. Retrived from <https://ifs.org.uk/uploads/PG_LEO_report_FINAL.pdf> (Download date: 2023.02.15)

Carnevale, A. P., Rose, S. J., & Ban Cheah, B. (2011). The College Payoff. Education, Occupations, Lifetime Earnings. Georgetown University. Retrived from <https://cew.georgetown.edu/wp-content/uploads/2014/11/collegepayoff-complete.pdf> (Download date 2021.10.09.)

Donina, D., & Jaworska, M. (2024). Higher Education Governance in Poland: Reform Pathway from the Communist Regime to Law 2.0. Higher Education Policy, 37(1), 40–58. <https://doi.org/10.1057/s41307-022-00293-x>

Ehrenberg, R. G., & Zhang, L. (2005). The changing nature of faculty employment. In R. Clark, & J. Ma (Eds.), Recruitment, retention and retirement in higher education: Building and managing the faculty of the future (pp. 32–52). Edward Elgar Publishing, Inc.

Jakab, N., Prugberger, T., & Tóth, H. (2020). A magyar munka- és a közszolgálati jogi szabályozás alakulása a rendszerváltás után [Developments in Hungarian Labour and Public Service Law Since the Change of Regime]. Polgári Szemle, 16(1–3), 287–313. <https://doi.org/10.24307/psz.2020.0718>

Keczer, G. (2014). Higher Education in Eastern Europe: Post Crisis Policies and Trend. In G. Pop, & V-M. Clinci (Eds.), Proceedings of the 10th Conference of ASECU (pp. 35–47). Babeş-Bolyai University Faculty of Economics and Business Administration, Cluj-Napoca, Romania. Retrived from <https://www.asecu.gr/files/proceedings_10th_conference.pdf> (Download date: 2020.03.10)

Kováts, G. (2023). University Governance Reform in an Illiberal Democracy. Public Interest Trusts in Hungary. In Broucker, B., Milsom, C., Calleja, J. & M. O'Hara (Eds.), Accelerating the Future of Higher Education (pp. 186–204). Brill.

Kováts, G., & Zsátku, B. (2023). The impact of institutional governance reforms on organizational culture—Two case studies from Finland and Hungary. Hungarian Education Research Journal, 13(1), 1–22. <https://doi.org/10.1556/063.2022.00165>

Ministry of Education (2002). Statisztikai tájékoztató Felsőoktatás 2000/2001 [Statistical Information Note Higher Education 2000/2001].

Ministry of Education and Culture (2006). Statisztikai tájékoztató Felsőoktatás 2005/2006 [Statistical Information Note Higher Education 2005/2006].

Odgen, E. (2023). Comparative Study of Higher Education Academic Staff Terms and Conditions Higher Education Policy Institute. HEPI. Retrived from <https://www.hepi.ac.uk/wp-content/uploads/2023/05/Comparative-Study-of-Higher-Education-Academic-Staff-Terms-and-Conditions.pdf> (Download date: 2023.12.15)

Polónyi, I. (2018). A gazdaságtudomány az ötvenes évektől a rendszerváltásig [Economics from the 1950s to the change of regime in Hungary]. Educatio, 27(1), 46–63.

Polónyi, I. (2020). A felsőoktatás politikai gazdaságtana [The political economy of higher education]. Gondolat Kiadó.

Polónyi, I. (2022). Is it Worth Getting a Doctorate? Central European Journal of Educational Research, 4(1). 142–149. <https://doi.org/10.37441/cejer/2022/4/1/10263>

Polónyi, I. (2023a). Bejutás a felsőoktatásba—növekvő egyenlőtlenségek [Access to higher education—growing inequalities]. Új Pedagógiai Szemle, 73(5–6), 80–99.

Polónyi, I. (2023b). A humán erőforrások és a vezető hatalmak a 21. század közepén [Human resources and the leading world powers in the mid-twenty-first century]. Világpolitika és Közgazdaságtan, 1(2), 49–69.

Polónyi, I., & Kozma, T. (2020). Gender and Higher Education: The Hungarian Case. In C. Fontanini, K. M Joshi, & S. Paivandi (Eds.), International Perspectives on Gender and Higher Education (pp. 93–11). Emerald Publishing Limited

Scott, P. (2007). Higher Education in Central and Eastern Europe. In J. J. F. Forest, & P. G. Altbach (Eds.), International Handbook of Higher Education. Springer International Handbooks of Education, vol 18 (pp. 423–441). Springer. <https://doi.org/10.1007/978-1-4020-4012-2_21>

UNESCO (1998). World Statistical Outlook on Higher Education: 1980–1995. Working Document World Conference on Higher Education Higher Education in the Twenty-first Century: Vision and Action UNESCO, Paris, October 5–9 1998.

3. Higher Education Academics in Slovakia

Dana Hanesová, Lenka Rovňanová & Patrícia Zólyomiová

ABSTRACT
The study presents an original synthesis of multi-layered data on academics in higher education (HE) in Slovakia, as existing sources (international and national reports) provide only partial insights. It begins with a historical context of HE in Slovakia—a former communist country—and continues with a comprehensive perspective on the current state of academics, giving evidence of the impact of post-Marxist legacies on current HE trends in post-communist Europe. After a description of reformed HE legislation, trends in student enrollment and attainment, the study presents characteristics the structure of academics by age, gender, academic degrees and seniority,—their ratio to HE students and, finally, the financial conditions under which academics perform their work are described. The research is based on a content analysis of international and national statistics, Slovak legislation and academic studies. Since it includes international data (primarily on Visegrád Four, OECD and EU countries), it allows for a comparative overview of the recent development of HE in post-communist countries. The authors highlight major challenges faced by Slovak academics: increasing demands for the development of global competencies, integration of students with special educational needs, and a more inclusive HE, as well as an increasingly internationalized HE environment.

Keywords: higher education, academics, institutions, Slovakia, students, ratio, salaries

Introduction

The aim of this study is to provide an original, comprehensive overview of data related to the profession of HE[1] academics in the Slovak Republic.[2] It focuses on the typical characteristics of academics in their wider historical, legislative, organizational and academic-pedagogical contexts, which directly influence their work performance. The study presents national and some international data on academics in Slovakia, including the ratio of academics to HE

1 In this study, we use the term "higher education" instead of "tertiary education." The data presented here on Slovak HE does not include ISCED level 5 (short cycle HE programs). It only includes levels ISCED 6 = bachelor's degree or an equivalent tertiary education level, ISCED 7 = master's degree or an equivalent tertiary education level and ISCED 8 = Doctoral degree or an equivalent tertiary education level. The reason is that the numbers of students in ISCED 5 are very small (2 800 in Slovakia in 2016/17II?). We also use the term "higher education" as a synonym for university education.

2 The official name of the country is the Slovak Republic, which we use in the article when referring to official names of institutions or documents. In all other cases, we use the commonly used name, Slovakia.

students and the distribution of academics by age, gender, and seniority. It also describes the financial conditions and current challenges faced by academics in Slovakia.

The study is based on four types of data sources which were analyzed, compared and synthesized in the form of tables or graphs:

- International statistics (World Bank, OECD, UNESCO, European Commission, European Education and Culture Executive Agency);
- Official national statistics from the Statistical Office, Ministry of Education, Science, Research and Sport, Slovak Accreditation Agency for Higher Education, and Slovak Centre of Scientific and Technical Information (CVTI);
- Laws of the Slovak Republic;
- Scientific and expert studies by Slovak authors related to the topic of HE and academics.

Several attributes of academics required calculations across multiple levels, necessitating an examination of research methodologies from various sources and the selection of comparable data according to established criteria (as detailed in the following chapters). Graphs from international organizations reveal that, in some countries, data were incomplete, or measurement methodologies varied in certain years. For Slovakia, international data were cross-verified with domestic official sources.

1. The Historical Context of Higher Education in Slovakia After 1989

Three historical events are of fundamental importance to comprehend the state of HE system in contemporary Slovakia: the anti-totalitarian Velvet Revolution that took place in former Czechoslovakia in November 1989; the constitution of the Slovak Republic in 1993 and joining the EU in 2004.

The process of HE transformation in Slovakia as a newly created democracy followed the political and societal events, especially the abolition of the Marxist state ideology in 1990–1991(Kosová & Porubský, 2011). Changes in the official state education policy were translated into new developmental conceptions which directed HE (Zacharová, 2013), such as the Conception of Development of HE in the Regions of Western, Central, and Eastern Slovakia from 1992, the subsequent Conceptions of HE Development in Slovakia (until 2000 and until 2010), and also the National Constantine Programme of Education and

Training (1994). The National Programme of Education and Training in the Slovak Republic for the next 15–20 years (Millennium, 2001) emphasized a humanistic, student-centered educational paradigm, which was already well-established in western educational systems. The rhetoric of academics began to focus increasingly on promoting the holistic development of students' personalities and adopting socio-cognitive and constructivist approaches. The transformation of HE included capitalization, globalization, economization, unification, informatization, virtualization and internationalization. Academics were expected to become reflective professionals and agents of innovative social change.

Since the 1990s, a number of legislative changes have been introduced into HE by the Ministry of Education, which has been led by 17 ministers since November 1989. The first law on higher education, Act No. 172/1990, aligned with the laws of Western European democracies in terms of the degree of autonomy, academic rights and freedoms it provided. It liberalized the concept of content and organization and emphasized the self-governance of HEIs, such as universities. The imperative was to create a strategy for HEIs development and their diversification, renewing their HE staff, streamlining internal organizational structures, enhancing the role of science in relation to teaching in HEIs and utilizing combined sources of HEIs funding (Zaťková 2024). So, in 2002 the Act No. 131/2002 Coll. on Higher Education came into force reassuring diversity of HEIs, depending on the founder (public, state and private HEIs). The diversification of HE in Slovakia primarily took the form of establishing new universities.

Although several new educational regulations have been issued and changes imposed on the status of academics, educational practice has not changed immediately due to a significant level of inertia and conservatism in the Slovak HE system. The fulfillment of most of these documents has lagged behind in concrete implementation or has not been fulfilled at all.

After 1990, Slovak HEIs became the subject of various international audits. One of the first major criticisms was the low (10%) proportion of HE students compared to the number of secondary school graduates and the need to increase it to at least 30%. Several independent private HEIs were established to address this growing demand for HEIs. The audit in 2008/2009 showed the 49.8% share of secondary school graduates continuing in HE studies (Zacharová 2013, p. 259). The original number of 17 HEIs expanded to 23 public and state universities and 13 private universities in 2015 (Hudoba, 2015).

In 1999, Slovakia became one of the signatory countries of the Bologna Process and later a partner in the European Higher Education Area (EHEA)

(2010). Based on the Bologna Agreement, structured HE programs began to be implemented in Slovakia starting from the 2004/2005 academic year: (1) first level—bachelor's study programs, (2) second level— master's study programs, and (3) doctoral (Ph.D.) study programs. Another major challenge that academics had to adapt to was the transition to the European Credit Transfer and Accumulation System (ECTS) assessment of students' performance. It became mandatory in Slovak HEIs starting from the 2005/2006 academic year.

2. Current Societal Context of HE in Slovakia

In accordance with Act No. 131/2002 and all its amendments up to 2023, the role of HEIs in building a knowledge society has been strengthened. Current Slovak HE legislation meets the fundamental pan-European criteria for the autonomy, academic rights and freedoms of HEIs and their academics.

2.1. Current Status and Structure of HEIs

The HEIs in Slovakia are recognized as legal entities and they are categorized based on their funding structure, ownership and location. *Public* HEIs are public service and independent institutions founded and closed by law. They operate with autonomy and self-governance, overseen by self-governing bodies that adhere to the internal regulations of the respective institutions. *State* HEIs include military and healthcare HE institutions. *Private* HEIs are legally established entities, specifically established for educational and research purposes. Authorization for private entities to function as private HEIs is granted by the Government of the Slovak Republic, after the approval by the Slovak Accreditation Agency for Higher Education (AAHE). In Slovakia, unlike public HEIs which basically offer tuition-free daily studies, private HEIs charge annual tuition fees for their study programs, similarly to HEIs in other OECD countries (OECD 2020). On average across the OECD, 17% of students are enrolled in private HEIs (OECD 2020). In Slovakia, 12% of HE students were enrolled in private HEIs in 2020. Top of Form Foreign HEIs provide HE in Slovakia in compliance with the legislature of their home country, based on the authorization granted by the Ministry of Education, Science, Research and Sport (MESRS) of the Slovak Republic (EC, 2020).

The highest number of faculties in the history of Slovakia was in 2012/2013—36 HEIs covering 132 faculties. In 2022, there were 128 faculties (Figure 3.1). In 2023, HE in Slovakia was facilitated by 20 public HEIs, 3 state HEIs, 10 private HEIS and 6 foreign HEIs.

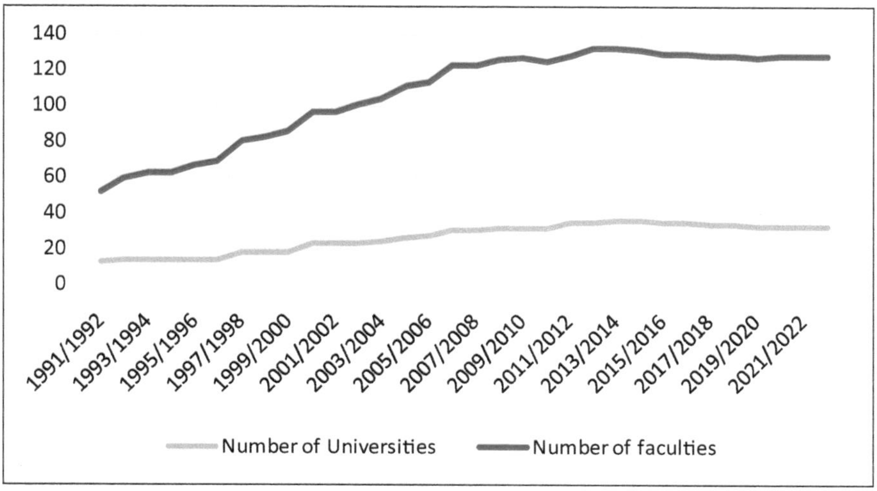

Figure 3.1: Numbers of HEIs and their faculties in Slovakia.
Source: Authors' own processing of data from CVTI.

In 2021, the Slovak Parliament approved the current HE reforms with the vision of "Modern and Successful Slovakia" as part of the "Slovak Recovery and Resilience Plan." It involves a comprehensive package of reforms and investments to be implemented in Slovak HE by 2026 (OECD 2021). On March 23, 2022, the Slovak Parliament approved an Act on Higher Education law that modifies Act No. 131/2002 Coll. on Higher Education in the area of the governance of HEIs (Sapała & Stanicek 2024). The objective of the reform is to improve the quality of administration and funding of HEIs, offer increased flexibility within HEIs, and foster entrepreneurial opportunities and international engagement within the academic community.

The system of HE study fields is administered by the MESRS of the Slovak Republic. HEIs have the prerogative to seek accreditation for their study programs by the AAHE which sets and evaluates the fulfillment of the HE accreditation criteria. The AAHE was established by Act No. 269/2018 Coll. in 2018 in response to the European Standards for Quality Assurance in Higher Education (ESG 2015). HEIs had to align their study programs with the new standards before August 31, 2022. HEIs have the right to offer study programs after an accredited internal system of quality assurance in place. HEIS regularly evaluate all their study programs on the basis of a) quantitative data (number of domestic/foreign applicants, admitted and enrolled students, proportion of students with specific needs, proportion of outgoing/incoming students and academics, quality of publications and research activities of academics, structure of academic staff by age, gender and degrees and teaching load); b) qualitative data (feedback from students, graduates and employer evaluations).

2.2. Current Trends in Numbers of HE Students and Graduates

The performance standards of academics according to the AAHE in Slovakia are directly related to other areas of the internal quality assurance system, predominantly those connected with HE students and graduates: (1) the criteria for student admission; (2) student achievements and the employment of graduates; (3) student support—a qualified support staff and environment related to diverse needs of all students (providing tutoring, counseling, administrative and other support services) at all parts of a HEI. For this reason, we consider it important to provide some data on HE students and graduates.

In Slovakia, since 2008 the number of newly admitted HE students among 19-years-olds has been decreasing every year. Between 2008 and 2018, the number of full-time HE students decreased by 27.79%, and the number of part-time HE students by 67.32%. In 2017, the median rate of enrolled HE students among the population aged 20–24 (in the EHEA) was 16.4%. All Visegrád Four countries Visegrád countries, including Slovakia, recorded a lower share (15.9% in Poland, 11.1% in Slovakia; EEC 2020, p.20). However, in 2021 and 2022, all showed a slight upward trend. This trend is also reflected in the ratio of the total number of HE students to the generation aged 20–24 (see Figure 3.2).

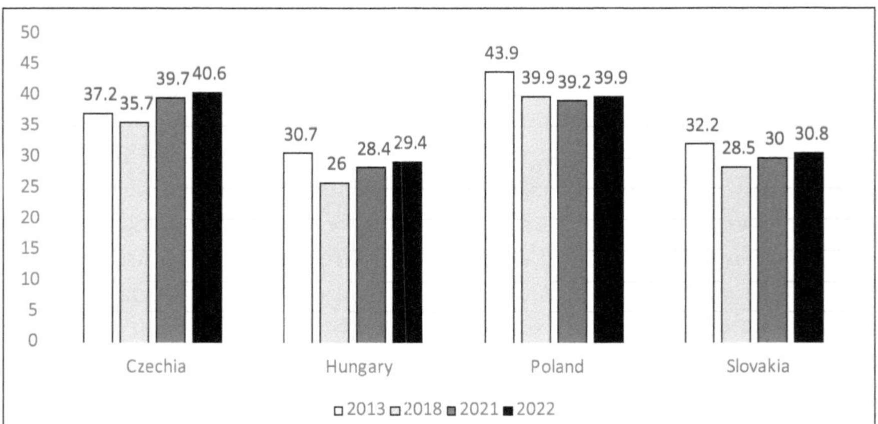

Figure 3.2: HE students as % of 20–24 years old in the Visegrád Four countries.
Source: Authors own processing of data from <https://ec.europa.eu/eurostat/>.

According to gross HE enrollment—the metric used by the World Bank, measuring the proportion of individuals in a specific age group enrolled in HEIs, in Slovakia the percentage of enrolled HE students decreased from 58% to 50.7% (from 2010 to 2021), whereas in neighboring Czechia as well as on average across OECD and EU countries, it has gradually increased. In the first decade of the twenty-first century, there was an overall increase of 14.8% in Slovakia whereas it was over 39% in Czechia (EEC 2020, p. 19). After 2011, the number of students enrolled in HE declined until 2019, when it saw a slight increase again (Figure 3.3).

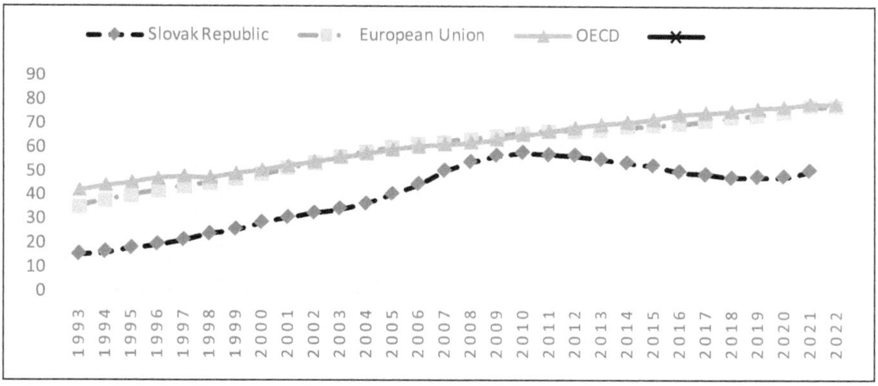

Figure 3.3: Gross enrollment rate of HE students in Slovakia.
Source: School enrollment, tertiary (% gross)—Slovak data (<worldbank.org>).

This decreasing trend cannot be solely attributed to demographic changes. The second cause of the lower numbers of HEI students in Slovakia is the growing emigration of a large portion of young people to HEIs abroad. According to the most recent OECD report, in 2016, as many as 17% of Slovak HE students studied abroad, whereas the OECD average was 2% and the EU average was 4% (Hall et al. 2019). In 2020, there was a momentary increase in the number of students, largely caused by the pandemic and the measures associated with it which resulted in fewer opportunities to study abroad. The rate of female HE students has been constantly over 50% since 2002/2023.

The number of Slovak Ph.D. students studying in Slovakia has also decreased over the last 10 years, with a 34% decrease in full-time Ph.D. studies and a 27% decrease in part-time Ph.D. studies. The number of external foreign students has also decreased by 30%. However, there has been an encouraging 270% increase in the number of foreign full-time Ph.D. students (CVTI, statistics in

2015, 2021, 2022, 2023). In 2013 the ratio of Ph.D. graduates per 1000 population aged 20–29 in Slovakia was 1.4. There has been a downward trend going down to one Ph.D. graduate per 1000, which exceeds most neighboring countries and the EU average (0.6–0.8).

On the other hand, in most OECD countries, including Slovakia, there is a logical overall trend toward an increasing share of individuals with tertiary attainment. The OECD average proportion of 25–34-year-olds attaining HE increased by 21%: from 20.2% in 2000 to 41.2% in 2021. In Slovakia, this increase occurred at an even faster pace, rising by 28.4% points: from 11% in 2000 to 39.4% in 2023 (Figure 3.4). In the previous decades, the proportion of graduates from HEIs in Slovakia used to fall far below the average of both EU and OECD nation. In 2017, Slovakia ranked among the six EU countries with the smallest percentage of individuals aged 25–34 holding university degrees.

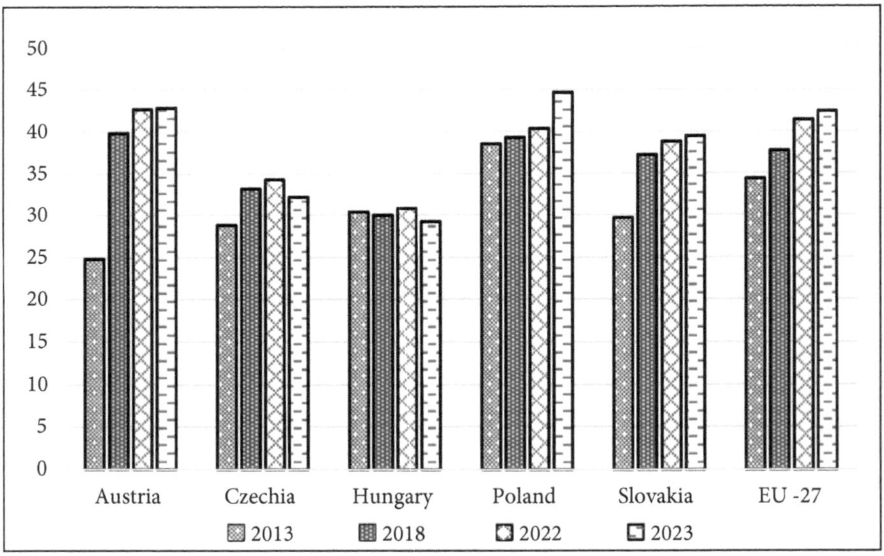

Figure 3.4: The proportion of HE graduates aged 25–34 (%)—international comparison. *Source*: Authors' own processing of data from <https://ec.europa.eu/eurostat/>.

The share of HE graduates aged 25–34 in Slovakia has increased for both men and women (from 16% to 30% for men and from 21% to 45% for women) since 2018. The total gender gap in favor of women with a HE degree has increased from 11.2% in 2013 to 17.6% in 2023. The highest gender difference reached was 23 percentage points in 2021, the second highest in the EU (EK 2022).

3. Academic Staff in Slovakia

According to Act No. 131/2002 and all its amendments up to 2023, the mission of academics in Slovakia is to cultivate the development of a well-rounded personality, along with knowledge, wisdom, ethical values and creativity in individuals. Additionally, they have to contribute to the advancement of education, science, culture and health for the benefit of society as a whole.

3.1. The Characteristics of Academics According to Slovak Legislation

The current understanding of the status of academics in HE in Slovakia is regulated by the amendment to Act No.131/2002 Coll. of February 21, 2002, on HEIs and on its amendments (2023). In Slovakia, similar to most EU countries, academics in HE hold the posts of professor, visiting professor, associate professor (so-called "docent"), assistant professor (so-called "odborný asistent," with Ph.D.), assistant lecturer (so-called "asistent") and lecturer (so-called "lektor"). Professors and associate professors are responsible for research and education in their field of education and science, technology or the arts. They participate in guaranteeing the quality and development of the study program pursued by the HEI. HE professors are members of state exam committees, supervise Ph.D. students and review students' theses. Assistant professor collaborate with professors or associate professors to fulfill the HEI's tasks in the areas of education and in science. They conduct lectures on selected topics, lead seminars, supervise and examine theses, administer state exams in undergraduate and master's programs, create study materials, provide consultations for students and organize field trips and professional internships for students. Assistant lecturers work under the guidance of professors and associate professors. They conduct practical exercises, evaluate students, contribute to the creation of study materials, engage in research, and organize scientific, professional, or artistic events. The duties of the lowest category of HE academic staff—lecturers—include teaching that does not require active participation in research or development, primarily conducting exercises, evaluating students, participating in other educational activities and contributing to the creation of study materials.

According to the Higher Education Law, HEIs in Slovakia have the authority to select their academics, including all assistant professors, associate professors and professors, based on a selection process announced in national media. The employment contract with an academic may be concluded on the basis of competition for a maximum period of five years. A HE academic may have a maximum of three employment contracts with the HEI. In cases where an associate professor or professor has had three contracts or if the total time in these positions has reached at least nine years, they acquire the right to a fixed-term employment contract with the HEI as a HE academic until they reach the age of 70. In the performance of their profession, all academics in HE in Slovakia are bound by a HEI Code of Ethics, which must be in accordance with the rules of the European Code of Ethics and Integrity in Research.

The Slovak Accreditation Agency (AAHE) establishes the following requirements for academics in Slovakia (Standards for the Higher Education Internal Quality Assurance System, Article 6—SAAVŠ, 2020):

- The selection process for academics should be transparent, objective, well-documented, and aligned with the long-term mission and plans of the receptive HEI;
- HEIs should be open enough to enable interinstitutional, intersectoral and international mobility of their academics;
- HEIs should have a sufficient number of academics with the required qualifications and workload allocation, corresponding to the number of students;
- academics in HE have the required qualifications to carry out both educational and research activities to ensure the expected learning outcomes of students in their study fields and thus provide for the promised level of qualification. The required qualifications of academics providing a study program are at least one degree higher than the qualifications achieved by its completion;
- Academics in HE continue in their professional development and the development of their linguistic, teaching, digital and transferable skills;
- The workload of academics should ensure the quality development of the study program, including the processes related to the supervision and assessment of final theses. Profile courses are typically provided by full-time professors or associate professors employed at the HEI.

Academics are required to engage in ongoing professional development. Their continuous education is regulated and managed by the regulations of their HEI. Most often they use the opportunity to develop their professional competencies through specialized activities at both the national and international levels, such as conferences, internships, and research and development projects. In Slovakia, they can apply for research projects through state-supported agencies (KEGA, VEGA, APVV), participate in Erasmus+ mobilities, respond to various research calls (under European Social Fund projects, Horizon 2030, etc.).

3.2. Statistics on Academics in HE

In most EHEA countries, there was an increase in the number of academics in HE between 2000 and 2017 (e.g., Albania 415%, Malta 200% and in the Visegrád Four countries: Hungary +13.5%, Poland +11.4%). In Slovakia, there was a slight decrease in the number of academics (–0.1%), in the Czech Republic the decrease was even greater (–6.6%).

3.2.1. HE student-to-academic staff ratio

The overall ratio of HE students per academic staff was highest during the peak population years in the first decade (22.2 in Poland in 2005, 18.4 in Hungary in 2007 and 18.9 in Slovakia in 2009). Since then, it has been gradually declining (Figure 3.5).

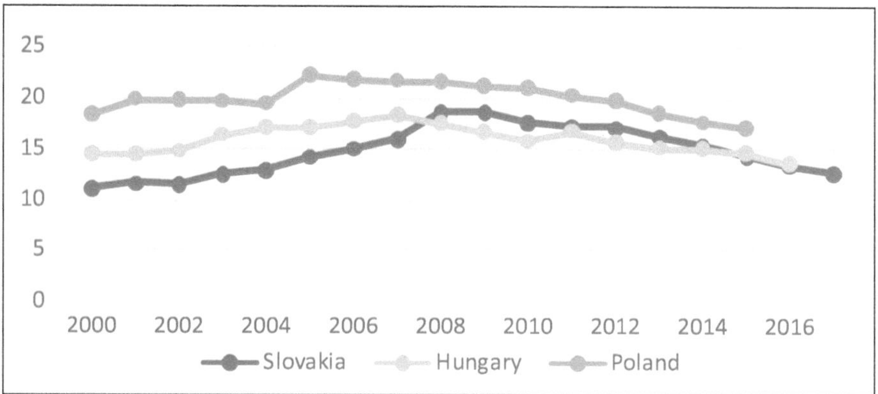

Figure 3.5: HE students-academic staff ratio 2000–2017 (Slovakia, Hungary, Poland).
Source: Authors' own processing of data from the World Bank: Students-teacher ratio, tertiary | Data (<worldbank.org>).

In 2020, OECD statistics showed a modest difference between this ratio in public HEIs and private HEIs. That year, there were 15.3 students per academic staff in public HEIs, compared to 17.3 in private HEIs on average across OECD nations. In some OECD countries, such as Poland, the ratio in private HEIs was even higher. In Slovakia, there were only 11 students per academic staff in public HEIs and 16 students per academic staff in private HEIs (Table 3.1).

Table 3.1: The number of HE students per academic staff in 2020

HE students-academic staff ratio in 2020	Public HEIs	Private HEIs
Slovakia	11.1	16
Czech Republic	16.2	16.4
Hungary	11.3	11.5
Poland	10.8	31.1
OECD average	15.3	17.3
EU22 average	14.3	17.1

Source: Authors' own processing of data from OECD 2020: <https://www.compareyourcountry.org/snaps/education-at-a-glance-2022/en/4579/2020>.

In Figure 3.6, two sets of data from the Visegrád countries are compared. The first is the ratio of enrolled HE students within the generation of 18-to-34-year-olds (in 2000 and 2017), and the second is the percentage change in the number of academics in HE between 2000 and 2017. The highest number of HE students was in Poland, where the ratio increased by 0.7%, from 15.2% in 2000 to 15.9% in 2017. At the same time, the number of academics also increased by 11.4%. In the Czech Republic, the most notable change was the decrease in the number of academics (–6.6%) between 2000 and 2017, compared to the increase in enrolled HE students (from 9.4% to 14.1% of 18–34-year-olds). In Slovakia, there was a minimal decrease in the number of academics by 0.1%, while the student ratio rose by 2.1%. In Hungary, both the number of HE students among the 18-to-34-year-old peers and the number of academics increased between 2000 and 2017—the ratio of students by 0.5%, and the number of academics by 13.5%—the highest growth of academics among Visegrád Four countries.

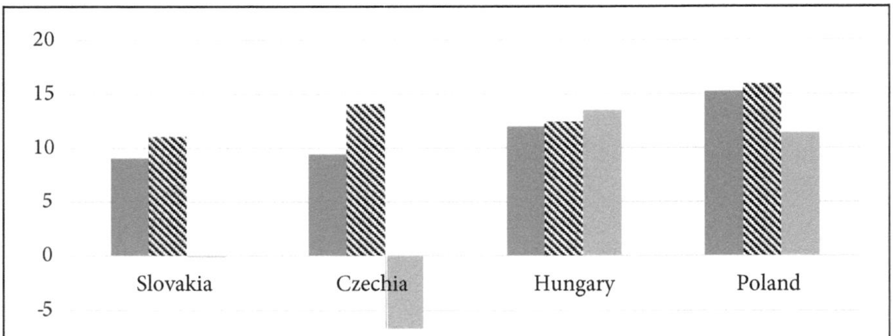

Figure 3.6: Comparison of the % ratio of enrolled HE students (within 18–34-years-old) in 2000 and in 2017 as well as the % change in the number of academics between 2000 and 2017 (Visegrád Four countries).

Source: Authors' own processing of data from the World Bank: Pupil-teacher ratio, tertiary | Data (<worldbank.org>).

In Slovakia, over the last 8 years (2015–2023), the number of students in bachelor's and master's programs has significantly decreased (by 9%), as well as the number of Ph.D. students (by 27%) and the number of academics (by 9%) (Table 3.2).

Table 3.2: The changes in numbers of HEIs, their students, and academics in Slovakia (2015–2023)

All HEIs	Universities	Faculties	All bachelor and master students	All doctorands	All academics in HE
31.10.2023	33	128	109156	6049	8583
31.10.2022	33	128	109800	6190	8764
31.10.2021	33	128	108385	6482	8764
31.10.2015	35	129	118862	8220	9422

Source: Authors' own processing of data from CVTI (2015, 2021, 2022, 2023).

3.2.2. Age structure of academics in HE

The analysis of the representation of various age categories among academics in HE revealed that Slovakia belongs to a group of countries with a relatively high number of academics over 50 years old. This proportion increased from 24.4% in 2005 to 43.4% in 2017. Large increases (higher than 17%) of the over 50 academics can also be found in Spain, Portugal and Finland. In some countries, the proportion of the over 50 academics has decreased, for example, in France, Denmark, also in Hungary from 43.6 in 2000 to 40.4 in 2017 (EEC, 2020, p. 23).

Academics often commence their careers at a relatively advanced age owing to the extensive duration of their educational qualifications. In Slovakia, merely 4% of academics are below the age of 30, a figure that falls short of the OECD average of 8%. Conversely, the proportion of academics aged 50 or older stands at 42%, surpassing the OECD average by a small margin of 2 percentage points (OECD 2020). The proportion of academics aged 50 or over has remained at 40% between 2015 and 2020 in the OECD countries. In Italy and Greece, more than half of academics are at least 50. In one third of OECD countries, including Slovakia, the academic workforce grew younger over the past 5 years.

In 2020, the age structure of academic staff in Slovak HEIs in 2020 was as follows: academics under 30—4.2%, 30–49 years old—53.7%, over 50 years old—42.1%. Academic staff under 30 years old represented on average only 9% of academics at bachelor's, master's and doctoral level in OECD countries. These young academics usually enter academic world, either during doctoral studies or directly after (Table 3.3).

The age structure of academics (including HE researching academics) in Slovakia in 2024 is presented in Table 3.4. A comparison with Table 3.3 shows that, compared to 2020, the percentage of academics aged 30–49 increased in 2024 (from 54% to 65%), while the number of academics over 50 years old decreased (from 42% to 31.6%). Over the last 4 years, the academic staff at HEIs in Slovakia has thus become significantly younger.

Table 3.3: Age distribution of academic staff/senior staff (OECD and Slovakia)

Age distribution of academic staff / senior staff (OECD 2020)	Slovakia < 30 years	OECD < 30 years	Slovakia 30–49 years	OECD 30–49 years	Slovakia ≥ 50 years	OECD ≥ 50 years	Slovakia all	OECD all
2015	5.5	9	50	51	44.5	40	100	100
2020	4	8.4	54	51.5	42	40	100	100

Source: Authors' own processing of data from OECD: Education at a Glance 2022 <https://www.oecd-ilibrary.org/docserver/bb6ee273-en.pdf?expires=1708846132&id=id&accname=guest&checksum=E7044A226447451D9EF18DE7AE6AAB88>.

Table 3.4: The age structure of HEI staff in Slovakia—% (2024)

Age	Number of academics in HE	Ratio (%)
0–29	555	3.01
30–39	7665	
40–49	4371	
30–49	12036	65.38
50–59	2822	
60–69	2161	
70 and more	835	
50 and more	5818	31.60
Together	18409	100

Source: Authors' own processing of data from Register zamestnancov vysokých škôl <https://www.portalvs.sk/regzam/stats/age?range=1&date=2023-12-31&day=30&month=6&year=2024>.

3.2.3. Distribution of academics in HE by gender

The number females in HE academic teams has been growing since 2005 in most OECD countries. Among academics under the age of 30 in OECD countries, women make up, on average, about half of the academic workforce. In half of the EHEA countries, more than 45 % of academics in HE were female in 2017 (median = 45.2). In the EU, women also accounted for around 45% of academics in 2017 (EC 2020). In Slovakia the ratio of female academics increased from 38.4% in 2000 to 45.8% in 2017. The share of female academics increased in almost all EU countries (with the exception of Albania, Greece, Luxembourg and Latvia). It grew also in Visegrád Four countries: in Poland (41% in 2000 and 45% in 2017) and in Hungary (38.5% in 2000 and 40.2% in 2017). In Czechia, the share of women among academics in 2000 and 2017 was the same (38.4%) (EC 2020, p. 24). In 2021, the share of females among academic staff of all ages reached 43.1% in EU and OECD countries, and 46.6% in Slovakia (The World Bank 2023) (Figure 3.7).

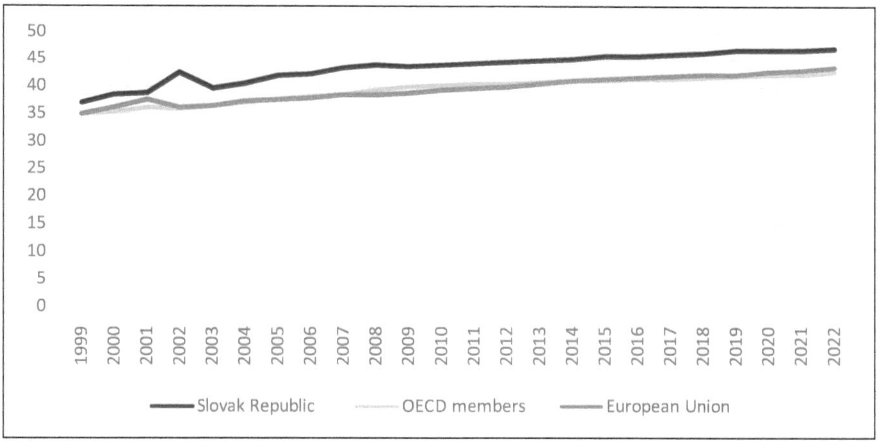

Figure 3.7: Proportion of females among Academics in HE in the EU/OECD and in Slovakia. *Source*: Authors' own processing of data based on Tertiary education, academic staff (% female) | Data (<worldbank.org>).

3.2.4. Primary function of academic staff

The primary role of academics in OECD countries is either teaching or research, or it may be both. In four EU countries, 100% of HEI academic staff must carry out both teaching and research. HEIs in 15 out of 21 OECD countries employ some academic staff only for research (24.7%—the highest percentage is in the Netherlands). In other 15 countries, 20–25% HEIs hire their academic staff only for teaching (around 20–25%, though some transatlantic countries employ a much higher number of staff teaching only—e.g., 64.9% in the U.S.A or 80% in Mexico). In Slovakia, the primary role of the majority of HEI academic staff is both teaching and conducting research (88.1%) and a relatively small portion (11.9%) are employed solely for research. This distribution of tasks of academics in Slovakia differs from the situation in Poland, where 67.3% of academics participate in research and teaching, 2.1% only in research, and almost 1/3 (30.5%) only in teaching, which is the highest proportion of such teaching HEI staff in the EU (OECD, 2020).

3.2.5. Distribution of academics in HE by seniority level

Seniority in academia "refers to a combination of the level of competence and the types of tasks and responsibilities… The seniority of academic staff is one of the strongest determinants of contractual stability." (OECD, 2020, pp. 412–413). There are four levels of seniority—junior, intermediate, senior and other academic staff. OECD defines *junior* as those who have been very recently recruited to start their academic career. In Slovakia, they often face stress and uncertainty in their position as they are usually employed on short fixed-term contracts or on a project basis. The *intermediate* encompasses academic personnel engaged in roles below the highest positions but surpassing entry-level positions. They are employed on more stable contracts. The *senior* has attained the highest degree or position in an academic career, and they often have permanent contracts with an HEI. Lastly, the "other" classification encompasses Academics in HE and researchers who are not following an academic career path and it "excludes doctoral candidates, teaching assistants and research assistants" (pp. 413–414). A similar situation was described by Aarrevaara et al. (2015).

In 2020, the academic staff in Slovak HEIs consisted of 12.0% senior, 70.8% intermediate, 5.3% junior, and 11.9% other personnel. The biggest academics group in Slovakia—in contrast to Poland and Hungary—consisted of middle-aged personnel. However, in some Visegrád Four countries, the situation was very different. In both Hungary and Poland, junior academics were the largest group (almost half of the whole academic personnel). The proportion of senior academics was quite similar (between 9.1 and 12%) (OECD, 2020) (Table 3.5).

Table 3.5: Distribution of academic staff by seniority (% in 2020)

Academic staff (2020)	Junior	Intermediate	Senior	Other
Slovakia	5.3	70.8	12	11.9
Hungary	44.5	33.8	9.1	12.6
Poland	50.2	20.3	11.4	18

Source: Authors' own processing of data from OECD: Education at a Glance, 2022.

In Slovakia, the achieved level of scientific-pedagogical activity of individual Academics in HE is also reflected in their degree-level qualifications ("professors" and "docents"—associate professors). For the time being, professors at HEIs are primarily persons appointed as professors by the President of the Slovak Republic on the basis of a recommendation from HEIs as a result of successful accomplishment of high scientific and pedagogical criteria, evaluated by the scientific councils of faculties and universities. Recently, the legislative possibility to hire a person into the functional position of a docent (associate professor) and even a professor without these academic achievements has been increasingly applied. They are called "university professors" and "university docents." The requirement for the third level in the academic position ranking—of assistant professors—is a Ph.D. degree. Assistant lecturer hold at least master's degree.

Logically, academics with Ph.Ds. form the largest group of academic staff, followed by the group of docents, and finally professors. Since 2003, the number of professors and associate professors has been growing, while the number of academics with Ph.Ds. has been decreasing. This trend indicates an increasing level of seniority among academic staff in Slovakia (Table 3.6).

Table 3.6: Distribution of academics in HE due to their academic degrees (Between 2003 and 2023, Slovakia)

Academic staff Slovakia (%)	Professors	Associate professors	Assistant professors with Ph.D.	Assistant lecturers
2003	13	23.49	62.46	1
2015	15.49	25.87	56.64	2
2021	16.05	29.71	52.07	2.17
2022	17	25.2	55.3	1.9
2023	17.36	34.3	45.26	3.08

Source: Authors' own processing of data from the Slovak Centre of Scientific and Technical Information (CVTI) (2003, 2015, 2021, 2022, 2023).

3.3. Current Challenges for Academics in HE

3.3.1. Requirements for a broader range of transversal competencies of academics

Nowadays, academics in Slovakia must fulfill the qualification requirements in accordance with Act No. 131/2002 on Higher Education Institutions and Act No. 269/2018 Coll. on Quality Assurance of Higher Education. The workload of 90% of academics in Slovakia involves not only research but also teaching HE students.

Their role is to apply the latest scientific findings from their research fields in their teaching, as well as insights from educational psychology, neuroeducation, and HE didactics, particularly focusing on the shift from content-focused HE to student-centered, competence-based HE.

In the legislation, there is no explicit requirement for teaching which raises the competencies of academics. In Czechoslovakia, there was a mandatory system for enhancing the pedagogical qualifications of academics in the 1970s and 1980s. Subsequently, this training was mandatory for academics according to Act No. 39/1980, § 78. Currently, HEIs in Slovakia address the development of teaching skills of their academics in various ways, often on a voluntary basis. Academics are encouraged to raise their teaching competence either by individual departments or faculties, or they undertake it out of their own interest or concern about defending their position in future selection processes. The educational standards for higher education pedagogy and courses in the context of Slovakia are currently not established (Petríková and Váradyová 2019). Based on the research by Zaťková (2024), "not even half of the Slovak public universities are aware of the need to acquire and develop the pedagogical competence of university academics ... Efforts for the support of academics in HE′ pedagogical education have been growing over the years and we are sure that it should be a well-established practice in the future of higher education." (Zaťková, 2024, p. 179).

Since 2010, influenced by international trends, the pressure on academics to focus their educational activities on the development of students' competencies has intensified. It concerns not only bachelor students but also master and Ph.D. students. In 2013, a survey conducted in Slovakia involved 2,453 HE graduates and other HE stakeholders. The evaluation of HE graduates' competencies by employers yielded negative results, reflecting concerns about their ability to apply their theoretical knowledge in practical settings and to work independently (Vančo et al., 2016). The Centre for Scientific and Technical Information (CSTI) in Slovakia conducted significant research among employers entitled "Assessment of the readiness of university graduates for practice in selected competencies" in 2015. A total of 2,671 business entities participated. Again, the outcomes revealed an unfavorable perception among employers regarding HE graduates' implementation competence, specifically in their application of theoretical knowledge in practical scenarios, ability to work independently, as well as their orientation and discussion skills (Janková, 2015).

The widespread integration of digital technologies within HE during the first decades of the twenty-first century has underscored the imperative of revising the professional development programs for academics in HE. Specifically, there may be a heightened requirement for additional support aimed at fostering the development of techno-pedagogical competencies among academics aged 50 and older (OECD, 2022).

In the post-COVID era, a deeper pedagogical and psychological issue has emerged for HEIs: how to ensure the well-being of their HE students and academics, with a focus on creating a positive learning environment and mitigating the effects of isolation, such as depression, neuroses, and increased cyber threats (Niklová 2023). Academics are not only required to incorporate the development of specific professional competencies in their students on their courses but also to nurture so-called global competencies in all HE students, including Ph.D. students. These general competencies are essential for employment and survival in the coming decades, for example: critical and creative thinking skills, the ability to collaborate, problem-solving, etc.) (WEF 2016). The question is whether they themselves possess these competencies that they are supposed to impart to the next generation of students.

3.3.2. Coordinating students with special educational needs and ensuring an inclusive approach

According to ESG 2015 and other aforementioned documents, academics in HE in Slovakia must tailor their study programs to meet the needs of all students, aiming to facilitate the cultivation of their personalities and the shaping of their profiles in accordance with their abilities and strengths. The Act No 131/2002 Coll. No. 131/2002 of the Act on Higher Education Institutions mandates the establishment of suitable study conditions for special education students to accommodate their specific study needs, without reducing the requirements for academic performance, as stipulated by Decree No. 458/2012 on the minimum requirements for students with specific needs. Slovakia is also dedicated to implementing the 2030 Agenda, as endorsed by the Government Resolution of 2016. This commitment aims to bolster inclusivity within the education system at the national level and ensure equality of opportunity. This initiative is outlined in documents such as the National Program for the Development of Living Conditions of Persons with Disabilities for 2014–2020 (Ministry of Education and Science, 2014) and the National Programme of Education and Training in Slovakia for 2018–2027.

In Slovak HEIs, students with special educational needs (SEN) constitute only a small percentage of the HE population. Students who decide to officially acknowledge their SEN are registered by their faculties every year. According to the central registry, in 2017 there were 992 students with specific needs enrolled in HEIs in Slovakia. Although their numbers have more than doubled over the past five years, they still represent less than 1% of the total HE population in bachelor and master studies. It is the lowest proportion across all levels of the education system (Hall et al. 2019). Inclusive education is still insufficiently covered in HE study programs in Slovakia, as reported in connection with HE courses for future teachers at lower levels of the educational system by the TALIS 2018 survey (see Hall et al., 2019).

In Slovakia, targeted and organized institutional care for SEN students at their selected HEIs began in 2012/2013 with the development of the first internal study guide for these students, which also outlined the conditions for inclusion in the SEN register. Faculty coordinators for working with SEN students were chosen from among academics and appointed by faculty deans. In 2014/2015, the position of HE coordinator for working with SEN students was established. Additionally, student volunteers provide effective social assistance to SEN students and their teachers. Cooperation among all parts has been essential for increasing the effectiveness of SEN students' studies.

Inclusive education places even greater demands on the competencies of academics than the integration of SEN students. The goal of the inclusive approach to students in HEIs is to enable each one to develop their talents and extract maximum value from their academic pursuits, ultimately contributing to a purposeful and fulfilling professional and personal life. Investigation into opinions on the quality of the inclusive environment among all groups of HE students and academics is necessary. Understanding the attitudes of SEN students can help HEIs and their teachers provide a more appropriate and useful perspective on the current situation and contribute to improving the quality of inclusive education (Vlachou & Papananou, 2018).

The aim of the action research in 2017/18 was to assess the attitudes of undergraduate SEN students toward the inclusive quality of the environment at the Slovak HEI where they studied. The research findings revealed that the attitudes of SEN students toward the quality of the inclusive environment were statistically significantly related to the effectiveness of the coordinator's—HE academic's—work. However, not all academics in HE, despite their education and professional and scientific work at the faculty, possess the necessary knowledge and experience to effectively work with SEN students (Belková & Zólyomiová, 2021).

3.3.3. Developing the dimension of internationalization in HEIs

In general, internationalization of HE consists of two main processes: internationalization abroad (approximately 10% of activities—Erasmus and other mobilities, international consortia of HEIs, international projects), and internationalization in the home environment (approximately 90% of activities—internationalization of study programs, focusing on global citizenship and development of the global competencies of HE graduates as well as academics in HE). Based on these requirements for internationalization, Slovak HEIs are not sufficiently internationalized yet. That is also the outcome from a national survey of the opinions of academics and HE students in Slovakia—called To dá rozum—(Hall, 2020). It showed that in 2020 only around 3% of Slovak domestic students went abroad for mobility. Only 8% of Ph.D. graduates in Slovakia were foreigners, while the OECD average was 25%. In 2021, Slovak HEIs signed the strategy for the internationalization of HE by 2030. It aims to increase the availability of international mobility opportunities and to modernize HE in the context of internationalization (EK, 2022).

Although the total number of students in Slovak HEIs has been mainly decreasing for two decades, the number of international students in Slovak HE has been slightly increasing. They have come from 118 different countries. They accounted for 5.8% of the HE student population in Slovak HE in 2013, whereas it was 15.6% in 2022. In recent years, the largest groups of international students were from Ukraine (10,067), then from the Czech Republic (2,934) and other countries (from Russia—931, from Hungary—710, and from Germany—64) (Blanár, 2022).

Most EU states receive more students than they send abroad. In Slovakia, the outflow of the HE student to HEIs abroad is greater than the arrival of foreign students to Slovak HEIs. Most students prefer Czech HEIs (Hall, 2020). In 2020 the results of a survey among HE students who were already studying abroad indicated strong motivation to leave Slovakia based on the conviction that foreign HEIs have a better reputation and a degree from a foreign HEI would open the door to better job opportunities than a degree from Slovakia (Hall, 2020). Figure 3.8 clearly illustrates a significant disparity in trends between Slovakia and other countries, with a considerably higher number of students leaving through Erasmus compared to those arriving in Slovakia.

The *To dá rozum* survey showed that, from the point of view of Slovak academics in HE, international mobility helps to build their relationships and partnerships with colleagues abroad, to expand their scientific knowledge, as well as to adopt innovative teaching methods (Hall et al., 2019). In particular, they value the opportunities that mobility brings to their Ph.D. students, that is, the chances to collaborate with partners from all over the world in their future careers, to acquire intercultural skills and to establish contacts with different research teams and institutions. The respondents highlighted also the variety of international collaboration between academics, in particular mutual international projects such as the Horizon 2020 program. The research data showed that academics, as well as HE students who participated in mobility, were more likely to be involved in the governance of their HEI than their counterparts who had not been abroad.

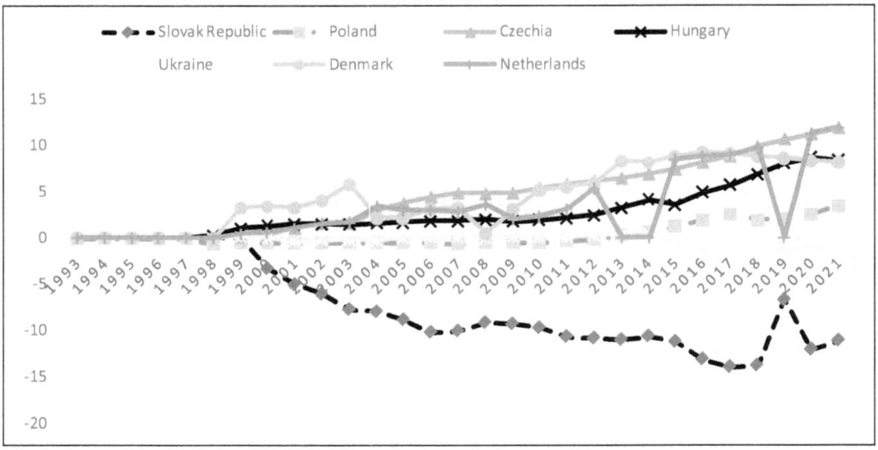

Figure 3.8: Net flow ratio of internationally mobile students (inbound–outbound), both sexes (%).

Source: Authors' own processing of data from UNESCO <http://data.uis.unesco.org/index.aspx?queryid=3800#>.

Regarding the international diversity of academics in Slovakia, in 2020 less than 6% of academics were from abroad, while at the best HEIs in the world this share was often around half of academics (at ETH Zurich up to 73%, at MIT 56%, at Oxford University 48%). Within the framework of European scientific grant schemes (Horizon 2020), which supported the international research and mobility activities as well as activities aimed at developing scientific capacity, Slovakian teams of academics were in 24th place out of 28 in EU, behind all the other Visegrád Four countries (Hall, 2020).

Slovakia has made sustained efforts to develop strategies for the internationalization of its HEIS. However, these strategies have been only partially implemented, largely due to a lack of a systematic approach and insufficient funding (Kupriyanova & Ferencz, 2022). The Slovak MESRS presented its draft HE internationalization strategy up to 2030 for public consultation in autumn 2021, with a major focus on the internationalization of study and human resources, especially on recruitment of international academics and researchers. According to this strategy, the goal is to increase the number of international doctoral students and academics by 15% and 10% respectively by 2030 (ibid., p. 23). In 2023, 31 HEIS and one consortium in Slovakia requested a total of 7,442 Erasmus+ mobilities. They included 4,396 student mobilities and 3,046 staff mobilities. Out of academics mobilities, 1,468 mobilities were for teaching purposes (an increase of 13.6% compared with 2022) and 1,578 mobilities for training purposes (an increase of

45.4% compared with 2022). Compared to the year 2022, the total number of requested mobilities increased by 703 (9%) (MŠVVM 2024).

4. Public Expenditure on Academics' Salaries

Public HEIs in Slovakia, similarly to other EU countries, are funded by state finances. Financing of academics in Slovakia is based on government expenditure on higher education as a percentage of Gross Domestic Product (GDP), with funds from the state budget in relation to annual GDP. Probably because of the economic crisis in 2008, public expenditure on HE decreased slightly in 17 out of 29 EU countries between 2004 and 2016. This is also the case of Slovakia, with a decrease in median public expenditure from 1.0 to 0.8% of GDP (including research and development) except in 2015. "The median public expenditure relative to GDP accounted for 0.95 % across the EHEA" in 2016 (EC, 2020, p. 27).

Further decrease in the share of public expenditure directed to HE was evident between 2009 and 2016, with the share of public expenditure on HE as a percentage of GDP decreasing in all EU countries except Estonia. The median annual expenditure per student in EHEA was 6,780 Euros in 2016. Over the previous two years public spending on HE in the other Visegrád Four countries increased (in Hungary from 2,938 Euros in 2014 to 3,443 Euros in 2016, in Poland from 3,310 in 2014 to 3,250 Euros in 2016). In the Czech Republic it rose from 3,154 Euros in 2014 to 3,514 Euros per student in 2016 (EC 2020). In Slovakia, it dropped down from 4,942 Euros in 2014 to 4,593 Euros in 2016. In this respect, Slovakia ranks last among all EU member states.

The trend of decreased public expenditure on HE has also continued in recent years—2021–2022 (UNESCO data). Figure 3.9 compares government expenditure on HE as a percentage of GDP (%) across all Visegrád Four countries, among which Poland invests the most in HE. Slovakia, with the exception of 2015, invests less annually, although in 2020 it invested more than the Czech Republic. Figure 3.9 compares the expenditures of these countries with Finland, a country known for its high level of education system. Since 1994, the state subsidy to public HE in Finland has been almost twice as high as in the Visegrád Four countries, although there has also been a decline after 2012.

As revealed by the TALIS 2013 study, Slovakia ranked last among 32 OECD countries, with 96% of teaching professionals disagreeing that their profession is valued in society (the OECD average was 69%). More recent data from TALIS 2018 confirmed Slovakia's position at the bottom among all OECD countries, with only 4.5% of respondents agreeing that the teaching profession is appreciated in society (the OECD average was 25.8%).

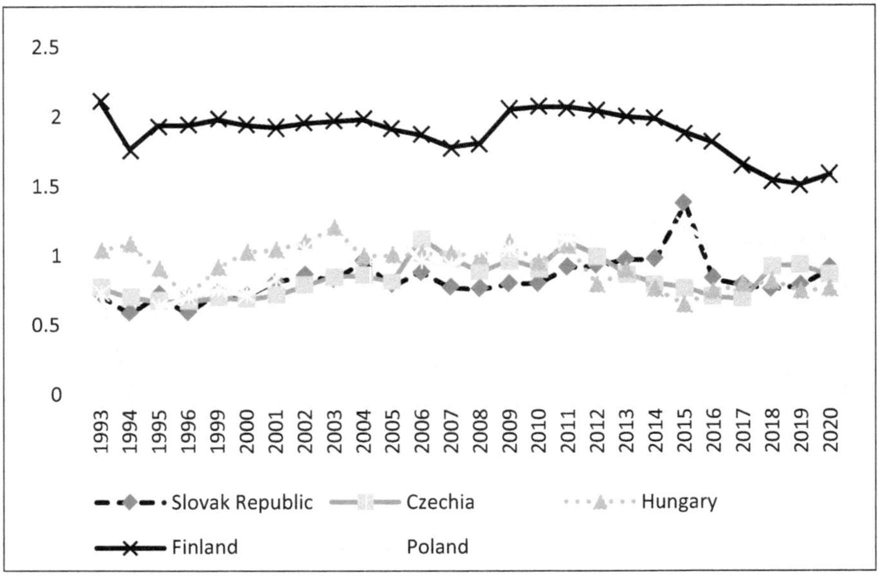

Figure 3.9: Government expenditure on HE as a percentage of GDP (%)—Visegrád Four and Finland.

Source: Authors' own processing of data from UNESCO <http://data.uis.unesco.org/index.aspx?queryid=3800#>.

As revealed by the TALIS 2013 study, Slovakia ranked last among 32 OECD countries, with 96% of teaching professionals in Slovakia disagreeing that their profession is valued in society (the OECD average was 69%). More recent data from the TALIS 2018 study confirmed Slovakia's position at the bottom among all other OECD countries five years later, with only 4.5% of respondents agreeing that the teaching profession is appreciated in society (the OECD average was 25.8%) (Hall et al. 2019). According to the perception of academics, social recognition of their teaching profession in Slovakia is the lowest among all OECD countries. The Ministry of Education of the Slovak Republic funds the salaries of academics primarily based on their scientific and research performance, and to a lesser extent on the number of students in HE study programs.

In Slovakia, expenditure per HE student exceeded spending in other levels of education, which is a trend that is reflected in most OECD countries. In 2016, the OECD average was $15,556 per HE student. Slovakia allocated $11,413 per capita to HE students (OECD 2019, p. 274). In 2021, $12,749 per year was spent in Slovakia, which exceeds spending at the primary level by approximately $4,800, and at the secondary level by $5,300 (0ECD 2022). Although this is below the OECD average, it is similar to many other countries. However, the average expenditure at HE ($17,559) is affected by high prices in some countries. Research and development (R&D) expenditure accounts for 21% of HE expenditure in Slovakia, which is below the OECD average (29%). In private HEIs in Slovakia, it amounts to 27%, slightly below the OECD average of 31% (OECD, 2022).

Figure 3.10 presents an international comparison of public expenditure on HE (% of government expenditure on education) from 2004 to 2021. After the exceptional year 2015 for HE, Slovakia invested a smaller share of state expenditure from the education budget into HE from 2016 to 2021 (20.2% in Slovakia compared to 22.4% the EU average in 2021).

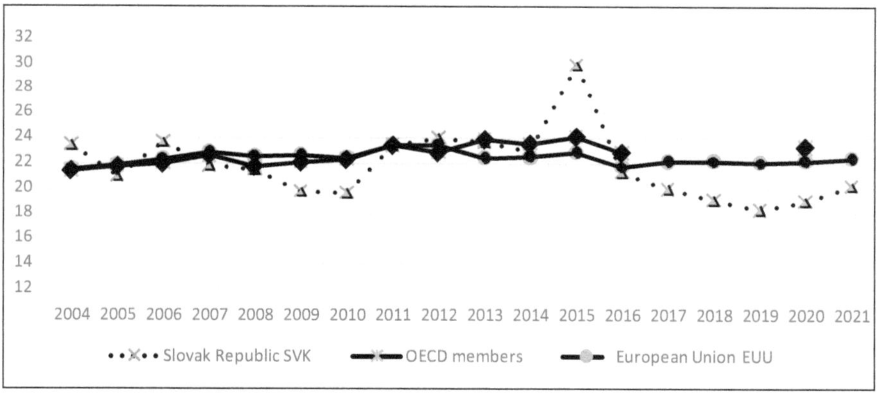

Figure 3.10: International comparison of public expenditure on HE (% of government expenditure on education) 2004–2021.

Source: Authors'own processing of data from Expenditure on tertiary education (% of government expenditure on education) | Data (<worldbank.org>), <http://data.uis.unesco.org/index.aspx?queryid=3800#>, <https://data.uis.unesco.org/index.aspx?queryid=3852>.

Between 2001 and 2020, the pattern of expenditure on salaries for academics mirrors that of total state spending on HE. When compared to the other Visegrád Four countries and Finland, it is evident that academics in Slovakia receive the lowest salaries, although their salaries are increasing (Figure 3.11).

Salary conditions for academics in Slovakia are determined by government legislation on the remuneration of educational staff—the Teaching Staff Remuneration Act. Academics are compensated through so-called salary tables. Salaries are calculated as a combination of salary grades and salary categories (ranging from 1 to 14) based on the type and difficulty of the work performed and increase with years of experience. The characteristics of the salary grades for activities involving a predominance of mental work in the performance of public

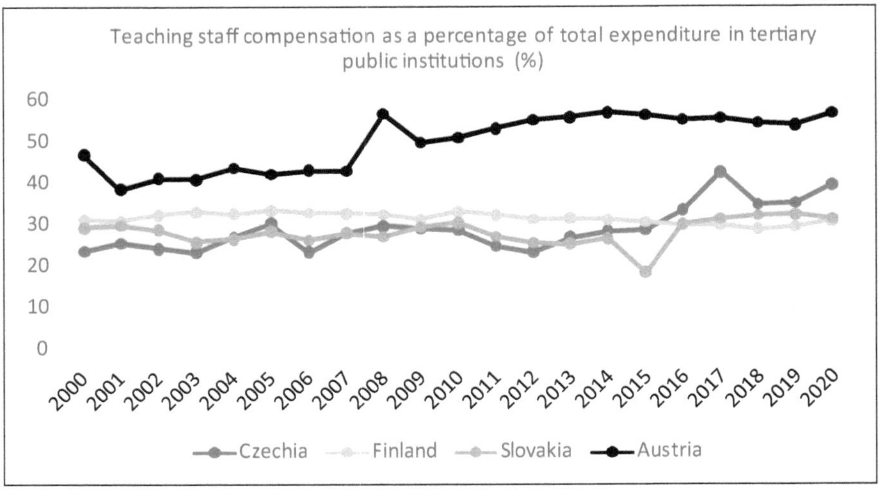

Figure 3.11: Academics' compensation as a percentage of total expenditure in public HEIs (%). *Source*: Authors' own processing of data from UNESCO <http://data.uis.unesco.org/index.aspx?queryid=3800#>.

service work are described in the Annex to Act No. 553/2003 on the remuneration of employees performing public service work. The Special Scale of Salaries for academics (2023) stipulates that the minimum salary for Grade 6 and Level 1 is €1,025.50 per month. The tariff salary for Grade 11 and Level 1 is €1,586.50. If the number of years of experience exceeds 40, the tariff salary is €1,394.50 in Grade 6 and Level 14, and €2,166 in Grade 11 and Level 14 (Eurydice, 2024).

A full-time Ph.D. student is entitled to a scholarship, which is paid monthly and funded by the university and faculty's own resources (2023). As a result, the number of newly admitted Ph.D. students has decreased by a half to two-thirds. There are few credits given for teaching, and the university exerts significant pressure on supervisors—academics—to ensure their Ph.D. students produce scientific outputs, for which they receive the most credits. According to Act No. 553/2003 Coll. on the remuneration of certain employees in the public interest and amendments to other laws as amended, before passing the dissertation exam, the student receives a monthly stipend (currently 807.50 euros). After passing the dissertation exam, the stipend is raised to at least the salary corresponding to the 7th pay grade (currently 940.50 euros per month) (Hamuľák, 2021).

According to a Slovak website on salaries of employees, the actual (2024) gross monthly salary range for people working in Education, Science & Research in Slovakia is typically from 1,047 EUR (minimum salary) to 1,936 EUR (highest average). The following sums are the total gross monthly salaries including bonuses: (1) A professor and associate professor may earn between 1,300 Euros and 2,305 Euros. On the overall salary scale in Slovakia, this job position takes 351st place. Women represent 49 percent of this category academy staff. (2) The other HE academic positions are rewarded by salaries between 1,278 and 1,932 Euros, this job takes 446th place in the salary scale. Females represent 65 percent of this category of academic staff. However, generalizing or averaging salary data has its limits, as salaries reflect not only age and level of education but also the individual's role (e.g., a member of the HEI management, performing additional functions).

Educational achievement (accomplished level of education) has the biggest influence on wage levels in the public HEI system. On average across the OECD, workers aged 25–64 who have completed upper secondary or postsecondary non-tertiary education earn 29 percent more than those with education below upper secondary level. Furthermore, individuals with an HE qualification earn approximately double the minimum income. In Slovakia, the earnings disparity between tertiary-educated workers and others was even more pronounced than the OECD average (OECD, 2020).

In Table 3.7 there is a summary of ratios between full professors, associate professors, assistant professors, assistant lecturers and lecturers in Slovakia in 2022. They were broadly in line with international practice, but the earnings ratios between assistant professors and assistant academics were below the international practice.

Table 3.7: The salary ratios of academics rank in HE in Slovakia (2022)

Function	Professor	Associate professor	Assistant professors	Assistant lecturer	Lecturer
salary ratios	1	0.76	0.59	0.48	0.48

Source: Authors' own processing of data from <https://www.minedu.sk/vyrocne-spravy-o-stave-vysokeho-skolstva/>.

Conclusions

As we demonstrate in this study, several phenomena in contemporary Slovak HE are the result of both national historical factors and current global educational trends. We highlighted how the laws have changed to enable the transition from a politically dominated, totalitarian system to a democratic, humanistically focused and diversified system of HEIs. Slovakia is a relatively young democracy—30 years old—whose HE is still influenced in several ways by the previous political regime. Certain structures, particularly the composition of academics based on academic titles, have remained stable for a long time, with older academics dominating in Slovakia.

On the other hand, Slovak HE is also influenced by global trends, such as the increasing pressure on the transversal or global competencies of academics (Theodoulides & Hanesová 2022), including their ability to work in an increasingly internationalized environment with international groups of students, as well as the growing need to integrate students with various special educational needs (SEN) into the teaching process. The present role of Slovak academics in HE involves generating new knowledge and facilitating competence development that addresses both societal and global challenges, thus ensuring the continued relevance of HE in the twenty-first century.

The data presented in this study concerning academics in Slovakia, allowed for a comparison with other countries and highlighted that the development of HEIS and their academics shows several similarities to other Visegrád post-communist countries. This is particularly evident in the comparable ratio of HE students per academic and the gender structure of academics, which is similar to that of other OECD countries. Collectively, the Visegrád Four countries differ from more developed EU democracies in having significantly lower government expenditure as a percentage of GDP and a smaller share of total government spending on education. The salary ratios of academics also do not vary significantly across these countries.

On the other hand, there are some notable differences between Slovakia and other countries. One key distinction is the approach of the new population of HE students to studying in Slovakia versus abroad—the proportion of outbound students to inbound students is significantly higher compared to other European democracies. Slovak HEIs also have a much higher proportion of older academic staff than in other Visegrád Four countries. In Slovak HE, the number of HE students has shown a more sharply declining trend, which can be explained not only by demographic trends but also by a higher number of students leaving to study abroad. Additionally, the number of Ph.D. students has been rapidly declining due to changes in salary policies—there are no direct subsidies from the ministry for Ph.D. studies, and HEIs must finance Ph.D. students from their own budgets based on their research performance.

Overall, the trends in Slovakia, in many respects similar to those in neighboring Central European countries, can be summarized as follows:

- Insufficient funding compared to international standards and other sectors, along with inadequate social status and recognition, particularly in the case of assistant professors.

- Increasing pressure on academics to secure funding through their performance (projects, publications), with a decreasing portion of stable state funding for HEIs.
- Decreasing number of academics staff due to an aging workforce.

In order to continuously improve the quality of study at HEIs, it is necessary for to be able to show innovation in the curricula of their study programs and teaching methods. Regular updating of teaching content, evaluation of the fulfillment of educational goals, effective collection and use of feedback on the quality of teaching, support of academics in the preparation and implementation of teaching and strengthening of interactive methods in HE—these are some of the measures to achieve change and make studying at Slovak HEIs more attractive. They result from the recommendations for improving the quality of education explored via the national survey (Hall et al. 2019).

More analyses and in-depth research studies with practical implications for HE are needed to determine in which areas it is possible to contribute to the quality of HE in Slovakia, whether in terms of the autonomy of HEIs and academics or in terms of their better financial compensation.

References

Belková, V., & Zólyiomiová, P. (2024). The attitude of university students with special educational needs to the inclusive environment at their university. *Acta Educationis Generalis, 11*(1), 1–13. <https://doi.org/10.2478/atd-2021-0001>

EC (European Commission), Directorate-General for Education, Youth, Sport and Culture (2021). *Education and training monitor 2021.* Retrived from <https://data.europa.eu/doi/10.2766/54808>

EC (European Commission. Eurydice) (2024). *Slovakia 7. Higher education.* Retrived from <https://eurydice.eacea.ec.europa.eu/national-education-systems/slovakia/types-higher-education-institutions>

EEC (European Education and Culture Executive Agency, Eurydice) (2020). *The European higher education area in 2020—Bologna process implementation report.* Publications Office. Retrived from <https://data.europa.eu/doi/10.2797/756192>

EK (Európska komisia—European Commission) (2022). *Monitor vzdelávania a odbornej prípravy 2022: Slovensko* [Education and Training Monitor—Slovakia]. Úrad pre vydávanie publikácií Európskej únie. Retrived from <https://op.europa.eu/webpub/eac/education-and-training-monitor-2022/sk/country-reports/slovakia.html>

ESG (2015). *Standards and Guidelines for Quality Assurance in the European Higher Education Area.* Retrived from <http://ehea.info/media.ehea.info/file/ESG/00/2/ESG_2015_616002.pdf>

Eurydice (2024). *Podmienky služby pre akademických zamestnancov vysokých škôl. Slovensko* [Terms of service for academic employees of universities. Slovakia]. Retrived from <https://eurydice.eacea.ec.europa.eu/sk/national-education-systems/slovakia/podmienky-sluzby-pre-akademickych-zamestnancov-vysokych-skol>

Hall, R. (2020). Otvorme vysoké školy svetu a zvýšme tým ich kvalitu [Let's open universities to the world and thereby increase their quality]. Denník, April 28. Retrived from <https://dennikn.sk/blog/1873581/otvorme-vysoke-skoly-svetu-a-zvysme-tym-ich-kvalitu/>

Hall, R., Dráľ, P., Fridrichová, P., Hapalová, M., Lukáč, S., Miškolci, J., & Vančíková, K. (2019). *Analýza zistení o stave školstva na Slovensku: To dá rozum* [Analysis of findings on the state of education in Slovakia: That makes sense]. MESA10.

Hamuľák, M. (2021). Doktorandi, doktorandské štúdium a zárobková činnosť [Doctoral students, doctoral studies and earnings employment]. *Personálny a mzdový poradca podnikateľa, 26*(11), 44–53.

Hudoba, I. (2015). Ponovembrové vysoké školstvo—veľké očakávania za málo peňazí [Post-November higher education—great expectations for little money]. *Denník*, March 6. Retrived from <https://dennikn.sk/65394/ponovembrove-vysoke-skolstvo-velke-ocakavania-za-malo-penazi/>

Janková, M. (2015). *Zamestnávateľský prieskum* [The Employers' Survey]. CVTI SR.

Kosová, B., & Porubský, Š. (2011). *Transformačné premeny slovenského školstva* [Transformational changes of Slovak education]. Pedagogická fakulta Univerzity Mateja Bela.

Kupriyanova, V., & Ferencz, I. (2022). *Attracting and Supporting International Ph.D. Students, Lecturers, and Researchers in Central-Eastern and South-Eastern Europe: Current Status and Recommended Improvements.* Academic Cooperation Association & UniWellis.

Millennium (2001). *Národný program výchovy a vzdelávania v SR na najbližších 15 až 20 rokov* [National education and training program in the Slovak Republic for the next 15 to 20 years]. Retrived from <https://www.nrsr.sk/dl/browser/document?documentid=163357>

MŠVVM (Ministry of Education, Science, Research and Sport of the Slovak Republic) (2024). *Informácia o účasti Slovenskej republiky na programe Erasmus+ v roku 2023* [Information about the Slovak Republic's participation in the Erasmus+ program in 2023]. Retrived from <https://www.minedu.sk/data/att/2ee/30715.f4b455.pdf>

Niklová, M. (2023). Virtuálne ohrozenia generácie Z—vybrané problémy [Generation Z virtual threats—selected issues]. *Paidagogos*, 1–2, 184–200.

OECD. (2019). *Education at a Glance 2019: OECD Indicators.* Retrived from <https://doi.org/10.1787/f8d7880d-en>

OECD. (2020). *Education at a Glance 2020: OECD Indicators.* Retrived from <https://doi.org/10.1787/69096873-en>

OECD (2021). *Improving Higher Education in the Slovak Republic.* Retrived from <https://doi.org/10.1787/259e23ba-en>

OECD (2022). *Education at a Glance: Slovak Republic.* Retrived from <https://www.oecd.org/en/publications/education-at-a-glance-2022_3197152b-en.html>

OECD (2023). *Education at a Glance 2023: OECD Indicators.* Retrived from <https://doi.org/10.1787/e13bef63-en>

Petríková, D., & Váradyová, T. (2019). Vysokoškolská pedagogika na Technickej univerzite v Košiciach v dimenziách štandardu IGIP [Higher Education Pedagogy at the Technical University of Košice in the Dimensions of the IGIP Standard]. In T. Šeben Zaťková (Ed.), *Pedagogicko-psychologické vzdelávanie na vysokej škole v retrospektíve a jeho perspektívy* (pp. 18–24). Nadlac.

SAAVŠ (Slovak Accreditation Agency for Higher Education). (2020). Standards for the Higher Education Internal Quality Assurance System. Retrived from <https://saavs.sk/wp-content/uploads/2020/12/Standards_for_the_Internal_System.pdf>

Sapała, M., & Stanicek, B. (2024). *Slovakia's National Recovery and Resilience Plan*. European Parliament.

SP (Slovak Parliament) (2022). *Zákon 37 z 23. marca 2022, ktorým sa mení a dopĺňa zákon č. 131/2002 Z. z. o vysokých školách a o zmene a doplnení niektorých zákonov v znení neskorších predpisov a ktorým sa menia a dopĺňajú niektoré zákony.* Ammendment of 137/2002 Act on Higher Education [Act 37 of March 23, 2022, amending and supplementing Act No. 131/2002 Coll. on Higher Education and on the Amendment and Supplementation of Certain Acts, as amended, and amending and supplementing certain laws]. Retrived from <https://www.slov-lex.sk/static/pdf/2022/137/ZZ_2022_137_20220425.pdf>

Theodoulides, L., & Hanesová, D. (2022). *Mastering Transversal Competencies in a Higher Education Environment: through Processes of Critical Thinking and Reflection*. Belianum.

Vančo, M., Srnánková, Ľ., Blanár, F., & Slovíková, M. (2016). *Analýza získavania prierezových kompetencií na slovenských vysokých školách* [Analysis of acquisition of cross-sectional competencies at Slovak universities]. CVTI SR.

Vlachou, A., & Papananou, I. (2018). Experiences and Perspectives of Greek Higher Education Students with Disabilities. *Educational Research, 60*(2), 206–221.

Zacharová, J. (2013). Komparácia vývinu vysokého školstva na Slovensku v XX. a v XXI. storočí [Comparison of the development of higher education in Slovakia in the XX. and in the XXI. Century]. *Pedagogika, 22*, 259–277.

Zaťková, T. Š. (2024). *What are the Models of Courses in Academic Teaching in Slovakia?* Document analysis and the survey of lecturers' opinions. University of St. Cyril and Methodius of Trnava.

Internet Websites (Assessed on September 10, 2024)

CVTI (Centrum vedecko-technických informácií SR—Slovak Center for Scientific and Technical Information). Retrived from <https://www.cvtisr.sk/en/about-scsti/general-information.html?page_id=3704, https://www.cvtisr.sk/cvti-sr-vedecka-kniznica/informacie-o-skolstve/statistiky.html?page_id=9230>

EUROGRADUATE Consortium (2022). Testing the Feasibility of a European Graduate Study. Retrived from <https://www.eurograduate.eu>

European ESO (European Sources Online). Retrived from <https://www.europeansources.info/advanced-search/?as=Slovakia%20higher%20education>

European Union. Education and training monitor 2022—Publications Office of the EU (europa.eu). Retrived from <https://op.europa.eu/en/publication-detail/-/publication/95063009-66f3-11ed-b14f-01aa75ed71a1>

EUROSTUDENT 8. (2022). Retrived from <https://www.eurostudent.eu/>

Ministry of Education, Science, Research and Sport of the Slovak Republic. Employees Portal. Retrived from <https://www.portalvs.sk/regzam/stats/age?range=1&date=2023-12-31&day=30&month=6&year=2024>

Ministry of Education, Science, Research and Sport Register of the Slovak Republic. Annual reports on the state of higher education. Retrived from <https://www.minedu.sk/vyrocne-spravy-o-stave-vysokeho-skolstva/>

Ministry of Education, Science, Research and Sport Register of the Slovak Republic. Revízie výdavkov [Expenditure revisions]. Retrived from <https://www.mfsr.sk/sk/financie/hodnota-za-peniaze/revizia-vydavkov/>

Salaries in the category: Education, Science and Research. Retrived from <https://www.platy.sk/en/salaryinfo/education-science-research>

Slovak Accreditation Agency for Higher Education. Retrived from <https://saavs.sk/en/agency/>

Slovakia's Recovery and Resilience Plan. Retrived from <https://commission.europa.eu/business-economy-euro/economic-recovery/recovery-and-resilience-facility/country-pages/slovakias-recovery-and-resilience-plan_en>

UNESCO, Institute for Statistics. Retrived from <https://uis.unesco.org/>

WEF (World Economic Forum) (2016). The Future of Jobs: Employment, Skills and Workforce Strategy for the Fourth Industrial Revolution. Retrived from www.weforum.org

World Bank. Retrived from <https://data.worldbank.org/>

Zákon č. 553/2003 Z. z.Zákon o odmeňovaní niektorých zamestnancov pri výkone práce vo verejnom záujme a o zmene a doplnení niektorých zákonov [Law no. 553/2003 Coll. Act on Remuneration of Certain Employees in the Performance of Work in the Public Interest and on Amendments to Certain Acts]

4. Academics in the Romanian Higher Education Context

Imre Tódor

ABSTRACT
There is a broad consensus that following the post-communist transition, higher education in Romania underwent significant transformations as a result of democratization and market liberalization. This study aims to explore how and in what direction have the Romanian higher education and the status of academic staff evolved since the transition. It seeks to identify the prevailing trends, as well as the international and national level social, economic and political factors that have driven these changes. The study analyses the year-to-year changes of both public and private higher education institutions and of the academic staff from the transition period to the present day, with particular attention given to the Hungarian language higher education network in Romania. The present paper is based on secondary data analysis obtained from the National Institute of Statistics, and for international comparisons, it relies on data from Eurostat and the World Bank. The results of the longitudinal data analysis indicate that by the fourth decade following the transition the number of higher education institutions in Romania, along with the associated changes in the number of faculties, student population, and academic staff, had normalized and stabilized. Currently, 90 percent of the entire academic staff teach in public higher education institutions, while only 10 percent are in private institutions. One-third of all academic staff are employed at universities in the capital city, Bucharest. Over half (55%) of the academic staff belong to the 40–54 age group, and women constitute more than half (52%) of the total academic workforce. From the quantitative data analysis, it can be concluded that in the near future Romanian higher education will face demographic challenges, emigration, and the need to maintain international competitiveness. In addition to these challenges, Hungarian language higher education must pay special attention to preserving the community's cultural and identity-related continuity while adapting to modern educational challenges.

Keywords: academic staff, higher education, Romania, Hungarian language higher education in Romania

Introduction

In the first part of the study, I provide an overview of (Hungarian Language) higher education in Romania, briefly highlighting some key elements of the post-1989 period. The second part of the study presents the network of higher education institutions in Romania, based on quantitative data. Firstly, I examine the changes in the number of higher education institutions in Romania from the post-communist transition period to the present day, according to the type of funding (public or private) received and by development regions. Subsequently, I analyze the changes in academic faculties and departments within these institutions, breaking down the data by development regions, counties, and university centers. Thirdly, I analyze government expenditures on education as a percentage of GDP, reflecting the level of funding and prioritization of the educational system in a given country. In addition, I present the numbers of student enrollment annually by type of institution. In the third part of the study, within the framework established earlier and also based on quantitative data, I present the main stakeholders of the Romanian higher education: the academic staff. First, an analysis of the student-staff ratio will be provided, then a detailed account of the annual changes in the number of academic staff is provided by development regions and institution types (public and private). Following this, I present the academic staff using various demographic indicators, including gender, age, academic rank, and career paths.

1. A Brief Overview of the (Hungarian Language) Higher Education in Romania After the Regime Change (1990–2023)

Following the events in 1989, higher education in Romania has undergone significant transformations as a result of democratization and market liberalization. Particularly, from the mid-1990s onward, numerous new universities have been established in both the public and private sectors (see Appendix 1 and 2). The newly accredited private higher education institutions have significantly contributed to increasing access to education. During the 1990s, the number of higher education institutions in Romania doubled, and concurrently, the number of students experienced explosive growth (see Appendix 5). However, this educational expansion did not necessarily lead to an improvement in quality (Ciolan et al., 2015). The rapidly increasing student population, along with the swift expansion of newly established institutions, often failed to ensure the necessary strengthening of infrastructure and academic staff.

Quality assurance systems have gradually developed but were long unable to effectively address the challenges posed by the increasing number of student population (Curaj et al., 2015b; Geven et al., 2015). Quality assurance and accreditation have been central elements of higher education reforms in Romania (see ARACIS: The Romanian Agency for Quality Assurance in Higher Education). As part of the Bologna Process, Romania committed to the development of quality assurance systems aimed at improving the standard of education and ensuring the recognition of degrees. The volume edited by Curaj et al. (2015a; 2022) illustrates how Romania has developed its own quality assurance system, which takes into account European standards while also adapting to local specificities. The accreditation process, which ensures that institutions meet national and European requirements, plays a crucial role in maintaining the quality of education. However, the authors highlight that the accreditation process is sometimes overly bureaucratic, which can slow down institutions' ability to adapt to new challenges (Curaj et al., 2015b; Vîiu & Miroiu, 2015).

The challenges related to funding, including the reduction of state fundings, have caused significant difficulties for institutions, particularly impacting smaller universities (Curaj et al., 2015a, 2015b). Romania's accession to the EU in 2007 brought about new directions and opportunities for the higher education system. Through alignment with EU standards and the implementation of the Bologna Process, the Romanian higher education system has become more unified and competitive on the European market (Szolár, 2014). The three-cycle degree system introduced under the Bologna Process (bachelor's, master's, and doctoral programs) has improved mobility and the comparability of the education system with those of other European countries (Florea & Wells, 2011). Since accession to the EU, significant progress has also been made in international cooperation and student mobility. Through the Erasmus program, more Romanian students and academic staff have participated in international exchange programs, contributing to the improvement of educational quality and the strengthening of international relations (Deca et al., 2015). A quantitative study conducted by Dolga and colleagues found that international mobility had a positive impact on students' personal and professional development, as well as on the competitiveness of national higher education institutions (Dolga et al., 2015).

Hungarian language higher education in Romania, as an integral part of the Romanian higher education system, has undergone significant changes following the regime change along with the broader developments in Romanian higher education. These changes influenced the educational opportunities available to the Hungarian minority and the institutional frameworks supporting them (Salat et al., 2010). After the fall of the communist regime, opportunities emerged for the reorganization and strengthening of Hungarian language higher education in Romania (Magyari, 2012). During the first decade after the regime change, the development of higher education in the mother tongue and the establishment of independent Hungarian universities became important objectives for the Transylvanian Hungarian minority (Tonk, 2010).

However, the political and social context of the time presented numerous challenges, causing the restoration of Hungarian language higher education to encounter difficulties in many cases (Magyari, 2012; Tonk, 2012). During this period, Babeş–Bolyai University of Cluj-Napoca (BBU) played a central role, where education programs in Hungarian language were partially reintroduced (Papp Z., 1998). At the same time, there were significant debates regarding the autonomy of Hungarian departments and programs, but full independence was not achieved. Magyari (2012) emphasizes that the establishment of Hungarian language higher education is not only a matter of education, but it is also crucial for the cultural and identity preservation of the community. The study argues that for Hungarians in Romania, creating an independent university would be one of the most important tools for asserting linguistic, cultural, and ethnic rights (Magyari, 2012).

A milestone in the development of Hungarian language higher education was the establishment of Sapientia Hungarian University of Transylvania (SU) in 2001, which is the first accredited private higher education institution in Romania specifically providing higher education opportunities for the Transylvanian Hungarian minority. The university operates with various faculties and campuses in Cluj-Napoca (Kolozsvár), Târgu Mureş (Marosvásárhely), Miercurea Ciuc (Csíkszereda), and Sfântu Gheorghe (Sepsiszentgyörgy), offering numerous programs in Hungarian language (Tonk, 2019). In addition to SU, the Partium Christian University in Oradea (Nagyvárad) also plays a significant role in Hungarian language higher education (János-Szatmári, 2012). Since the mid-2000s, Hungarian higher education in Romania has faced substantial challenges, including funding difficulties, the need for educational infrastructure development, and ongoing political debates over the institutionalization of Hungarian language education (Salat et al., 2010). During the first two decades following the regime change, Hungarian higher education gradually expanded, with new programs being launched and student enrollment increasing (Tonk, 2019). Nevertheless, in the fourth decade following the regime change, both Romanian and Hungarian language higher education in Romania is confronted with serious challenges, such as demographic decline and emigration, which are also evident in the trends in student numbers (see Appendix 5).

The comprehensive reform of the Romanian (higher) education system is detailed in the "Educated Romania" ("România Educată") a national project initiated and directed by the President of Romania, Klaus Iohannis. The program officially commenced in 2016, with its fundamental objective to improve the quality of education in Romania over the long term, providing a modern, efficient, and equitable educational system for students, teachers, and society as a whole (Raport, 2021). In the first phase of the project, various professional events were held across the country (see <https://www.presidency.ro/ro/angajamente/romania-educata>). The final document was adopted by the government in 2021 and includes several new proposals. According to the vision outlined in the document for higher education, Romanian higher education is expected to be equitable and of high quality for all students by 2030 (Raport, 2021). One of the project's goals concerning higher education is to enhance the international competitiveness of Romanian universities and to make them more internationalized (see Deca et al., 2015; Deca, 2016). This will be achieved by supporting research, developing university infrastructure, and encouraging international collaborations. The project supports the integration of Romanian universities into international networks. Additionally, it promotes the involvement of international students and academic staff, as well as the international accreditation of academic programs (see Raport, 2021; Deca, 2016; Deca-Santa, 2020).

To sum it up, the Romanian higher education system over the three and a half decades after the 1989 Revolution can be characterized by the following features: 1) the development and diversification of the higher education system, 2) the massification of higher education, 3) the internationalization of the education system, 4) the transition to the Bologna Process, 5) the decline and aging of the domestic population, 6) globalization, 7) the digitization of the system, and 8) the emigration of skilled labor. Additionally, these factors can be further compounded by the instability of the governmental system, as Romania has experienced 32 different Ministers of Education over the past 34 years.

2. The Network of Higher Education Institutions in Romania

The network of higher education institutions in Romania will be presented based on data from the National Institute of Statistics, comparing the results on public and private higher education institutions from 1990 to 2023. Subsequently, data will be presented by regions (macro-regions, development regions), counties, and cities as well.

2.1. Development of Higher Education Institutions in Romania Between 1990 and 2023

The figure (see Figure 4.1 and Appendix 1) clearly shows that during the academic year after the regime change (1990–1991), there were only public higher education institutions, totaling 48. In the year of the transition, Romania had 40 public higher education institutions, while private institutions did not yet exist. This reflects the legacy of the communist system, where the state held a monopoly on education. Starting from the following academic year, private higher education institutions began to emerge gradually, with their precise numbers appearing in the statistics from 1995, when the first graduating classes of newly initiated programs completed their four-year university education. Thus, in the 1995/1996 academic year, there were already 95 universities, comprising 59 public and 36 private institutions, meaning that Romania's network of higher education institutions had doubled in five years. This period is characterized by the emergence of private higher education institutions, although the number of public institutions also increased to 59, reflecting the heightened demand for higher education.

At the turn of the millennium and during the following five years (2000–2006), the network of higher education institutions in Romania experienced its greatest expansion, with the number of universities rising above 120. The number of institutions continued to grow in both sectors, although during this period, there was a notable increase in the number of private institutions, which exceeded the number of public institutions for six academic years (from 1999/2000 to 2005/2006). For instance, in the 2002/2003 academic year, private universities accounted for 56 percent of the total. This expansion is attributed to both the democratization of higher education and the need to meet market demands.

In the past decade, the total number of higher education institutions has shown a declining trend, primarily driven by a decrease in the number of private universities, while the public higher education network has remained relatively constant over the past five years. In the last four academic years, the distribution of the higher education network by type of institution has remained relatively stable. This stabilization reflects market saturation and the tightening of quality assurance requirements. In the academic year of 2022/2023, the Romanian higher education network comprised 87 accredited institutions, including 53 public and 34 private institutions. Public higher education institutions account for 61 percent of the total, while the private sector represents 39 percent.

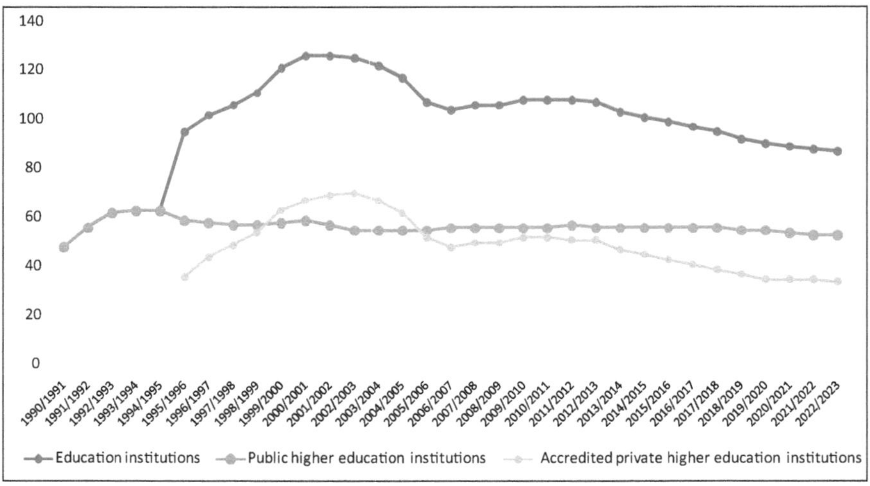

Figure 4.1: The evolution of the total number and types of Romanian higher education institutions (1990–2023).

Source: Compiled by the author, based on data available at INS Tempo Online. Table SCL101D, retrieved on August 14th, 2024.

The structure of the Hungarian language higher education network in Romania, as interpreted by Tonk (2019), can be represented by a "*3 + 3 + 1*" composition. According to this "formula," the first trio refers to the three independent Hungarian language higher education institutions (Sapientia Hungarian University of Transylvania—Cluj-Napoca; Partium Christian University—Oradea; and the Protestant Theological Institute—Cluj-Napoca), which belong to the accredited private university sector. The other three universities (Babeş-Bolyai University—Cluj-Napoca; "George Emil Palade" University of Medicine, Pharmacy, Sciences, and Technology—Târgu Mureş; and the University of Arts—Târgu Mureş) that also have Hungarian departments are part of the public higher education sector. It should be noted that, according to Article 262 of the law on higher education, the three public universities mentioned above are "*State higher education institutions teaching in the language of national minorities, which retain their status as multicultural and multilingual higher education institutions, according to this law*" (art. 262, PR 199/2023). The final digit of the formula, which is one (1), refers to training programs offered by Hungarian higher education institutions outside Hungary, which do not constitute part of the accredited higher education network in Romania.

In the following portion, higher educational institutions will also be analyzed by macro-regions (NUTS-I), development regions (NUTS-II), and counties (NUTS-III). Romania has a total of eight development regions, which were established in 1998 in response to the EU's request (David, 2020). The table (see Table 4.1) lists only those counties within the respective development regions that have universities. It is evident that the majority of higher education institutions are located in the Bucharest-Ilfov region, which accounts for 35.63 percent of the institutions, followed by the North-West and North-East regions. The lowest number of higher education institutions is found in the South and South-West regions, which can be attributed to the southern location of the capital and largest city of Romania (Bucharest). In terms of macro-regions (NUTS: Nomenclature of Territorial Units for Statistics), the III macro-region, which includes the Bucharest-Ilfov and South regions, contains the highest number of universities (35 higher education institutions), while the IV macro-region, which includes the South-West and West development regions, has the fewest (13 higher education institutions).

The higher education institutional network is most prominently represented in Bucharest (see Appendix 2), where more than one-third (34.5%) of the higher education institutions are located. Over two-thirds (67.81%) of the universities are concentrated in the six university cities listed in the table (see Table 4.2). Two-thirds (66%) of the public universities and 41.17% of the private universities

Table 4.1: Higher educational institutions by macro-regions, development regions, and counties, types (2022/2023 academic year)

Macro-regions (NUTS-I)	Development regions (and counties) NUTS-II (NUTS-III)	Higher educational institutions		
		Total	Public	Private
I.	North-West (Bihor, Cluj)	13	7	6
	Center (Alba, Braşov, Mureş, Sibiu)	8	7	1
II.	North-East (Bacău, Iaşi, Neamţ, Suceava)	11	7	4
	South-East (Constanţa, Galaţi)	7	4	3
III.	South (Argeş, Dâmboviţa, Prahova)	4	3	1
	Bucharest-Ilfov	31	16	15
IV.	South-West (Dolj, Gorj)	3	3	0
	West (Arad, Hunedoara, Timiş)	10	6	4
	Total	**87**	**53**	**34**

Source: Compiled by the author, based on data available at INS Tempo Online. Table SCL101A, retrieved on August 14th, 2024.

are situated in these cities. Prior to the regime change, the so-called classical universities, established in the nineteenth century and the first half of the twentieth century, were located in these very cities (University of Bucharest—Bucharest, Babeş-Bolyai University—Cluj-Napoca, Alexandru Ioan Cuza University—Iaşi, West University of Timişoara—Timişoara, etc.). Therefore, the four largest university centers remain Bucharest, Cluj-Napoca, Iaşi, and Timişoara.

Table 4.2: The largest higher education centers (2022/2023 academic year)

Largest centers	Higher educational institutions		
	Total	Public	Private
Bucharest	30	16	4
Cluj-Napoca	9	6	3
Iaşi	7	5	2
Timişoara	5	4	1
Constanţa	4	3	1
Oradea	4	1	3
N	**59**	**35**	**14**

Source: Compiled by the author, based on data available at INS Tempo Online. Table SCL101A, retrieved on August 14th, 2024.

2.2. The Development of Faculties in Romanian Higher Education Institutions Between 1990 and 2023

The diagram depicting the evolution of higher education institutions in Romania is closely aligned with the diagram (see Figure 4.2), which illustrates the development of faculties between the 1990–2023 academic years. On the one hand, it is logical that the number of faculties increases in parallel with the number of universities. On the other hand, let us highlight some key elements. From the early 1990s until 2007, there was a continuous increase in both the number of faculties and academic programs, reflecting the diversification of higher education offers and the growing demand for specializations. Since the 2006/2007 academic year, a slight decline or stagnation has been observed, which can be attributed to demographic changes, a decrease in student numbers (see Figure 4.4 and Appendix 5), and shifts in labor market demands.

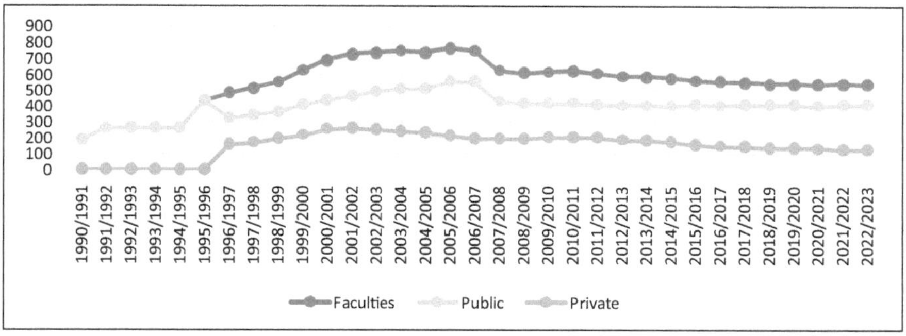

Figure 4.2: The evolution of the faculties of Romanian higher education institutions (1990–2023).

Source: Compiled by the author, based on data available at INS Tempo Online. Table SCL101E, retrieved on August 15th, 2024.

In the academic year 2022/2023 a total of 542 faculties were operational across 87 universities. When examined by source of funding, faculties in public higher education institutions account for three-quarters of all faculties (N=411; 75.83%), while private universities contribute a quarter (N=131; 24.17%). Faculties located in universities based in the capital of Romania, Bucharest, represent more than a quarter (27.5%) of the total faculties (see Appendix 3).

2.3. Government Expenditure on Higher Education in Romania

As previously noted, the network of higher education institutions in Romania has expanded and grew in numbers following the regime change. However, it remains to be seen how much importance the country places on investing in education. This question will be explored further through a single indicator: expenditures on education as a percentage of GDP. This economic indicator reflects the level of funding and priority given to a country's educational system. It demonstrates the proportion of the GDP that the government allocates to support the education sector. This indicator also reflects political commitment and long-term investment, as well as aspects such as academic staff salaries and training, infrastructure development, and student scholarships.

In Romania, government expenditure on education as a percentage of GDP is very low and significantly below the EU average (see Appendix 4). Over the past twenty years (2000–2021), it has averaged 3.4%. In the early 2000s, it represented a relatively low value, fluctuating around 3–4%. During the period around Romania's accession to the EU (between 2006 and 2009), Romania aimed to gradually increase its education expenditures, reaching an average of 4.1% (4.3% in 2006). However, after this period, a downward trend emerged. The lowest point occurred in 2011 and 2012, influenced by the global financial crisis, with expenditures dropping to just 2.8%. Following this, the indicator remained just above 3.5%.

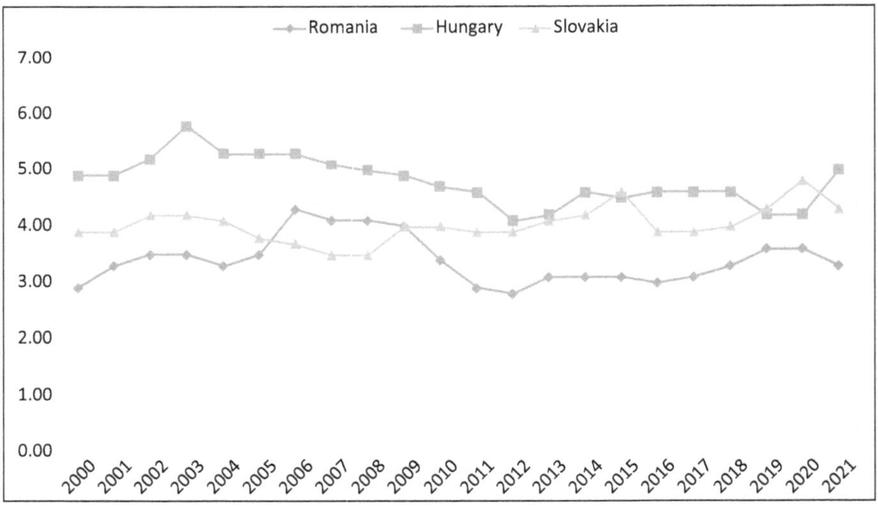

Figure 4.3: Government expenditure on education (% of GDP)—Romania, Hungary, Slovakia. *Source*: <https://data.worldbank.org/indicator/SE.XPD.TOTL.GD.ZS>.

In an international context, it is observed that in 2021, the average government expenditure on education as a percentage of GDP across the 27 member states of the EU was 5%. The figure (see Figure 4.3) presents data for Romania,

Hungary, and Slovakia. Among these countries, Hungary had the highest expenditure, reaching the EU average in 2021. Conversely, Slovakia, although it has increased its spending on education over the past decade compared to Romania, still falls short of the EU average. Between 2006 and 2009, Slovakia allocated less to education relative to GDP compared to Romania. Over the period from 2000 to 2021, Hungary's average expenditure was 4.8%, whereas Slovakia's was 4.03%, with the EU average at 4.97% (see Appendix 4). Countries such as Sweden, Denmark, Belgium, and Finland consistently allocate over 6% of their GDP to education, reflecting their strong educational policy priorities, whereas Romania is positioned in the lower third of the list (see World Bank data).

In relation to the Romanian higher education institution network described above and the international perspective, it is important to note that none of the Romanian higher education institutions have been included in the Shanghai Ranking (ARWU) global top 1000 universities in the past two years (neither in 2024 nor in 2023). In contrast, this year Hungary is represented by four institutions, Serbia by two, Slovakia by one, and Ukraine by one institution in the ranking.[1] In previous years, when the ranking was expanded from 500 to 800 and then to 1000, Babeş-Bolyai University (BBU) appeared on the ARWU 1000 list for six consecutive years (2017–2022), while the University of Bucharest was listed for two years (2018–2019). In the annual national meta-ranking[2] of the top 30 higher education institutions, out of 53 public universities, 28 made the list, and out of 34 private universities, two were included, one of which is the Sapientia Hungarian University of Transylvania (27th place).

---

1 The criteria used in the Shanghai Ranking are as follows: "Quality of education (10%: number of the alumni of an institution winning Nobel Prizes and Fields Medals); Quality of faculty (40%: number of the staff of an institution winning Nobel Prizes and Fields Medals; number of highly cited researchers); Research output (40%: number of research articles published in *Nature* and *Science*, and number of papers indexed in Science Citation Index-Expanded and Social Science Citation Index); Per Capita Performance (10%: per capita academic performance of an institution)." <https://www.shanghairanking.com/methodology/arwu/2024>.

2 The methodology for compiling the national meta-ranking is based on the scores achieved by universities in eight global higher education rankings (ARWU, CWUR, CWTS Leiden Ranking, NTU Ranking, QS World University Ranking, SCImago Institutions Ranking, THE, URAP). It is important to note that, among these, no Romanian higher education institution appears in two global rankings (ARWU and NTU). <https://www.edu.ro/sites/default/files/_fişiere/Minister/2024/div/Raport_metaranking_2023.pdf>.

2.4. Changes in the Number of Students Enrolled to Higher Education Institutions in Romania Between 1990 and 2023

In the final section of this chapter, I will describe the evolution of student enrollment numbers at universities, their faculties, and departments based on the logical framework previously outlined, specifically analyzing these trends annually from the post-communist period onward. The overall trend in student numbers shows a notable increase, as observed in case of both universities and faculties (see Appendix 5). From the late 1990s to the early 2010s, student enrollment grew exponentially, peaking during the 2007–2009 academic years (ca. 900,000 students: ca. 500,000 in public institutions and ca. 400,000 in private institutions). This peak reflects increased demand for higher education and a desire for social mobility. Starting from the 2010s, a decline in student numbers has been observed in both sectors, particularly in the private education sector. This decline can be attributed to demographic decline, decreasing birth rates, youth emigration, and changing interests in higher education. Although the diagram shows an increase starting from the 2014/2015 academic year (ca. 100,000 students), this is due to the fact that from this academic year onward, the National Institute of Statistics includes not only undergraduate students but also those participating at all levels of higher education (BA, MA, Ph.D.) in the statistics. In this context, no significant deviation is observed, with the most noticeable reality being the low enrollment rates in MA and Ph.D. programs within the private education sector.

In the 2022/2023 academic year, a total of 538,720 students were enrolled in higher education, with 88.3% in public and 11.7% in private institutions. In terms of regional distribution, the largest proportion of students are enrolled in the Bucharest-Ilfov region (30%), which encompasses the majority of universities and faculties, followed by the North-Western region (18%) (Cluj and Bihor counties). The regions with the fewest students are the southern (4%) and South-western (6%) regions, according to the data presented (see Tables 4.1–4.2). In the indicated academic year, over three-quarters of the students (76.15%) were enrolled in undergraduate programs, nearly 19.75% in master's programs, and 4.1% in doctoral or postdoctoral programs (see INS Tempo Online SCL103L).

Data on students learning in Hungarian language in Romania is not available from the National Institute of Statistics, neither from the Ministry of Education, or any other official body, and must be obtained directly from the universities. Based on data collected directly from universities, Tonk (2019) reports that the number of students participating in Hungarian language programs is approximately 10,500, which has remained stable over the past decade. Therefore, it can be stated that this student population represents just under 2% of the national student population, with just under half (approximately 5,000 students) enrolled at Babeş-Bolyai University (BBU) and 20% (about 2,200 students) at the Sapientia Hungarian University of Transylvania (SU) (Tonk, 2019).

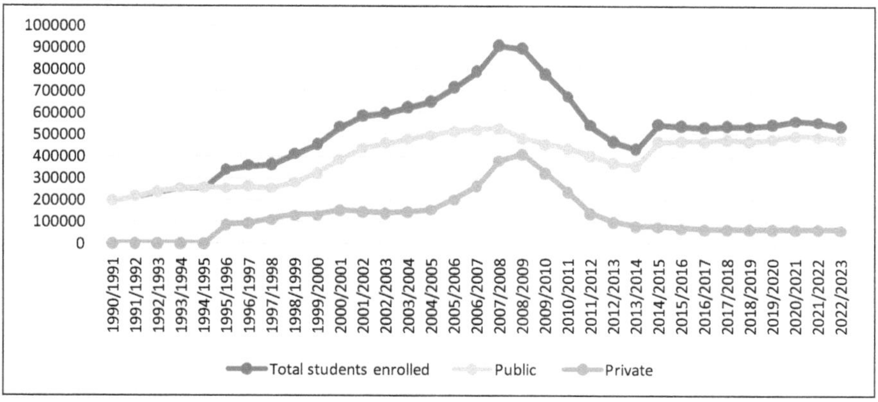

Figure 4.4: The evolution of the number of students enrolled in Romanian higher education institutions (1990–2023).

Source: Compiled by the author, based on data available at INS Tempo Online. Table SCL103L, retrieved on August 14th, 2024.

3. Academic Staff in Romanian Higher Education Institutions

In what follows the developments in the number of academic staff in Romanian higher education after the regime change will be presented based on quantitative data. First, the student-academic staff ratio will be examined, followed by an analysis of sociodemographic indicators such as gender, age, and academic rank.

3.1. Student-Academic Staff Ratio

The first part of the analysis regarding academic staff in higher education examines the evolution of student-academic staff ratio in Romanian higher education institutions. The student-academic staff ratio is a crucial indicator of the quality of the education system, as it directly impacts teaching effectiveness, the quality of education, and students' academic performance. In Romania, this ratio has undergone significant changes between 1990 and 2023 (see Figure 4.5), influenced by various social, economic, and political factors. The rapid expansion of newly established private and public higher education institutions led to substantial growth in student numbers, while the increase in the number of academic staff did not fully keep pace with this trend. Consequently, the ratio of students per academic staff has increased.

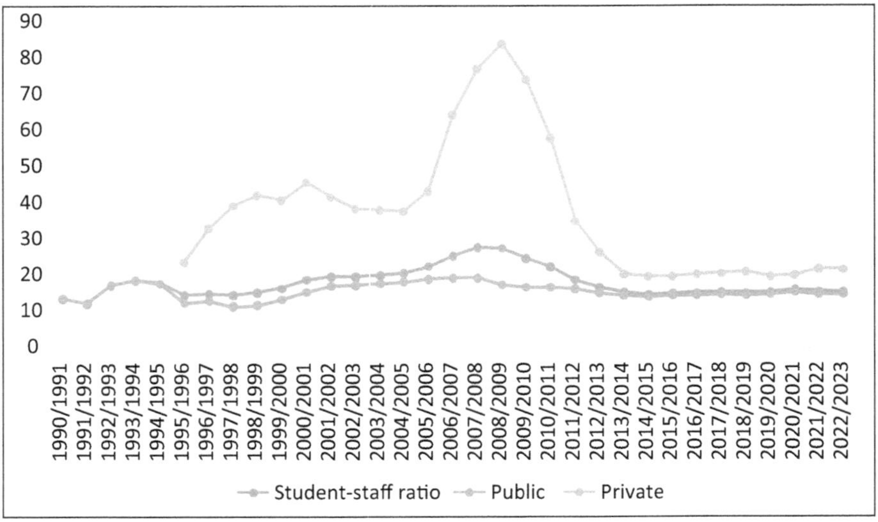

Figure 4.5: Ratio of students-to-academic staff, by type of institution (1990–2023).
Source: Compiled by the author, based on data available at INS Tempo Online. Table SCL103L and SCL104C, retrieved on August 15th, 2024.

Starting from the early 2000s, the ratio of student per staff gradually rose, remaining high throughout this period. During this time, the number of academic staff also began to increase (see Appendix 7), although the growth rate of student numbers continued to surpass that of the academic staff. For example, in the 2009/2010 academic year, there was a substantial difference in the student-academic staff ratio between the two higher education sectors: in the public sector, the ratio was 16.9, while in the private sector, it was 74.2, meaning that there were 74 students per academic staff in the private sector and 17 students per academic staff in the public sector. In the 2022/23 academic year, the total number of students (see Appendix 5) was 775,319 (452,982 from the public sector and 322,337 from the private sector), while the number of academic staff (see Appendix 7) was 31,103 (26,757 from the public sector and 4,346 from the private sector). From the 2010s onwards, the growth in student numbers began to slow down in parallel with the closure of universities and programs (see Appendix 5), partly due to demographic changes and economic factors. Concurrently, the number of academic staff stabilized, leading to a decrease in the ratio of student per academic staff.

In the past decade, the student-staff ratio has been approximately 15–16 students per academic staff, marking a significant decrease compared to the pre-2010 period, when the ratio was around 25 students per academic staff. For the

2022/2023 academic year, the ratio was 15.4. The ratio values show a significant disparity between public and private education sectors. In private education, the number of students per academic staff remains higher compared to public education. In the past two academic years, the difference in the ratio values between public and private education has been around 7 students per academic staff (see Appendix 6).

In international comparison (see Eurostat[3]), the student-academic staff ratio in the EU is traditionally lower than in Romania. Generally, the EU sees a ratio of 7–10 students per academic staff (in 2022, the average for the EU-27 was 12.4), particularly in countries with more developed educational systems, such as Finland (7.6 in 2022), Germany (9 in 2022), Luxembourg (8.6), etc. Among EU member states, the previously mentioned Scandinavian countries and Germany have lower ratios (7–10 students per academic staff), while other countries, such as Slovenia or France, show higher ratios (17–18 students per academic staff). Among neighboring countries, Romania had the highest ratio of student per academic staff in 2022 (14.3), with Serbia at the lowest (10.8), Slovakia at 11.1, and Hungary at 12.6. A lower student-academic staff ratio provides opportunities for academic staff to dedicate more time to research and innovation, thereby further enhancing the competitiveness of educational systems on a global scale.

3.2. Changes in the Number of Academic Staff in Higher Education Between 1990 and 2023

The number of academic staff in Romanian higher education has shown significant growth after the regime change (see Figure 4.6 and Appendix 7). This period marks an era of expansion in higher education, a consequence of the political regime changes and the shift toward a market economy. Growth continued into the early 2000s, followed by a stabilization observed at the end of the decade, which was then succeeded by a slight decrease. Educational policy reforms, the implementation of the Bologna Process, and the optimization of student numbers have also contributed to the transformation of the higher education structure. Starting from the 2010s, a decline in the number of academic staff has been observed, continuing up to 2023 with minor fluctuations. This decline is logically linked to the decrease in both the number of education institutions and student enrollment.

---

3 *Ratio of pupils and students to teachers and academic staff by education level and program orientation* (online data code: educ_uoe_perp04). Source of data: Eurostat.

Starting from the 1995/1996 academic year, the number of academic staff in the private sector increased, although this growth represented a smaller proportion relative to the total number. Between the academic years of 2005/2006 and 2009/2010, the number of academic staff in the private sector was at its peak, after which it either stabilized or declined. From the 2010/2011 to the 2022/2023 academic years, a similar decline in the number of academic staff is observed in the private sector, in alignment with the decrease in student enrollment and economic constraints.

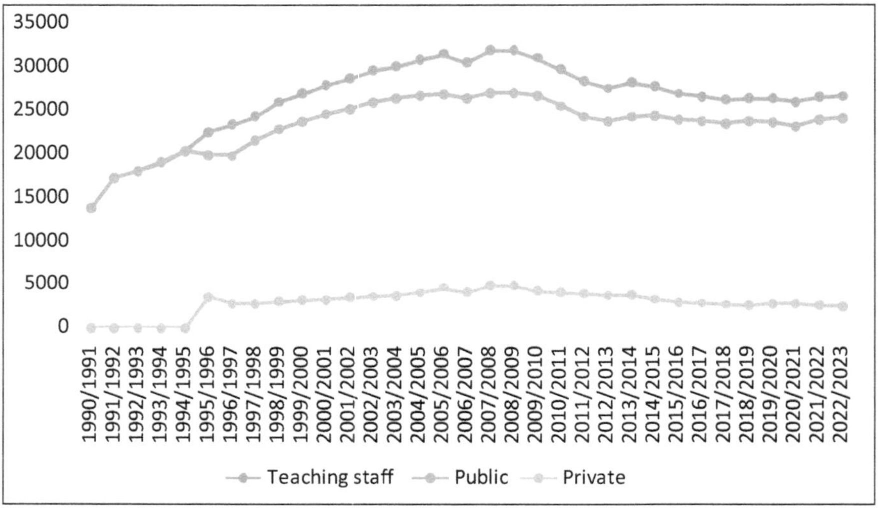

Figure 4.6: Academic staff in higher education institutions, by academic year (1990–2023).
Source: Compiled by the author, based on data available at INS Tempo Online. Table SCL104C, retrieved on August 15th, 2024.

Official data on academic staff at Hungarian language higher education institutions in Romania is also unavailable. According to Tonk (2019), based on data he directly collected from universities, the number of tenured academic staff involved in Hungarian language programs was approximately 750–800 during the years of 2012/2013 to 2018/2019, remaining stable over the past decade. Thus, it can be stated that this number constitutes about 3% of the total academic staff population (with a proportion between 2.85% and 2.91%) (Tonk, 2019). The student-academic staff ratio during these academic years ranged from 12.8 to 13.8, which is close to the national average.

In the following analysis, the distribution of academic staff by development regions will be examined. In Romania, the distribution of academic staff across

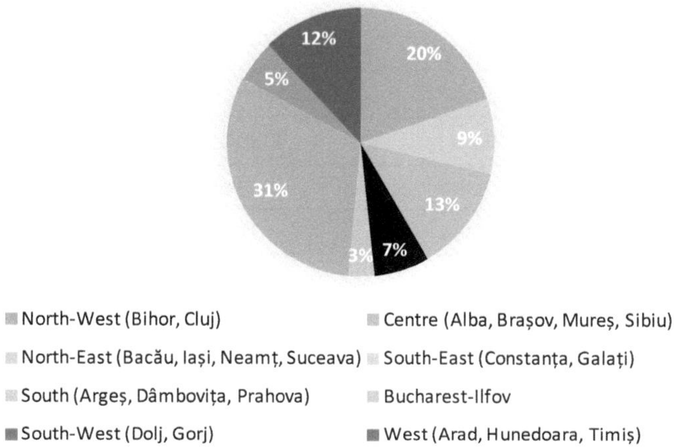

Figure 4.7: Academic staff in higher education institutions by macro-regions, development regions, and counties (2022–2023 academic year).

Source: Compiled by the author, based on data available at INS Tempo Online. Table SCL104C, retrieved on August 15th, 2024.

development regions shows significant variations influenced by various educational, economic, and social factors. It is crucial to consider Romania's eight development regions for this analysis. As depicted in the diagram (see Figure 4.7), nearly one-third of academic staff are located in the development region encompassing the capital (Bucharest) and Ilfov County. This is corroborated by previous data, as the highest number of higher education institutions operates in this region. It is not surprising that 20% of academic staff are found in the North-Western development region, given that this region's largest university center is located in Cluj-Napoca, which is also one of the country's most important educational hubs, leading to a high concentration of academic staff in this area. Together, these two development regions account for half (51%) of the academic staff, while the remaining half is distributed among the other six regions. Academic staff are found in the lowest proportions in the southern (3%) and South-western (5%) development regions. The differences in the number of academic staff between regions are primarily influenced by educational traditions, economic development, followed by demographic factors, and naturally, the concentration of higher education institutions. Largest university centers, such as Bucharest, Cluj-Napoca, Iaşi, and Timişoara, host a larger number and higher concentration of higher education institutions, and thus employ more academic staff (see Table 4.3).

Table 4.3: The largest higher education centers, by academic staff numbers (2022/2023 academic year)

	Academic staff		
Largest centers	**Total**	**Public**	**Private**
Bucharest	8354	7147	1207
Cluj-Napoca	4055	3773	282
Iași	2871	2745	126
Timișoara	2553	2465	88
Craiova	1212	1212	0
Oradea	1042	916	126
N	**20087**	**18258**	**1829**

Source: Compiled by the author, based on data available at INS Tempo Online. Table SCL104C, retrieved on August 15th, 2024.

As observed in Chapter 2, universities, faculties, and students are concentrated in the capital, and consequently, the majority of higher education academic staff are also located in Bucharest. For example, during the 2022/2023 academic year, Bucharest hosted 8,354 academic staff. Practically, every third academic staff works at an educational institution in Bucharest (31.34%). The cities with the largest academic staff bases align with the largest university cities, with Craiova being the sole exception. Unlike Constanța, which has four universities, Craiova hosts only two universities. However, these institutions are notably larger, particularly the University of Medicine and Pharmacy. In the 2022/2023 academic year, which shows no significant deviation from previous years, the six university cities listed in the table (see Table 4.3) account for three-quarters (75.37%) of the academic staff working in higher education, across both public and private sectors. The table presents university cities with more than a thousand academic staffs. Regarding the distribution of academic staff by types of educational institution, 90.7% are employed in public higher education institutions, while 9.3% work in private higher education institutions.

In the table (see Table 4.4), we have listed six university cities with the largest number of academic staff in private institutions, where the number of academic staff exceeds 100. These cities account for 87% of the private education sector. Bucharest also has the highest number of academic staff, representing nearly half (48.9%) of those employed in private universities. When comparing this with the data presented in Table 4.3, we found that in Arad, the highest proportion of academic staff work in private universities, similarly to Galaţi. In Timişoara and Craiova, the number of academic staff working in private universities does not reach 100. Notably, Craiova does not have any private universities, while in Timişoara, among the five universities, only one belongs to the private sector.

Table 4.4: The largest private higher education centers, by academic staff numbers (2022/2023 academic year)

Largest private higher education centers	Teaching staff numbers
Bucharest	1207
Arad	299
Cluj-Napoca	282
Iaşi	126
Oradea	126
Galaţi	108
N	**2148**

Source: Compiled by the author, based on data available at INS Tempo Online. Table SCL104C, retrieved on August 15th, 2024.

3.3. Distribution of Academic Staff in Romania by Gender

The gender distribution among academic staff in Romanian higher education institutions has changed from 1990 to the present, influenced by various factors including changes in social norms, educational policy reforms, and labor market dynamics. Based on the data presented in the diagram (see Figure 4.8), four distinct phases can be identified. At the time of the regime change, nearly three-quarters of the academic staff in Romania were men (72% male). This imbalance can be attributed to the legacy of the communist era, during which women had access to higher education, but higher positions and advancement in academic careers were predominantly reserved for men. The dominance of male academic staff at universities remained strong, particularly in fields such as engineering, natural sciences, and management.

Over the years, the gender gap between female and male academic staff has gradually narrowed. By the turn of the millennium, the proportion of male academic staff had decreased by 12%, resulting in a male representation of 60%, while the proportion of female academic staff began to slowly increase to 40%. This shift can be attributed to changing social norms and the increasing participation of women in higher education, both as students and as academic staff. It is noteworthy that educational policy reforms introduced alongside European integration also contributed to promoting gender equality. The Bologna Process and EU regulations have encouraged the advancement of gender equality at all educational levels. Starting from the 2010s, the proportion of female academic staff continued to rise, and in some academic fields (such as humanities, social sciences, and educational sciences), women's representation has approached or even surpassed that of men.

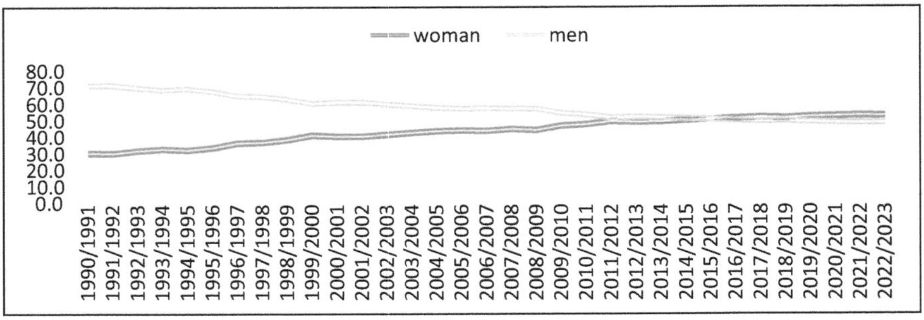

Figure 4.8: Female and male academic staff in the Romanian higher education (1990–2023; in percentages).

Source: Compiled by the author, based on data available at INS Tempo Online. Table SCL104A, retrieved on August 16th, 2024.

In the 2015/2016 academic year, the ratio of female to male academic staff reached parity at 50–50%. While prior to the 2014/2015 academic year there were more male academic staff (50.6%) than female (49.4%), the trend reversed following the 2015/2016 academic year. Consequently, the proportion of women among academic staff has been steadily increasing (see Appendix 8). In the 2022/2023 academic year, the proportion of female academic staff reached 52.3%, continuing the upward trend observed in recent years. According to data from the National Institute of Statistics (INS Tempo Online SCL104B), the proportion of women in managerial academic positions also increased, reaching 42.6% in the 2022/2023 academic year.

3.4. Distribution of Academic Staff in Romania by Age Groups

The distribution of academic staff by age group for the 2022/2023 academic year is as follows. The diagram (see Figure 4.9) illustrates a normal distribution (Gaussian curve) across five-year age intervals. The proportion of academic staff under the age of 30 is only 2.8%, reflecting a decreasing presence of younger academics. This is due to the extended duration of doctoral programs and the difficulties associated with starting an academic career, which delay younger individuals from pursuing academic staff positions.

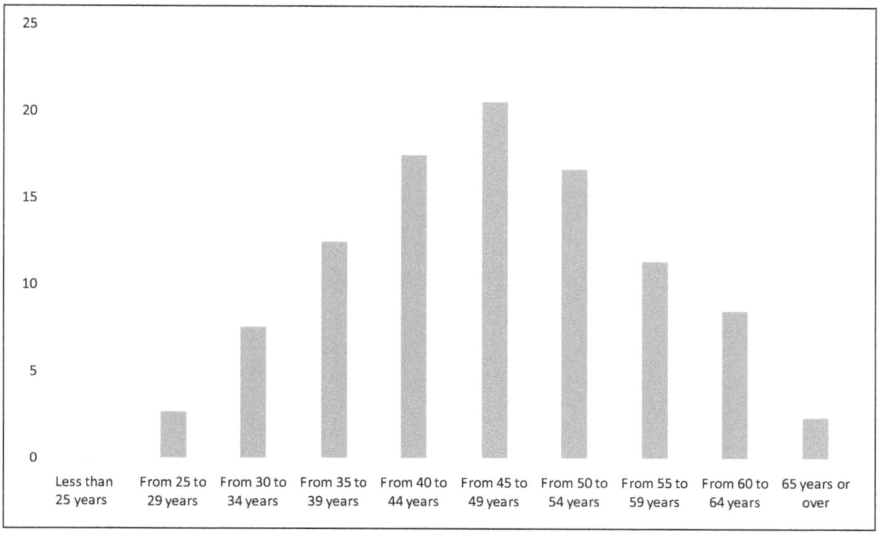

Figure 4.9: Distribution of academic staff in Romania by age groups (2022/2023 academic year).

Source: Compiled by the author, based on data available at Eurostat (online data code: educ_uoe_perd02), retrieved on August 16th, 2024.

More than half of the academic staff in Romania (54.8%) falls within the 40 to 54 age group, which is the dominant age group among academic staff. The majority of active academic staff are in this age range, as they are likely to be at the peak of their careers during this period. The generation ten years younger and ten years older than this group is evenly distributed, accounting for 20.1–22.3% of the academic staff. It can also be noted that academic staff in Romania are, on average, around 45 years old. The proportion of academic staff under 45 is 40.4%, while those over 50 constitute 39%, and those aged 45–49 make up 20.6%. Clearly, the average age of academic staff in Romania ranges between 45 and 50 years, which is higher compared to previous years (see Figure 4.10).

Over the past decade (see Figure 4.10), the average age has increased, a trend partly attributable to the rise in the retirement age and the lack of younger academic replacements. I have reduced the ten age groups presented by Eurostat to four: less than 30 years, from 30 to 39 years, from 40 to 54 years, and 55 years or over. In the past decade, the number of academic staff in the 40–54 age group has increased, while concurrently, the younger generation (ages 30–39) has shown a decreasing trend. The growth in the former age group indicates that a significant part of academic staff is concentrated in this middle-aged bracket, likely due to career advancement and job stability. The dramatic decrease in the number of

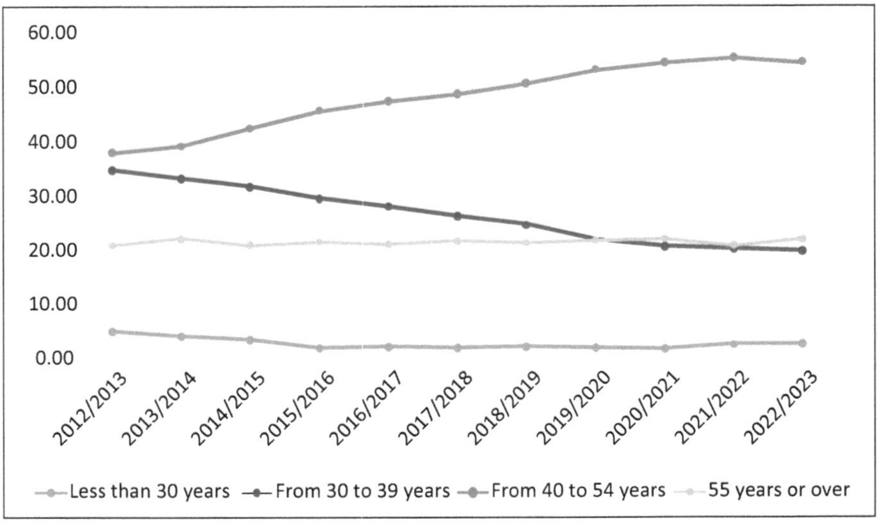

Figure 4.10: Distribution of academic staff in Romania by age groups (2012–2023; in percentage).

Source: Compiled by the author, based on data available at Eurostat (online data code: educ_uoe_perd02), retrieved on August 16th, 2024.

younger academic staff and the increase in the proportion of middle-aged academic staff clearly signal the aging of the academic workforce. This trend has been influenced by demographic changes, the transformation of career opportunities, as well as institutional strategies and reforms (cf. Harper, 2016; Musselin, 2001; Yudkevich et al., 2016). The number of academic staff under 30 has shown a dramatic decline during the analyzed period. While there were 1,435 young academic staff in higher education in 2012/2013, this number fell to 695 by 2022/2023. This decrease represents a roughly 50% drop, reflecting significant demographic shifts. The attractiveness of an academic career to younger generations has diminished due to both lower salaries and uncertainties related to research funding opportunities.

According to Eurostat data,[4] the average age of academic staff in the EU member states is increasing in a manner similar to the trends observed in Romania. The average age generally ranges between 45 and 50 years, though there are significant variations between countries. Similar to Romania, other Eastern European countries also have a low proportion of younger academic

---

4 *Source*: Eurostat. Online data code: educ_uoe_perd02. <https://doi.org/10.2908/EDUC_UOE_PERD02>.

staff and a dominance of older academic staff. This phenomenon can be partly explained by comparable socio-economic conditions.

3.5. Distribution of Academic Staff in Romania by Academic Rank

The 199/2023 law on higher education (PR 2023) defines the career advancement system for academic staff and researchers at higher education institutions in Romania, including the requirements and conditions for entering various academic positions (art. 200, 199/2023). Below, I outline the career advancement system according to the main academic rank. Paragraph 200 of the law on higher education specifies the academic rank, maintaining the hierarchical structure established by previous educational laws. According to this structure, the academic hierarchy is organized as follows: Assistant Lecturer (asistent universitar), Assistant Professor (lector universitar/şef de lucrări universitar), Associate Professor (conferenţiar universitar), and Professor (profesor universitar). Previously, the position of Instructor (preparator) was also included.

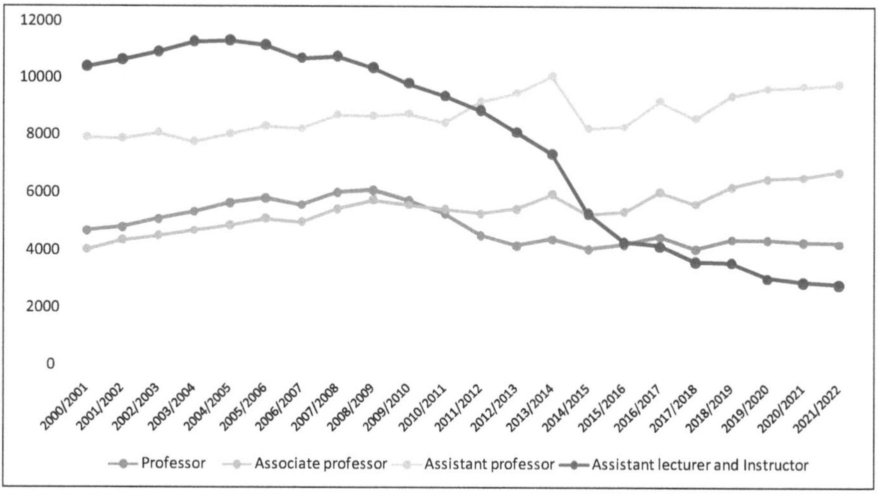

Figure 4.11: Academic staff in Romanian higher education institutions, by academic rank (2000–2022; in numbers).

Source: Compiled by the author, based on data available at INS Tempo Online. Table SCL104A, retrieved on August 16th, 2024.

Based on the data presented in the figure (cf. Figure 4.11 and Appendix 9), it can be stated that cyclical increases and decreases in academic staff positions have been observed over the past two decades, particularly among Professors and assistant lecturers. The number of associate professors has shown a relatively stable increase, while the number of assistant lecturers (and Interns) has indicated a continuous decline, reflecting a reorganization in the distribution of academic staff in higher education. Over time, the academic staff employed in higher education institutions has been rearranged according to the hierarchical dynamics of career progression.

The period from the early 2000s to 2009 is characterized by gradual growth, during which the number of professors increased continuously from 4,722 (2000/2001) to 6,128 (2008/2009). A parallel increase is observed among associate professors, from 4,051 to 5,789. In the subsequent period, the number of professors began to decrease after 2008, falling from 6,128 (2008/2009) to 4,571 (2011/2012), while the number of associate professors gradually increased. The most noticeable change is in the position of assistant lecturers, which can be partly explained by the growth of doctoral and postdoctoral positions that replaced the former assistant lecturer roles. Additionally, generational shifts within the academic staff have also contributed to the reduction in the number of assistant lecturers. After Romania's accession to the EU, universities increasingly sought to employ higher-qualified academics over assistant lecturer, thereby enhancing the quality of education and international competitiveness.

The diagram (see Figure 4.12) does not display data for associate teaching staff (with limited-time work contract), whose numbers have fluctuated differently compared to those in tenured teaching staff ("*titular*," with permanent contract).[5] Between 2018 and 2022, the number of associate teaching staff significantly increased from 7,423 to 11,332. This growth is observed in all academic positions, with higher values particularly noted among assistant professors and assistant lecturers. From this, we can infer that universities are placing greater emphasis on involving individuals with expertise in scientific activities, which is expected to have a positive impact on improving the quality of education.

5 "*Recruitment to a teaching or research position shall be for an indefinite-time or a limited-time. Employment for an indefinite-time in any teaching or research position shall be possible only through an open competition organized by the higher education institution.*" (art. 202. (1), PR 199/2023).

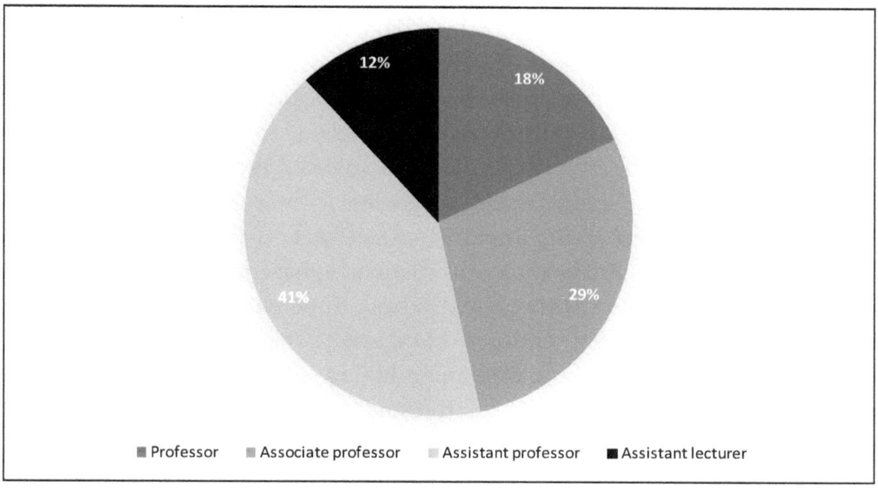

Figure 4.12: Academic staff in Romanian higher education institutions, by academic rank (2021–2022 academic year; in percentage).

Source: Compiled by the author, based on data available at INS Tempo Online. Table SCL104A, retrieved on August 16th, 2024.

In the last academic year examined (2021/2022), based on the percentage distribution of academic positions among tenured academic staff in Romania (see Figure 4.12), it can be observed that assistant professors constitute the largest proportion of the academic staff, making up nearly half of the total (41%), while assistant lecturers represent the smallest proportion (12%). The proportion of academic staff in higher positions (associate professors and professors) together accounts for 47%, indicating an almost equal distribution between those in lower and higher academic ranks. The distribution of the entire academic staff (including associate teaching staff) differs slightly: the proportion of assistant professors and assistant lecturers is approximately two-thirds (63%), while those in professor and associate professor positions together account for just over one-third (37%). Notably, there is a significant discrepancy in the proportion of assistant lecturers between the two types of employment arrangements (tenured academic staff: 12%, associate teaching staff: 21%).

Summary

The present study intended to trace the transformation of Romanian higher education following the regime change, with a focus on the network of Hungarian language higher education institutions. It is evident that from the mid-1990s, numerous higher education institutions were established in both the public and private sectors in Romania, leading to the expansion of higher education. The rapid development of institutions posed significant challenges to education policy, particularly in addressing shortcomings related to infrastructure and academic staff support. The structural reforms introduced as a result of the Bologna Process, along with the significant advancements in international academic staff and student mobility following Romania's accession to the EU, have greatly contributed to the internationalization of Romanian higher education. Furthermore, during the post-communist transition period, opportunities emerged for the reorganization and strengthening of Hungarian language higher education, which is an integral part of the Romanian higher education system, leading to the establishment of the "3+3+1" institutional structure of the Transylvanian system of Hungarian language higher education network as it is known today.

In the past decade, the number of higher education institutions has decreased, reaching a more normalized and stabilized level, particularly due to the decline in the number of private universities, which also resulted in a reduction in the number of faculties, students, and academic staff. Behind these trends, particularly after Romania's accession to the EU, lie factors such as demographic decline and emigration. To address the challenges of the twenty-first century, the President of Romania's flagship educational project, the so-called "Educated Romania" national project, aims at the long-term development of Romanian higher education and enhancing its competitiveness by 2030.

What have we learned about the current situation of academic staff in higher education? Based on data from the last academic year (2022/2023), we can state that the number of academic staff has remained constant over the past decade, around 26,000. During the period from 2018 to 2023, the number of associate academic staff significantly increased by 65%. Nearly all academic staff (99.4%) work full-time. 90% of the total academic staff teach in public higher education institutions, with only 10% in private education. More than half of the academic staff (55%) belong to the 40–54 age group. Female academic staff make up 52% of the total academic staff. The student-academic staff ratio was 15.5 students per academic staff, which represents a decrease compared to previous years; the number of students per academic staff is higher in private education (22 students) than in public education (15 students). One in three academic staff works at a university in Bucharest, and three-quarters of the academic staff in one of the six largest university centers.

From the analysis of quantitative data, we can conclude that in the near future, Romanian higher education will have to face demographic challenges, emigration, and the need to maintain international competitiveness. Undoubtedly, digitalization and globalization will continue to play a defining role in the development of the higher education system. In addition to the aforementioned challenges, Hungarian language higher education must pay particular attention to the preservation of the community's culture and identity while adapting to modern educational challenges.

References

Ciolan, L., Păunescu, M., Fartuşnic, C., Iucu, R., & Hintea, C. (2015). The Role of Impact Evaluation in Evidence-Based HE Policy Making: The Contribution of Transparency Tools. In A. Curaj, L. Deca, E. Egron-Polak, & J. Salmi (Eds.), *Higher Education Reforms in Romania* (pp. 25–42). Springer Cham. <https://doi.org/10.1007/978-3-319-08054-3_2>

Curaj, A., Deca, L., & Egron-Polak, E. (2015a). *Higher Education Reforms in Romania. Between the Bologna Process and National Challenges*. Springer Cham. <https://doi.org/10.1007/978-3-319-08054-3>

Curaj, A., Deca, L., & Hâj, C. M. (2015b). Romanian Higher Education in 2009–2013. The Bologna Process and Romanian Priorities in the Search for an Active European and Global Presence. In A. Curaj, L. Deca, E. Egron-Polak, & J. Salmi (Eds.), *Higher Education Reforms in Romania* (pp. 1–24). Springer Cham. <https://doi.org/10.1007/978-3-319-08054-3_1>

Curaj, A., Salmi, J., & Hâj, C. M. (2022). *Higher Education in Romania: Overcoming Challenges and Embracing Opportunities*. Springer Cham. <https://doi.org/10.1007/978-3-030-94496-4>

David, E-K. (2020). Debating Regionalisation in Romania. Historical Review and Current Draft Laws on Territorial Administration. *Forschungshorizonte Politik und Kultur*, *4*(8), 1–8.

Deca L. (2016). Understanding the internationalization of higher education as a policy process: the case of Romania. Doctoral dissertation, University of Luxembourg. Retrived from <https://hdl.handle.net/10993/31206>

Deca, L., & Santa, R. (2022). Educated Romania—Focusing on Inclusive Policy-making After 30 Years of Shifting Reforms in the Romanian Education System. In A. Curaj, J. Salmi, & C. M. Hâj (Eds.), Higher Education in Romania: Overcoming Challenges and Embracing Opportunities (pp. 1–19). Springer Cham. <https://doi.org/10.1007/978-3-030-94496-4_1>

Deca, L., Egron-Polak, E., & Fiţ, C. R. (2015). Internationalisation of Higher Education in Romanian National and Institutional Contexts. In A. Curaj, L. Deca, E. Egron-Polak, & J. Salmi (Eds.), *Higher Education Reforms in Romania* (pp. 127–147). Springer Cham. <https://doi.org/10.1007/978-3-319-08054-3_7>

Dolga, L., Filipescu, H., Popescu-Mitroi, M. M., & Mazilescu, C. A. (2015). Erasmus Mobility Impact on Professional Training and Personal Development of Students Beneficiaries. *Procedia—Social and Behavioral Sciences*, 191, 1006–1013. <https://doi.org/10.1016/j.sbspro.2015.04.235>

Florea, S., & Wells, P. J. (2011). *Higher Education in Romania*. UNESCO,

Geven, K., Sârbu, O., Santa, R., Maricuţ, A., & Sabic, N. (2015). Why Do Romanian Universities Fail to Internalize Quality Assurance? In A. Curaj, L. Deca, E. Egron-Polak, & J. Salmi (Eds.), *Higher Education Reforms in Romania* (pp. 43–61). Springer, Cham. <https://doi.org/10.1007/978-3-319-08054-3_3>

Harper, S. (2016). *How population change will transform our world*. Oxford University Press, Oxford.

János-Szatmári, Sz., Horváth, G., & Tolnay, I. (2012). Az erdélyi magyar közösséget szolgáló "magánegyetem": a nagyváradi Partiumi Keresztény Egyetem [The "private university" serving the Hungarian community in Transylvania: the Partium Christian University in Oradea]. *Pro Minoritate*, *15*(1). 83–92.

Magyari, T. (2012). A romániai magyar egyetem ügyének vitája a 90-es években [The debate on the Hungarian university in Romania in the 1990s]. *Pro Minoritate, 15*(1). 50–68.

Musselin, C. (2001). *La longue marche des universités françaises*. Presses universitaires de France.

Papp, Z. A. (1998). A romániai magyar oktatás helyzete 1989 után [The Situation of the Hungarian Minority Education in Romania after 1989]. *Magyar Kisebbség, 4*(3–4). <https://epa.oszk.hu/02100/02169/00010/m980321.htm>

Parliament of Romania (PR) (1995). Legea învăţământului nr. 84/1995 [Law on education] (in Romanian). Monitorul Oficial al României [Official monitor of Romania], Nr. 606/10.XII.1999.

Parliament of Romania (PR) (2011). Legea educaţiei naţionale nr. 1/2011 [Law on national education] (in Romanian). Monitorul Oficial al României [Official monitor of Romania], Nr. 18/10.I.2011.

Parliament of Romania (PR) (2023). Legea învăţământului superior nr. 199/2023 [Law on higher education] (in Romanian). Monitorul Oficial al României [Official monitor of Romania], Nr. 614/5.VII.2023.

Raport (2021). România Educată—Proiect al Preşedintelui României. Retrived from <http://www.romaniaeducata.eu/wp-content/uploads/2021/07/Raport-Romania-Educata-14-iulie-2021.pdf>

Salat, L., Papp, Z. A., Csata, Zs., & Péntek, J. (2010). Az erdélyi magyar felsőoktatás helyzete és kilátásai. In M. Szikszai (Ed.), *Az erdélyi magyar felsőoktatás helyzete és kilátásai* (pp. 9–126). Ábel Kiadó.

Szolár, É. (2014). The Bologna Process in Romania. In T. Kozma, M. Rébay, A. Óhidy, & É. Szolár, (Eds), *The Bologna Process in Central and Eastern Europe* (pp. 183–222). Springer VS. <https://doi.org/10.1007/978-3-658-02333-1_8>

Tonk, M. (2010). Present and Future of Higher Education in the Hungarian Language in Romania. *Acta Universitatis Sapientiae, European and Regional Studies, 1*(2). 149–160.

Tonk, M. (2012). Lehetőségek, modellek, kihívások a kisebbségi felsőoktatás-politikában [Possibilities, models, and challenges in Minority Highed Education Policy]. *Pro Minoritate, 15*(4). 69–82.

Tonk, M. (2019). Adalékok a romániai magyar felsőoktatási stratégiához: demográfiai, oktatáspolitikai, nemzetpolitikai kihívások [Factors Determining the Strategy of Hungarian Higher Education in Romania: Demographic and Educational Challenges]. *Kisebbségi Szemle, 4*(2). 49–62.

Vîiu, G. A., & Miroiu, A. (2015). The Quest for Quality in Higher Education: Is There Any Place Left for Equity and Access? In A. Curaj, L. Deca, E. Egron-Polak, & J. Salmi (Eds.), *Higher Education Reforms in Romania* (pp. 173–189). Springer, Cham. <https://doi.org/10.1007/978-3-319-08054-3_9>

Yudkevich, M., Altbach, P. G., & Rumbley, L. A. (2016). *The Global Academic Rankings Game. Changing Institutional Policy, Practice and Academic Life.* Routledge.

Websites

Agenţia Română de Asigurare a Calităţii în Învăţământul Superior [The Romanian Agency for Quality Assurance in Higher Education]. Retrived from <https://www.aracis.ro>

Eurostat. Retrived from <https://ec.europa.eu/eurostat/en/>

Institutul Naţional de Statistică [National Institute of Statistics]—Tempo Online statistical data. Retrived from <http://statistici.insse.ro:8077/tempo-online/#/pages/tables/insse-table>

Ministerul Educaţiei [Ministry of Education]. Retrived from <https://www.edu.ro>

Preşedintele României [President of Romania]. Retrived from <https://www.presidency.ro>

Shanghai Ranking. Retrived from <https://www.shanghairanking.com>

World Bank. Retrived from <https://www.worldbank.org/en/home>

Appendices

Appendix 1: The evolution of the total number and types of Romanian higher education institutions (1990–2023)

	Higher education institutions		
Academic year	Total	Public	Private
1990/1991	48	48	:
1991/1992	56	56	:
1992/1993	62	62	:
1993/1994	63	63	:
1994/1995	63	63	:
1995/1996	95	59	36
1996/1997	102	58	44
1997/1998	106	57	49
1998/1999	111	57	54
1999/2000	121	58	63
2000/2001	126	59	67
2001/2002	126	57	69
2002/2003	125	55	70
2003/2004	122	55	67
2004/2005	117	55	62
2005/2006	107	55	52
2006/2007	104	56	48
2007/2008	106	56	50
2008/2009	106	56	50
2009/2010	108	56	52
2010/2011	108	56	52
2011/2012	108	57	51
2012/2013	107	56	51
2013/2014	103	56	47
2014/2015	101	56	45
2015/2016	99	56	43
2016/2017	97	56	41
2017/2018	95	56	39
2018/2019	92	55	37
2019/2020	90	55	35
2020/2021	89	54	35
2021/2022	88	53	35
2022/2023	87	53	34

Source: Compiled by the author, based on data available at INS Tempo Online. Table SCL101D, retrieved on August 14th, 2024.

Appendix 2: Higher Education Institutions in Romania, by type of institution (conform HG nr. 367/2023, cu modificările şi completările ulterioare)

Nr.	Higher education institutions	Location	Public/ Private	Note
1.	*Politehnica* University of Bucharest	Bucureşti	Public	
2.	Technical University of Civil Engineering of Bucharest	Bucureşti	Public	
3.	*Ion Mincu* University of Architecture and Urbanism of Bucharest	Bucureşti	Public	
4.	The University of Agricultural Sciences and Veterinary Medicine of Bucharest	Bucureşti	Public	
5.	University of Bucharest	Bucureşti	Public	
6.	*Carol Davila* University of Medicine and Pharmacy of Bucharest	Bucureşti	Public	
7.	Academy of Economic Studies of Bucharest	Bucureşti	Public	
8.	National University of Music Bucharest	Bucureşti	Public	
9.	National University of Arts of Bucharest	Bucureşti	Public	
10.	*Ion Luca Caragiale* National University of Theatre and Cinematography of Bucharest	Bucureşti	Public	
11.	National Academy of Physical Education and Sports of Bucharest	Bucureşti	Public	
12.	National School of Political Sciences and Administration Bucharest	Bucureşti	Public	
13.	*Dimitrie Cantemir* Christian University of Bucharest	Bucureşti	Private	
14.	*Titu Maiorescu* University of Bucharest	Bucureşti	Private	
15.	*Nicolae Titulescu* University of Bucharest	Bucureşti	Private	
16.	*Romanian-American* University of Bucharest	Bucureşti	Private	
17.	*Hyperion* University of Bucharest	Bucureşti	Private	
18.	*Spiru Haret* University of Bucharest	Bucureşti	Private	
19.	University *Bioterra* of Bucharest	Bucureşti	Private	
20.	The *Ecological* University of Bucharest	Bucureşti	Private	
21.	University *Athenaeum* of Bucharest	Bucureşti	Private	
22.	University *Artifex* of Bucharest	Bucureşti	Private	
23.	*Baptist* Theological Institute of Bucharest	Bucureşti	Private	
24.	*Pentecostal* Theological Institute of Bucharest	Bucureşti	Private	
25.	Theological Institute Evangelicals *Timotheus* of Bucharest	Bucureşti	Private	
26.	*Romanian-American* Business School	Bucureşti	Private	****
27.	Military Technical Academy *Ferdinand I* of Bucharest	Bucureşti	Public	*
28.	National Defense University *Carol I* of Bucharest	Bucureşti	Public	*

(*Continued*)

Appendix 2: (*Continued*)

Nr.	Higher education institutions	Location	Public/ Private	Note
29.	*Mihai Viteazul* National Intelligence Academy of Bucharest	Bucureşti	Public	*
30.	*Alexandru Ioan Cuza* Police Academy of Bucharest	Bucureşti	Public	*
31.	*Technical* University of Cluj-Napoca	Cluj-Napoca	Public	
32.	University of Agricultural Sciences and Veterinary Medicine of Cluj-Napoca	Cluj-Napoca	Public	
33.	*Babes-Bolyai* University of Cluj-Napoca	Cluj-Napoca	Public	
34.	University of Medicine and Pharmacy Iuliu Hatieganu of Cluj-Napoca	Cluj-Napoca	Public	
35.	*Gheorghe Dima* Academy of Music of Cluj-Napoca	Cluj-Napoca	Public	
36.	University of Art and Design of Cluj-Napoca	Cluj-Napoca	Public	
37.	*Avram Iancu* University of Cluj-Napoca	Cluj-Napoca	Private	***
38.	*Bogdan Voda* University of Cluj-Napoca	Cluj-Napoca	Private	
39.	*Protestant* Theological Institute of Cluj-Napoca	Cluj-Napoca	Private	**
40.	*Sapientia* Hungarian University of Transylvania	Cluj-Napoca	Private	**
41.	*Gheorghe Asachi* Technical University of Iaşi	Iaşi	Public	
42.	*Ion Ionescu de la Brad* University of Agricultural Sciences and Veterinary of Iaşi	Iaşi	Public	
43.	*Alexandru Ioan Cuza* University of Iaşi	Iaşi	Public	
44.	*Grigore T. Popa* University of Medicine and Pharmacy of Iaşi	Iaşi	Public	
45.	University of Arts George Enescu of Iaşi	Iaşi	Public	
46.	*Mihail Kogalniceanu* University of Iaşi	Iaşi	Private	***
47.	*Petre Andrei* University of Iaşi	Iaşi	Private	
48.	*Apollonia* University of Iaşi	Iaşi	Private	
49.	*Politehnica* University of Timişoara	Timişoara	Public	
50.	*Banat* University of Agricultural Sciences and Veterinary Medicine *King Mihai I of Romania*	Timişoara	Public	
51.	*The West* University of Timişoara	Timişoara	Public	
52.	*Victor Babes* University of Medicine and Pharmacy of Timişoara	Timişoara	Public	
53.	*Tibiscus* University of Timişoara	Timişoara	Private	
54.	*Ovidius* University of Constanţa	Constanţa	Public	
55.	*Maritime* University of Constanţa	Constanţa	Public	
56.	*Andrei Saguna* University of Constanţa	Constanţa	Private	
57.	*Mircea cel Batran* Naval Academy	Constanţa	Public	*

Nr.	Higher education institutions	Location	Public/ Private	Note
58.	University of Oradea	Oradea	Public	
59.	*Agora* University of Oradea	Oradea	Private	
60.	*Emanuel* University of Oradea	Oradea	Private	
61.	*Partium* Christian University	Oradea	Private	**
62.	*Lucian Blaga* University of Sibiu	Sibiu	Public	
63.	*Romanian-German* University of Sibiu	Sibiu	Private	***
64.	*Nicolae Balcescu* Land Forces Academy	Sibiu	Public	*
65.	*George Emil Palade* University of Medicine, Pharmacy, Science and Technology of Târgu-Mureş	Târgu-Mureş	Public	
66.	University of Arts of Târgu-Mureş	Târgu-Mureş	Public	
67.	*Dimitrie Cantemir* University of Târgu-Mureş	Târgu-Mureş	Private	
68.	*Aurel Vlaicu* University of Arad	Arad	Public	
69.	*Vasile Goldis* West University of Arad	Arad	Private	
70.	*Vasile Alecsandri* University of Bacău	Bacău	Public	
71.	*George Bacovia* University of Bacău	Bacău	Private	
72.	*Transilvania* University of Braşov	Braşov	Public	
73.	*Henri Coanda* Air Force Academy	Braşov	Public	*
74.	University of Craiova	Craiova	Public	
75.	University of Medicine and Pharmacy of Craiova	Craiova	Public	
76.	University Dunarea de Jos Galaţi	Galaţi	Public	
77.	Danubius University of Galaţi	Galaţi	Private	
78.	Decembrie 1, 1918 University of Alba-Iulia	Alba-Iulia	Public	
79.	*Dragan* European University of Lugoj	Lugoj	Private	
80.	University of Petrosani	Petrosani	Public	
81.	*Constantin Brancoveanu* University of Pitesti	Pitesti	Private	
82.	*Petroleum and Gas* University of Ploiesti	Ploiesti	Public	
83.	*Stefan cel Mare* University of Suceava	Suceava	Public	
84.	*Valahia* University of Targoviste	Targoviste	Public	
85.	*Constantin Brancusi* University of Târgu-Jiu	Târgu-Jiu	Public	
86.	Adventist Theological Institute of Cernica	Cernica	Private	

Source: Compiled by the author, based on data available at ME (<https://www.edu.ro/universitati_stat_civile; https://www.edu.ro/institutii_inv_superior_militare>; <https://www.edu.ro/universitati_particulare_acreditate>), retrieved on August 15th, 2024.

Notes: *Higher education institutions with military profile; **Hungarian Language University; ***Specializations/Programs of undergraduate studies in the structure of the higher education institution enter into liquidation starting with the academic year 2014–2015; 2016–2017, 2020–2021; ****University education—second cycle.

Appendix 3: The evolution of the faculties and types of Romanian higher education institutions (1990–2023)

	Faculties		
Academic year	**Total**	**Public**	**Private**
1990/1991	186	186	:
1991/1992	257	257	:
1992/1993	261	261	:
1993/1994	262	262	:
1994/1995	262	262	:
1995/1996	437	:	:
1996/1997	485	324	161
1997/1998	516	342	174
1998/1999	556	361	195
1999/2000	632	411	221
2000/2001	696	438	258
2001/2002	729	465	264
2002/2003	742	489	253
2003/2004	754	513	241
2004/2005	742	510	232
2005/2006	770	554	216
2006/2007	755	558	197
2007/2008	631	432	199
2008/2009	617	420	197
2009/2010	624	417	207
2010/2011	629	422	207
2011/2012	614	410	204
2012/2013	596	405	191
2013/2014	590	405	185
2014/2015	583	403	180
2015/2016	567	409	158
2016/2017	560	405	155
2017/2018	554	406	148
2018/2019	545	406	139
2019/2020	546	407	139
2020/2021	541	404	137
2021/2022	543	409	134
2022/2023	542	411	131

Source: Compiled by the author, based on data available at INS Tempo Online. Table SCL101E, retrieved on August 14th, 2024.

Appendix 4: Government expenditure on education (% of GDP)

	Government expenditure on education			
Year	**Romania**	**Hungary**	**Slovakia**	**European Union**
2000	2.90	4.90	3.90	4.90
2001	3.30	4.90	3.90	5.10
2002	3.50	5.20	4.20	5.20
2003	3.50	5.80	4.20	5.10
2004	3.30	5.30	4.10	5.00
2005	3.50	5.30	3.80	5.10
2006	4.30	5.30	3.70	5.00
2007	4.10	5.10	3.50	4.70
2008	4.10	5.00	3.50	5.00
2009	4.00	4.90	4.00	5.50
2010	3.40	4.70	4.00	5.30
2011	2.90	4.60	3.90	5.10
2012	2.80	4.10	3.90	4.90
2013	3.10	4.20	4.10	5.00
2014	3.10	4.60	4.20	5.00
2015	3.10	4.50	4.60	4.90
2016	3.00	4.60	3.90	4.80
2017	3.10	4.60	3.90	4.60
2018	3.30	4.60	4.00	4.60
2019	3.60	4.20	4.30	4.60
2020	3.60	4.20	4.80	4.90
2021	3.30	5.00	4.30	5.00
Average	**3.40**	**4.80**	**4.03**	**4.97**

Source: <https://data.worldbank.org/indicator/SE.XPD.TOTL.GD.ZS>.

Appendix 5: The evolution of the number of students enrolled in Romanian higher education institutions (1990–2023)

	Students enrolled		
Academic year	Total	Public	Private
1990/1991	192810	192810	:
1991/1992	215226	215226	:
1992/1993	235669	235669	:
1993/1994	250087	250087	:
1994/1995	255162	255162	:
1995/1996	336141	250836	85305
1996/1997	354488	261054	93434
1997/1998	360590	249875	110715
1998/1999	407720	277666	130054
1999/2000	452621	322129	130492
2000/2001	533152	382478	150674
2001/2002	582221	435406	146815
2002/2003	596297	457259	139038
2003/2004	620785	476881	143904
2004/2005	650335	495034	155301
2005/2006	716464	513678	202786
2006/2007	785506	520263	265243
2007/2008	907353	526844	380509
2008/2009	891098	480239	410859
2009/2010	775319	452982	322337
2010/2011	673001	433063	239938
2011/2012	539852	399464	140388
2012/2013	464592	364916	99676
2013/2014	433234	353988	79246
2014/2015	541653	464149	77504
2015/2016	535218	465012	70206
2016/2017	531586	464642	66944
2017/2018	538871	471376	67495
2018/2019	533749	467931	65818
2019/2020	543299	475823	67476
2020/2021	560490	491943	68547
2021/2022	554007	486520	67487
2022/2023	538720	475546	63174

Source: Compiled by the author, based on data available at INS Tempo Online. Table SCL103L, retrieved on August 14th, 2024.
Note: Between the academic years 1990/1991 and 2013/2014, only the numbers of students enrolled in BA courses are shown, and from the following academic year until today, the numbers of students enrolled in all types of courses (BA, MA, Ph.D.) are shown.

Appendix 6: Ratio of students-to-academic staff, by type of institution (1990–2023)

	Student-staff ratio		
Academic year	**Total**	**Public**	**Private**
1990/1991	13.8	13.8	:
1991/1992	12.4	12.4	:
1992/1993	17.6	17.6	:
1993/1994	18.8	18.8	:
1994/1995	18	18	:
1995/1996	14.8	12.5	23.8
1996/1997	15.1	13.1	33.4
1997/1998	14.7	11.5	39.6
1998/1999	15.6	12	42.5
1999/2000	16.7	13.5	41.1
2000/2001	19	15.5	46
2001/2002	19.9	17.3	42
2002/2003	19.8	17.5	38.7
2003/2004	20.3	18	38.5
2004/2005	20.8	18.4	38.2
2005/2006	22.7	19.1	43.5
2006/2007	25.6	19.6	64.4
2007/2008	28	19.5	77.3
2008/2009	27.8	17.7	84.1
2009/2010	24.9	16.9	74.2
2010/2011	22.6	16.9	58.1
2011/2012	19	16.4	35.2
2012/2013	16.9	15.3	26.6
2013/2014	15.4	14.5	20.5
2014/2015	14.8	14.1	19.9
2015/2016	15.2	14.7	19.9
2016/2017	15.3	14.7	20.6
2017/2018	15.5	14.9	20.7
2018/2019	15.3	14.6	21.1
2019/2020	15.4	14.9	19.8
2020/2021	16.1	15.6	20.3
2021/2022	15.7	15	21.9
2022/2023	15.4	14.8	21.7

Source: Compiled by the author, based on data available at INS Tempo Online. Table SCL103L and SCL104C, retrieved on August 15th, 2024.

Appendix 7: Academic staff in higher education institutions, by academic year (in numbers; 1990–2023)

	Teaching staff		
Academic year	**Total**	**Public**	**Private**
1990/1991	13927	13927	:
1991/1992	17315	17315	:
1992/1993	18123	18123	:
1993/1994	19130	19130	:
1994/1995	20452	20452	:
1995/1996	22611	19994	3580
1996/1997	23477	19897	2794
1997/1998	24427	21633	2794
1998/1999	26013	22955	3058
1999/2000	26977	23809	3168
2000/2001	27959	24686	3273
2001/2002	28674	25174	3500
2002/2003	29619	26029	3590
2003/2004	30137	26400	3737
2004/2005	30857	26790	4067
2005/2006	31543	26881	4662
2006/2007	30583	26464	4119
2007/2008	31964	27044	4920
2008/2009	31973	27089	4884
2009/2010	31103	26757	4346
2010/2011	29746	25618	4128
2011/2012	28365	24372	3993
2012/2013	27555	23805	3750
2013/2014	28211	24342	3869
2014/2015	27772	24467	3305
2015/2016	26949	23978	2971
2016/2017	26618	23776	2842
2017/2018	26266	23566	2700
2018/2019	26384	23822	2562
2019/2020	26429	23621	2808
2020/2021	25991	23204	2787
2021/2022	26555	23992	2563
2022/2023	26649	24181	2468

Source: Compiled by the author, based on data available at INS Tempo Online. Table SCL104C, retrieved on August 15th, 2024.

Appendix 8: A Higher education female and male academic staff (in percentages; 1990–2023)

	Teaching staff	
Academic year	**Woman**	**Men**
1990/1991	28.0	72
1991/1992	27.9	72.1
1992/1993	29.6	70.4
1993/1994	30.8	69.2
1994/1995	30.1	69.9
1995/1996	31.8	68.2
1996/1997	34.7	65.3
1997/1998	35.1	64.9
1998/1999	36.9	63.1
1999/2000	39.8	60.2
2000/2001	39.0	61
2001/2002	39.0	61
2002/2003	40.2	59.8
2003/2004	41.4	58.6
2004/2005	42.5	57.5
2005/2006	42.9	57.1
2006/2007	42.8	57.2
2007/2008	43.9	57.1
2008/2009	43.3	56.7
2009/2010	45.9	54.1
2010/2011	46.8	53.2
2011/2012	48.7	51.3
2012/2013	48.5	51.5
2013/2014	48.6	51.4
2014/2015	49.4	50.6
2015/2016	50	50
2016/2017	50.8	49.2
2017/2018	51.3	48.7
2018/2019	50.9	49.1
2019/2020	51.7	48.3
2020/2021	52.1	47.9
2021/2022	52.4	47.6
2022/2023	52.3	47.7

Source: Compiled by the author, based on data available at INS Tempo Online. Table SCL104A, retrieved on August 16th, 2024.

Appendix 9: Academic staff in Romanian higher education institutions, by academic rank (2000–2022; in numbers)

	Academic rank			
Academic year	Professor	Associate professor	Assistant professor	Assistant lecturer and instructor
2000/2001	4722	4051	7942	10431
2001/2002	4840	4369	7889	10680
2002/2003	5115	4538	8090	10955
2003/2004	5374	4723	7766	11295
2004/2005	5688	4896	8046	11352
2005/2006	5842	5148	8341	11196
2006/2007	5614	5020	8240	10725
2007/2008	6036	5477	8741	10785
2008/2009	6128	5789	8687	10396
2009/2010	5767	5609	8773	9845
2010/2011	5312	5461	8455	9410
2011/2012	4571	5319	9223	8903
2012/2013	4209	5475	9517	8134
2013/2014	4425	5988	10111	7376
2014/2015	4071	5299	8258	5319
2015/2016	4240	5380	8317	4314
2016/2017	4495	6066	9236	4183
2017/2018	4090	5651	8606	3635
2018/2019	4413	6239	9428	3615
2019/2020	4392	6511	9688	3063
2020/2021	4315	6576	9758	2930
2021/2022	4260	6768	9835	2835

Source: Compiled by the author, based on data available at INS Tempo Online. Table SCL104A, retrieved on August 16th, 2024.

Notes: The status of Instructor (preparator) was not included in the 1/2011 Education Law, nor is it present in the current Higher Education Law (199/2023). Therefore, it was not displayed separately in the table but was combined with the assistant lecturer position. Additionally, the previous Education Law (128/1997) included another position, namely Consultant Professor (profesor universitar consultant), which is no longer present in the last two education laws. Consequently, these positions have been categorized under "other" in the table, but they are not displayed, as they have been phased out over the years and no longer exist.

5. Characteristics of the Higher Education System and Academic Staff in Serbia

Elvira Kovács & Zoltán Papp

ABSTRACT
The Serbian higher education system has undergone significant changes, particularly following the Bologna reforms of 2005. There is a consensus among researchers that these reforms have aimed to integrate Serbian institutions into the European Higher Education Area, yet challenges remain in fully achieving this integration. However, there is still debate regarding the effectiveness of these reforms in improving the quality of education and the accreditation processes of Serbian higher education institutions. This study seeks to address these gaps by examining the impact of these regulations on faculty appointment and employment policies, the composition of academic staff, and their career progression. The research questions focus on how these regulations affect the distribution of faculty and students between public and private universities, and the statistical analysis of student enrollment and graduation rates. The study utilizes a dataset provided by the Statistical Office of the Republic of Serbia. Data on higher education is collected by regular annual surveys. Data on students enrolled in tertiary education and academic staff in faculties and academies refer to the beginning of the winter semester, that is, when students were enrolled. Data on graduated students, specialists, Master of Arts/Science, and Ph.Ds. relate to the calendar year. Key analytical methods include descriptive and comparative statistics. The findings reveal significant disparities in faculty distribution and student outcomes between public and private institutions, highlighting areas for policy improvement. These results have important implications for the future of higher education in Serbia, suggesting that targeted reforms could enhance both academic and practical outcomes.

Keywords: Serbian higher education, Bologna Process, faculty distribution, academic staff, student outcomes, accreditation, policy analysis

Introduction

The educational system plays a crucial role in social development, considering that its quality is closely linked to economic development and its level of excellence (Branković, 2021; European Council 2000; Kočović, 2020; Kolarski, 2021; Škorić, 2008). Consequently, the design of the educational system needs to align with labor market requirements (Avramović, 2013) and provide high-quality education to students (Jarić & Vukasović, 2009; Lungulov, 2015).

Serbian higher education reforms after 2005 brought significant changes to the structure and operation of the higher education system (Lungulov, 2011, 2015). These reforms were part of the Bologna Process, aimed at harmonizing and standardizing the European Higher Education Area. The primary goal was to make Serbian higher education compatible with European systems, thereby facilitating student mobility (Jerotijević & Aleksić Glišović, 2019) and mutual recognition of diplomas and qualifications within EU member states. Within the framework of the Bologna Process, mobility provides opportunities for students to access various learning and training options at all study levels. Additionally, it offers researchers, teachers, and non-teaching staff opportunities for research and training.

The Bologna Process has two main advantages in comparison to the old higher education system: it is the student-centered education, which reduces the potential flaws of the old system of university studying and makes it more vibrant, and it is based on the European university framework that facilitates employment after graduation (Osmanović Zajić & Maksimovic, 2023).

The study begins by analyzing the impacts of introducing the Bologna System in Serbia's higher education system, which marked a significant shift toward harmonizing educational standards across Europe. The study then addresses The challenges of implementing the accreditation process, highlighting the hurdles faced by institutions in meeting the stringent criteria necessary to ensure quality education. A detailed analysis of the structure and characteristics of the higher education system provides insight into the organizational framework and educational paradigms that shape Serbian academia. The study also reviews the academic qualification requirements in higher education, scrutinizing the standards set for academics and their impact on teaching efficacy. In a comparative analysis of state and private universities in Serbia, the study contrasts the two models, shedding light on their operational differences and the implications for students and faculty. This is complemented by an examination of trends in student enrollment and graduation rates, which offers a statistical perspective on the shifting demographics and academic outcomes within the system. Further, the study investigates the structure and characteristics of the higher applied education system, focusing on vocational and technical training as vital components of Serbia's educational landscape. It also contemplates the prestige of the academic career in Serbia, discussing the societal value placed on academia, the opportunities for emerging talent, and the potential trajectories for future development. The study concludes with a summary that encapsulates the key findings, emphasizing the need for ongoing reform and support to foster an environment conducive to educational excellence and innovation. It posits that embracing change and addressing current challenges head-on will be crucial for Serbia's higher education system to thrive in the global academic arena.

1. Impacts of the Bologna Process on the Serbian Higher Education System

The introduction of the Bologna Process not only enhanced the quality and efficiency of higher education (Osmanović Zajić & Maksimovic, 2023; Janićijević et al., 2005; Vukasanovic, 2007) but also contributed to the international competitiveness of Serbia's higher education system. This integration paved the way for Serbia's accession to the EU, which is a crucial step in the further development and modernization of Serbian higher education (Lungulov, 2011). Additionally, the Bologna Process aims to enhance the competitiveness of European higher education globally (The U.K. HE Europe Unit, 2005).

In Serbian higher education during the 2000s, many students either dropped out of their studies or took unreasonably long to complete their studies. Until the adoption of the new Higher Education Law in 2005, the expected duration of undergraduate studies at Serbian state universities was four to six years. However, statistical data reveal that the officially expected study time often transformed into significantly longer average durations (from enrollment to graduation): the average duration for four-year programs was 6.76 years, 7.51 years for five-year programs, and 7.62 years for six-year programs (Jarić & Vukasović, 2009). Overburdened students and strict educational regulations were cited as reasons for this extended study period (Turajlić et al., 2004).

Another important aspect of the reforms was the transformation of curricula and teaching methods. Modernizing curricula and making teaching methods more innovative allowed students to acquire knowledge and skills more effectively (Osmanović Zajić & Maksimovic, 2023: 702). Essentially, the purpose of the Bologna higher education system is to facilitate students' learning experiences in every way possible. It aims to bring the necessary curriculum closer to students most efficiently and engagingly. At the end of their undergraduate studies, students would have the opportunity to continue with master's programs, and later, upon completing their master's studies, they could pursue doctoral programs within their chosen field.

The reforms also impacted other areas of higher education. The broadening of study programs and training fields allowed students to choose from a wider range of academic areas and appropriately shape their professional specializations. This encouraged student mobility, contributing to the enrichment of cultural and professional experiences (The Sorbonne Declaration, 1998; Bergen Communiqué, 2005; Budapest-Vienna Declaration, 2010; Rome Ministerial Communique, 2020).

Another innovation introduced by the Bologna higher education system is the ECTS. ECTS is a unique system that facilitates easier recognition and comparison of various educational programs and institutions across European countries (Bologna Declaration, 1999; Berlin Communiqué, 2003; Budapest-Vienna Declaration, 2010; Kolarski, 2021; The Sorbonne Declaration, 1998). The system is based on credit points that depict students' workload during the acquisition of a specific study program (60 points per academic year, 30 points per semester, 20 points per trimester). Implementing the ECTS system in university practice contributes to student mobility within the European Higher Education Area, allowing for transferring and accumulating points earned at different institutions. This forms the basis for inter-university collaboration for both students and academics alike (Šofranac & Damjanović, 2010; Marinković-Nedučin & Lazetić, 2002).

In Serbian higher education, this credit transfer procedure is often referred to simply as "points." Essentially, these points indicate the effort a student invested in a mandatory or elective course at the university, reflecting the quality of knowledge acquired. Naturally, assignments such as homework, seminar papers, tests, or quizzes can be counted, making it easier for students. While the original intention of the ECTS concept was to reduce students' burdens, many students feel that it has had the opposite effect: points weigh heavily on them, and the focus shifts from quality education to acquiring points (Kolarski, 2021).

According to Kolarski (2021), the adoption of the Bologna Declaration and entry into the European Higher Education Area brought innovations such as reduced academic workload for students, shorter study durations, higher average grades, and enhanced mobility opportunities.

In the Bologna higher education system, lectures and practical sessions are mostly mandatory. This has its advantages because students can more easily retain the material during lectures and practical sessions. Consequently, they have a solid foundation when preparing for colloquia or exams, provided they pay attention during lectures and practicals.

During practical sessions, teaching assistants encourage students to engage with relevant literature, which aids their preparation for future exams. However, there is one drawback related to literature: in many departments, students have access to outdated books for certain subjects (Kolarski, 2021). Compared to the pre-Bologna system, Serbia has not made significant progress in updating the literature. In many cases, the same content from earlier textbooks is still used, albeit in a condensed form due to combining material from various sources.

In the Bologna higher education system in Serbia, certain problems might occur: insufficient space for teaching, insufficient number of academic staff, a large number of students in comparison to the number of academics and facilities, insufficiently developed student body, inadequate use of human, financial, and infrastructural resources (Osmanović Zajić & Maksimovic, 2023).

Lisman is particularly critical of the Bologna Process, which aims to create a unique European education system enabling comparability and mobility for both academics and students (Liessmann, 2008). Lisman's critique extends to the organization of studies into modules-units that can be assembled or even exchanged like puzzle pieces. In Lisman's view, this approach overlooks the fact that science has its specific systematic structure, which does not allow for arbitrary omissions or combinations of elements. Furthermore, it disregards the sequence of processing and assimilating scientific facts.

As a key element of the Bologna reforms, each educational program must precisely define the expected outcomes at the end of the learning process. These outcomes represent the skills and competencies acquired by students. In practical terms, every curriculum must clearly and comprehensively describe the specific abilities students should possess upon successful completion of their studies within a particular field (Antolović & Petković, 2010).

After the introduction of the Bologna system, Serbian higher education witnessed a paradigm shift. The emphasis increasingly shifted toward student-centered education, aiming to support students' personal development and enhance their practical skills. As a result, smaller group sessions, project-based learning, and interactive teaching methods became more widespread.

The Bologna reforms also led to the transformation of curricula and subjects. Instead of overly specialized traditional content, more flexible, multidisciplinary study programs were established, better aligned with changing labor market demands and societal challenges.

Furthermore, the establishment and strengthening of a quality assurance system were integral parts of the reforms, ensuring high standards in teaching and research (Lungulov, 2011). Within this framework, various quality control and assessment mechanisms were introduced, contributing to the continuous improvement of teaching and research quality.

Therefore, after the implementation of the Bologna system, Serbian higher education underwent significant development, resulting in modernized structures and processes that better adapt to European higher education trends and expectations.

2. Challenges in Implementing the Accreditation Process Within the Serbian Higher Education System

The dynamic development of the reform process received renewed momentum with the adoption of accreditation, self-assessment, and external quality control standards in 2006. These standards defined the quality expectations for higher education institutions and study programs, establishing the framework for initiating the accreditation process. The goal of this measure was to strengthen and enhance the quality of higher education in Serbia, as well as to promote more effective operation of educational institutions and the delivery of quality education to students.

The introduction of these standards facilitated objective evaluation of the quality of higher education institutions and study programs, while also regulating the accreditation process. It encouraged institutions to engage in self-assessment and continuous improvement, enhancing transparency and reliability within the higher education system.

Thanks to these reforms, higher education institutions and study programs have consistently improved their quality, contributing to better education for students and more effective responsiveness to labor market demands. Furthermore, ongoing development of the accreditation process offers additional opportunities for further improvements and enhancements in the education system in the future.

Since its establishment, the National Entity for Accreditation and Quality Assurance in Higher Education (NEAQA), as an institution, financially, administratively, and professionally independent body, has, in accordance with the Higher Education Law starting from 2017, created the conditions for the operation by adopting new regulations and instructions. The introduction of a new methodology allowed for the independent conduct of accreditation procedures and external quality control for higher education institutions. This methodology includes the development of rules and instructions related to the accreditation of institutions and study programs, all aimed at ensuring and maintaining the quality of higher education. Accreditation decisions based on the new methodology rely on the reports of the reviewing committees.

The adoption of modern software has become essential for more efficient work and timely decision-making. As part of the new methodology, requirements have been established for digital accreditation processes for higher education institutions and study programs. The NAT 2019 software package, developed by the Faculty of Technical Sciences at the University of Novi Sad, has been actively in use since July 2019. With the introduction of this software, accreditation data management now occurs using modern and efficient tools that fully align with the new accreditation requirements. The unique database allows higher education institutions to provide information about their accreditation-related activities. The software automates the calculation of parameters for both institutions and study programs, facilitating data analysis.

The mission of the National Entity for Accreditation and Quality Assurance in Higher Education is to ensure that only higher education institutions that meet strict standards can provide education. This ensures that the professionals entering the job market and the professions aligned with their training meet the challenges of the Fourth Industrial Revolution. (Kočović, 2020). The most talented professionals across all social strata must constitute a high-quality workforce, possessing knowledge and skills aligned with modern practices. Their role in promoting technological development and innovation is indispensable for progress. Serbia's future partly depends on the extent to which the National Entity for Accreditation contributes to maintaining stability within the higher education system. It is essential that only institutions consistently meeting requirements and providing their students with quality knowledge and skills remain operational.

The new accreditation execution methodology must contribute to more efficient assessment and fulfillment of accreditation standards for higher education institutions and study programs. The key role should be entrusted to the most talented professionals across all segments of society, individuals equipped with quality qualifications and skills aligned with modern practices. Without a high-quality workforce that drives technological development and innovation, progress is unattainable (Kočović, 2020).

2.1. Structure and Characteristics of Serbia's Higher Education System

In the Serbian higher education system, there are two types of studies:

a) academic studies, primarily organized at universities, and
b) applied studies, organized at faculties of applied studies or within universities.

The academic study system comprises three cycles:

- Undergraduate studies, which typically last 4 years with 240 ECTS, but 3-year, 180 ECTS bachelor programs are also available.
- Master's studies typically last 1 to 2 years and correspond to 60 to 120 ECTS credits, while specialized academic studies last 1 year, with 60 ECTS credits.
- Doctoral studies (Ph.D.) typically last for at least three years of study or 180 ECTS credits.

The applied study system comprises two cycles:

- Undergraduate applied studies, which last for three years and carry 180 ECTS credits, and specialized applied studies with a duration of 1 year, with 60 ECTS credit.
- Master's applied studies, which last for 1 to 2 years, correspond to 60 to 120 ECTS credits.

Figure 5.1. presents a schematic organization of the Serbian higher education system.

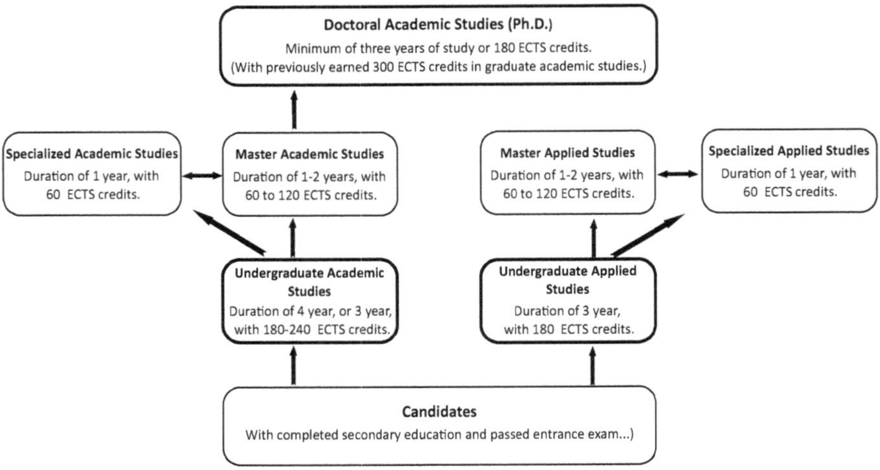

Figure 5.1: Serbian higher education system.

Source: Republic of Serbia, Ministry of Education, Science and Technological Development: National Qualifications Framework of the Republic of Serbia.

Summarizing the information provided, in Serbia, higher education is organized within universities, faculties, and colleges. According to the 2011 census, 10.59% of the population in Serbia held a higher education degree, while the 2022 data indicates a growth to 16.40% (Census of Population, Households and Dwellings, 2022). Every individual with a four-year high school diploma is entitled to higher education. Higher education institutions offer a wide range of study programs and specializations, allowing students to choose from various academic paths.

2.2. Review of the Academic Qualification Requirements for Academics in Higher Education

According to the law on higher education, the academic staff consists of academics, researchers, and associates. The non-teaching staff of higher education institutions includes individuals who perform professional, administrative, and technical tasks.

In Serbia, obtaining the title of an academic in higher education is subject to extremely strict requirements. Applicants are evaluated based on various criteria, including their academic qualifications, scientific or professional achievements, teaching experience, and other important factors. These criteria have been established to ensure the high standards and expertise of academics, as well as the excellent level of education provided to students. The rigorous requirements play a crucial role in maintaining the reputation of higher education institutions and promoting scientific excellence in Serbia. Therefore, the selection of academics is not only an individual decision but also an important consideration within the broader context of the quality and credibility of the entire educational system.

In Serbian higher education institutions, the titles for academics encompass various levels, including lecturer of applied studies, senior lecturer of applied studies, professor of applied studies, assistant professor, associate professor, and full professor (Law on higher education "Official Gazette of RS," No. 88/2017, 73/2018, 27/2018—consolidated text, 67/2019, 6/2020—consolidated texts, 11/2021—authentic interpretation, 67/2021, 67/2021— consolidated text, and 76/2023). Academics holding the titles of lecturer of applied studies, senior lecturer of applied studies, or professor of applied studies are authorized to conduct teaching exclusively within applied study programs. Academics with the titles of assistant professor, associate professor, and full professor are authorized to teach across all types of study programs.

To be appointed as an academic, a candidate must meet specific criteria, including possessing relevant professional, academic, scientific, or artistic qualifications acquired through accredited study programs and higher education institutions, as well as demonstrating pedagogical competence.

According to the law on higher education, the title of lecturer of applied studies can be awarded to an individual who holds the academic title of master, or at least the professional title of specialist in academic studies.

The title of senior lecturer of applied studies can be awarded to an individual who holds the scientific title of Doctor of Science, or an artistic title of Doctor of Arts. To attain the title of professor of applied studies, candidates must have relevant scientific or professional works published in scientific journals or proceedings, along with reviews, or provide evidence of artistic achievements.

According to the law on higher education, the title of assistant professor can be awarded to an individual who has completed previous levels of study with an average grade of at least eight, has at least three years of teaching experience at a higher education institution, holds a scientific title of Doctor of Science or an artistic title of Doctor of Arts, and has relevant scientific or professional works published in scientific journals or proceedings, accompanied by reviews or artistic achievements. Additionally, the title of associate professor can be conferred upon an individual who, in addition to meeting the basic requirements, has a significant number of scientific works contributing to the development of science in a specific specialized field. These works should be published in international or leading domestic journals, along with accompanying reviews. Furthermore, candidates may have multiple artistic achievements in their artistic field, such as original projects, studies, and patents, as well as experience in leading or participating in scientific or artistic projects. Publishing textbooks, monographs, practical guides, or collections of tasks, as well as presenting works at international or domestic scientific conferences, further enhances the qualifications for the title of associate professor. The title of full professor can be conferred upon an individual who, in addition to meeting the basic requirements, has a significantly larger number of scientific works that are significant for the development of scientific thought in their specialized field. These works should be published in international or leading domestic journals, accompanied by relevant reviews. Additionally, candidates may have a greater number of recognized artistic achievements that are of great importance for progress in the arts. Furthermore, it is necessary to have a considerable number of scientific works and presentations at international or domestic scientific conferences, as well as published textbooks, monographs, or original professional accomplishments. Additionally, candidates should demonstrate results in developing the scientific and teaching the younger generation at the faculty, as well as participation in final projects in specialized and master academic studies.

An individual appointed to the titles of lecturer, senior lecturer, assistant professor, or associate professor receives the title and enters into employment for a period of five years.

An individual appointed to the titles of professor of applied studies or full professor receives the title and enters into permanent employment.

According to the law on higher education, the titles of associates include teaching assistant, assistant, and assistant with a doctorate. A higher education institution appoints an individual to the title of assistant who has completed each of the previous levels of study with an average grade of at least 8.00/10.00 and demonstrates an aptitude for teaching.

According to the law on higher education, higher education institutions can engage academics from other independent higher education institutions outside the territory of the Republic of Serbia. This can be done under the title of visiting professor, without the need for a public competition.

The number of academic staff starting from the 2009/10 academic year until the 2022/23 academic year is presented in Figure 5.2. According to Figure 5.2, the number of academic staff has shown a positive trend, increasing from 14812 to 17009 academics. Despite minor fluctuations, the overall direction shows an increasing trend with some variations.

Within the academic staff, the distribution of academics and associates is presented in Figure 5.3. The number of academics is rising, while the number of associates is slightly decreasing. Figure 5.3 also shows that there are approximately twice as many academics as there are associates.

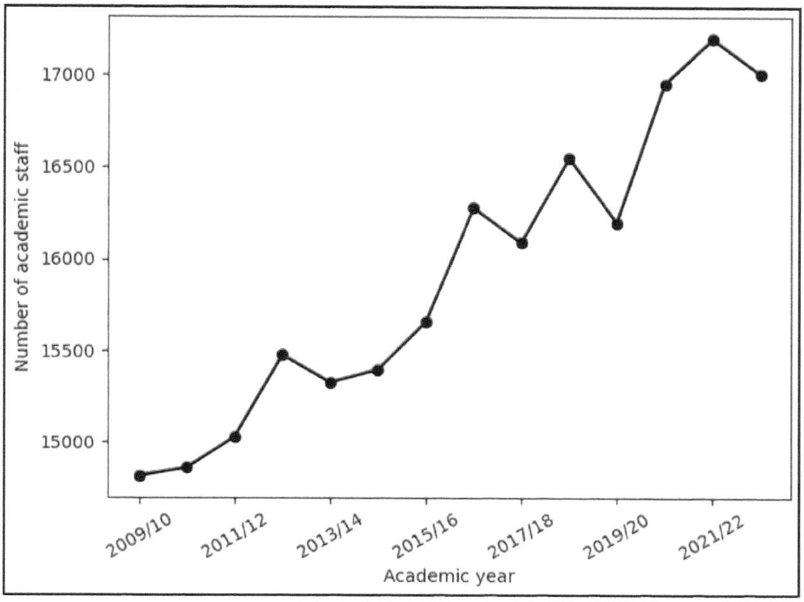

Figure 5.2: Number of academics and associates.
Source: Statistical Office of the Republic of Serbia.

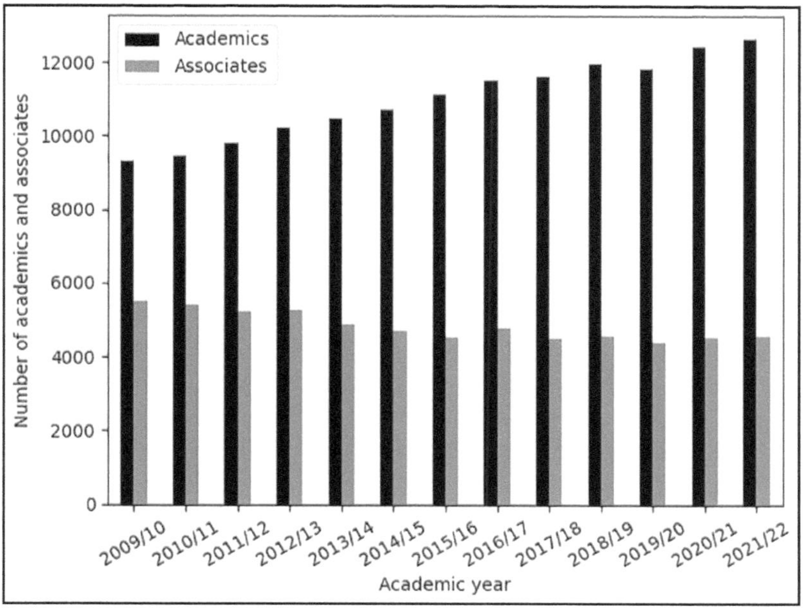

Figure 5.3: Distribution of academics and associates.
Source: Statistical Office of the Republic of Serbia.

The Statistical Office of the Republic of Serbia has been consistently providing data on male and female academic staff since the 2009/10 academic year. The gender distribution is presented in Figure 5.4.

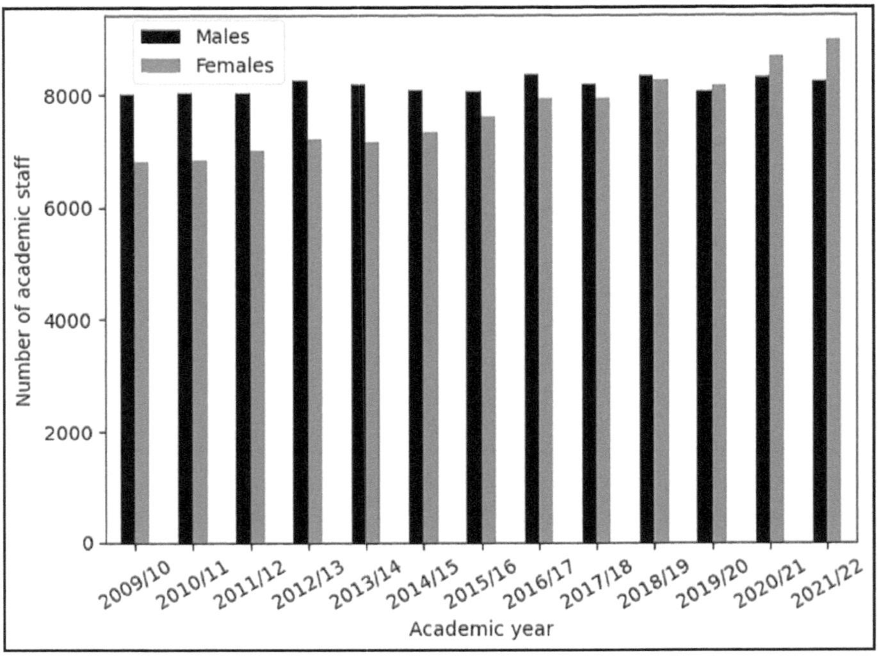

Figure 5.4: Distribution of male and female academic staff.
Source: Statistical Office of the Republic of Serbia.

Figure 5.4 indicates that from the 2009/10 academic year to the 2021/22 academic year, there has been a consistent pattern where the number of male academic staff in higher education in Serbia has remained constant, while the number of female academic staff has steadily grown. From 2009 to 2018, the number of male academic staff exceeded that of female academic staff. However, starting from the 2019/20 academic year, the number of female academic staff has surpassed that of male academic staff. Figure 5.5 presents the distribution of academic staff by gender and academic title.

It shows a consistent but slow rate of incline in the number of male Ph.D. holders, which was the most numerous group. The number of female Ph.D. holders is increasing at a faster rate. In the 2021/22 academic year, the number of male Doctor of Arts and Sciences was 5805, while the number of female Doctor of Arts and Sciences was 5754, almost as high as for males. The counts for both

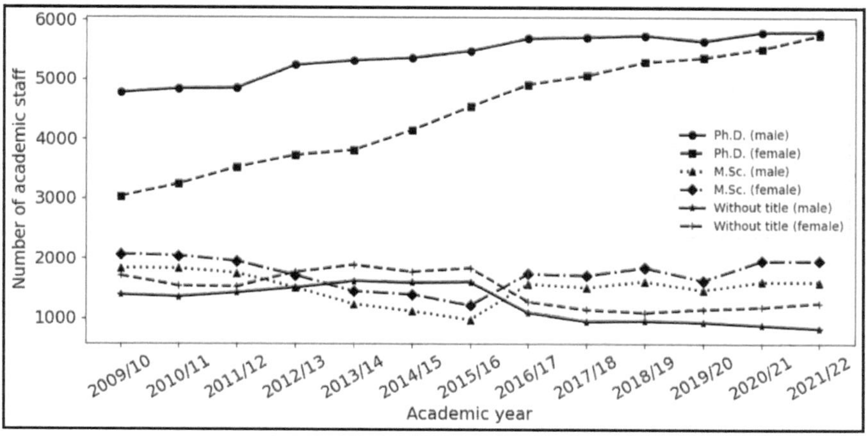

Figure 5.5: Distribution of academic staff by gender and title.
Source: Statistical Office of the Republic of Serbia.

male and female M.Sc. holders, as well as those without any title, remain relatively flat and significantly lower than their Ph.D. counterparts. In each case, the number of female academic staff is higher than that of male academic staff. The total number of male and female academic staff from the 2009/10 academic year to the 2021/22 academic year is given in Figure 5.4. The data reveals a consistent but gradual rise in the number of male academic staff, while the female academic staff has experienced more rapid growth. Between the 2009/10 and 2018/19 academic years, the male academic staff population was larger. However, starting from 2019/20, the female portion of the academic staff overtook that of males.

2.3. Comparative Analysis of Public and Private Universities in Serbia

The higher education landscape in Serbia has undergone significant transformations over the past two decades. Before 2005, higher education in Serbia was predominantly state-controlled, with a limited presence of private institutions. According to The Ministry of Education of the Republic of Serbia, as of the 2022–23 academic year, there were eight public universities in Serbia without AP Kosovo and Metohia. These universities are:

- University of Belgrade: founded in 1808.
- University of Arts in Belgrade: established in 1957.
- University of Novi Sad: established in 1960.
- University of Kragujevac: founded in 1976.
- University of Nis: founded in 1965.

- State University of Novi Pazar: founded in 2006.
- University of Defense: established in 2011.
- University of Criminal Investigation and Police Studies: established in 2018.

The Higher Education Act of 2005 liberalized the sector, leading to the establishment of numerous private universities. This period witnessed a proliferation of private universities, catering to niche areas of study and attracting students seeking alternative educational experiences. According to the Statistical Office of the Republic of Serbia, as of the 2022–23 academic year, there were ten private universities:

- Megatrend University: established in 1989.
- Alpha University: established in 1992.
- Singidunum University: founded in 1999.
- University of Business Academy: founded in 2000.
- University Union: established in 2005.
- University of Novi Pazar: established in 2006.
- Educons University: founded in 2008.
- Metropolitan University: established in 2010.
- University Union—Nikola Tesla: established in 2010.
- European University: accredited in 2012.

Historically, state universities enjoyed a reputation for quality education and research, often benefiting from government funding and resources. Concerns regarding the quality and accreditation of private universities persisted, although efforts were made to establish accreditation mechanisms to ensure standards.

Over the years, both state and private universities in Serbia have expanded their academic programs and international cooperation. The Bologna Process has played a pivotal role in reforming higher education, aligning Serbian universities with European standards. The number of higher education institutions has changed over time, as presented in Table 5.1.

While the number of public higher institutions fluctuated within a relatively narrow range over the years, starting from the academic year 2020/21, the number of public higher institutions declined. This decrease can be attributed to the restructuring of vocational colleges into academies of applied studies, a process that began in 2019. Conversely, the number of private higher institutions experienced more variability, with fluctuations and a noticeable drop starting from the 2013/14 academic year, followed by growth starting from 2018/19.

Table 5.1: Number of higher education institutions

Academic year	Public higher institutions	Private higher institutions
2010/11	120	69
2011/12	120	67
2012/13	121	62
2013/14	120	59
2014/15	123	59
2015/16	123	58
2016/17	123	57
2017/18	123	58
2018/19	125	62
2019/20	122	62
2020/21	101	63
2021/22	102	66
2022/23	103	66

Source: Statistical Office of the Republic of Serbia.

The distribution of enrolled students in public and private higher institutions is given in Table 5.2 in percentage. The number of enrolled students has fluctuated, with public higher institutions consistently showing higher enrollment rates than private institutions. State higher institutions continue to attract those seeking traditional academic paths and state-funded education. Meanwhile, private institutions have seen a steady expansion of enrollment, particularly among students pursuing specialized programs, preferring smaller class sizes, or requiring flexible scheduling options. From Table 5.3, we can deduce that between 2009/10 and 2016/17, enrollment numbers at state universities steadily rose from 188294 to 229284. Conversely, private universities declined from 38478 to 33249 during the same time frame. Post-2016/17, state universities experienced a slight decrease in enrollment, dropping to 207370 in 2021/22, followed by a modest rise to 209367 in 2022/23. On the other hand, private universities experienced enrollment fluctuations until 2019/20, hitting a low of 33249. A significant rebound occurred from 2020/21 to 2022/23, with enrollments climbing to 39141. These trends may be attributed to various factors such as economic conditions, governmental policies, shifts in perception and reputation, and the market demand for certain programs. Overall, state universities have exhibited more consistent growth leading to stabilization, whereas private universities have shown greater variability, with a marked increase in recent years.

Table 5.2: Distribution of enrolled students in public and private higher institutions

Academic year	Total number of students	Public higher institutions (%)	Private higher institutions (%)
2009/10	226772	83.03	16.97
2010/11	228531	82.89	17.11
2011/12	231661	83.99	16.01
2012/13	238945	85.15	14.85
2013/14	242848	85.60	14.40
2014/15	241054	86.82	13.18
2015/16	251162	87.12	12.88
2016/17	262108	87.48	12.52
2017/18	256172	87.34	12.66
2018/19	249771	86.43	13.57
2019/20	241968	86.26	13.74
2020/21	242550	85.78	14.22
2021/22	243730	85.08	14.92
2022/23	248508	84.25	15.75

Source: Statistical Office of the Republic of Serbia.

Among other factors, the difference between public and private higher institutions is reflected in the hiring policies of academic staff. Table 5.3 displays the number of academic staff at public and private higher education institutions.

Table 5.3: Distribution of academic staff in public and private higher institutions

Academic year	Public higher institutions	Private higher institutions	Total number of academic staff
2015/16	13042	2355	15397
2016/17	13477	2621	16098
2017/18	13377	2511	15888
2018/19	14158	2625	16783
2019/20	13221	2713	15934
2020/21	13830	3125	16955
2021/22	13758	3442	17200
2022/23	13531	3478	17009

Source: Statistical Office of the Republic of Serbia.

The number of academic staff in public institutions has shown some fluctuations but generally appears to have diminished slightly over the years from 2015/16 to 2022/23. In private institutions, the number of academic staff has generally gone up over the same period, although there are some fluctuations from year to year. This indicates potential differences between public and private institutions in hiring practices, financial resources, or institutional priorities. To elucidate the year-to-year fluctuations, we can examine whether there exists a correlation between the enrollment of students and the presence of academic staff in both public and private higher institutions. Figure 5.6 illustrates that in public higher institutions, there is no discernible correlation between the number of enrolled students and the number of academic staff. This observation is further supported by a Pearson correlation coefficient of −0.26. Conversely, for private higher institutions, Figure 5.6 suggests a positive linear relationship between the enrollment of students and the number of academic staff. This trend is corroborated by a Pearson correlation coefficient of 0.92. However, due to the limited availability of data spanning only eight years, conducting a reliable correlation analysis is not feasible. These differences in the trends between public and private institutions may suggest disparities in hiring practices, financial resources, or institutional priorities.

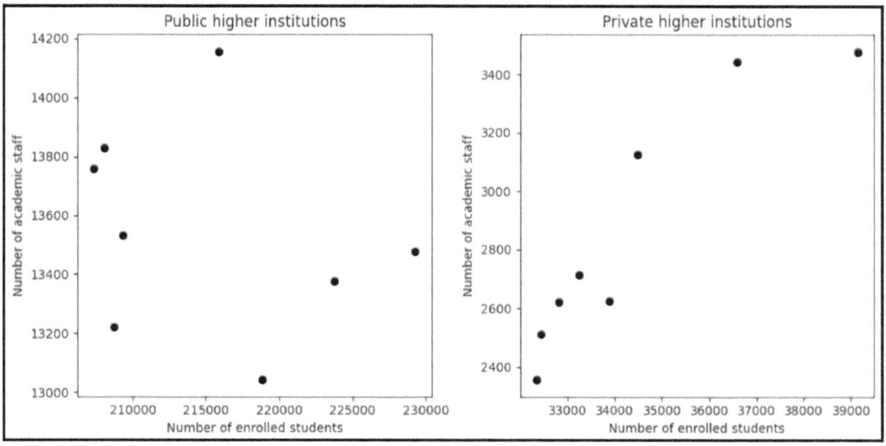

Figure 5.6: Number of enrolled students vs. the number of academic staff.
Source: Statistical Office of the Republic of Serbia.

The student-to-academic staff and student-to-lecturer ratio are presented in Figure 5.7. It illustrates that academic staff in private higher institutions typically work with smaller groups of students.

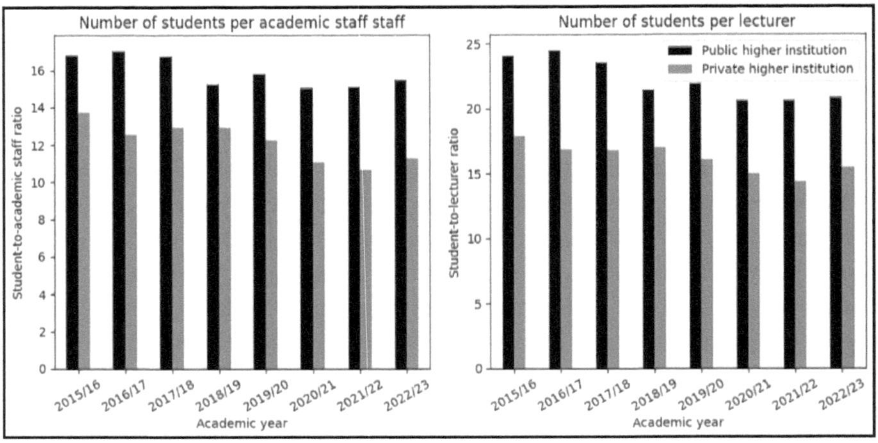

Figure 5.7: Number of students per academic staff/lecturer.
Source: Statistical Office of the Republic of Serbia.

If we consider the student-to-academic ratio, the differences between the numbers of students per academic are even higher. The basic descriptive statistics are given in Table 5.4.

Table 5.4: Descriptive statistics of students-to-academic staff and students-to-lecturer

	Students-to-academic staff		Students-to-lecturer	
Descriptive statistics	**Public higher institutions**	**Private higher institutions**	**Public higher institutions**	**Private higher institutions**
mean	15.89	12.16	22.16	16.16
standard deviation	0.82	1.08	1.62	1.19

Source: Statistical Office of the Republic of Serbia.

Additionally, the data suggests that the student-to-academic staff ratio in public institutions fluctuates less than the student-per-lecturer ratio over the years. When considering students-to-academic staff, the fluctuation in private institutions is higher than in public institutions. This indicates that private institutions may have been adjusting their academic staff numbers to accommodate changes in student enrollment, leading to a decrease in the student-to-academic staff ratio over time. On the other hand, when considering the student-to-lecturer ratio, fluctuation in public institutions is higher than in private institutions. This may indicate that public institutions promoted more academic staff to lecturers, thereby decreasing the number of students per lecturer.

2.4. Trends in Student Enrollment and Graduation Rates Within Serbian Higher Education

In Serbia, the academic landscape is marked by a vibrant pattern of enrollment and graduation. Figure 5.8 illustrates the proportion of newly enrolled students relative to the total number of enrollments, as well as the proportion of students who have graduated in comparison to the total number of enrollments.

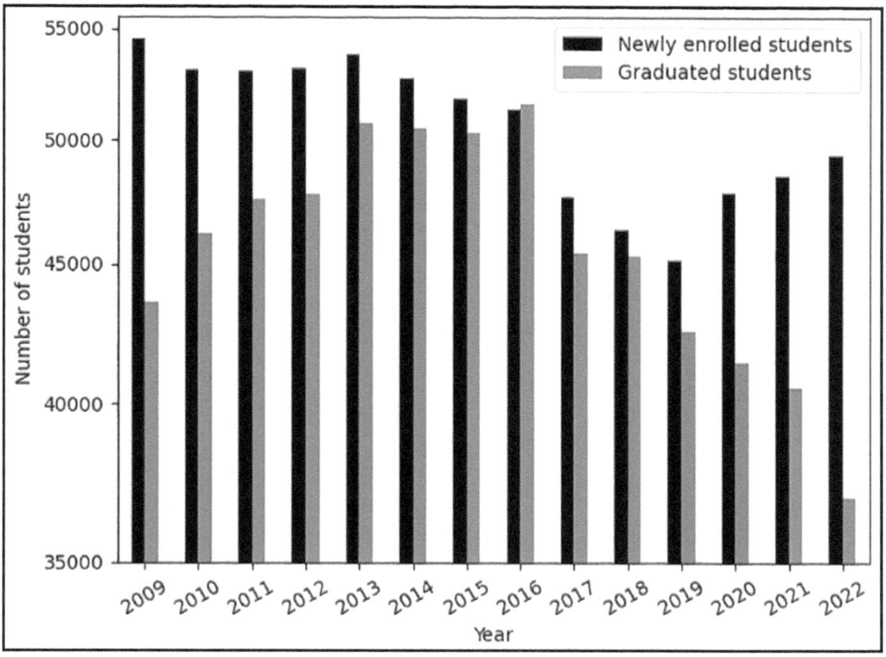

Figure 5.8: Number of enrolled and graduated students.
Source: Statistical Office of the Republic of Serbia.

From Table 5.2 and Figure 5.8, we observe a downward trend in both the number of newly enrolled students and their ratio relative to the total number of enrolled students up until the year 2018. This decline in the ratio is attributed to a decrease in the number of newly enrolled students alongside an increase in the total number of enrolled students. From 2019 onwards, the number of newly enrolled students has been increasing, while their ratio relative to the total number of enrolled students has remained consistent. The number of graduated students and their proportion was rising until 2016. However, starting in 2017, there has been a sharp decline in the number of graduated students, accompanied by a steady decrease in their ratio relative to the total number of students.

Considering the distribution of newly enrolled male and female students as depicted in Figure 5.9, it is evident that the number of newly enrolled female students exceeds that of male students. The data indicates a downturn in enrollment for both genders in 2017, 2018, and 2019. However, from 2020 onwards, there has been a notable upward trend in the enrollment of female students, while the number of male students has remained relatively stable.

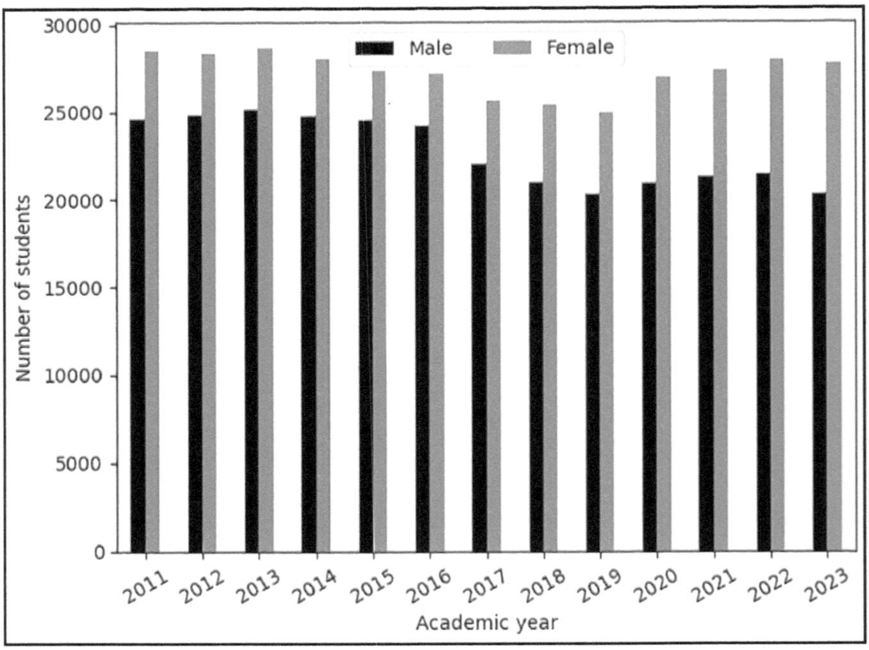

Figure 5.9: Distribution of newly enrolled male and female students.
Source: Statistical Office of the Republic of Serbia.

Serbia is divided into four statistical regions:

a) Vojvodina,
b) Belgrade,
c) Sumadija and Western Serbia, and
d) Southern and Eastern Serbia.

The distribution of newly enrolled students in the four regions of Serbia is presented in Figure 5.10, which reveals that the region of Belgrade has the highest number of newly enrolled students, followed by the region of Vojvodina. The number of newly enrolled students in Sumadija and Western Serbia is slightly higher than in southern and Eastern Serbia.

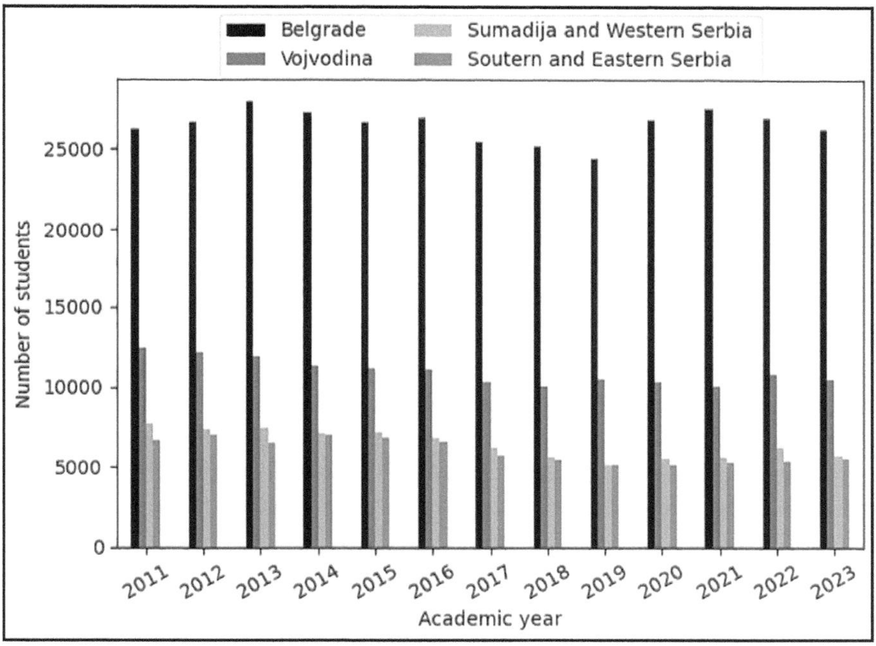

Figure 5.10: Distribution of newly enrolled students across Serbia's statistical regions. *Source*: Statistical Office of the Republic of Serbia.

2.5. Structure and Characteristics of Serbia's Higher Applied Education System

In parallel with the development of university education in Serbia, the development of education of applied sciences progressed. At the end of the 1950s, the state began establishing higher applied education institutions in the larger cities and industrial centers of that time. The exceptionally dynamic development of society, especially the industry at that time, demanded well-educated professionals. Thus, cities such as Subotica, Novi Sad, Belgrade, Zrenjanin, Kragujevac, Trstenik, Krusevac, and others, acquired higher applied education institutions. They were formed following the example of highly respected German higher vocational institutions of that time. The duration of education in these institutions lasted between two and three years, and the study profiles and programs were always in line with the current level of science and technology worldwide and the needs of the environment. Higher applied education institutions in Serbia have always played a significant role and made a huge contribution to the development of society and the economy not only in local communities but also at the regional and national levels. Until the beginning of the 2000s, the higher education system in Serbia was tailored to the needs of society and the economy. It consisted of six universities and around forty higher applied education institutions.

The alignment with educational systems in Europe began in 2001. Preparations lasted for almost five years. A new regulation was adopted in 2005, creating opportunities for the transformation of the higher education system in Serbia. The legal solutions embraced the basic principles of the Bologna Declaration and introduced many innovations. The first accreditation of institutions and study programs began in 2007. The new law on higher education was first implemented in institutions of applied sciences. This led to the transformation of these institutions, resulting in the establishment of the first higher vocational colleges. After the accreditation and transformation of higher applied institutions, the accreditation of universities followed. This new stipulation, among other things, defines the category of the Academy of Applied Studies. According to the law, the Academy of Applied Studies is an independent higher education institution that integrates educational, research, professional, and artistic work in carrying out its activities, as components of a unified higher education process. These academies can be formed by the transformation of existing higher vocational colleges or by the merger of multiple vocational colleges into a new higher education institution—the Academy of Applied Studies. The formation of the Academies of applied studies started in 2019. The plan was to integrate all public vocational colleges into fourteen academies of applied studies. However, the Ministry of Education did not manage to carry out the plan. The process of transition is given in Table 5.5.

Table 5.5: The transition from vocational colleges to academies of applied studies

Academic year	2018/19	2019/20	2020/21	2021/22	2022/23
Number of vocational colleges	43	2	9	10	10
Number of academies of applied studies	0	38	10	10	11
Total number	43	40	19	20	21

Source: Statistical Office of the Republic of Serbia.

As of now, there are eleven academies of applied studies and eleven higher vocational colleges. The transformation of higher vocational colleges to academies of applied studies is not characteristic of private higher education. In the academic year of 2022/23, Table 5.6 provides the number of public and private universities, as well as the number of faculties in universities and academies of applied sciences, along with vocational colleges.

Table 5.6: Distribution of higher education institutions

	Number of universities	Number of faculties	Number of academies of applied studies together with vocational colleges
Public	8	82	21
Private	10	51	15
Total number	18	133	36

Source: Statistical Office of the Republic of Serbia.

2.6. Wage Ratios of Higher Education Staff and Wage Ratios Relative to Labor Market Wages

Between 2005 and 2010, significant changes occurred in Serbia's higher education sector, which also impacted the salaries of academics. By the mid-2000s, Serbia's economy slowly began to recover, resulting in some improvements in the education sector. As a result, several higher education institutions raised the salaries of academics to make the profession more attractive. However, during the period from 2005 to 2010, the issue of academic salaries remained significant in Serbia. Government expenditures were limited, and higher education institutions faced challenges in securing adequate funding. Consequently, academic salaries either stagnated or increased only minimally, failing to align with their work and expertise.

In the early 2010s, higher education institutions continued to grapple with financial difficulties and limited government resources. As a result, academic salaries generally remained unsatisfactory, leading many to seek higher pay and better working conditions abroad.

However, by the mid-2010s, there was some improvement in higher education financing in Serbia. Educational institutions received government support and external funding, allowing them to increase academic salaries and enhance working conditions. Economic growth and political stability further contributed to progress. While academic salaries generally rose by the end of the 2010s, there remained a significant gap between different institutions and various fields of expertise. Some institutions implemented strategies to make faculty positions more competitive by offering higher pay and additional benefits.

However, in the 2020s, the COVID-19 pandemic posed further challenges for academics in Serbia's higher education sector. The economic impact of the pandemic reduced government and institutional funding, affecting academic salaries. Additionally, the transition to remote teaching due to the pandemic presented additional challenges for academics, impacting both working conditions and compensation.

Funds for the salaries of academics and associates are determined as the product of the salary calculation base and the complexity coefficient for permanent employees. The salary calculation base is uniform for all academics and associates and is determined for each budget year by the Budget Law of the Republic of Serbia, after obtaining the opinion of the Social and Economic Council of the Republic of Serbia on the proposed amount of the base during the preparation of this law. and the salary calculation base established by applicable regulations.

The complexity coefficient expresses the value of all the requirements for the performance of the duties of the workplace. The complexity coefficients for financing the salaries of faculty academics and associates at faculties and universities are given in Table 5.7.

Table 5.7: Complexity coefficients for financing the salaries

Academic staff	Complexity coefficient
full professor, independent artistic associate, and scientific advisor with a doctorate	30.19
associate professor, senior research associate, and senior artistic associate with a doctorate	28.01
independent professional associate at an academy or faculty of arts with a doctorate	27.46
assistant professor, research associate, artistic associate, librarian advisor, and university general secretary with a doctorate	25.65
senior professional associate at an academy or faculty of arts with a doctorate	22.62
assistant doctor of science	21.75
senior lecturer at a university	20.96
assistant with a master's degree, research associate, assistant artistic associate, and lecturer	20.17
professional associate at an academy or faculty of arts	19.78
assistant trainee	18.58
professional associate	17.91

Source: Official Gazette of RS, No. 15/2002, 100/2004, 26/2005, 38/2007, and 110/2007.

The salary base in Serbian dinar, as reflected in Figure 5.11, decreased from April 2014 to January 2024, but then consistently rose, with the most significant increases occurring in the final three years, culminating in a peak by January 2024. Since the complexity coefficients are fixed, and the salary is the product of the salary base and the complexity coefficient, the trend of salary changes for academic staff depends solely on the complexity coefficients in a proportional manner.

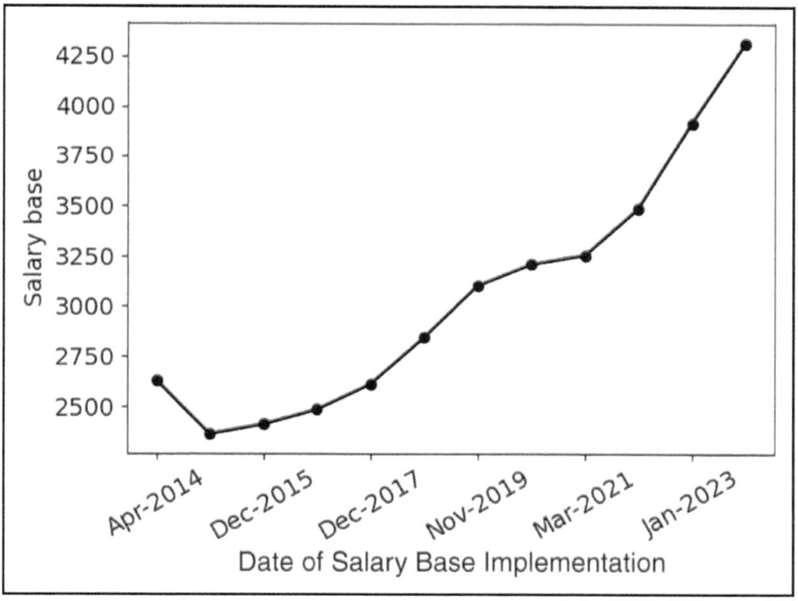

Figure 5.11: The trend of net salary bases in higher education.
Source: Statistical Office of the Republic of Serbia.

We can conclude that academic salaries depend on changes in the education system and economic circumstances. Increasing academic salaries remains an important task for the government and educational institutions to provide attractive working conditions and adequate benefits for academics, thereby supporting the quality of education and the development of the higher education sector.

In this context, it is important to consider how the salaries of academics compare to those of other public professionals in Serbia, such as elementary and secondary school teachers, theater actors, and primarius medicine doctors.

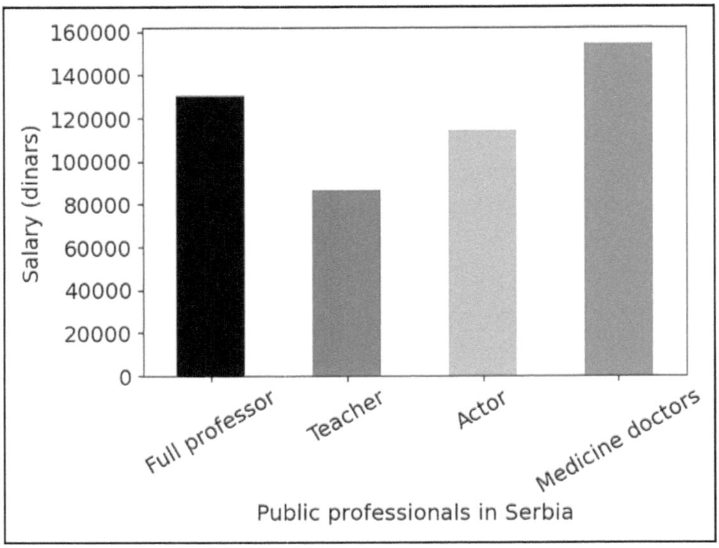

Figure 5.12: Salary comparison of public professionals in Serbia.
Source: Statistical Office of the Republic of Serbia.

Academics in higher education generally earn more than teachers in elementary and secondary schools, reflecting the higher qualifications and specialized expertise required. However, when compared to other professions, disparities become apparent. Theater actors, despite their cultural significance, tend to receive lower salaries, while primarius doctors, who hold a prestigious title in the medical field, often earn salaries comparable to or exceeding those of academics. These variations underscore the need for continued efforts to improve academic salaries, ensuring that they are competitive with other professional fields, and to maintain the attractiveness of the teaching profession within the broader socio-economic landscape of Serbia.

3. The Prestige of the Academic Career in Serbia, Prospects for the Future, and Talent Development

In society, an earlier opinion persists that a diploma is an important factor in an individual's social status and prestige. This notion continues to influence employment and social positions. The academic career in Serbia carries a certain authority and respect, especially within intellectual circles and scientific communities. It is often regarded as a symbol of intellectual superiority and knowledge. However, in a broader social context, the perception of prestige may be less pronounced, particularly compared to other more prominent or higher-paying professions. In terms of financial appeal, academic careers are generally less competitive than other sectors. Most academic positions in Serbia do not offer high salaries, and career opportunities are often limited.

However, for many professionals, the allure of an academic career cannot be measured solely in monetary terms. Passion for research, teaching, and intellectual work motivates them. Academic work provides a degree of autonomy and creativity, which can be attractive to those who value intellectual freedom.

The majority of accredited faculties, whether public or private, now admit students to doctoral programs. Initially, some faculties were hesitant, but during the accreditation process for bachelor's and master's programs, they were required to authorize doctoral studies as well. These standards indicate whether a given faculty has a high-quality academic staff, adequate educational facilities, sufficient equipment, and quality scientific and research tools.

Thanks to the Bologna study system, many students now complete their bachelor's and master's degrees with exceptionally high average grades. This achievement allows them to meet the minimum requirement of an average grade of 8 or higher for admission to doctoral programs. This represents a significant change compared to earlier times when only exceptional students achieved an average grade above eight. Once, academic education was accessible to only a few, and the title of "doctor" was reserved for truly outstanding individuals at Serbian universities.

From the perspective of academics, becoming a mentor requires not only an appropriate scientific doctoral degree but also specific teaching and scientific recognitions. Additionally, over the past decade, candidates must have at least five scientific publications in designated impact factor journals.

For doctoral students, faculties and institutes now represent the sole opportunity for employment in the labor market. Opportunities are extremely limited at Serbian universities, and only a small percentage of them manage to find positions within the institutions. As a result, both the educational system and the university community have witnessed increased competition among academics (Jerkovic et al., 2011). Currently, a critically important question arises in our society: whether every person with a doctoral degree can find an opportunity to utilize their knowledge and abilities for the benefit of society.

Summary

The Bologna Process played a significant role in transforming higher education, resulting in Serbian universities aligning more closely with European standards. As a consequence, there has been an increase in student and staff mobility, and more modern curricula have been introduced. As a result, Serbian higher education has undergone significant changes in the past two decades. Among these, there has been an observed increase in the number of private universities in recent years (since 2018/19), while the number of state institutions has slightly decreased. Overall, state higher education institutions have a higher enrollment rate, but the growth in enrollment rates is emphasized in private institutions, particularly among students requiring special programs, smaller class sizes, or flexible schedules. However, based on the general trend, state universities have shown more consistent growth.

It can be concluded that there has been a significant decline in the number of graduates in recent years.

In terms of gender, there has been a remarkable increase in newly enrolled female students, while the number of male students has remained stable. Regarding geographical distribution, it is observed that Belgrade has the highest number of newly enrolled students, followed by the Vojvodina region.

As for academics, it is evident that the number of female academics has consistently grown, whereas the number of male academics has remained stable. Surprisingly, the data indicate that the male academics count exhibited gradual, slower growth, while the female academics count experienced much faster growth.

Differences can be observed in the trend of academic staff numbers between state and private institutions in recent years. While the academic staff count in state institutions has slightly decreased, it has generally increased in private institutions. The ratio of academic staff between state and private universities has decreased from 5.53 to 3.89. This difference in the trend may be influenced by admission practices, financial resources, and institutional priorities. State institutions face limitations that could lead to a decrease in academic staff numbers, whereas private institutions can more flexibly strive for expansion.

The variability in academics' numbers within private institutions suggests that these institutions have adjusted their academics' count based on changes in student enrollment. As a result, the ratio of students per academic staff has decreased.

The Serbian Higher Education Law provides detailed requirements for academic qualifications and performance criteria for academics positions, such as assistant professors, associate professors, and full professors. Over the past decade and a half, these requirements have become more stringent, likely influenced by the political direction closely related to academic qualification procedures and expectations for higher education quality.

We believe that in our country, the scientific career can still carry prestige, even though financial rewards are generally limited. Nevertheless, for many, the love of the profession, the intellectual challenges, and the pursuit of outstanding results in their research provide sufficient motivation for choosing a scientific career.

From the perspective of the development of Serbian higher education, it would be fundamentally important for educational policymakers to review the situation of academics and find solutions to eliminate obstacles that hinder progress.

References

Antolović, M., & Petković, V. (2010). Studio Bolognese i Bolonjska reforma visokog obrazovanja u Srbiji (Studio Bolognese and Bologna Process in Serbia). *Pedagoška stvarnost, 56*(3–4), 196–206.

Avramović, Z. (2013). *Obrazovanje u tokovima društva znanja* (*Education in the Currents of the Knowledge Society*). Zavod za udžbenike.

Branković, J. (2021). Ekonomska relevantnost znanja: percepcije o ulozi univerziteta u ekonomskom razvoju Srbije (The Economic Relevance of Knowledge: Perceptions of the Role of Universities in the Economic Development of Serbia). In Gazela Pudar, D., & Pavlović, A. (Eds), *Univerzitet u Srbiji i njegova društvena odgovornost (The University in Serbia and Its Social Responsibility*) (pp. 59–89). Beogradski Univerzitet, Institut za filozofiju I društvenu teoriju; Institut za demokratski angažman jugoistočne Evrope.

Janićijević, N., Baucal, A., & Cvejić, S. (2005). Formulisanje standarda i unapređenje kvaliteta nastave na Univerzitetu u Beogradu (Standardization and Enhancement of the Quality of Teaching at Belgrade University). In A. Mimica, & Z. Grac (Eds.), *Visoko obrazovanje u Srbiji na putu ka Evropi četiri godine kasnije* (pp. 35–42). Alternativna akademska obrazovna mreža.

Jarić, I., & Vukasović, M. (2009). Bolonjska reforma visokog školstva: mapiranje faktora niske efikasnosti studiranja (Bologna Reform in Higher Education in Serbia: Mapping Factors of Low Efficiency of Studding). *Filozofija i društvo, 2*(3), 119–151. <https://doi.org/10.2298/FID0902119J>

Jerotijević, D., & Aleksić Glišović, M. (2019). Bolonjska deklaracija danas i njena primena u Srbiji (History of the Bologna Declaration). In D. Mizdrak, & D. Slijepčević (Eds.), *Zbornik radova Međunarodni naučni skup Visoko obrazovanje u Republici Srpskoj—Stanje, putevi i perspektive* (pp. 287–297). Banja Luka.

Kočović, J. (2020). *Izazovi u sprovođenju postupaka akreditacije po novoj metodologiji i uloga NAT u obezbeđenju kvaliteta u visokom obrazovanju (Challenges in Implementing Accreditation Procedures by New Methodology and Role of the Neaqa in Quality Assurance of Higher Education*). XXVI Skup Trendovi razvoja: „Inovacije u modernom obrazovanju". Kopaonik 16–19.02.2020.

Kolarski, Lj. (2021) Bolonjski proces: perspektive i izazovi Republike Srbije u procesu implementacije (Bologna Process: The Republic of Serbia's Perspectives and Challenges in the Implementation Proces). *Administracija i javne politike, 16*(2), 73–87. <https://doi.org/10.22182/ajp.1622021.4>

Liessmann, K. P. (2008). *Teorija neobrazovanosti: zablude društva znanja (The Theory of Unlearning: The Errors of the Knowledge Society).* Jesenski i Turk.

Lungulov, B. (2011). Ishodi učenja u visokom obrazovanju kao indikatori kvaliteta obrazovanja (Learning Outcomes in Higher Education as Indicators of the Quality of Education). *Pedagoška stvarnost,* 7(9), 610–623.

Lungulov, B. (2015). *Analiza ishoda učenja kao indikatora kvaliteta visokog obrazovanja (Analysis of Learning Outcomes as Indicators of the Quality of Higher Education)* Doctoral dissertation. Novi Sad, Filozofski fakultet Univerziteta u Novom Sadu. Retrived from <https://nardus.mpn.gov.rs/handle/123456789/4506>

Marinković-Nedučin, N., & Lazetić, P. R. (2002). *Evropski sistem prenosa bodova u visokom školstvu* (*The European Credit Transfer System in Higher Education*). Vodič kroz ECTS. Alternativna akademska obrazovna mreža.

Osmanović Zajić, J., & Maksimovic, J. (2023). The Bologna in the Field of Social Sciences and Humanities: A Precondition for Successful University Education. *Athens Journal of Education, 10*, 1–15. <https://doi.org/10.30958/aje.10-4-8>

Rančić, M., Jašin, D., & Eremić, Ž. (2017). Aktuelno stanje u visokom strukovnom obrazovanju (Current State in Higher Applied Education). XXIII Conference Trends in Development: "Position of Higher Education and Science in Serbia." Zlatibor, 22nd–24th February 2017.

Škorić, S. (2008). About reform of high education. *Pravo—teorija i praksa*, *25*(11–12), 76–91.

Šofranac, R., & Damjanović, R. (2010). *Bolonjski proces i kvalitet visokog obrazovanja* (*The Bologna Process and the Quality of Higher Education*). Pobjeda.

Turajlić, S., Andrejić, M., Rudić, L., & Todorović, Lj. (2004). *Visoko obrazovanje u Srbiji. (Higher Education in Serbia).* Ministarstvo prosvete i sporta.

Vukasović, M. (2007). *Higher Education and Social Stratification in Serbia 1990–2005.* University of Aveiro.

Documents

Bergen communiqué (2005). The European Higher Education Area—Achieving the Goals, Communiqué of the Conference of European Ministers Responsible for Higher Education. Retrived from <https://iqaa.kz/images/doc/Bologna/Ministerial%20Communique%20(Bergen,%202005).pdf(11.02.2024.)>

Berlin Communiqué (2003). "Realising the European Higher Education Area" Communiqué of the Conference of Ministers responsible for Higher Education in Berlin on September 19, 2003. Retrived from <https://www.wg.aegee.org/ewg/berlincommunique.htm(11.02.2024.)>

Bologna Declaration (1999). Joint declaration of the European Ministers of Education of June 19, 1999. Retrived from <https://iqaa.kz/images/doc/Bologna/The%20Bologna%20Declaration%20(1999).pdf(11.02.2024.)>

Budapest-Vienna Declaration (2010). Joint declaration of the European Ministers of Education of March 12, 2010. Retrived from <https://ehea.info/Upload/document/ministerial_declarations/Budapest_Vienna_Declartion_598640.pdf(11.02.2024.)>

Census of Population, Households and Dwellings (2022). Knjiga 4. *Školska sprema, pismenost i kompjuterska pismenost (Educational Attainment, Literacy and Computer Literacy).* Beograd. ISBN 978-86-6161-236-7

European Council (2000). *Presidency conclusions.* Lisbon European Council, March 23–24, 2000. Retrived from <https://www.europarl.europa.eu/summits/lis1_en.htm(06.03.2024.)>

Law on Higher Education. *Official Gazette of the Republic of Serbia*, Nos. 88/2017, 73/2018, 27/2018—other law, 67/2019, 6/2020—other laws, 11/2021—authentic interpretation, 67/2021, 67/2021— other law, and 76/2023.

Regulation on Norms and Standards for Working Conditions at Universities and Faculties for Activities Financed from the Budget. *Official Gazette of the Republic of Serbia*, Nos. 15/2002, 100/2004, 26/2005, 38/2007, 110/2007.

Republic of Serbia, Ministry of Education, Science and Technological Development (2017). *National Qualifications Framework of the Republic of Serbia.* Retrived from the World Wide Web <http://noks.mpn.gov.rs/wp-content/uploads/2019/10/Национални-оквир-квалификација-у-Републици-Србији.pdf(15.02.2024)>

Republic Statistical Office (2011–2023). *Statistical Pocketbook of the Republic of Serbia*. Belgrade. ISSN 1820-6794.

Republic Statistical Office (2011–2023). *Statistical Yearbook of Serbia for 2011–2023.* Belgrade. ISSN 0351-4064.

Rome Declaration (2020). Joint declaration of the European Ministers of Education on November 19, 2020 Retrived from <https://iqaa.kz/images/doc/Ministerial%20Communique%20(Rome,%202020).pdf (11.02.2024.)>

Strategy of the National Accreditation Body (NAT) for the Period 2019–2022. Management Board of NAT. Retrived from <https://www.nat.rs/strategija-nat/(01.03.2024.)>

The Sorbonne Joint Declaration (1998). Joint declaration on harmonisation of the architecture of the European higher education system. Paris the Sorbonne, May 25 1998 Retrived from <https://www.ehea.info/media.ehea.info/file/1998_Sorbonne/61/6/1998_Sorbonne_Decaration_French_552616.pdf(11.02.2024.)>

The U.K. HE Europe Unit (2005). *Guide to The Bologna Process*. Retrived from <http://www.unl.pt/data/qualidade/bolonha/guide-to-the-bologna-process.pdf (11.02.2024.)>

6. Challenges in Higher Education and for Academics in Ukraine

Katalin Pallay

ABSTRACT
The present study offers a comprehensive account of the development of higher education in Ukraine from the period of independence to the present day. It examines the manner in which the modernization and restructuring of higher education, which had its roots in the Soviet era, proceeded after the Declaration of Independence. The paper presents an analysis of the structural and content-related changes that resulted from Ukraine's accession to the Bologna Process in 2005. Firstly, the study provides an overview of the political and social changes in Ukraine that have an impact on the higher education system. Specific focus is dedicated to the evolution of the student and doctoral populations. The second half of the study will analyze the characteristics of those engaged in teaching and instruction in higher education. Subsequently, an investigation will be conducted into the structure and evolution of professional roles within the higher education sector, the total number of academic staff in Ukraine, the proportion of those with academic qualifications and titles, and the gender distribution of university professors. In conclusion, the remuneration system for academic staff will be subjected to analysis.

Keywords: Higher education in Ukraine, academic staff, Bologna Process, educational reforms

Introduction

Since Ukraine gained independence in 1991, its higher education system has undergone significant transformation, mainly influenced by political, social and economic changes. The transition from a Soviet-era model to a more modern, European-style education system, particularly following Ukraine's accession to the Bologna Process in 2005, has brought about structural changes. Researchers such as Kozma (2006) have described these reforms as part of a wider effort to align Ukraine's educational framework with European standards. However, the effectiveness and depth of these changes have been debated, particularly in the wake of the 2014 Maidan events, which marked a turning point in the country's socio-political landscape.

The present study aims to explore the development of higher education in Ukraine, with a focus on modernization efforts following the country's independence. It examines both structural and substantive changes, particularly in the composition of academic staff, student enrollment trends and the impact of various policy reforms. The paper also examines the remuneration system for academic staff and the challenges facing higher education in the context of the ongoing conflict.

Data for this study were collected from a number of sources, including the State Statistical Service of Ukraine, the Wittgenstein Centre and various academic publications. The period under study spans from 1991 to 2023, with a particular focus on the period following Ukraine's accession to the Bologna Process. A combination of descriptive statistics and trend analysis was used to provide a comprehensive picture of the evolution of the higher education system. While previous research (Orosz, 2012) has largely focused on policy implications, this study includes a more detailed examination of faculty composition and its impact on academic quality.

1. Higher Education in Post-Regime Ukraine: Trends and Changes

The transformation of higher education in Ukraine following the regime change has been considerable. After gaining independence, Ukraine committed itself to modernizing its higher education system. The aim was to bring it more into line with European standards. The increased autonomy afforded to higher education institutions has facilitated the development of their curricula and research areas to a greater extent. The reforms affecting higher education in Ukraine have been gradual. This can be attributed to the necessity for the country to undergo a transformation not only of its higher education system but also of the structure of the nascent state, which is in a state of flux. Kozma (2006) characterizes the second phase of higher education policies in the years following the regime change as a consolidation phase. The period spanning the second half of the 1990s to the turn of the millennium was marked by the consolidation of relations between power elites and civil society. During this period, Ukraine's higher education policy became increasingly centralized, with the restoration of national culture emerging as the dominant ideology. Additionally, there was a restructuring of power within the field of higher education, which sought to achieve greater autonomy and independence (Kozma, 2006).

Following Ukraine's 2004 presidential election and the subsequent "Orange Revolution" (Yekelchik, 2007), the country focused on consolidating its nation-state identity with an emphasis on strengthening the role of the Ukrainian state language. Education was identified as the most effective tool for this purpose, leading to reforms that prioritized Ukrainian language instruction. The overarching aim was to transform Ukraine into a de facto monolingual state.

2. The Bologna System in Ukraine

Kozma (2006) defines the third phase of change in higher education policy as a process of re-nationalization. This process took place in the late 1990s.

Although Ukraine is not a member of the European Union, it saw the Bologna Process as an opportunity and a stepping stone toward EU accession. Joining the Bologna system had a significant impact on the country's higher education policy (Orosz, 2009).

In 1999, the Bologna Declaration was signed in Bologna by the education ministers of 29 countries, launching a major reform of higher education known as the Bologna Process (Hrubos, 2005; 2021). The reform aimed to structurally harmonize the higher education systems of EU countries and make them interoperable by introducing a credit system, thus contributing to the unification of the EU. The previous five-year university education, common in most countries, was divided into two levels. Ukraine joined the Bologna Process on May 19, 2005. As a result of the reforms, the structure of higher education was restructured, but many elements of the Soviet education system were retained (Kovács, 2014; Pallay, 2019).

Ukraine moved to multilevel training and credit systems. One of the most important effects of joining the Bologna Process on higher education is that the structure of higher education has changed. Higher education in Ukraine was initially divided into four levels:

- Baccalaureus (BSc, BA);
- Specialist (SSc);
- Master's degree course, (MSc, MA);
- Candidate (Doctoral studies, Ph.D.)

1. Bachelor's degree—BA/BSc level (Baccalaureate)—Bachelor's degree courses at colleges and universities, for which candidates with a school-leaving certificate can apply with the results of external independent test exams. The course lasts four years, after successful completion of which students receive a bachelor's degree. The four-year duration of the course is explained by the fact that young people in Ukraine graduate at the age of 17. In the traditional education system, students who graduate from high school usually complete their secondary education at the age of 18. The one-year-longer basic education aims to provide an adequate professional and theoretical basis and to allow students develop their general education.
2. Specialist level—a one-year course sandwiched between bachelor's and master's degrees, leading to a diploma equivalent to a master's degree upon successful completion (Orosz, 2012). The last time this type of training was open to people with a bachelor's degree was in 2016. The specialist level was abolished in 2017. It has been replaced by a one-and-a-half or two-year master's program. The BSc/BA is expected to be reduced to three years but is currently a four-year course (cf. law on higher education of Ukraine).

3. Master's degree course—(MA/ MSc), students who have completed a bachelor's degree and hold a BSc/BA degree can apply for this level of education. This level has now become the second level of the Bologna system in Ukraine as well. The master's degree corresponds to the university degree obtained before the introduction of the Bologna system, which students could obtain after the fifth year of university studies in the undivided system. After obtaining a master's degree, young graduates can find a job in the labor market or apply for a Ph.D. (Orosz, 2005). In Ukraine, the duration of a master's degree course is 1.5 to 2 years.
4. Candidate/Aspirancy (Doctoral studies, Ph.D.) currently the third level of higher education that can be applied for with a master's degree. The doctoral program lasts for four years, during which the doctoral student is required to fulfill the requirements set by the higher education institution and to complete the doctoral dissertation by the end of the training period (Moisieieva & Usachov, 2014).

Since joining the Bologna system, Ukraine has also seen an increase in the proportion of graduates. However, the figure shows that Ukraine falls behind its neighbors, except for Moldova, in terms of the growth rate of higher education graduates (Figure 6.1).

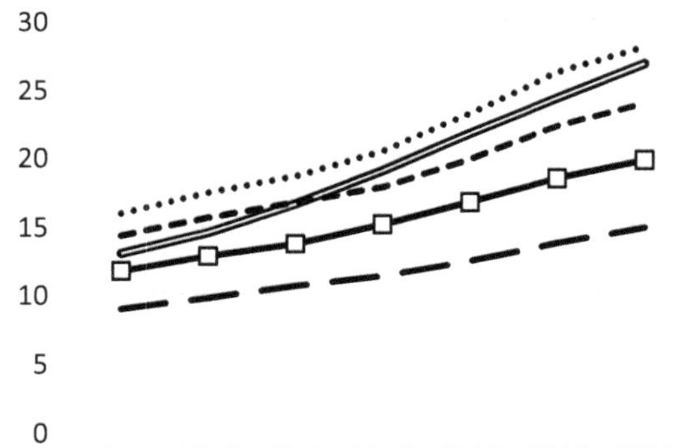

	1990	1995	2000	2005	2010	2015	2020
Ukraine	11.7	12.8	13.7	15.1	16.7	18.4	19.7
Hungary	13	14.5	16.6	19	21.7	24.3	26.8
Russia	15.9	17.4	18.6	20.4	23.2	26.2	28
Moldova	8.9	9.7	10.6	11.3	12.4	13.7	14.8
Belarus	14.3	15.6	16.7	17.8	19.8	22.2	23.9

Figure 6.1: Share of population aged 15 and over with tertiary education, by country.
Source: Based on data from the Wittgenstein Centre.

Ukraine's accession to the Bologna system has triggered a number of educational policy developments in the country. On July 4, 2005, the President of Ukraine, Viktor Yushchenko, issued a decree on the measures necessary *to ensure the functioning and development of education in Ukraine*, aimed at reducing corruption, improving the quality of secondary education and integrating the Ukrainian education system into the European model. In order to implement the decree, the Ukrainian Center for Quality Assessment of Education (Ukrainian: Український центр оцінювання якості освіти) was established in 2005 to assess the factual knowledge of applicants. A unified admission system based on the Bologna system was introduced. As a result, an advanced level examination, the so-called external independent test examination, must be taken at independent examination centers. The unified entrance system aims to ensure equal opportunities in the entrance examination. On July 13, 2007, the then Ukrainian Minister of Education, Stanislav Nikolayenko, ordered that from the 2008/2009 academic year, all applicants to higher education in Ukraine, regardless of their course of study, would have to take a test exam in Ukrainian language and literature at an advanced level. According to Viktor Yushchenko, the existence of a developed European state depends on the existence of a single state language (Orosz, 2009; Csernicskó, 2012). According to the decree of Stanislav Nikolayenko, in addition to the advanced level of Ukrainian language and literature, applicants must take an optional exam in Ukrainian language and literature and an optional exam in history or mathematics, depending on the subject. The decree stipulates that all candidates must take this exam in Ukrainian. The next Minister of Education, Ivan Vakarchuk, amended his predecessor's decree of December 25, 2007, allowing graduates of national schools to use a specialized vocabulary for the exam (Ministerial Decree No. 1171).[1]

From 2017, all school leavers are required to take the independent test exams, regardless of whether they intend to study at a higher education institution in Ukraine or even if they do not intend to apply to a university or college. Ukrainian language and literature are still compulsory for all students, while the other subjects are optional: history of Ukraine, mathematics or biology. A third subject is compulsory if the student intends to study at a higher education institution. The results of an independent test examination are the basis for both the admission score and the final grade (Csete et al., 2010; Ukrainian Center for

1 <https://zakon.rada.gov.ua/laws/show/z0005-08#Text>.

Education Quality Assessment;[2] Ministry of Education and Science of Ukraine: Admission Requirements for 2018[3]).

The Table 6.1 shows that in the years following the regime change, Ukraine was also characterized by an expansion of higher education. The decline after 2014 was partly due to shortcomings attributed to higher education, such as corruption, the global devaluation of Ukrainian university degrees, the mismatch of education with labor market expectations, and the financial and technical weakness of institutions. The Ukrainian Ministry of Education and Science has started to optimize the number of universities, which led to the closure of some institutions (Fastovets, 2020). The number of students decreased due to the introduction of a new admission procedure in 2008. By 2011, when all year groups were admitted to higher education through an external, independent examination, the number of students had started to decline across the country. It posed a challenge to higher education institutions. Both applicants and the academic staff had to adapt to the new admissions process.

Table 6.1: Higher education institutions and student numbers (Undergraduate, bachelor, master, and postgraduate)

Academic year	Number of higher education institutions	Number of students
1990/91	149	881 300
1991/92	156	876 200
1992/93	158	855 900
1993/94	159	829 200
1994/95	232	888 500
1995/96	255	922 800
1996/97	274	976 900
1997/98	280	1 110 000
1998/99	298	1 210 300
1999/2000	313	1 285 400
2000/2001	315	1 402 900
2001/2002	318	1 548 000
2002/2003	330	1 686 900

2 <https://testportal.gov.ua/>.

3 <https://mon.gov.ua/ua/osvita/visha-osvita/arhiv-vstupnoyi-kampaniyi-2017-2020/vstupna-kampaniya-2018/umovi-prijomu-na-navchannya-do-zakladiv-vishoyi-osviti-ukrayini-v-2018-roci>.

Academic year	Number of higher education institutions	Number of students
2003/2004	339	1 843 800
2004/2005	347	2 026 700
2005/2006	345	2 203 800
2006/2007	350	2 318 600
2007/2008	351	2 372 500
2008/2009	353	2 364 500
2009/2010	350	2 245 200
2010/2011	349	2 129 800
2011/2012	345	1 954 800
2012/2013	334	1 824 900
2013/2014	325	1 723 700
2014/2015[1]	277	1 438 000
2015/2016[1]	288	1 375 200
2016/2017[1]	287	1 369 400
2017/2018[1]	289	1 330 000
2018/2019[1]	282	1 322 300
2019/2020[1]	281	1 266 100
2020/2021	515	1 142 000
2021/2022	386	1 047 000
2022/2023	347	1 054 000

Source: Author's calculations based on data from the State Statistics Service of Ukraine.[4]

3. Development of Higher Education in Ukraine After Maidan

The so-called Orange coalition, led by President Yushchenko and Prime Minister Tymoshenko, soon destabilized the domestic political situation in Ukraine as the differences between the two parties escalated (Yekelchik, 2007). In 2010, Yanukovych won the presidency, and his government promoted regionalization, passing a law in 2012 that allowed minority languages official status in areas where minorities comprised at least 10 percent of the population. Despite initial talks with the EU, Yanukovych declined to sign an association treaty in favor of closer ties with Russia, sparking widespread protests known as Euromaidan.

4 <https://www.ukrstat.gov.ua/>.

Following escalating violence, Yanukovych fled to Russia in February 2014, and Ukraine's Parliament replaced him with Oleksandr Turchynov. A new coalition government was then formed under Arseniy Yatsenyuk (Deák, 2014; Sz. Bíró, 2014; Csernicskó, 2016).

Maidan changes also affected higher education in Ukraine. On September 6, 2014, the new law on higher education[5] entered into force. The adoption of the law was primarily a political step, which clearly reflected the alignment of the Ukrainian education system with the European education space. Students played a key role in initiating the reform process in higher education. The first steps were made possible by the blockade of the Ministry of Education and Science, then headed by Dmytro Tabachnyk. On February 21, 2014, the students presented two concrete demands to the minister: firstly, the suspension of classes in higher education institutions until the situation of the Maidan protests was resolved, and secondly, an end to the repression of students supporting the Maidan. On February 23, 2014, the Supreme Council acquitted Tabachnyk. The new Minister of Education became Serhiy Kvit. Student opinion continued to dominate, and they imposed a number of conditions on the newly appointed minister, which were included in the Roadmap for the Development of Education in Ukraine. The students' demands included decentralization of the higher education system and a more student-centered approach. As the conflict escalated, the higher education system faced several new challenges. The annexation of the Autonomous Republic of Crimea and the deteriorating situation in the Donbass region made it necessary to address issues related to the transfer of students and staff. The rapid increase in the number of refugees within the country made it difficult to implement planned reforms in higher education. The concept of so-called 'universities in exile' emerged in Ukraine. By early 2015, 26 educational and research institutions, including 16 universities and 10 research institutes, had been evacuated from the occupied territories (Shchudlo, 2015).

4. The Impact of the Russian-Ukrainian War on Higher Education

In 2021, Russia began to increase its military presence on the Russian side of the border in eastern Ukraine. Vladimir Putin's decision on February 21, 2022, heightened concern among Ukrainian and European leaders to recognize the independence of the two breakaway Ukrainian administrative entities of Donetsk

5 Про вищу освіту. Закон України №1556-18 від 1.07.2014 // Відомості Верховної Ради (ВВР).—2014.—№ 37-38. <https://zakon.rada.gov.ua/laws/show/1556-18#Text>.

and Luhansk. On February 24, the Russian army invaded Ukraine, marking the beginning of the Russo-Ukrainian war. Western countries, including the European Union, strongly condemned the Russian aggression, defended Ukraine's territorial integrity and imposed sanctions against the aggressor (official website of the Council of the EU and the European Council[6]).

The armed conflict posed significant challenges to the higher education system in Ukraine. In the two weeks following the outbreak of the war, classes were suspended, and in March, most Ukrainian higher education institutions introduced distance learning for the spring semester. The war destroyed some of Ukraine's higher education institutions. The institutions directly affected have suffered losses in several areas: infrastructure, material and human resources. The number of universities classified as "in exile" is increasing. A number of higher education institutions originally located in Luhansk, Kherson, Zaporizhzhya and the Crimean region are now operating in other Ukrainian provinces. The relocation of these institutions has brought about a significant change in the educational institutional system in the regions concerned. The competitiveness of the relocated institutions has decreased and regional disparities in higher education institutions have increased (Lugovyi et al. 2023).

Following the imposition of martial law, it was recognized that the admissions process could not continue as before. On March 24, 2022, the Supreme Council of Ukraine, citing the state of emergency, introduced an amendment to the law on simplified admission procedures.[7] A decree[8] on the new admission procedure was adopted at the end of April. The most significant change was the replacement of the External Independent Evaluation with a National Multi-subject Test. The National Multi-subject Test is a complex examination consisting of three subjects: Ukrainian language, Mathematics and History of Ukraine. The multi-subject test was administered online and consisted of far fewer test questions per subject than the previous external independent test.

The Russian invasion forced millions of Ukrainian citizens to leave their homes. Most of those who fled abroad went to neighboring EU countries. In response, Ukrainian examination centers were set up in 46 locations in 23 countries (21 EU member states, the United Kingdom and Moldova). The supplementary test was held at 35 locations in 26 countries (19 EU member states, the United Kingdom, Georgia, Canada, Moldova, Switzerland, Turkey and the United States).[9]

---

6 <https://www.consilium.europa.eu/hu/european-council/>.

7 <https://zakon.rada.gov.ua/laws/show/2157-20#Text>.

8 <https://zakon.rada.gov.ua/laws/show/z0487-22#Text>.

9 <https://testportal.gov.ua/wp-content/uploads/2022/10/Zvit_NMT_2022.pdf>.

The results of the multi-test were used to apply for state-funded places. For fee-paying places and courses in private higher education institutions, with the exception of a few prestigious courses such as medicine and law, it was possible to apply with a letter of motivation. The introduction of a low threshold for the multiple-choice test and letters of motivation meant that the requirements for applicants were significantly lower than in previous years. Despite this, the number of students in Ukraine has neither decreased nor increased drastically. This is due to the fact that online distance learning is still allowed in areas where active fighting is taking place and that the war situation in the country has led many young people to start their studies abroad.

Kyiv is the city with the highest student population in Ukraine. The capital is followed by Kharkiv, a major university center. Next are Dnipropetrovsk, Odessa and Lviv, which are also important centers of higher education in Ukraine. These cities stand out in the country not only in terms of the number of students but also in the excellent higher education institutions that are located there. No statistics are available on the number of students in the Russian-occupied territories (Figure 6.2.)

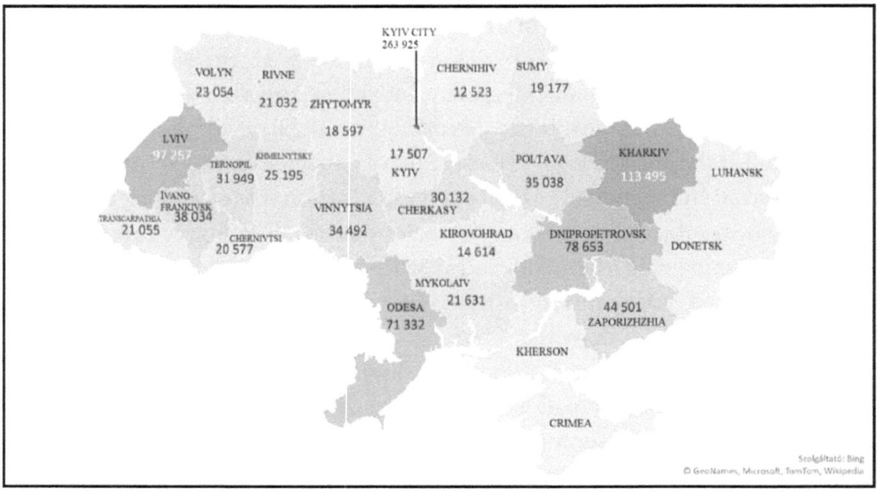

Figure 6.2: Number of students by field for the academic year 2022/23.[10]
Source: Author's calculations based on data from the Statistical Office of Ukraine.

[10] We do not have data on the current number of students in the areas currently under Russian occupation.

The martial law and the simplified admission processes have had a significant impact on the composition of students enrolled in higher education. Many older students who failed the previous admission procedure took advantage of this opportunity. The increase in the number of male students is due to the exemption from military service. Broken down by age group, it is striking to note that the proportion of males aged 20 and under in higher education decreased by 17% from 2021 to 2022 and by 21% in 2023. The proportion of males aged 20–29 increased significantly, almost tripling in 2022 compared to the previous year. For those aged 30–39, the increase is even more marked, with a 15-fold increase in 2022, and for those aged 40+, participation rates increased 17-fold in 2022 and 31-fold in 2023 compared to 2021 (Figure 6.3). In their study, Lugovyi et al. (2023) conclude that such a change in the student contingent could have a negative impact on the quality of higher education in Ukraine and could pose a risk to the Ukrainian economy in the future.

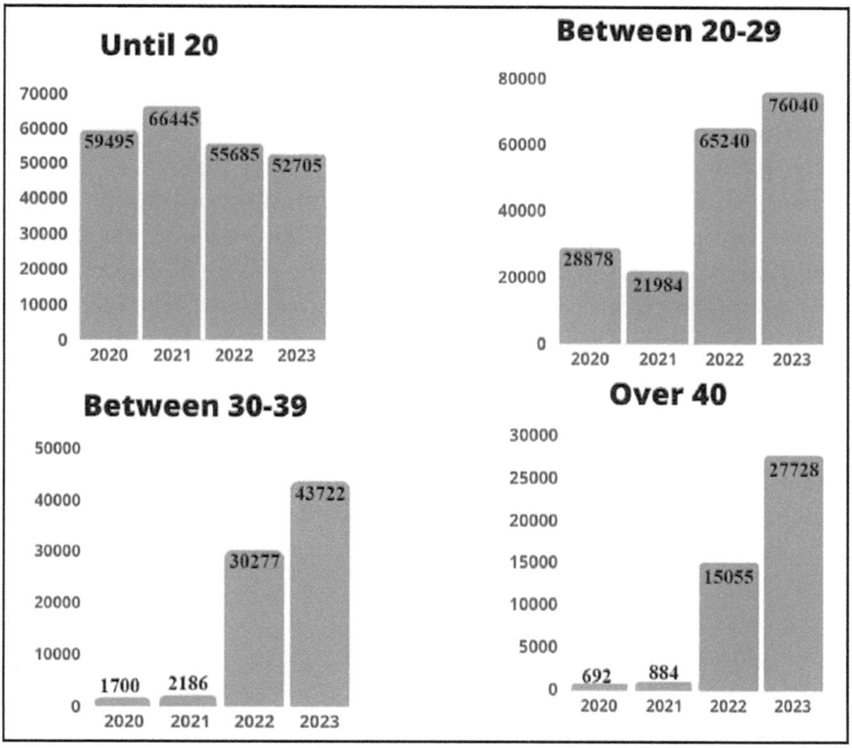

Figure 6.3: Growth in the number of male students by age group over the past four years.
Source: Author's calculations based on statistics from the Ministry of Education and Science of Ukraine.

After the outbreak of the Russian-Ukrainian war, the number of male students at bachelor's and master's levels increased, as did the number of doctoral students (candidates). In 2022, 13.386 doctoral students started their studies, of which only 2.231 were women. From the regime change until the mid-2010s, doctoral studies in Ukraine were followed by a candidate's degree. Again, the higher education system was considered to be in line with EU standards, but the influence of the Soviet education system was still felt (Rumyantseva et al., 2018). The current law on higher education, adopted in 2014, has brought changes in the area of doctoral degrees. After the law came into force, the Candidate of Sciences degree became equivalent to the Ph.D. degree, and the traditional system of Candidate of Sciences degrees was changed to the Ph.D. degree in line with international practice. The main aim was to harmonize Ukrainian doctoral education with European and international standards. The introduction of the new system will facilitate the international recognition of Ukrainian doctoral degrees, which is an essential step for the international cooperation of the scientific community and researchers. Those who started their studies after 2014 will have obtained a doctoral degree instead of the previous candidate's degree. However, those who started their studies earlier but defended their dissertation after 2014 will continue to hold a candidate's degree (law on higher education of Ukraine[11]).

There are currently 384 higher education institutions in Ukraine offering full-time and part-time doctoral programs with state support and fees. The proportion of doctoral students increased since the change of regime in 2010, partly due to the expansion of higher education in Ukraine. The increasingly mass higher education has required an increasing number of academic staff, which has led to a gradual increase in the number of doctoral students. The events of 2014 also created a precarious situation in higher education, with a gradual decrease in the number of Ph.D. students. In the year of the outbreak of the war, however, there was a sharp increase. As mentioned above, the exemption from military service for full-time students played a role in the background.

---

11 <https://zakon.rada.gov.ua/laws/show/1556-18#Text>.

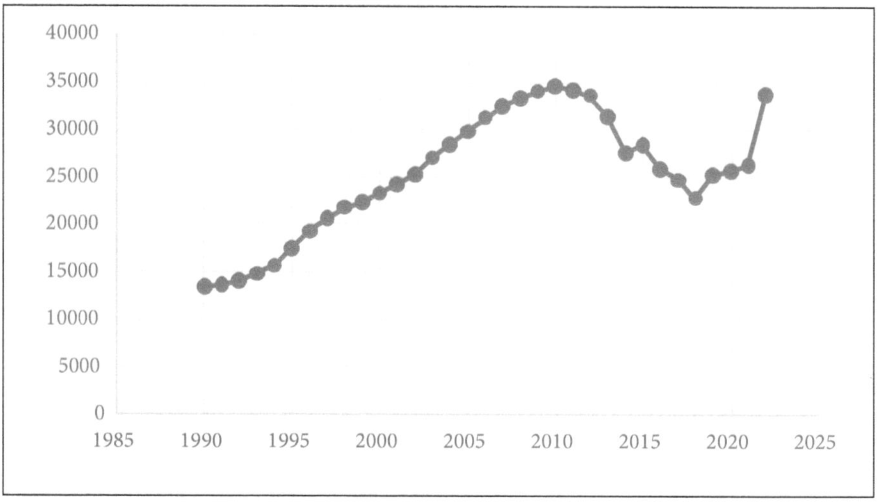

Figure 6.4: Number of Ph.D. students in Ukraine from the regime change to the present.
Source: Author's calculations based on data from the Statistical Office of Ukraine.

In terms of age, doctoral students are predominantly young. 4.392 of them are between 22 and 25 years old, indicating that they started their doctoral studies immediately after graduation. Forty percent of the students, 13.598, are between 26 and 30 years old. 136 started their doctoral studies at the age of 60 or more. The distributions are shown in the graph.

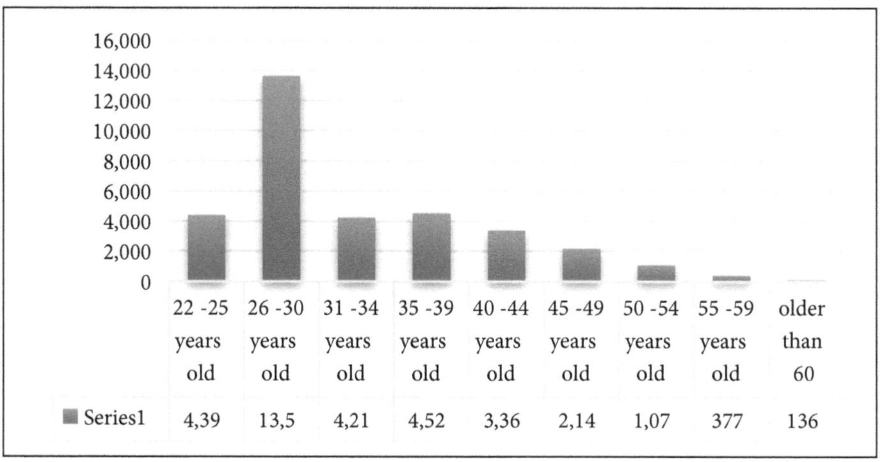

Figure 6.5: Ph.D. students in Ukraine by age group.
Source: Author's calculations based on data from the Statistical Office of Ukraine.

5. Employment Regulations for Academic Staff in Higher Education of Ukraine

In Ukraine, persons who meet the so-called licensing (tender) conditions approved by the Cabinet of Ministers of Ukraine in Resolution No. 1187[12] may be employed in higher education. The conditions include 20 points, of which at least four must be fulfilled over a period of five years in order to be employed as academic staff:

1. At least five publications in journals listed in the Ukrainian list of peer-reviewed publications, as well as in scientific metrics databases, including Scopus, Web of Science Core Collection;
2. A patent for an invention;
3. One published textbook or monograph (with at least 5 author sheets), including co-authored publications (with at least 1.5 author sheets per co-author);
4. At least three educational aids and methodological guides;
5. A doctoral degree;
6. Supervisory role for a doctoral student;
7. Participation as an opponent in reviews or scientific evaluations, membership of a scientific committee;
8. Editors-in-chief, members of editorial boards, proofreaders of Ukrainian or foreign indexed journals;
9. Member of the National Agency for Higher Education Quality Assurance, Accreditation Commission, expert or member of three expert councils of the Ministry of Education and Science;
10. Participation in international scientific and/or educational projects;
11. Scientific advice to research institutions for at least three years;
12. At least five scientific or professional studies;
13. Teaching in a foreign language (except for language training specializations) for at least 50 hours per academic year;
14. Tutoring a student who has won a prize at the first or second stage of a Student Olympic games or as a member of the organizing committee or jury of the All-Ukrainian Student Olympic games, international competitions, festivals, etc.;
15. Tutoring a student who has been awarded a place in the "Minor Academy of Sciences of Ukraine," participation in the jury;
16. Active participation in the armed struggle in Ukraine;
17. Participation in international peacekeeping and security operations under the auspices of the United Nations;
18. Participation in international military exercises (training) involving the armed forces of NATO member states;
19. Membership in professional organizations;
20. At least five years of non-specialized professional experience.

---

12 <https://zakon.rada.gov.ua/laws/show/1187-2015-%D0%BF#Text>.

In addition, in Ukrainian higher education, the employment of academic staff is based on whether their educational and professional qualifications meet the educational components of the mandatory elements of the applicant's training program. Evidence of compliance with these components is a university degree, a degree in the same field as the diploma, at least five years of professional experience, a doctoral thesis in Ukraine or abroad, publications in at least five Ukrainian journals and/or journals indexed in scientific metrics databases (Scopus, Web of Science (WoS)). The professional activity requirements do not apply to academic staff with less than three years' experience, staff who have fought on the front line, and to part-time academic staff (Decision 1187).

It can be concluded that in Ukrainian higher education over the past five years, research activity has gained increasing emphasis for academics and has become a primary task. This aligns with Kwiek's (2016) perspective, who argues that only those who prioritize research activities and subordinate all other university roles can be considered part of the research elite.

Also, academic staff in Ukrainian higher education institutions must undergo an annual performance evaluation regulated independently by the relevant academic institutions. These include Government Decree No. 411 of April 13, 2011[13] on *"Issues Related to Further Training of Scientific and Scientific-Pedagogical Staff in Foreign Educational and Scientific Institutions,"* Government Decree No. 800 of August 21, 2019[14] on *"In-Service Training of Pedagogical and Scientific-Pedagogical Personnel"* (as amended by Decree No. 1133 of December 27, 2019[15]), Decree of the Ministry of Education and Science of Ukraine No. 1341 of October 30, 2020[16] on *"Methodological Recommendations for Professional Development of Scientific-Pedagogical Personnel."* On this basis, higher education institutions are required to develop regulations for the in-service training of academics. Ukrainian academic staff are re-certified every five years. During the five-year period, credits must be accumulated through in-service training in accordance with the standards of the ECTS. Forms of professional development may include participation in seminars, workshops, training courses, webinars, and master classes. Internships for academic staff and certain types of professional activities (e.g., participation in conferences) may also be recognized as professional development. How credits are earned is left to the academic staff to decide. For example, they may attend one training course in the first year to obtain the required 6 credits at once, or they may

---

13 <https://zakon.rada.gov.ua/laws/show/411-2011-%D0%BF#Text>.

14 <https://zakon.rada.gov.ua/laws/show/800-2019-%D0%BF#n18>.

15 <https://zakon.rada.gov.ua/laws/show/1133-2019-%D0%BF#Text>.

16 <https://mon.gov.ua/ua/npa/pro-zatverdzhennya-metodichnih-rekomendacij-dlya-profesijnogo-rozvitku-naukovo-pedagogichnih-pracivnikiv>.

attend short courses once a year for one or two weeks to obtain 1–2 credits. The topics of the training courses must be relevant to the subjects taught by the academic staff. Academic staff may also attend professional training courses abroad in compliance with *Government Decree No 411 of April 13, 2011*[17] *on "The Training of Students and Doctoral Candidates and Issues Related to the Training of Academic and Scientific-Pedagogical Staff in Foreign Educational and Scientific Institutions."*

Regular in-service training provides academics with the opportunity to learn about current pedagogical methods, professional trends and new information that can contribute to the development and application of effective teaching and methodological practices. In addition, in-service training can help academics acquire up-to-date professional knowledge that contributes to improving the quality of teaching and the relevance of the curricula.

6. The Structure of Academic Staff of the Ukrainian Higher Education

At the initiative of the Ministry of Education and Science of Ukraine, the Ministry of Economics, Trade and Agricultural Development approved the Professional Standard of *Academic Staff of Higher Education Institutions* by Decree No. 610 of 23.03.2021.[18] The decree stipulates that in higher education in Ukraine, academics can be organized in the positions of assistant, instructor, assistant professor, associate professor and professor. Early-career academic staff can aim for *assistant* positions, which require a higher education degree in the field of specialization and scientific research in line with the profile of the department. Previous employment is not a criterion. The *lecturer* posts require a university degree or a Ph.D. or candidate's degree in the relevant discipline, academic work relevant to the profile of the department and at least two years of academic experience. Lecturers are expected to have completed three years of doctoral studies. For *assistant professors*, a university degree in a discipline relevant to the field, at least five years of teaching and research experience (minimum 5 published scientific publications, at least 6 conferences attended), and in the case of an existing Ph.D.

17 <https://zakon.rada.gov.ua/laws/show/411-2011-%D0%BF#Text>.

18 <https://mon.gov.ua/storage/app/media/pto/standarty/2021/03/25/Standart%20na%20hrupu%20profesiy_Vykladachi%20zakladiv%20vyshchoyi%20osvity_25.03.pdf>.

degree, at least 3 years of teaching and research experience. An assistant professor lecturer is required to obtain a Ph.D. or candidate's degree[19] within five years.

The associate professor position requires a minimum of five years of teaching and research experience, a candidate or Ph.D. degree and/or an associate professor title, methodological publications, a monograph or textbook, a paper published in Ukrainian journals or a Scopus or WoS indexed journal. Academics in an associate professor's post are encouraged to supervise students' doctoral thesis and prepare the Ph.D. students for their thesis over a period of five years. To be considered for *a professorial* position, academic staff must hold a professorial academic title and/or an associate professorship with a doctorate degree (Doctor of Science), have at least ten years of teaching and research experience, and be the author of textbooks, monographs, papers published in Ukrainian journals or journals indexed by Scopus or WoS. Professorial staff should be involved in the organization of student competitions or scientific conferences, as well as national and international research projects.

In addition to jobs in higher education, there are also opportunities to obtain academic titles. According to Decree No. 13 of January 14, 2016[20] on *Approval of the Procedure for Awarding Scientific Titles to Researchers and Scientific Staff*, it is possible to apply for the titles of Associate Professor, Senior Research Fellow and Professor in Ukraine. In the case of the title of *associate professor*, the scientific council of the higher education institution first examines whether the candidate is eligible for the title of associate professor. If the candidate meets the requirements and the council finds him/her suitable, the candidate is submitted to the Ministry of Education and Science of Ukraine. In Ukraine, the requirements for the title of associate professor include a doctoral or postdoctoral degree, a foreign language certificate of at least intermediate level (B2) in a complex language or equivalent, at least five years of professional experience in higher education, independent scientific achievement, recognized publications in the relevant field, postdoctoral research published in a Scopus or WoS indexed journal, regular participation in pedagogical and professional training courses, supplemented by international mobility. The candidate must have given a public lecture at the institution to be awarded the title of Associate Professor.

---

19 Candidate of Sciences is an academic degree that can be earned by the holder of a master's or specialist's qualification. The standard time of study in the postgraduate department is 3 years (daytime) or 4 years (extramural). The last admission to the Candidate of Sciences' programs was in 2015.

20 <https://zakon.rada.gov.ua/laws/show/z0183-16#Text>.

To be awarded the title of *Senior Research Fellow*, the candidate's application must be supported by at least six staff members of the higher education institution or research institute holding a scientific degree. The title of *Senior Research Fellow*, which is equivalent to that of the Associate Professor, is open to researchers who hold a doctorate or postgraduate degree and have at least five years' professional experience, of which at least one year must have been as a senior researcher, senior research fellow, associate professor, professor, head or deputy head of a research institute, head of department, rector, deputy rector for science, director, deputy director for scientific work, and scientific secretary. In addition, the program requires at least an intermediate level (B2) or equivalent in a foreign language, or at least ten publications in English in Scopus or WoS journals, and participation in international research projects and international conferences. Proof of professional competence must be provided via the publishing of at least two studies in Scopus or WoS journals following the writing of the dissertation.

The *professor's title* may be awarded to a person with a doctorate in higher education who has already obtained the title of associate professor and who regularly participates in professional training and international research projects. He or she must also have at least 10 years of professional experience. Other requirements include at least an intermediate level (B2) in a language of the EU or ten publications in a journal indexed by Scopus or WoS. Professional competence must be demonstrated by at least two of the person's own publications in Scopus or WoS journals.

7. Number of University Academic Staff in Ukraine

On July 13, 2011, the Cabinet of Ministers of Ukraine adopted a Resolution on the Creation of a Unified State Electronic Education Database (Resolution No. 752).[21] The document states that the Unified State Electronic Education Database is an automated system of collection, registration, processing, storage and protection of information and data on education. The Unified State Electronic Education Database is owned by the state, administered by the Ministry of Education and Science of Ukraine, and technically managed by the state enterprise Inforesource.[22] The inclusion of higher education institutions in the Unified State Electronic Education Database started in 2012. All lecturers' qualifications, titles, degrees and training certificates are recorded in the unified system.

21 <https://zakon.rada.gov.ua/laws/show/752-2011-%D0%BF#Text>.
22 <https://www.inforesurs.gov.ua/>.

The number of academics also increased in line with changes in the number of higher education institutions and Ph.D. students until 2020. The COVID-19 pandemic and the subsequent Russian aggression led to a reduction in the number of Ukrainian academics. The measures taken in the wake of the epidemic and the subsequent Russian aggression also posed a significant challenge to higher education, especially in war zones. In their research, Tsybuliak et al. (2023) point out that the war has increased burnout among the members of higher education staff. Women have been negatively affected by the relocation of universities and associated migration processes, but the prolonged war also leads to emotional exhaustion among men. Some academics have also emigrated and given up their careers. These factors may have contributed to the decline in the number of academics in universities and colleges. The reduction of the teaching workload from 900 to 600 hours per year has also contributed to the decline in the number of academic staff. As a result, student autonomy has increased while the number of university staff has not. There are also plans to reduce the number of hours spent on the tuition of bachelor's and master's theses (Stavytskyy, 2018).

The reduction in the number of faculty can be attributed to the emigration of academic staff. Since Ukraine's independence, the emigration of highly skilled professionals ("brain drain") has posed a significant challenge for the country's scientific community. The main wave of emigration began in the 1990s, as numerous researchers and scientists left Ukraine due to political and economic instability. Between 1991 and 2000, 420 researchers migrated to the United States, of whom 343 held a Candidate of Sciences degree and 77 held a Doctor of Sciences degree, while 251 went to Germany, including 208 Candidates of Sciences and 43 Doctors of Sciences. Although the emigration rate later declined, the 2014 Maidan protests marked another sharp increase, with 1,781 scientists leaving the country, including 1,436 Candidates of Sciences and 345 Doctors of Sciences. According to Popp & Kirda (2024), this emigration of researchers has resulted in substantial economic losses, with Ukraine estimated to have lost $36 billion due to the outflow of scientists by 2014. OECD and World Bank data from 2020 indicate that Ukraine's R&D expenditures accounted for only 0.41% of GDP, far below the levels seen in developed countries. Even prior to the war, low funding levels and limited development opportunities led many scientists to seek employment abroad (Medina & Pendur, 2014). The Russian-Ukrainian war starting in 2022 has further aggravated the situation. According to a survey of 2022 entitled "*Rebooting Science After the War*,"[23] 14.6% of Ukrainian

[23] Research report: Проєкт «Наука в небезпеці» березень 2023 <scienceatrisk.org>.

researchers have been forced to relocate abroad since the war began, with most of them moving to Germany (26.8%) and Poland (25.1%). Internal migration poses additional challenges, as 38% of researchers and academic staff have been forced to relocate within Ukraine due to the conflict, disrupting research networks and collaborative efforts. Since 2015, the Statistical Office of Ukraine has not maintained records on the emigration of academic staff and researchers (Nikitenko, 2019).

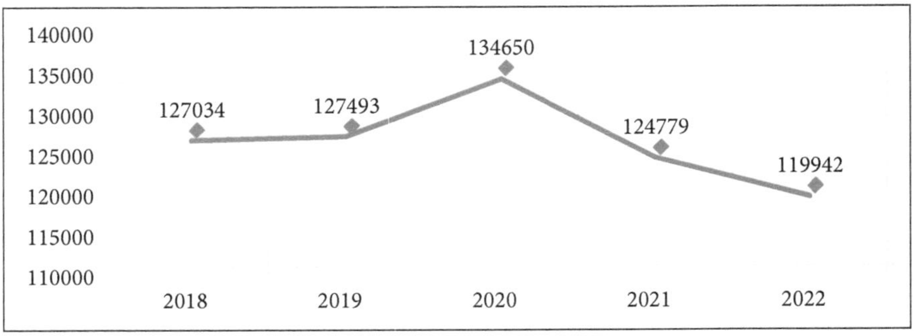

Figure 6.6: Change in the number of Ukrainian academic staff over the last five years (N).

Source: Author's calculations based on data from the State Statistics Service of Ukraine.

Based on the statistical data for 2022 analyzing the composition of the higher education staff in Ukraine, it can be observed that slightly more than half of the academic staff (50.82%) have a Ph.D. degree, and 1.59% have a doctorate. The reason for this imbalance is that Ukraine switched from candidate to doctoral training in 2016. Ph.D. students study for a period of four years, so the number of Ph.D. degrees in the country is still relatively low. Students who started their studies before 2016 but defended their dissertation after 2020 are still studying for a candidate's degree today. 16.1% have a doctorate (Doctor of Science). 31.58% of academics do not have a doctorate; they have a master's degree. Almost half of Ukrainian academics have an academic title: 36.76% have the title of associate professor, and 12.25% have the title of professor.

In 2022, the proportion of women in higher education in Ukraine was high at 59.44%, well above the average proportion of women in the Visegrád Four countries in previous years (Figure 6.8).

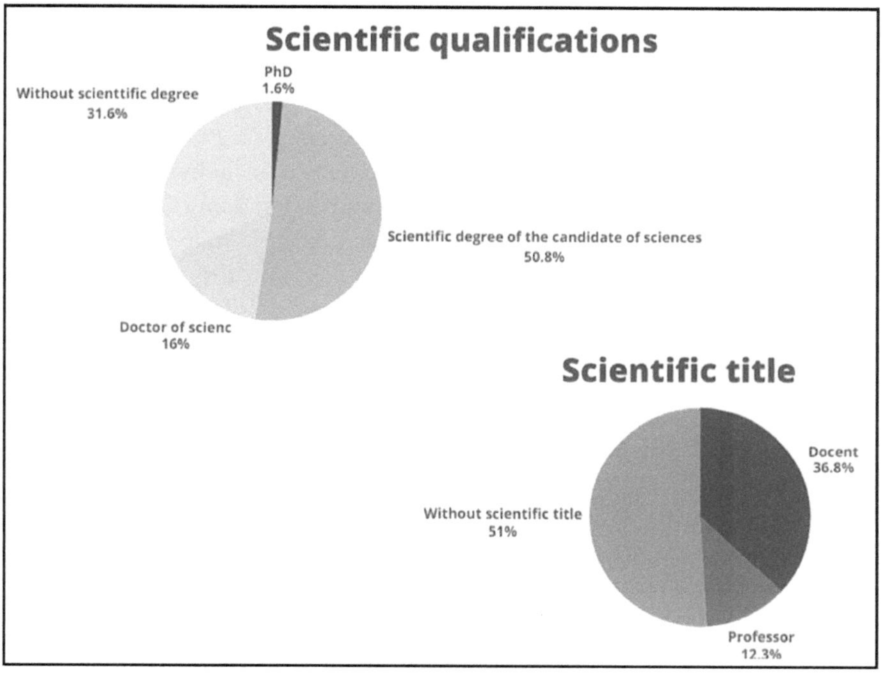

Figure 6.7: Distribution of academic degrees and titles among Ukrainian academics (%).
Source: Author's calculations based on data from the Ukrainian Statistical Office.

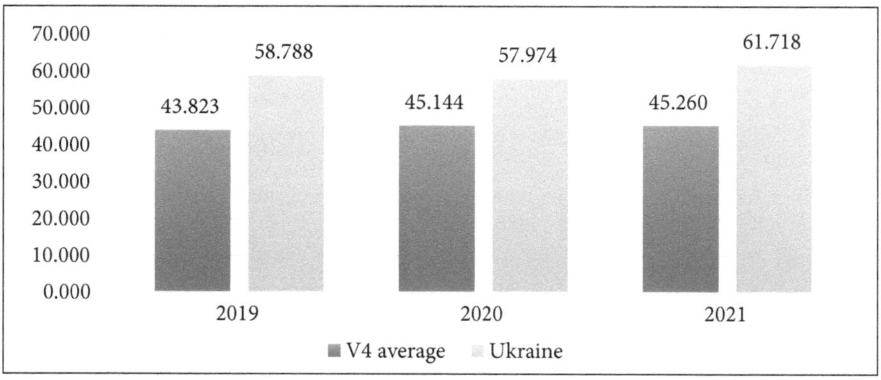

Figure 6.8: Share of women of academic staff in Ukraine and the Visegrád countries.
Source: Author's calculations based on data from the World Bank and Statistics of Ukraine.

8. Salaries of Academic Staff in Ukraine

In 2002, a decision[24] was adopted on a unified salary scale and salary coefficients for employees of institutions, establishments and organizations in specific sectors of the public sector, which was last amended on January 12, 2024.[25] According to the decision, the salaries of public employees in Ukraine, including academic staff and researchers, are determined by a so-called unified tariff scale (UTS) based on different salary categories. In higher education, academic staff and researchers are divided into salary categories based on their academic degrees, professional experience and other professional criteria. The pay grades for academics are all above the Ukrainian living wage, which, according to the Law of Ukraine on the State Budget of Ukraine for 2024,[26] will be UAH 7100 (EUR 168) from January 1, 2024 and is expected to rise to UAH 8,000 (EUR 190) from April 1. Different allowances will be added to the amount set for each pay-scale category. For example, for more than ten years of professional experience, a 20% bonus is added to the salary determined for the tariff category, 15% for a scientific degree, 25% for the title of associate professor and 33% for the title of professor. Nevertheless, the average monthly salary of academic staff in Ukraine is significantly lower than in the Visegrád Four countries (see Figure 6.9).

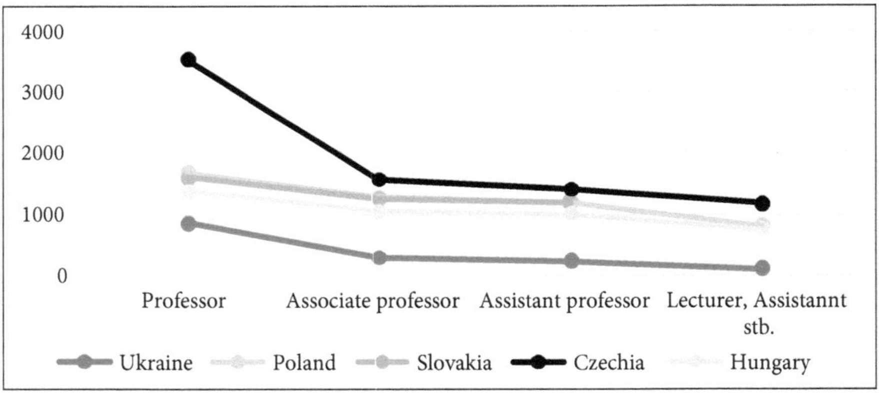

Figure 6.9: Average salary of academic staff in Ukraine and Visegrád countries in Euro.
Source: Author's calculations based on data from Glassdoor.

[24] <https://zakon.rada.gov.ua/laws/show/1298-2002-%D0%BF#n78>.
[25] <https://zakon.rada.gov.ua/laws/show/23-2024-%D0%BF#n2>.
.[26] <https://zakon.rada.gov.ua/laws/show/3460-20#Text>.

Summary

Higher education in Ukraine has undergone significant changes since the change of regime. After gaining independence in 1991, the adoption of new laws and the reorganization of educational institutions made it a priority for the country to modernize higher education and overcome the Soviet tradition. Ukraine's accession to the Bologna system in 2005 has led to significant structural changes in the higher education system and closer links with foreign educational institutions, facilitating student and teaching mobility and the integration of foreign students and academics into the Ukrainian education system. A unified admissions system has been developed to create equal opportunities and reduce corruption. Political and economic changes in the country have also had an impact on higher education. Following the Maidan Square Protest in 2014, the higher education system has also sought to align itself more closely with the standards of the European Higher Education Area. However, the escalating Russian-Ukrainian conflict has had a negative impact on higher education in Ukraine. In many cases, universities in Russian-occupied areas have become *universities in exile*, meaning that they continue to operate in other parts of the country. Another challenge for higher education is that Russia attacked Ukraine in February 2022. This has triggered a demographic wave that has led to a decline in the number of higher education institutions and faculties. The pandemic and the war have led to relaxed admissions, allowing students who could not meet the previous admission requirements to enter higher education. Despite the relaxed admissions system, the number of applicants to higher education has not increased massively due to the high proportion of young emigrants. Since the outbreak of the war, the number of older male students has soared, probably due to the military exemption for full-time students. Despite these difficulties, over the past decade, Ukrainian higher education has become increasingly aligned with European trends in higher education: higher expectations of academic staff, compliance with licensing rules, requirements for specific programs and subjects taught, and the introduction of performance assessment. Academics are paid according to different salary scales, with additional allowances for academic degrees, academic titles and length of service. However, the salaries of Ukrainian academics are still significantly lower than those of their counterparts in the EU and even in the Visegrád Four countries.

The outcome of the Russia-Ukraine war is likely to bring significant changes to higher education in Ukraine. The war is creating severe economic and social challenges for the country, which will have a significant impact on the education system. There has already been a decline in the number of higher education institutions, academics and state-funded places.

References

Csernicskó, I. (2012). *Megtanulunk-e ukránul? A kárpátaljai magyarok és az ukrán nyelv.* [Will we learn Ukrainian? Hungarians in Transcarpathia and the Ukrainian language]. PoliPrint.

Csernicskó, I. (2016). *Nyelvpolitika a háborús Ukrajnában.* [*Language policy in war-torn Ukraine*]. Autdor-Shark.

Csete, Ö., Papp Z. A., & Setényi, J. (2010). A kárpát-medencei magyar oktatás az ezredfordulón. [Hungarian education in the Carpathian Basin at the turn of the millennium]. In Bitskey, B. (Ed.), *Határon túli magyarok a 21. században.* [*Hungarians living abroad in the twenty-first century*] (pp. 44–55). KEH.

Deák, A. (2014). Kifulladásig—Az orosz-ukrán konfliktusról. [On the Russian-Ukrainian conflict]. *Figyelő, 36*, 18–19.

Fastovets, N. (2020). Higher Education in Ukraine: Reality and Perspectives. *Management, 32*(2), 153–164.

Hrubos, I. (2005). A peregrinációtól az Európai Felsőoktatási Térségig. [From Peregrination to the European Higher Education Area]. *Educatio, 14*(2), 223–243.

Hrubos, I. (2021). *A bolognai tornyok üzenete Tanulmányok az európai felsőoktatási reformról és a nemzetközi trendekről.* [The Message of the Bologna Towers: Studies on European Higher Education Reform and International Trends]. Gondolat.

Kovács. K. (2014). The Bologna Process in Ukraine. In T. Kozma, M. Rébay, A. Óhidy, & É. Szolár (Eds.), *The Bologna Process in Central and Eastern Europe* (pp. 321–354). Springer VS.

Kozma, T. (2006). Regionális átalakulás és térségi visszhang. A „partiumi" felsőoktatás esete. [Regional transformation and spatial resonance. The case of higher education in the "Partium" region]. In E. Juhász (Ed.), *Régió és oktatás. A „Regionális egyetem" kutatás zárókonferenciájának tanulmánykötete*. [Region and education. Proceedings of the final conference of the "Regional University" research] (pp. 13–25). Doktoranduszok Kiss Árpád Közhasznú Egyesülete.

Kwiek, M. (2016). The European research elite: a cross-national study of highly productive academics in 11 countries. *Higher Education, 71*(3), 379–397.

Lugovyi, V., Kalashnikova, S., Talanova, Z., & Vlasov, I. (2023). Transformation of higher education in Ukraine: Impact of the war and objectives for post-war recovery. *European Journal of Education. Research, Development and Policy, 58*(4), 611–628.

Medina, T., & Pendur, N. (2014). Intellectual migration from Ukraine: causes and consequences. *Релігія та Соціум, 1–2*(13–14), 150–157.

Moisieieva, F. A., & Usachov, V. A. (2014) = Ф.А. Моісєєва & В.А. Усачов (2014). Європейська інтеграція вищої освіти України в контексті болонського процесу. [European Integration of Ukrainian Higher Education in the Context of Bologna Process]. *«Наука. Релігія. Суспільство»*, 1, 36–40.

Nikitenko, L. (2014). = Нікітенко Лілія (2014). «Відтік мізків» та його наслідки для України. ["Brain Drain" and Its Consequences for Ukraine]. *Правове забезпечення інтеграції України в європейський політичний, економічний, безпековий, інтелектуальний простір: матеріали Всеукраїнської науково-практичної конференції (м. Хмельницький, 23 квітня 2019 року).* Abstract book (pp. 245–249). Retrived from <https://jlsouk.donnu.edu.ua/article/view/6822/6854 09/03/2025>

Orosz, I. (2005). *A magyar nyelvű oktatás Kárpátalján az ukrán államiság kialakulásának első évtizedében. [The Hungarian language education during the first decade of Ukrainian statehood].* PoliPrint.

Orosz, I. (2009). Bolognai rendszer—balkáni módszer. [Bologna system—Balkan method]. In Z. Karmacsi, & A. Márku (Eds.), *Nyelv, identitás és anyanyelvi nevelés a XXI. században. Nemzetközi tudományos konferencia előadásainak gyűjteménye. [Language, identity and mother tongue education in the twenty-first century. Collection of papers from an international scientific conference]* (pp. 129–141). II. Ferenc Rákóczi Transcarpathian Hungarian College—Antal Hodinka Institute.

Orosz, I. (2012). A magyar nyelvű oktatás helyzete. [The situation of Hungarian teaching language education]. In I. Orosz (Ed.), *Két évtized távlatából. [From the perspective of two decades]* (pp. 192–193). PoliPrint.

Pallay, K. (2019). Az ukrán oktatáspolitika hatása a kárpátaljai magyar tannyelvű felsőoktatásra. [The Impact of Ukrainian Education Policy on Hungarian Language Higher Education in Transcarpathia]. *Neveléstudomány. Oktatás—Kutatás—Innováció,* 7(2). 56–72.

Popp, R., & Kirda, A. (2024). Mihratsiini protsesy v naukovomu seredovyshchi Ukrainy (1991–2023) [Migration processes in the scientific environment of Ukraine (1991–2023)]. *Problemy humanitarnykh nauk: zbirnyk naukovykh prats Drohobytskoho derzhavnoho pedahohichnoho universytetu imeni Ivana Franka. Seriia Istoriia—Problems of Humanities. History Series: a collection of scientific articles of the Drohobych Ivan Franko State Pedagogical University, 15*(57), 127–134.

Rumyantseva, N., & Logvynenko, O. (2018). Ukraine: Higher Education Reforms and Dynamics of the Institutional Landscape. In J. Huisman, A. Smolentseva, & I. Froumin (Eds.), *25 Years of Transformations of Higher Education Systems in Post-Soviet Countries Reform and Continuity* (pp. 407–433). Palgrave Macmillan.

Shchudlo, S. (2015) = Світлана Щудло (2015). Освіта після майдану: експектації та реалії. [Education after Maidan: expectations and realities]. Релігія та Соціум. [*Religion and Society*] *1–2*(17–18), 117–120.

Stavytskyy, A. (2018). Challenges for Higher Education: The Case of Ukraine. In J. A. Valsiner, & A. A. Lutsenko (Eds.), *Sustainable Futures for Higher Education. The Making of Knowledge Makers* (pp. 115–123). Springer

Sz. Bíró, Z. (2014). Ukrajnai tanulságok. [Lessons from Ukraine] *Mozgó Világ, 1.* 72–78.

Tsybuliak, N., Suchikova, Y., Shevchenko, L., Popova, A., Kovachev, S. & Hurenko, O. (2023). Burnout dynamic among Ukrainian academic staff during the war. *Nature Science Report*, *13*(1), 17975.

Yekelchyk, S. (2007). *Ukraine. Birth of a Modern Nation*. Oxford University Press.

Websites

Amendment to the law of March 24, 2022. Retrieved from <https://zakon.rada.gov.ua/laws/show/2157-20#Text> March 18, 2024.

Council of the EU and the European Council. Retrieved from <https://www.consilium.europa.eu/hu/european-council/ March, 14, 2024>.

Decision No. 1187 on Approval of the Licensing Conditions for Conducting Educational Activities. Retrieved from <https://zakon.rada.gov.ua/laws/show/1187-2015-%D0%BF#Text March 22, 2024>.

Decision No. 752 on the Establishment of the Unified State Electronic Database on Education No. 752. Retrieved from <https://zakon.rada.gov.ua/laws/show/752-2011-%D0%BF#Text March 29, 2024>.

Decree of the Ministry of Education and Science of Ukraine No. 1341 of October 30, 2020. Retrieved from <https://mon.gov.ua/ua/npa/pro-zatverdzhennya-metodichnih-rekomendacij-dlya-profesijnogo-rozvitku-naukovo-pedagogichnih-pracivnikiv> March 28, 2024.

Government Decree No. 411 of the Issues of training of students and internships (scientific internships) of postgraduate students, adjuncts and doctoral students, researchers and scientific and pedagogical staff in leading higher education institutions and scientific institutions abroad. Retrieved from <https://zakon.rada.gov.ua/laws/show/411-2011-%D0%BF#Text March, 25, 2024>.

Glassdoor. Retrieved from https://www.glassdoor.com/Salaries/index.htm March 27, 2024.

Language Law (2012). Retrieved from <https://zakon.rada.gov.ua/rada/show/v1185835-12#Text> March 8, 2024.

Law of Ukraine on the state budget of Ukraine for 2024. Retrieved from <https://zakon.rada.gov.ua/laws/show/3460-20#Text> March 30, 2024.

Law on Higher Education of Ukraine (2014). Retrieved from <https://zakon.rada.gov.ua/laws/show/1556-18#Text> March 12, 2024.

Ministerial Decree No 1171. Retrieved from <https://zakon.rada.gov.ua/laws/show/z0005-08#Text> March 19, 2024.

Ministerial Decree of the Procedure for Admission to Higher Education in 2022 27.04.2022 Nº 392. Retrieved from <https://zakon.rada.gov.ua/laws/show/z0487-22#Text> March 16, 2024.

Ministerial Decree of the Some issues of professional development of pedagogical and scientific-pedagogical staff in 2019. 08. 21. Nº800. Retrieved from <https://zakon.rada.gov.ua/laws/show/800-2019-%D0%BF#n18 March 23, 2024>.

Ministerial Decree on Amendments to the Procedure for Professional Development of Pedagogical and Scientific and Pedagogical Workers No. 1133 of December 27, 2019. Retrieved from <https://zakon.rada.gov.ua/laws/show/1133-2019-%D0%BF#Text> March 25, 2024.

Ministerial Decree on Approval of the Procedure for Awarding Academic Titles to Research and Scientific and Pedagogical Employees No 13 of January 14, 2016. Retrieved from <https://zakon.rada.gov.ua/laws/show/z0183-16#Text>: March 29, 2024.

Ministerial Decree On Remuneration of Employees on the basis of the Unified Tariff Scale of Categories and Coefficients for Remuneration of Employees of Institutions, Establishments and Organizations of Certain Sectors of the Public Sector No.1298 of August 30, 2002. Retrieved from <https://zakon.rada.gov.ua/laws/show/1298-2002-%D0%BF#n78> March 21, 2024.

Ministerial Decree Some Issues of Remuneration of Employees of Institutions, Establishments and Organizations of Certain Sectors of the Public Sector No. 22. of January 12, 2024. Retrieved from <https://zakon.rada.gov.ua/laws/show/23-2024-%D0%BF#n2> March 24, 2024.

Ministry of Education and Science of Ukraine: Admission requirements for 2018. Retrieved from <https://mon.gov.ua/ua/osvita/visha-osvita/arhiv-vstupnoyi-kampaniyi-2017-2020/vstupna-kampaniya-2018/umovi-prijomu-na-navchannya-do-zakladiv-vishoyi-osviti-ukrayini-v-2018-roci.> March 4, 2024.

Professional Standard of Lecturers of Higher Education Institutions by Decree No 610 of 23.03.202. Retrieved from <https://mon.gov.ua/storage/app/media/pto/standarty/2021/03/25/Standart%20na%20hrupu%20profesiy_Vykladachi%20zakladiv%20vyshchoyi%20osvity_25.03.pdf> March 29, 2024.

Report on the results of the National Multi-subject Test (2022). Retrieved from <https://testportal.gov.ua/wp-content/uploads/2022/10/Zvit_NMT_2022.pdf> March 17, 2024.

State Enterprise Inforesource. Retrieved from <https://www.inforesurs.gov.ua/> March 24, 2024.

State Statistics Service of Ukraine. Retrieved from <https://www.ukrstat.gov.ua/> March 8, 2024,

Ukrainian Center for Education Quality Assessment: <https://testportal.gov.ua/> Retrieved March 2, 2024.

PART II

Well-Being of Academics in Central and Eastern Europe

7. Performance Assessment: A New Dimension of Institutional Culture

Gabriella Pusztai, Zsuzsanna Demeter-Karászi & Katalin Pallay

ABSTRACT
The importance of the introduction and impact of performance assessment systems in higher education institutions is widely recognized, particularly in relation to their impact on organizational culture and the effectiveness of academics. However, there is still debate about how these systems are implemented in different institutional cultures and the extent to which they influence the performance and satisfaction of academics. This study examines the extent to which and the form of the influence of performance evaluation systems on the work of academics in Hungarian higher education institutions in the Carpathian Basin. The research used a qualitative method, in which focus group interviews were conducted between July and October 2022 with 41 academics from nine higher education institutions in five Carpathian Basin countries. The interviews focused on the institutional culture, the effectiveness of teaching and the implementation of performance appraisal systems. In the analysis, four types of institutional culture were identified, and the interpretations of academics effectiveness were also grouped into four main types. The results show that the introduction of performance appraisal systems has had different effects in different institutional cultures and in different ways and has led to different attitudes among academics. The study shows that the introduction of performance appraisal has a significant impact not only on the performance of academics but also on the institutional culture, particularly in terms of organizational development in higher education institutions and job satisfaction of academics.

Keywords: institutional culture, performance evaluation, teaching effectiveness, higher education in the Carpathian Basin

Introduction

The relevance of our study is that today's higher education in Central and Eastern Europe is undergoing new transformations, which are most visible in the institutional culture. This culture can be understood through different interpretive communities, and while some approach the phenomenon by looking at the dimensions of student society and student life (Pusztai, 2015; Rizzi, 2019; Demeter-Karászi, 2023; Ceglédi & Dabney-Fekete, 2023; Dusa & Dabney-Fekete, 2024), others see it through the interpretive communities of institutional leaders, academics and researchers (Mohammadi et al., 2010; Florenthal & Tolstikov-Mast, 2012; Masouleh & Allahyari, 2017; Barton, 2019; Batugal & Tindowen, 2019; Dabney-Fekete, 2020). From the point of view of the different interpretive communities, institutional culture can be examined from different dimensions. The question arises as to what these dimensions might be, and whether they are stable or possibly changing over time. The novelty of our study lies in understanding institutional culture through the interpretive community of academics. It aims to refine dominant conceptions by including performance evaluation in academics' narratives, which we expect will accurately infer the basic features of institutional culture.

In the theoretical part of our study, we will first present the processes that have contributed to the multidimensional transformation of higher education in the region over the last three decades. We will do this in order to better understand the current changes in higher education. In the second section of our theoretical part, we will discuss performance assessment in higher education, and in the third section we will present the teaching community's understanding of institutional culture and the possible dimensions of this perspective.

1. Theoretical Background

1.1. Higher Education at Scale

To understand the current transformations, it is first important to look back at the region's three decades of higher education after the regime change. Over these years, higher education has undergone a multidimensional transformation. Many of these were forced by political and social changes, such as expansionism or the Bologna Process. Expansion has followed a stifled higher education system in Central European countries in terms of social participation. As a result, the number of students in higher education has increased, and the number of institutions, courses and academics has also increased, albeit to a lesser extent (Kozma, et al., 2017). This institutional and staffing growth has fundamentally changed the institutional culture from what had previously been a traditional one, with student, teacher and administrator roles radically redefined from the elite phase of higher education.

The most important element of the Bologna Process, of structural change in higher education, aimed at making higher education more flexible and adaptable to the masses, was the introduction of multi-cycle education, which came into power in the region in the mid-2000s. In an extensive system of higher education institutions, few universities were able to offer a wide range of master's and doctoral programs, most institutions offered a variety of undergraduate courses, thus increasing the differences in the academic performance and prestige of the institutions, and their organizational culture also varying, with more and more specific features becoming descriptive.

The twenty-first century has brought further challenges for the higher education institutional sector. In its marketized world competing for students, and R&D resources, institutions have become uniform thanks to the monkey policy of international ranking fetishism (Hrubos, 2012; Berger et al., 2021). However, in the pluralistic, globalized social environment of the twenty-first century, the question may arise as to what extent an institutional environment with similar characteristics will be able to exert a unique attraction and satisfy the pluralistic, diverse social needs. As a result, in the competition for students, the importance of individual characteristics, such as differences in the culture of each higher education institution, may increase (Demeter-Karászi, 2023).

On this basis, a key question arises whether, in the force field of the changes that have affected all higher education institutions in recent decades, and to what extent institutions have become identical or different, and to what extent we can talk about a uniform institutional culture, or how far we can capture the specific characteristics that lie along its lines.

1.2. Valuing and Evaluating the Performance of Higher Education Institutions

There is a consensus in the literature that the transformation of higher education over the last few decades has brought about a radical, unprecedented change in the status of academics. The changes have overturned what we traditionally thought of as uniformly prestigious higher education profession. But changes affecting academics cannot be understood without understanding the transformation of higher education systems. Perhaps the most striking interpretation of these changes is that of Marginson (2016), who has directly questioned the validity of previous theories of expansion in higher education (Marginson, 2016). He argued that what has now been proven is that the most popular theory about the massification and democratization of higher education, Martin Trow's theory, is not true. Trow argued that the elite-selective model of higher education was gradually moving through the mass phase toward a universally accessible model, and that a socially open, democratic, equal-opportunity higher education was emerging (Trow, 1972). According to Marginson, however, by the twenty-first century, economically developed, urbanized societies had developed so-called "High Participation Systems," but these did not result in equal access to quality higher education. Mass entry, the devaluation of the distinctive role of the diploma and the resulting desperate competition for more advantageous social positions between the most ambitious students and their families, and the constraints on higher education funding have put higher education institutions in different positions. The internal vertical differentiation of higher education, which previously appeared unified, has increased, inequalities within and between higher education systems have become more pronounced, and positional differences between higher education institutions have led to strong stratification. Two distinctive institutional strata can be identified everywhere, the so-called leading research university (LRU) group of institutions with a track record of research excellence and greater access to resources, and the group of institutions that educate and generate resources for the masses of students. In addition, an ever-shrinking pool of cutting-edge research institutions has access to abundant resources, reinforcing the concentration of opportunities.

This has led to serious inequalities in both the student and teaching communities (Marginson, 2018). Marginson has already pointed out that, in addition to macro-level participation statistics, global and institutional-level effects, that is, the interests of academics and students, should also be examined (Marginson & Rhoades, 2002). The persistence and even amplification of inequalities in student access and achievement in higher education, in the context of massification, has been the subject of several studies (Triventi, 2013; Pusztai, 2015; Ceglédi et al., 2022), but few studies have focused on how this affects higher education in different countries. Kwiek (2019), analyzing data on higher education in 11 European countries, explains in detail how the world of higher education has become stratified and academic professionals have become highly internally divided (Kwiek, 2022). This means that the segments of the profession may not only be very far apart in the vertical hierarchy of prestige but also surrounded by a very different workplace subculture. There is no doubt that the increasing stratification between higher education systems and institutions at the micro level reinforces the diversity of institutions and institutional cultures and thus has a significant impact on the careers of academic staff (Kwiek, 2019; 2022). Kwiek's analysis identified three key dimensions of teacher stratification. The most significant, and most influential, differences between academics are along the lines of stratification by research output and academic and publication output. This is to some extent linked to another structuring factor, namely internationalization and the involvement in the international research community, and another strong stratification factor is wage inequality (Kwiek, 2018; 2019). The research and publication output of a narrow, elite group of academics is internationally recognized, their articles are published in the most prestigious international indexed journals, and they have access to the most research resources both at national and international levels, as they are strongly embedded in international networks.

It is striking that teaching activities are not included in any of the merits of the most outstanding academics, and in fact the group is characterized by the lowest teaching load and the lowest student population (Kwiek, 2022). Already at the turn of the millennium, Schimank and Winnes (2000) indicated that the Humboldtian model of the unity of teaching and research had been replaced by the so-called post-Humboldtian model, in which teaching and research tasks have been differentiated and have a markedly different organizational background and resources (Schimank & Winnes, 2000).

The stratification of tertiary education society is evident not only in terms of the different tasks assigned to each group, but also in terms of working hours, workload and disposable income (Kwiek, 2022).

In parallel with the above processes, the formal organizational act of performance assessment, familiar from the market sector and some public education systems, has also become established in higher education, precisely because of the increasing competition between institutions. There are several arguments for the usefulness of performance appraisal, some of which relate to enhancing the efficiency and productivity of the institution, others to making the employee more motivated, and satisfied, encouraging him or her to develop professionally (Cintron & Flaniken, 2011; Dasanayaka et al., 2021). The negative interpretation is competitive, ranking and selection (Bradley, 1992).

Performance appraisal starts with setting the goals of the institution. This is built upon to develop valid and reliable individual indicators, measurement practices and data assessment, and feedback on performance and areas of improvement. This also ideally provides the academic staff with directions on what and how to improve and as well as on how to train (Dasanayaka et al., 2021). In this formative appraisal model, incentives (promotion, salary supplements, additional non-material recognition) play an important role in keeping the system evolving. Although performance appraisal systems are present worldwide at the beginning of the twenty-first century, their positive impact on institutional and individual progress has not yet been conclusively demonstrated by research, but studies are being conducted on the uptake, experience, development, motivation and job satisfaction of performance appraisal (Cintron & Flaniken, 2011; Dasanayaka et al., 2021).

The future prospects and opportunities of an institution are not independent of the quality of the human resources available (Kaplan, 2009). In highly stratified higher education, some institutions strive to bring world-class research results to the table, attract the best students internationally and improve their position in international rankings (Kwiek, 2019; 2022). However, the institution-level objectives, reflecting the expectations of institutional owners and managers, may be quite different in other strata of higher education. In education-centered institutions, the number of students enrolled and admitted, the proportion of graduates, student dropout rates, the rates of students' further education between different educational levels, and the employability indicators of graduates can be institutional targets. In order to improve these indicators, institutions of this type could give greater weight to teaching outcome indicators generated on the basis of how satisfied students are with individual teachers and courses.

1.3. Institutional Culture

Whereas the transformation of higher education has become a focus of attention for researchers, the complexity and diversity of institutional culture is a little researched topic. Although, institutional diversification in higher education has become increasingly important (Teichler, 2008).

Over the last few decades, cultural studies have become an increasingly active area of research among researchers in higher education. A deeper understanding of different cultures has become vital not only for researchers, but also for individuals who want to create an innovative institutional climate that allows higher education to have a positive impact on society (Tierney & Lanford, 2018). In the literature, the concept is known as both institutional and organizational culture. Research on organizational culture has been spread mostly in the field of economics and focused mainly on individual organizations (Bess & Dee, 2012). It was only much later that researchers began to see higher education institutions as complex organizations (Bess & Dee, 2012), mainly after it became clear that understanding culture could provide partial solutions to problems within an organization (Warter, 2019) and that culture could be linked to organizational effectiveness and efficiency (Mohammadi et al., 2010; Warter, 2019). Based on these findings, the question arises: what can influence the efficiency and effectiveness of an institution? Effectiveness and efficiency can, however, be influenced by a number of factors, but some researchers (Masouleh & Allahyari, 2017) believe that human resources are one of the most important assets in a competitive organization, as effective and motivated individuals play a key role in driving organizational life forward. And organizational culture plays a key role in this (Masouleh & Allahyari, 2017).

The culture of higher education institutions is seen by some through the perspectives of governance, teaching and academic research (Barton, 2019; Batugal & Tindowen, 2019), while others see it through the perspectives of student society, student life, (Rizzi, 2019) and faculty (Mohammadi et al., 2010; Florenthal & Tolstikov-Mast, 2012; Masouleh & Allahyari, 2017). These are communities that interpret the institutional culture of higher education (Warter, 2019). The teaching profession also deserves particular attention in terms of organizational efficiency and effectiveness. Institutions themselves are increasingly recognizing the importance of academics for organizational success (Florenthal & Tolstikov-Mast, 2012; Masouleh & Allahyari, 2017), as it has been shown that it is the academics, the employees, who, if committed to their institution, will make the effort to make the organization successful. For, they interpret its purpose as their own (Masouleh & Allahyari, 2017). The engagement of academics is an important determinant of institutional culture, as researchers believe that culture exists in social relationships and can be strengthened through engagement (Masouleh & Allahyari, 2017). Organizational culture can also be approached through the perceptions of faculty, as institutional culture influences faculty attitudes, behavior, the quality and quantity of work done, attitudes toward the institution, and community life, while institutional culture can influence faculty, departments, the quality and effectiveness of teaching and research, and even faculty careers (Mohammadi et al., 2010; Florenthal & Tolstikov-Mast, 2012).

It can be concluded that higher education institutions are complex social organizations with a distinctive culture and different communities that interpret that culture (Warter, 2019), which can be analyzed based on different dimensions.

Different concepts and paradigms have been developed to describe and study institutional culture. Positivist or social constructivist approaches to institutional culture are known as such paradigms (Bess & Dee, 2012). Positivist researchers have created a concept of culture that can be generalized, so that all institutions can be categorized according to certain criteria. In contrast, social constructivists believe that it is the individual characteristics that are displaced by the positivist view, questioning the existence of a single description of organizational culture and believing that each institution can be understood as a distinct entity. Its meaning can best be captured through qualitative methods. In fact, qualitative methods are seen as a way of making the concept of institutional culture more tangible, thus revealing a deeper layer of culture that can only be captured by the perspective of individuals who are familiar with the institutional culture (Bess & Dee, 2012; Gaus et al., 2017).

Among the social constructivist approaches, the conceptual framework developed by Tierney is the most promising for a multidimensional, dynamic approach to institutional culture (Tierney, 1988; Bess & Dee, 2012). Tierney identified six concepts to describe institutional culture in higher education, including the dimensions of mission, environment, socialization, information, strategy and governance. First, in the case of mission, the framework examined how institutions and individuals define their mission, and to what extent there is agreement and/or disagreement between individual and institutional mission definitions. An essential element of institutional culture is whether institutional actors believe that institutional decisions are in line with the declared objectives. Second, it looks at the environment to answer questions such as how members of the institution identify with their environment and how the institution relates to its environment, whether it perceives it as supportive or hostile. The third key aspect in Tierney's concept is socialization, which seeks to understand how new members socialize in the institution, how they learn their roles and perhaps find their place within the institution, and what individuals need to do to be successful in the institution. Fourth, the most important starting point for information is what constitutes it within an institution. An important feature of institutional culture is whether the information distributed is relevant to the individual, or whether, in the interests of the institution, the individual is given only the minimum amount of information necessary, with the dominant members of the organization making the decisions. The fifth dimension of strategy is one of the most complex areas of institutional culture. If leaders do not respect values and expectations, internal legitimacy is shaken, and it becomes difficult to gain/maintain institutional trust. In studying institutional strategy, Tierney looks for answers to questions such as how the organization makes decisions, who is involved in decision-making, and whether there are consequences for the outcomes of good and bad decisions. Sixth, the governance dimension of institutional culture seeks to answer questions about what the institution and individuals expect from leaders and whether the power of leaders is formal or informal (Tierney, 1988; Bess & Dee, 2012).

In the extensive literature on institutional culture, several dimensions of this concept have been identified and studied, but perceptions of teacher effectiveness have not previously been considered as a dimension in its own right, but rather as a subset of other dimensions. Due to changes in higher education policy, the importance of performance measurement and performance assessment has been reinforced in an unconventional way, and, in our view, it has itself become a very influential dimension of institutional culture. Our qualitative research therefore aims to contribute to refining the dominant concepts of institutional culture. Our research question is whether different institutional cultures of higher education entail specific perceptions of teacher effectiveness. Our expectation is that perceptions of faculty performance can be used to infer with high accuracy the basic features of institutional culture. These features might include the following: what faculties perceive as valuable performance, how they view the performance prized and encouraged by the institution, and how that performance characterizes an institution in a way similar to the previously identified dimensions of institutional culture (e.g., communication, governance, mission, strategy, environment, socialization).

2. Methodology

The database of our qualitative research is a corpus of seven focus group interviews with 41 academics, averaging 100–150 minutes, The national economic justification of regular physical activity in Hungary for a sustainable and safe environment within the framework of the research project "Social, professional background, institutional characteristics and effectiveness of academics in the Carpathian Basin," conducted in the summer of 2022 by the research group "Sport Economics Research Group for the Health and Well-being of Academics of Higher Education Institutions in the Carpathian Basin." The research was carried out in Hungary, Romania, Serbia, Slovakia and Ukraine. Each country has a Hungarian language higher education institution, in areas where both Hungarian language HE institutions exist alongside ones run in the state-recognized language. The core population consisted of academics from higher education institutions from all institutional sectors in these countries.

The interview survey explores trainers' views on well-being, health and performance along ten dimensions. The interview guide covers the profile of the academics, their views on professional effectiveness, the challenges of teaching and research, the culture and climate of their higher education institution.

In the present research, we focus on the culture of higher education institutions based on the discourses of academics and seek to answer the question: to what extent have institutions become identical or different as a result of the various changes affecting them, to what extent is it possible to speak of a uniform institutional culture, and do different institutional cultures entail specific interpretations of educational effectiveness. Transcripts of the interviews were made and used to create a text corpus for the study, which was analyzed using Atlas.ti text analysis software. The text material was subjected to thematic coding. The coding process was hybrid, using both deductive and inductive coding. In deductive coding, dimensions were identified prior to the analysis to provide the subsequent master codes, while in inductive coding, individual interpretations were identified. In the deductive coding process, the six dimensions of institutional culture of Tierney (1988) were used as a basis for defining the dimensions that would later become the main codes, while the inductive process outlined the dimension of academics' perceptions of effectiveness. To increase reliability, intra-coding was employed, whereby one researcher coded the documents four times, with each coding being performed with a one-week variation. In this case, we could not count on the principle of personal triangulation (Sántha, 2015), but in order to minimize subjectivity, we included two additional researchers in the analysis process. By analyzing the corpus of texts associated with the codes, we have created a typology of institutional culture based on the perceptions of the academics, as well as types of teacher effectiveness. In the analysis of the interviews, our aim in creating the codes was to map out what types of institutional culture are drawn in the discourses of the academics and how the interpretation of effectiveness is represented in these discourses.

The ethical permission was granted by the Doctoral School of Education of the University of Debrecen (no: 4/2022). The data were collected anonymously and voluntarily, in compliance with ethical rules. The results were reported honestly, the submitted work is original, and the authorship reflects the consent of the individuals.

3. Results

3.1. The Types of Institutional Culture

During our research, we used the six dimensions of institutional culture by Tierney (1988) as a basis, and we examined the context in which the parts describing each dimension appear in the academics' responses and how they contribute to the description of institutional culture. By analyzing the text corpus, we identified the types of institutional culture that emerge from the perceptions of the academics. The two main axes of typification are the community-individualist axis and the institutional goals, individual goals axes. As regards empirical facts and the characteristic features of individual interpretations, four types of institutional culture were outlined, namely supportive institutional cultures that define their strength by unity, cohesive micro-communities, the lonely crowd, and egocentric monumental institutional cultures. Following the basic principles of the qualitative research approach, we did not name the types on the basis of theories or literature, but according to an inductive logic, taking into account the most characteristic features of empirical facts and individual interpretations. One of the results of our analysis is that despite the complexity of the descriptions and the variety of interpretations, we were able to form institutional culture types and classify the higher education institutions in which the focus group interviews took place. Furthermore, institutional culture types emerged that not only allow the classification of the institutions that were the subject of the study but also allow additional institutions to be classified in each category. A further result is that institutional culture types have emerged that not only allow the institutions under study to be classified, but additional institutions can also be fit into each category. What is more, the finding that a particular type of institutional culture may be applied to the institution as a whole, while smaller units therein, such as departments, institutes, or faculties, may reflect a different culture. In what follows, we describe the types of institutional culture that have emerged in detail.

Establishments belonging to a supportive institutional culture type, the strength of which is in unity, find their teaching environment to be infrastructurally appropriate. In addition to the infrastructural environment, the university also creates a unifying educational and cultural space for the region's s many ethnic groups, which suggests a social and cultural function that is wider than the perceived traditional function of higher education. Its mission is seen as based on its responsibility for the society of a region that is in many ways peripheral, therefore, for the academics the role of the institution in society is unquestionable. For the most part, this type of institutional culture can be used to describe those institutions which, in addition to being institutions intended to serve the majority nation, are also universities for the minority, providing it with academic and cultural environments as well as spheres for socialization. A key element of the strategy in these universities is to approach the staff with support and appreciation that goes beyond the relationship of employer and employee. The broad institutional role and operation in peripheral regions imply extended involvement in teaching, additional performance, and aid for teaching and research provided by the institution. The university might even stand by the academics and employees in the event of personal and family problems. The atmosphere of supportive institutional cultures which see their strength in unity, is positive and familial, something true not only of the smaller university units but also of the institution as a whole. The institutions described by this culture especially focus on students, ascribe great importance to knowing their students personally, give priority to showing empathy and establishing a trusted relationship, follow their students' future careers, and feel responsible for them. This type is therefore characterized by identification with the goals of the institution and the community, their success lying in supporting each other, in unity, and in community cohesion. They provide an appropriate environment for the fulfillment of their traditional functions, such as teaching, research and learning, but they also put emphasis on the function that the institution fulfills in social and cultural life.

The second type of institutional culture differs from the previous one mainly in the degree of institutional cohesion. This type of institutional culture is characterized by a loose set of cohesive micro-communities. Institutions of this type typically include a larger number of academics and students. Of course, from the outside, these institutions also give the impression of unity, but this is due to the unified image and the dominant culture that is characteristic of the institution. However, at the same time, it is the individual cultural interpretations of the smaller communities that are of real importance in the lives of the academics. This may be partly similar to and partly different from the dominant culture of the institution, so that its influence is undoubtedly felt in the institutional culture of the micro-communities. According to the perceptions of the academics, they can be defined as "a small community, a micro-community within a larger community" (Focus Group 4). These micro-communities can usually be spelled out at the level of the institute or department, and a common interpretation of certain dimensions of institutional culture can only be captured at this level. The dominant culture of their institution is usually not even within the focus of the individuals' attention. Their atmosphere is characterized by familiarity, inclusiveness, and support, similarly to the previous type of supportive institutional culture that defined their strengths in unity, but here they no longer attribute this support to the institution, but to their own community, which often includes their students. Within their own circles, they seek to improve focus on students, but there is also an emphasis on the relationship between individuals working together. Typically, they also have good relations with the leadership of their institute or department, defined by "paying attention, direct communication, and informality" (Focus Group 4). The cohesiveness of their community is outstanding, and these cohesive micro-communities can be explained both intellectually and physically (spatially). In the case of this type, the own goals of micro-communities that guide their strategies can be defined. These micro-community goals do not go against the dominant institutional culture, but rather integrate into it and shape it, building on their individual characteristics. The vulnerability of these types of institutional cultures may be that the lack of coherence and stability at the institutional level that also has an impact on micro-communities. They essentially differ from the supportive institutional culture type defined by unity, while that institutional culture type can bring the institution as a whole together, the cohesive micro-communities institutional culture type only provides the basis for small communities within a large unit to function together effectively.

We have identified third type of institutional culture as the "lonely crowd." Institutions belonging to this institutional culture type have a smaller student population compared to institutions of the previous types, yet unity is seen at the level of small communities. The institution-wide culture is either perceived as incomplete or unsupportive.

When looking at the dimensions of strategy and leadership, the characteristics of abandoned employees also emerge. In many cases, the workload is distributed asymmetrically across the teaching staff, but those who are effective are not valued enough. Compared to the previous types, the environmental dimension of the lonely crowd type of institutional culture is not adequate either, the employees in these institutions struggle with a lack of space, equipment, and facilities, the improvement of which is not a priority for the institution, which is obviously struggling to survive. As in the previous types, the student focus is also present in this type of institution, with students being given priority alongside teaching, research, and administrative work. This type of institutional culture embodies the institutions characterized by a student-focused, lonely, abandoned teaching community.

We have defined the egocentric monumental institutional culture as the fourth type. Similarly to the culture of cohesive micro-communities, the institutions which belong to this type have a large student population, and the culture of the micro-communities is influenced by the dominant culture of the institution, which can become unstable due to constant environmental changes. The institutional change that is being enhanced by the appearance of performance evaluation fundamentally influences this type of institutional culture, and all the dimensions of institutional culture that we have examined are affected by this change. Their atmosphere is highly variable, it is partly determined by the functioning micro-communities, but dominated by the changes that affect the institution, and therefore it can be characterized as such: an institutional atmosphere that could be corrected, can be rated as mediocre, fluctuating, and subject to improvement. In the case of relations, it is not the relations within the institution but those outside of the institution that are relevant, but "cooperation within the institution is becoming less and less effective" (Focus Group 6). The deterioration of cooperation within the institution is reflected in the transformation of relationships. The institutions belonging to this type are located at the top of the list of rank-fetishist higher education, but the culture of divisiveness and the assertion of individual interests is associated with a lack of identification with institutional goals.

The Table 7.1 illustrates the types of institutional culture with excerpts and keywords from the interviews.

Table 7.1: Types of institutional culture and its characteristics

Types of institutional culture	Supportive institutional cultures that define their strength by unity	Cohesive micro-communities	Lonely crowd institutional culture	Egocentric monumental institutional culture
Interview excerpt	*"Our building is our glory. Our institute is a citadel of the Hungarian community. It is the stronghold of all those who wish to be connected with the Hungarian people on some level"* (FG 3)	*"… every year we organize team-buildings, informal departmental meetings, which is really good for us"* (FG 7)	*"All lay loads on a willing horse, even more load"* (FG 5)	*"Cooperation within the institution is becoming less and less effective"* (FG 6)

(Continued)

Table 7.1: *(Continued)*

Types of institutional culture	Supportive institutional cultures that define their strength by unity	Cohesive micro-communities	Lonely crowd institutional culture	Egocentric monumental institutional culture
Keywords in the interviews	Support from the institution; recognition of each other's work; institutional motivation, good relations between colleagues	Family-friendly, small department; student-friendly institution; celebrations with colleagues; direct contact with the head of the department; team-building events	Micro-environments; lack of organizational culture and positive feedback	Hostile atmosphere among the colleagues

Note: Based on research interviews, compiled and edited by the author.

3.2. Types of Effectiveness of Academics

Regarding the attitudes of the academics toward performance evaluation, based on the focus group interviews, we have differentiated four types. The typology was defined based on the empirical facts recalled in the interviews and their individual interpretations. The four different types—those who are enthusiastic about research performance, those who are enthusiastic about teaching, those who consider research and publishing a (superfluous) nuisance and those who approach teaching from the perspective of an employee—were linked to workplace characteristics such as administrative work and the attitude of the academics toward it. The results of our research show that although the interviews were conducted with academics from institutions in different countries within the higher education region, with different cultural backgrounds, respondents face similar difficulties in teaching, research, and administrative tasks. In the countries surveyed, performance evaluation for the teaching staff has been introduced recently, which often creates tensions within the society of an institution. In many cases, in addition to research and teaching tasks, higher education staff are also burdened with administrative workload. Below, we present the types of that we have developed, examining for each type whether the academics do administrative work, and how it affects their effectiveness.

Academics who are enthusiastic about research performance put academic activity at the forefront of their work, for them, research is more important than teaching. Academics in this group consider themselves to be successful if they achieve professional success in the area of academia. Academics in this category also do administrative work, which they see as a burden. Academics enthusiastic about research perceive the recently introduced performance evaluation as positive. They believe that this gives the heads of the institutions an objective overall picture of the academic performance of their academics and that they see mutual feedback between the leadership and staff as important.

The vast majority of the academics interviewed could be classified as enthusiastic about teaching. This type includes academics who put teaching before research. They point out as a problem that teaching has to take a back seat to expectations when it comes to science metrics. They see mentoring, talent management, launching students, and preparing them for the National Scholarly Student's Association (national competition) as their most important tasks. Most of the people who are enthusiastic about teaching do administrative work, even if it is partially done to measure and possibly to recognize performance. In many cases, interviews revealed that they do not even enjoy accounting for their own performance. Some of the academics who are enthusiastic about teaching are happy to do administrative work and enjoy it. This category of academics mostly highlighted administrative tasks that are also related to teaching activity and student affairs. They had similar views on performance evaluation. They said that measurement was necessary, but that student feedback, rather than academic performance, should be the focus of performance evaluation. They did not consider measurements that evaluate academic performance to be objective, because they believed that higher education should primarily take into account the perspective of the students.

From the interview transcripts, it was clear that the most successful academics are those who are enthusiastic about both teaching and research. They believed that research is essential to teaching. The best way to provide up-to-date information is to be up-to-date with findings of the latest research. Many also stressed that they can encourage students to pursue a research career only if they themselves carry out research. Those enthusiastic about both research performance and teaching were the most positive about the introduction of performance assessment in higher education institutions. With regards to performance evaluation, those equally committed to research and teaching stressed that this way their results could be quantified, making them more valued within the institution. Furthermore, for those on the axis of these two types, performance evaluation acts as a motivating force.

The results of our interview survey revealed that, among those who are enthusiastic about both teaching and research, a large proportion of the respondents are involved in administrative tasks in addition to teaching and research. The overwhelming majority of respondents said that taking on administrative tasks takes time away from research and class preparation. This is therefore seen as a hindrance: "What I enjoy is teaching and research, and what I don't like so much but unfortunately have to do are administrative activities." (FG 1). Nevertheless, these results of the interview research highlight that those who are more successful in both teaching and research are those who also perform administrative functions. Presumably, the reason for this is that those who are committed to both teaching and research can take a heavier workload, they have a better understanding of the requirements, and the employer is more willing to entrust an administrative task to an effective academic. Furthermore, they suggest that, although the administrative role takes a lot of time away from teaching and research, it does not change the force field itself.

In the third type, we have included academics who consider research and publication a (superfluous) nuisance. The interview research also revealed that some academics see academic work, which is essential for higher education, as a burden. Those in this category believe that the academic demands of performance evaluation often come at the expense of teaching. Several highlighted that the evaluation system does not provide realistic information on the work of academics and that tensions between colleagues have increased significantly since its introduction. Among academics who consider research and publication to be an unnecessary burden, only one academic takes on administrative tasks. This person says that in administrative work they are able to fulfill their potential. The remaining majority who consider research and publication a superfluous burden prefer teaching, though their responses show that they are not really committed to it. They are close to our fourth type.

The fourth type identified was those who approach teaching from the perspective of an employee. Of the academics surveyed, this category was the least numerous. Academics in this category are less motivated to teach and are also less enthusiastic about research tasks. None of those in the fourth category have an administrative position. They have a negative view of performance evaluation: they do not consider research performance or student feedback to be objective.

The Table 7.2 illustrates the interview excerpts and keywords from the interviews that belong to each type of effectiveness.

Table 7.2: Types of effectiveness and their characteristics

Type of effectiveness	**Enthusiastic about research performance**	**Enthusiastic about teaching**	**Consider research and publication a (superfluous) nuisance**	**Approach teaching from the perspective of an employee**
Interview excerpt	*"Basically, I prefer to think of science, the scientific path, as the fulfillment of an academic."* (FG 5)	*"The problem is that people are judged by science metrics. So, the those who have a lot of publications can get ahead."* (FG 6)	*"I would certainly make a very big distinction between the academic career and the teaching career. An academic who has dedicated his life to research, but because has to teach, is going to put in minimal effort."* (FG 7)	*"Anyone can stand in front of the projector and read the text, thus presenting the lesson."* (FG 2)
Keywords in the interviews	Recommend publications, administrative tasks at the expense of scientific research, feedback from the management	Mentoring, talent management, administrative tasks, student feedback, job placement as a performance indicator	Negative evaluation of teaching and research expectations	Lack of motivation; student disinterest

Note: Based on research interviews, compiled and edited by the author.

3.3. Institutional Culture and Interpretations of Effectiveness

During our analysis, we have established that certain conceptions of effectiveness are dominant in certain types of institutional cultures, but there are interpretations of effectiveness that are present in more than one type of institution:

The efficacy of supportive institutional cultures whose strength is in unity lies in the excellence of their academics' teaching, research, and administration. They consider teaching to be the most important, since their institutional mission is to focus on fulfilling other social and cultural capacities. This ensures learning in the mother tongue and the supply of qualified staff for various fields. In addition to teaching, research plays a prominent role among the teaching staff, and the institution provides the necessary conditions and venues for research, such as libraries, various international databases, and adequately equipped classrooms. Institutions that have this institutional culture not only expect their academics to perform but also strive to create the conditions necessary for productive teaching. These institutions do their utmost to guarantee their survival and continuous development, so that, in addition to their traditional jobs (teaching and research), academics also perform administrative duties where necessary, which they usually do not see as a burden. This perception of effectiveness is true for most of the members of the institution, as it is seen as a result of unity and cooperation.

The institutional culture of the cohesive micro-communities showed very similar characteristics to those of the supportive institutional culture. However, while individuals belonging to the latter think of their institution as a whole as an indivisible unit, individuals belonging to the former only perceive their own micro-community in a similar way. This implies that the academics in cohesive micro-communities have the same understanding of effectiveness, the same importance for teaching, research, and administrative functions, while they do not think at the institutional level, but exclusively at the level of their own micro-community.

In case of the academics that belong to the lonely crowd institutional culture, teaching has a prominent role in interpreting effectiveness. Still, in terms of this activity as well, they are typically considered a community left to their own devices. Their institution does little or nothing to create the conditions that would enable effective teaching and research. They often suffer from a shortage of teaching space, personal and community areas, but also from inadequate infrastructure. These individuals often feel that their concerns are not listened to and are not a priority for the institution. This way, given this absence, the institution's standards that are set for the academics cannot be met.

Academics in the egocentric monumental institutional culture prioritize individual interests, focus little on teaching, they take on administrative jobs in exchange for renumeration, and prefer research work. They are mainly adept at the performance evaluation of the institution, they do not strive to develop as a community but rather as an individual, and they favor their own interests.

4. Discussion

In our qualitative interview research, we sought to answer the question: to what extent the changes affecting higher education in general have made uniform the culture of each institution, and whether the different types of institutional culture in higher education entail specific interpretations of academic performance? Our results suggest that, despite the fact that higher education institutions face the same challenges and that the region in which they operate has different characteristics

Table 7.3: Evaluation of the academic effectiveness of each type of institutional culture

Types of institutional culture	**Supportive institutional cultures that define their strength by unity**	**Cohesive micro-communities**	**Lonely crowd institutional culture**	**Egocentric monumental institutional culture**
Evaluation of academic effectiveness	excelling in teaching, research and administrative activities not only expect performance from their academics, but also strive to create the conditions necessary for effective teaching	see their own micro-community as a unit attach equal importance to education, research and administrative functions, and do not think at the institutional level, but only at the level of their micro-communities	education is a priority in their understanding of effectiveness, but they are also typically understood as a community left to their own devices in this activity their institution does little or nothing to create the conditions that would promote effective teaching and research	academics prioritize individual interests, have little focus on teaching, take on administrative functions in return for an allowance, research work is what they prefer are mainly aligned to benchmarking, they do not seek to develop as a community, but individually, prioritizing their own interests

Note: Based on research interviews, compiled and edited by the author.

compared to other European regions, they are characterized by a significantly different institutional culture (Table 7.3). Drawing on the multidimensional research model of institutional culture, the academics' perceptions of the institutional mission, the relationship with the environment, institutional socialization, the nature of information flow, the way of strategizing and managing, but also the understanding of the academics' effectiveness as a separate dimension emerged as a result of the academics' narratives. Building on these, we were able to identify four types of institutional culture and four further interpretations of effectiveness. Overall, it can be concluded that performance-based evaluation has entered very different institutional worlds today. In the first two types, institutional and individual objectives are better harmonized. A supportive institutional culture that defines its strengths as a unit belongs to a cohesive, effective institutional model, while a culture characterized by cohesive micro-communities belongs to a fragmented, but still effective model that functions as a unit. In the other two institutional cultures, organizational members put their individual sense of purpose ahead of the institutional purpose, individual effectiveness does not coincide with institutional effectiveness, and the institution is not able to align all organizational members with its purpose. So, on the one hand, the burden is unevenly distributed within the organization, and, on the other hand, in the pursuit of individual goals, institutional goals are often overlooked, ultimately leading to the institution not functioning effectively.

Comparing academics' views on effectiveness and performance appraisal, we found that there are also significant differences between academics in this area. Those who identify themselves primarily as researchers also consider scientific results to be measurable, so performance appraisal is very positively received. This is mainly because of the positive feedback and the need for recognition. Those who see themselves primarily as academics do not see the purpose of their institution or their own work in research, rather, teaching and talent management are more critical to be done by the academic. Their expectation of performance assessment is that it should measure educational effectiveness. A combination of the first two types also occurs, and they were the most positive about performance appraisal, hoping that it would be able to detect the work they invested in education and research, also providing an opportunity to value that work.

The third and fourth interpretations of effectiveness can be grasped practically by their negatives, since academics who find research and publication a nuisance are not only skeptical about the validity of benchmarking. It is seen as a dangerous phenomenon that upsets the status quo within the organization and is predicted to increase conflict and even hostility, that is, they have only negative expectations. As with the former, the fourth concept of teaching effectiveness is characterized by the fact that the academic identifies himself or herself through failure, as being unsuccessful or burned out in teaching. This type also does not believe in the validity of the results of performance measurement, especially student assessment, and is not prepared to explain possible poorer results. Overall, it seems that, on the one hand, there are huge differences between academics' perceptions of their profession. On the other hand, performance appraisal is a long-awaited and hopeful act for some academics, while others see it as an unnecessary or harmful intervention. Moreover, our analysis also shows that the introduction of competitive assessment in institutions is not without risk, because some academics expect praise and recognition. The lack of such accolades may lead to disillusionment among better performers. The skeptics, however, already have their negative scenario of discord and conflict ready. At the same time, the diversity of occupations and work styles identified here highlights the need for performance evaluation in higher education institutions, given the inequalities in workload and the phenomena that undermine the effective functioning of organizations.

Comparing the typology of institutional culture with the typology of effectiveness, it is clear that the institutions that are home to a supportive institutional culture that defines their strength in unity and a cohesive micro-communities institutional culture are most characterized by academics who are enthusiastic about both education and research. Lone mass institutional culture academics are not satisfied with the incentives and conditions provided by the institution and therefore consider research productivity to be unattainable. Teaching, however, is of paramount importance to them. Despite the aforementioned lack, they are student-centered, and talent management and mentoring are in their eyes essential. On this basis, we can say that the academics from this culture type can be predominantly classified as enthusiasts for education. In the self-centered monumental institutions, the type of academic who is motivated by individual success, who values performance appraisal positively, and who wants to be at the forefront of academic achievement, emerges. They belong to the achievement type of those who are enthusiastic about research performance. Those who feel that education or research, or both, are a burden are mainly found in the lonely crowd and the self-centered monumental institutional culture.

Conclusion

Our research has shown that, despite facing essentially the same social and policy challenges, the institutions studied have been able to develop very different institutional cultures. The diversity of academics' perceptions of profession is reflected in the diversity of their views on effectiveness. Although the vast majority of respondents consider teaching to be their main activity, their views on performance appraisal reflect the fact that there are some academics who do not feel comfortable in either role and are also afraid of performance appraisal.

The limitations of our research are due to the specificity of the focus group interview. On the one hand the number of respondents is small compared to the population, on the other hand it reflects their composition only in a few aspects. What is more, the influence of the respondents on each other during the interviews and the resulting silence of opinions must also be taken into account in this type of data collection. In the present research, respondents reflect the organizational and national diversity of the institutional palette and also represent institutions by gender and discipline. In this case, though, there were also some invited respondents who declined to participate, so, in practice there may be additional faculty opinions and views. Albeit respondents seemed to openly express even contradictory views during the data collection, the lack of educational or research-publication results can be stigmatizing in this context, and it is possible that the self-assessments expressed in this context were not entirely reliable. We believe that the focus group interview seemed to be an appropriate method for the exploratory phase of the research, and that we were able to identify a wide range of opinions. As a continuation of the research, we have developed a measurement tool for the multidimensional assessment of institutional culture based on the views revealed in this study.

The policy use of the results can be helpful even at this stage, as the institutions being studied are in the process of improving their performance evaluation systems and, more importantly, the managers of the institutions are in a position to make decisions based on the data. Managers may choose to challenge the reality of the performance gaps identified and maintain the usual system of hierarchy and recognition. Even so, this may result in the disillusionment of those who expect recognition from performance appraisals and who are doing a hard job well.

References

Barton, A. (2019). Preparing for Leadership Turnover in Christian Higher Education: Best Practices in Succession Planning. *Christian Higher Education*, *18*(1–2), 37–53.

Batugal, M. L. C., & Tindowen, D. J. C. (2019). Influence of Organizational Culture on Teachers' Organizational Commitment and Job Satisfaction: The Case of Catholic Higher Education Institutions in the Philippines. *Universal Journal of Educational Research*, *7*(11), 2432–2443.

Berger, P., Grace, D., & Fokas, E. (2021). *Religious America, Secular Europe. A Theme and Variations*. Routledge.

Bess, J. L., & Dee, J. R. (2012). *Understanding College and University Organization. Theories for Effective Policy Practice*. Stylus Publishing.

Bradley, G. (1992). Increasing student retention. *Youth Studies*, *11*(1), 37–42.

Ceglédi, T., Fényes, H., & Pusztai, G. (2022). The effect of resilience and gender on the persistence of higher education students. *Social Sciences*, *11*(3), 93.

Ceglédi, T., & Dabney-Fekete, I. D. (2023). Curricular and Extracurricular Learning among Students with Resilience Potential. Social Inequalities in Higher Education. *Central European Journal of Educational Research*, *5*(1), 37–42.

Dabney-Fekete, I. D. (2020). *Nemzetköziesedő tudomány—A felsőoktatásban dolgozó oktatók nemzetközi aktivitása* [Internationalisation of science—International activity of higher education staff]. CHERD-Hungary.

Dasanayaka, C. H., Abeykoon, C., Ranaweera, R. A. A. S., & Koswatte, I. (2021). The Impact of the Performance Appraisal Process on Job Satisfaction of the Academic Staff in Higher Educational Institutions. *Education Sciences*, *11*(10), 623.

Demeter-Karászi, Zs. (2023). *A felekezeti felsőoktatás intézményi kultúrája hallgatói perspektívából. Szektorközi összehasonlító kutatás egy határmenti régióban* [Institutional Culture in Denominational Higher Education from the Students' Perspective. Intersectoral Comparison in a Border Region] Doctoral dissertation, University of Debrecen.

Dusa, Á. R., & Dabney-Fekete, I. D. (2024). Nemzetközi hallgatók magyar kultúrához való viszonyulása egy kelet-magyarországi egyetemen [International students' attitudes toward Hungarian culture at a university in Eastern Hungary]. In G. Pusztai, Á. Engler, A. Hrabéczy & Á. Bencze (Eds.), *Mesterség és intelligencia az oktatáskutatásban* [Teaching artificiality and intelligence in education research]. CHERD-Hungary.

Cintron, R., & Flaniken, F. (2011). Performance appraisal: A supervision or leadership tool. *International Journal of Business and Social Science*, *2*(17), 29–37.

Florenthal, B., & Tolstikov-Mast, Y. (2012). Organizational Culture: Comparing Faculty and Staff Perspectives. *Journal of Higher Education Theory and Practice*, *12*(6), 81–90.

Gaus, N., Tang, M., & Akil, M. (2017). Organisational culture in higher education: mapping the way to understanding cultural research. *Journal of Further and Higher Education*, *43*(6), 1–13. <https://doi.org/10.1080/0309877X.2017.1410530>

Hrubos, I. (2012). *Elefánttoronyból világtorony. A felsőoktatási intézmények misszióinak bővülése, átalakulása* [From elephant tower to world tower. Expanding and transforming the missions of higher education institutions]. AULA Kiadó Kft.

Kozma, T., Polónyi, I., & Pusztai, G. (2017). Higher Education Systems and Institutions: Hungary. In P. N. Teixeira & J. C. Shin (Eds.), *Encyclopedia of International Higher Education Systems and Institutions* (pp. 1–9). Springer. <https://doi.org/10.1007/978-94-017-9553-1_544-1>

Kwiek, M. (2018). International Research Collaboration and International Research Orientation: Comparative findings about European academics. *Journal of Studies in International Education*, *22*(1), 1–25. <https://doi.org/10.1177/1028315317747084>

Kwiek, M. (2019). *Changing European academics: A comparative study of social stratification, work patterns and research productivity*. Routledge.

Marginson, S. (2016). The worldwide trend to high participation higher education: Dynamics of social stratification in inclusive systems. Higher Education, 72, 413–434.

Marginson, S., & Rhoades, G. (2002). Beyond national states, markets, and systems of higher education: A glonacal agency heuristic. *Higher Education*, *43*(3) 281–309.

Masouleh, Z. D., & Allahyari, M. S. (2017). The predictability of organisational culture for commitment among faculty members: evidence from Iran higher education. *International Journal of Management in Education*, *11*(1), 94–109.

Mohammadi, M., Yeganeh, E. M., & Rad, T. D. (2010). The Relationship between Faculty Members' Perception of Organizational Culture Types and their Preferences for Instruction and Counselling in Iranian College of Education and Psychology. *Procedia Social and Behavioral Sciences*, *5*, 1841–1848.

Pusztai, G. (2015). *Pathways to success in higher education: Rethinking the social capital theory in the light of institutional diversity.* Peter Lang.

Rizzi, M. (2019). Defining Catholic Higher Education in Positive, Not Negative, Terms. *Journal of Catholic Education*, *22*(2), 1–25. <http://dx.doi.org/https://doi.org/10.15365/joce.2202012019>

Sántha, K. (2015). *Trianguláció a pedagógiai kutatásban* [Triangulation in pedagogical research]. Eötvös József Könyvkiadó.

Schimank, U., & Winnes, M. (2000). Beyond Humboldt? The relationship between teaching and research in European university systems. *Science and Public Policy*, *27*(6), 397–408.

Teichler, U. (2008). Diversification? Trends and Explanations of the Shape and Size of Higher Education. *Higher Education*, *56*(3), 349–379.

Tierney, W. G. (1988). Organizational Culture in Higher Education. The Journal of Higher Education, 59(1), 2–21. <https://doi.org/10.1080/00221546.1988.11778301>

Tierney, W. G., & Lanford, M. (2018). Institutional Culture in Higher Education. In P. N. Teixeira & J. C. Shin (Eds.), *Encyclopedia of International Higher Education Systems and Institutions* (pp. 1–9). Springer. <https://doi.org/10.1007/978-94-017-9553-1_544-1>

Triventi, M. (2013). The Role of Higher Education Stratification in the Reproduction of Social Inequality in the Labor Market. *Research in Social Stratification and Mobility*, *32*, 45–63. <https://doi.org/10.1016/j.rssm.2013.01.003>

Trow, M. (1972). The Expansion and Transformation of Higher Education. *International Review of Education*, *18*(1), 61–84.

Warter, L. (2019). The Impact of Organizational Culture in Higher Education. Case Study. *Journal of Intercultural Management and Ethics*, *2019*(2), 173–200.

8. (Inclusive) Teaching Practice and Well-Being Among Higher Education Academics in Central and Eastern Europe

Anett Hrabéczy & Zsófia Kocsis

ABSTRACT
Higher education is constantly expanding, diversifying and attracting more students from different backgrounds. To meet the long-term needs of the learning society, higher education needs to be able to accommodate learners, innovate teaching and learning methods. Previous research and policy have highlighted that higher education, as a labor-intensive sector, can ensure quality only through the well-being of its academics. However, we have limited data on the well-being of specific groups in the educational community and how well-being is related to educational activities and the quality of education in the case of these groups. Our research seeks to answer the question of what pedagogical approaches and activities are prevalent among the distinguished groups of academics (teaching-focused academics, academics with an administrative focus, research-focused academics, academic leaders), whether the inclusive approach appears among them, and how these approaches relate to the well-being of the academics studied. To investigate this, we applied a quantitative research method and used a questionnaire to survey academics working in higher education in Central and Eastern Europe (N=853). One of the most important findings of our research is that time- and energy-consuming pedagogical activities and approaches do not negatively affect academics' well-being, but these pedagogical activities can only be performed with sufficient efficiency if high levels of well-being are present. Our findings can be an important starting point for policymakers and university leaders to improve the efficiency and quality of their education.

Keywords: well-being, inclusion, higher education, higher education pedagogy

Introduction

Over the last decade, higher education has been transformed over a generation, bringing about a series of political, structural and institutional changes (Walsh, 2018). The changes in higher education are being driven by factors such as globalization, digitalization, decolonization and the development of a knowledge-based society. The massification of higher education has led to the emergence of heterogeneous groups of students in terms of age, occupational status, geographical and social background. Higher education institutions are less likely to have a monopoly on the provision of education services. The need for lifelong learning, and the competitive environment of change require higher education institutions to be responsive and flexible. To meet the long-term needs of the learning society, higher education must be able to innovate (Fitzgerald, 2012).It is continuously confronted by new challenges, having to meet ever-widening economic and social expectations, thus, along with the function of training up intellectuals, it is becoming more and more important for higher education institutions to raise up professionals with specialized knowledge, developing competencies according to the needs of the labor market and society. Both adapting to challenges and changes reflect the policy decisions, which constantly call for higher education institutions' supply of courses to meet the demands of the knowledge-based economy (Castro & Levy, 2001; Hurtado, 2007; Teichler, 2011, Harrison, 2017; Enslin & Hedge 2024).

In parallel with expansion, the reinterpretation of the role of the state has led to a rapid worldwide invasion of higher education in the last decade, rooted in neo-liberal public policy concepts of business and cost-effectiveness, which understand the institution to be a competitive market actor struggling to increase revenue, the academics as workers describable by quantitative performance indicators, and the students as consumers or products (Neave, 1998; Amaral, 2008). We can also see in international special literature that more and more the questions of effectiveness move to the forefront: how can an institution become successful? how can dropout be decreased? how can skills needed in the labor market be improved upon? how can an institution support teaching and learning? Higher education is a sector that greatly needs labor, where it can ensure appropriate quality by leaning upon the skillsets of its employees. Therefore, the most important actor and former in the above processes is the academic staff (Elliott, 2017; Kálmán, 2021; Pusztai et al., 2022; Dabney-Fekete 2020; Pusztai et al. 2015). In our study, we strive to uncover how academics in higher education feel about their teaching activities and about their support of students. Alongside discovering the characteristics of teaching activities, we also focus on the well-being of the academics. After all, in order for academics to take on the above challenges more successfully, their well-being is paramount. For, if the academics are undermotivated and have high stress levels, the institution cannot operate effectively either (Bell et al., 2012).

Teichler & Höhle (2013) highlight that access to research funding is the lowest among the various categories of resources, facilities and personnel for academics in Europe, and while there is little enthusiasm for academic work conditions, there are no major complaints. The expansion of higher education has significantly increased the number of academics, leading to a more differentiated profession with varying norms, working habits, and incomes across countries, generations, and disciplines (see EUROAC project). Ongoing academic restructuring has made the work environment more complex and stressful than in previous decades, with further changes expected.

Given the increasing complexity and hurdles in the academic profession, our research is essential in exploring teaching approaches, teacher competencies, and student support, particularly in relation to workplace well-being. Understanding these factors can help address the evolving demands of higher education and contribute to improving academic work conditions. The first part of the study deals with teaching approaches, teacher competencies and student support, and with the most critical theoretical approaches regarding workplace well-being. In the following section, we will introduce the methodological aspects of the study and will explain the results of the quantitative research. Following the discussion of the results will be the introduction of limitations, and the detailing of suggestions.

1. Theoretical Background

1.1. Changing Higher Education

Higher education is growing faster, diversifying and attracting more and more students from different backgrounds. The heterogeneous groups of students entering higher education through expansion have increased the scope for institutions to address and, where possible, compensate for inequalities arising from objective disadvantages. Through internationalization, another fundamental task and interest of higher education is not only to increase opportunities for students from different social and economic backgrounds, but also to make their higher education institution attractive to foreign students through successful international cooperation (Lewis, 2017). What is more, the accelerated pace of the information revolution and scientific progress is changing the skills that can be acquired in higher education. This change requires the transfer of practical knowledge alongside theoretical knowledge. Moreover, this requires information about the needs of the labor market, so institutions must play an economic role in addition to their academic one and develop partnerships with labor market players. It is of particular importance that academics are also in-informed about the stipulations of the knowledge economy (Teichler, 2011; Elliott, 2017). The modernization of training course content implies improvements be made to pedagogical and methodological culture. Institutions must increase the effectiveness of education by improving their pedagogical and pedagogical approaches to higher education, the delivery of knowledge, the organization of education, and the widespread use of new knowledge-sharing techniques. Adjustments will also be made in the development of an active learning environment, and the practical knowledge and competences expected and used in the labor market (Hurtado, 2007; Teichler, 2011). The changing world is a common topic of interest in higher education. Much research analyses change, much teaching about it is being done, and great efforts are being made by higher education staff to prepare students for it. Yet, employers are increasingly reporting that graduates are not adequately equipped for that world, as the world of work itself has also shifted significantly (Harrison, 2017). The varying demands on graduates are also driven by the process of internationalization and globalization (Kivinen & Nurmi, 2003; Teichler, 2011). Higher education institutions no longer have a monopoly on educational services, as a new competitive situation has emerged in the learning society, and lifelong learning has become a lifelong necessity for almost everyone. This kind of need requires continuous flexibility and rapid response from higher education institutions. In this context of constant change, the roles of education providers are increasingly blurred, as higher education no longer involves the full-time commitment of both academics and students. And for higher education to be able to accommodate learners and meet the long-term needs of the learning society, a change in teaching and learning methods is essential (Cross, 1987). For this renewal to be a successful, the work and role of academics, and their well-being, are irreplaceable. The international literature also highlights that changes in higher education have altered the position of academics and the higher education institution as a workplace. Higher education used to be a flexible, secure, relaxed and socially recognized workplace, and these factors protected academics from workplace stress. After the expansion of higher education, this is less true. The massification, diversification, internationalization and service-orientedness of higher education has led to a broadening of the tasks and roles of academics and, consequently, to higher expectations (Dabney-Fekete et al., 2024). Demands and requirements are emerging as a major stress factor, negatively affecting the well-being of academics (Bell et al., 2012; Kinman, 2014; Malik et al., 2017).

1.2. Defining the Characteristics of Teacher Activities

According to the literature, one of the key tasks of educational institutions, beyond the transfer of knowledge, is to provide feedback on students' skills. Consequently, the assessment of students' competencies and the development of skills based on these assessments are becoming increasingly important in higher education as well <https://www.mdpi.com/2227-7102/13/10/1024> (Smith & Sodano, 2011; Teichler, 2011; Harrison 2017). As a result, the assessment of students' competencies and the skill development built upon these assessments are gaining increasing prominence in higher education (Enslin & Hedge, 2024).

In relation to international research, studies in increasing number address teacher identity in higher education. Certain studies examine how it is possible for academics to maintain such an identity that comprises in itself care teaching in the present higher educational system, which often gives priority to the metrics of generating income and doing research over transformative teaching (Nairz-Wirth & Feldmann, 2019). Multiple factors contribute to the formation of the teacher identity of academics. While they considered maintaining contact with students and the development programs of colleagues elements that strengthen teacher identity, they viewed the broader higher education context as a restricting effect. Furthermore, they felt the effect of the immediate work environment to be either strengthening or restricting, depending on whether the instruction at the department is evaluated or not. Competencies, the feeling of belonging and appreciation, and commitment and envisioning of a future career path all play a role in forming teacher identity. The results point to the formation of teacher identity as a rough/ difficult process occurring in a higher education environment (Lankveld et al., 2017). Teaching has become a more problematic, more controlled, and more complex activity, their research approaches identity as a form of specifying the various levels of academic work (Laiho et al., 2020).

Teichler & Höhle (2013) examine various teaching methods in higher education. Based on their results, classroom lecturing is the most common teaching method, used by 95% of respondents, but other methods play a crucial role in student motivation and competence development. University professors and senior academics at other higher education institutions employ various approaches, including individualized instruction (66%), project-based learning (46%), practice instruction or laboratory work (44%) and ICT-based learning (30%). Academics in the United Kingdom and Finland use the most diverse teaching methods, followed by those in Ireland, Croatia, and Italy. In contrast, Austria has the least variety, with Germany also showing a limited range of teaching approaches. Academics in Croatia are strongly practice-oriented. Academics at universities in Poland clearly differ from those in other countries as regards teaching: they spend a relatively large amount of their time on teaching and express relatively often preference for teaching. Among junior staff at higher education institutions, those in Poland spend much time on teaching activities. Less than one-fifth of university professors in some European countries state that teaching and research are hardly compatible. This is the case for almost half in Poland and three quarters in Croatia.

A key task of modern higher education is to align curricula and qualifications with the skill demands of the knowledge economy, ensuring graduates are well-prepared for the labor market (Gill, 2018; Lexis et al., 2021). However, as Pabian et al. (2011) highlight, political and economic transitions in post-communist countries have made this transformation particularly complex. At the international level, the function of teaching-learning and the improvement of the quality of education in higher education is becoming increasingly valued, and academics are key players in this process, but in Central and Eastern Europe, research has been conducted on the identity and mindset of academics (Kálmán, 2019; 2021), the quality of education (Kovács, 2016; Kováts & Temesi, 2018) and students' perceptions of teaching methods (Berényi & Deutsch, 2018; Kocsis & Pusztai, 2024), educational development opportunities (Pleschová, 2024) or importance of skills (Gawrycka et al., 2021; Horváthová et al. 2022; Poláková et al., 2023). Higher education developmental projects are aiming for learning-oriented education culture more and more, thus, in the course of moving from teaching-oriented to learning-oriented, the role of academics also changes from knowledge-bearer to learning-promoter. This process clearly affects the professional identity of academics (Trautwein, 2018). Academics' views on teaching and learning both have an impact on their teaching practice, in how effective and how open to innovation they are (Trigwell et al., 1994). The teaching view mainly refers to how academics form the definition of good teaching, while the mode of teaching approach is the holistic interpretation of teaching, which covers an academics' teaching strategies and intentions (Kálmán, 2021; Rotidi et al., 2017). In the interest of discovering what academics think about their teaching activities, besides the teaching approaches, we also examine teacher competencies. Teacher competencies partially refers to the examining of academics' views, an important starting point for this could be teacher development, and thus we can get a more nuanced picture of teacher activities alongside the courses and weekly classes (Kálmán, 2021; Lankveld et al., 2017). In the professional context, competency means complex, psychological attributes which mutually comprise in themselves attitudes, skills, and abilities (Aziz et al. 2014). At the international level, multiple studies deal with the formational of teachers' competency framework (see: Ödalen et al., 2019; Kálmán, 2021).

1.3. The Inclusive Teaching Approach in the Light of Academic Work

The movement toward learning-centeredness parallel with the diversification of the student society also brought academics face-to-face with a new type of challenge. It became expected of institutions and teaching policy to, along with taking into account students' varied abilities and individual needs, make knowledge accessible for the widest range of students.

One of the lessons to be learned from the fresh and the past century's researches is that the problems that arose, from the beginning of inclusive higher education up to today, seem to researchers to be unsolvable. Among these problems, the special literature counts institution accessibility (included here is the approachability of classrooms, which can affect how an academic staff views the participation and progression in class by students with handicaps), access to teaching material and study aids, an academic staff's attitude, the insufficient flow of information (communication between student and academic staff, the accessibility or lack thereof of websites, and electronic information systems), the existence, acceptance, and insurance of institutional services by academics. Since the 1950s the above-mentioned factors have been the most pronounced research questions in the field, but these mainly come from non-traditional students, fewer studies were published dealing with the analysis of academic perspectives. The results in connection with this show that, according to academics' own admission, they have a positive attitude toward students with disabilities, and they work hard to stay informed about what their responsibilities are in teaching and supporting those who have some kind of disability (Debrand & Salzberg, 2005; Murray et al., 2008; Salzberg et al., 2002). Despite this, however, the affected students most often experience the opposite (Kurth & Mellard, 2002). Institutional and teacher activities comprise in themselves the appearance of inclusivity, but despite appearances, students with disabilities still end up on the fringe (Holloway, 2001). His conclusions show, in order to overcome this, steps must be taken at a faculty level. In connection with this, though, results can vary from major to major, discipline to discipline, depending on what institutional culture is typical of the given course, and what the quality and quantity of interactions are between the majority of students and academics (Heubeck & Latimer, 2002; Hrabéczy, 2019).

Kálmán (2013) writes about three learning-centered approaches in the case of special student groups, one of these is the approach based on learning attributes. In regard to this, Kálmán (2013) says that compensating for learning disabilities is no longer a part of today's practice, since the changed learning environment is a challenge for all students. Thus, he finds it more important to offer support through various programs, promoting becoming a self-regulated learner. The question may arise, what role academic staff can play in this, during everyday classes. Previous research shows that earlier it was typical to compensate for hardships that arose in learning, namely after researchers in the 1980s started examining students with learning disorders and creating all sorts of programs for them (Cordoni, 1982; Hoy & Gregg, 1986; Nelson & Lignugaris-Lraft, 1989; Robinson, 1986; Sicoli, 1985; Stalcup & Freeman, 1980; Strichart & Mangrum, 1986; Vogel, 1983). Academics and public opinion confused those with learning disabilities and those with mental disabilities. What is more, they did not understand some of the basic characteristics of certain disabilities (e.g., to academic staff, a student with a disability simply meant a student in a wheelchair) (Chard & Couch, 1998; Hadjikakou & Hartas, 2008; Kalivoda & Higbee, 1998; Hill, 1996; Reindal, 1995; Tinklin & Hall, 1999). There are results regarding how academics, lacking knowledge about students with disabilities, attribute the learning problems of the students with disabilities to the individual's preparedness, and completely ignore the need to understand the combination of students' learning problems and needs [(Heubeck & Latimer, 2002; Ryan 2005). In this regard, how the development and training of academics' inclusive approach will be done has become a real R&D problem. These studies mainly present the preliminary measurements of the results, upon which programs can be built (Cunningham, 2013; Langørgen & Magnus, 2018; Karlovicz, 2013; Kendall, 2017; Martins et al., 2017; Moriña, 2018).

1.4. The Ties Between the Work and Well-Being of Academics

The changes affecting higher education also weighed upon the situation of academics, since these changes transformed the higher education institutions, as workplaces, as well. The previously sure, calm, flexible, and socially recognized position that was the academic staff changed significantly in the internationalization and diversification of higher education. Academic tasks and roles expanded, requirements multiplied, which meant more stress factors and greater negative effect on well-being (Bell et al., 2012; Malik et al., 2017). Well-being is the combination of positive emotions, engagement, relationships, meaning, and accomplishment (PERMA) (Seligman, 2011). Workplace well-being is an employee's satisfaction with his work life (Akram, 2019). In the job demands-resources (JD-R theory) model the resources related to the job and the negative work conditions are mentioned, as they directly affect the employees' stress levels and health. By negative factors, we mean such characteristics as intense cognitive, emotional, and physical and/or psychological burdens, which require significant effort to complete a task (Bakker & Demerouti, 2014).

Iyali et al. (2020) sets apart the stress factors that have ties to workplace requirements (long hours, pressure to publish, administrative loads), and those which restrict effectiveness (bad communication, lack of technical support, etc.). Besides all this, they shine light on certain stress factors, the existence of which also comes with negative consequences, such as lack of respect and workplace safety, personal conflict, or harassment. The factors exuding stress come from the factors connected to work, such as the overload of taking the initiative, a goal-oriented culture, due to the behavior of students, or a result of high expectations. Furthermore, negative environmental and occupational characteristics also bear weight on well-being (conflict of roles, difference in views, inconsistent workloads, fear of evaluation).

The above stress factors' effect on physical and psychological well-being (Alqarni, 2021), along with their effect on the balance of work and private life are undergirded by countless studies (Winefield et al., 2014), just like the role that long-term workplace stress plays in burnout. Experiencing positive emotions, being in a good mood, and having the positive social support of colleagues all function as resources. Along with the social and cultural factors, individual psychological attributes also contribute to the well-being of academics (Jin et al., 2021; MacIntyre et al., 2019). The academics who have access to a great extent to these resources will enjoy their jobs more and be more committed (Han et al., 2020). The well-being of academics is irreplaceable not only on the individual level, but on the organizational level as well, since, if academics are undermotivated, tired, and do not feel well (Bell et al., 2012), their high stress levels and low well-being will negatively influence the operation of the organization. Higher education institutions need to actively react to the results of worker well-being, to strive to create an effective, supportive, academic environment (Brewster et al., 2022).

Aside from several Hungarian studies (see: Kálmán, 2019; 2021; Alpár et al., 2018) we know little about what academics think about their own work in teaching, about teaching itself, and about what ties their teacher activities have with their well-being. In our study, therefore, we also seek an answer to the question: amid the expectations placed on today's higher educational environment and academics, besides continuous methodological innovation, are academics capable of implementing their inclusive approach into their practice? And also, what sort of ties exist between openness toward this implementation and academics' well-being? Our study's novelty comes from the formation of academic staff and teacher activity types, as well as the previous factors connected to academic well-being.

2. Materials and Methods

Following the theoretical overview, the following research questions were formed: how do academics understand their own teaching activities, and what differences can be found between academic types? Also, among our research questions was: what differences can be discovered between academic types regarding inclusive teaching practice?

Based on the special literature, we surmised that it would be most typical of teaching-focused academics to have student-centered, practice-oriented teaching, since they seem to care much more for teaching. While among research-focused academics these attributes take a back seat, information transmission is what they strive for (Nairz-Wirth & Feldmann, 2019). We further presumed that academics whose teaching is defined by practice-orientedness, student-centeredness, and reflectivity can be characterized by lower workplace well-being, for, these activities demand far greater investments of time and energy (Alqarni, 2021; Iyali et al., 2020; Laiho et al., 2020). According to our third hypothesis, the inclusive teaching practice also characterizes teaching-focused academics to a great degree, and, among academics typified by teaching methodology preparedness, and a more colorful methodology toolbox, inclusive teaching opportunities appear in greater number as well (Heubeck & Latimer, 2002; Ryan, 2005).

2.1. Sampling

In the first part of the research project, focus group interviews were conducted with academics from Hungary, Romania, Slovakia, Serbia and Ukraine. The interviews covered a wide range of issues related to the work and situation of the academics. After analyzing and processing the interviews (Kovács et al. 2024), we compiled the questionnaire on which this volume is based, which was translated into English, Serbian, Slovak, Ukrainian and Romanian and sent out 2 or 3 times in an online format, with the permission of the head of the institution. It was dispatched to all academics of the institutions surveyed in spring 2023, thus ensuring a probability sample. In Hungary, we surveyed higher education institutions in two disadvantaged regions, the North Great Plain Region and the South Transdanubian Region (University of Debrecen [n=356], Reformed Theological University of Debrecen [n=7], University of Nyíregyháza [n=14] and University of Pécs [n=104]). While in the case of institutions beyond the border, we mainly targeted minority Hungarian institutions, we sent the questionnaire to all academics in the majority population language as well. A total of 853 people completed the questionnaire, and after data cleaning the final number of items was 821. The database was named Central and Eastern European Teachers in Higher Education (CEETHE 2023).

2.2. Participants

Among respondents 514 were Hungarian (61.8%), 115 were Ukrainian (14.1%), 113 were Romanian (13.8%), 40 were Serbian (4.9%), and 36 were Slovakian (4.4%), and, in the case of three persons, we were unable to identify the institution and the country of origin. Less than half, 43.7% of the respondents were men, 56.3% women, the average age was 46 years old (SD=10.71), and the average number of years worked in higher education was 17 (SD=11 years). Among academic fields, most represented medicine (16.1%), teacher education (13.6%), and humanities and social sciences (12.9% and 8.2%). The smallest ratio of respondents came from theology (1.1%), art mediation (1.9%), and law (1.5%). The ratio of those selecting other fields was 2.6 to 2.7%. The respondents' 21.1% did not have a degree, 46.4% possessed a Ph.D./DLA degree, 17.1% were academics with habilitations, and 9.4% held a DSc. Among traditional academics positions, most were adjuncts (29.6%) and associate professors (26.8%) in our sample, 11.3% were college or university professors, and almost the same ratio of assistant lecturers (11.2%) were teachers—2.6% senior professor, and 4% professors (language-, physical education, academics of professional subjects). There are far fewer academics with researcher status: 2.3% assistant research fellows, 1.8% research fellows, 1% senior research fellows and 1.2% research professors (with habilitations). 6% selected the „other" category, being mostly academics. The ratio of those who are not in a leadership role was 69.3%, but 1.8% fill institutional, 3.7% faculty, 16.6% institute and department, 3.9% center-leadership roles. Here too, 5.1% selected the „other" category.

2.3. Measures

2.3.1. Clusters of academics

Based on the experience of the focus group interviews prior to the quantitative research, we ranked the teaching jobs and asked respondents to rate on a scale of 1 to 4 how much they consider these to be their job responsibilities. Based on the responses, factor and cluster analyses were carried out and four types of academics were identified: teaching-focused academics (33.4%), academics with an administrative focus (19.7%), research-focused academics (20.3%) and academic leaders (26.6%). For more information about the clusters of academics see the Introduction of the volume.

2.3.2. Well-being

To measure well-being, we used Warr's (1992) well-being scale and asked academics how often they had felt different positive and negative emotions in the past few weeks (12 items, Chronbach α=.879, KMO=.908, p=000, explained variance 75.773%). The principal component was converted into a 0–100-point scale, with 0 indicating if the principal component was not at all present and 100 if it was completely present. The statistical values for the principal component of well-being are M=59.75, SD=18.89, N=797.

2.3.3. Teaching practice

We conducted the examination of the teaching approach on the basis of 12 statements (Table 8.1), and we analyzed teachers' competencies with the help of 10 statements (Table 8.2), which are based on Kálmán (2021). Nevertheless, we decreased the number of statements. While in the previous study (Kálmán, 2021) respondents evaluated teacher competencies on a scale of 1 to 10, regarding importance and perceived effectiveness, in the present study, the statements in both question blocks in the current study had to be evaluated using a five-point Likert scale (1: not characteristic at all, 5: completely characteristic). The 5-point

Likert scale is a widely used tool in social sciences for measuring attitudes and perceptions. Its popularity stems from its simplicity and clarity, which facilitate respondent understanding. The 5-point scale provides a balanced range of responses while minimizing respondent fatigue. In addition to the simplicity of responding, we are aware of the potential limitations, as some research points out that 5-point scales may lack the sensitivity to capture subtle differences in respondent evaluations (Finstad, 2010). Also, we did not ask respondents about the importance or effectiveness of the activities, but rather about how often the academics apply the mentioned areas.

Table 8.1: The teaching approach (N=818)

	Mean	SD
It is necessary to link theory with practice in the tasks.	4.33	.77
It is important that current data appear in classes.	4.22	.84
I give tasks that develop students' skills.	4.21	.85
I strive to initiate conversation about the topic learned in class.	4.18	.87
I use multiple methods (lecture, debate, student presentation, etc.).	4.10	.94
I build up the course content by students' practice tasks.	3.88	.90
I determine course content based on students' prior knowledge.	3.78	.97
In classes, students need to reflect on their own and their classmates' work.	3.69	1.12
I consider students' interest when designing the course.	3.65	.97
I take into consideration labor market expectations.	3.56	1.09
I give tasks which require students to cooperate with one another.	3.44	1.05
I make an effort to introduce lots of data in class.	3.41	1.04

Table 8.2: The existence of teacher competencies (N=812)

	Mean	SD
Evaluation of student results, giving feedback.	4.25	.90
Analysis of student feedback.	3.68	1.14
Evaluation of one's own teaching practice.	3.58	1.14
Participation in individual training.	3.49	1.26
Training/major development, monitoring.	3.42	1.23
Aiding and mentoring the learning and integration of new arrivals to the training.	3.24	1.28
Recruiting, popularization of a major.	3.22	1.28
Participation in methodological training that can be used in education.	3.17	1.31
Carrying out activities meant to help students catch up.	3.07	1.20
Helping students with special educational needs.	2.94	1.31

We rotated the teaching approach and teacher competency variables with the varimax method and used maximum likelihood estimates. The factor structure explains 51% of statements (KMO=0.911, p=0.001). During the factor analysis five factors developed regarding teaching activity: (1) practice-centered, (2) student-centered, (3) reflective, (4) development-oriented, and (5) data-/information-oriented.

The practice-centered factor emphasizes activities and teaching approaches that actively engage students in practical, skill-based learning such as considering students' interests during course design, customizing course content based on students' prior knowledge and taking labor market expectations into account when designing course materials and objectives. Key activities under this factor include the following: assigning tasks that develop various student skills, using multiple teaching methods to address diverse learning needs, designing tasks that require students to connect theoretical concepts with practical applications, promoting self-reflection and peer evaluation by asking students, facilitating discussions to encourage deeper understanding of topics covered in class.

The student-centered factor focuses on creating a learning environment tailored to individual student needs and fostering active participation. This factor emphasizes the importance of mentorship, inclusion, and personalized support to enhance the overall student experience such as aiding and mentoring the learning and integration of new arrivals to the training, helping students with special educational needs, recruiting, popularization of a major and monitoring analysis of student feedback.

The reflective factor highlights the importance of self-assessment and feedback in the teaching profession. This factor focuses on continuous improvement through thoughtful analysis of teaching practices and outcomes. Key activities within this factor include evaluating one's own teaching practices to identify strengths and areas for improvement and assessing student results and providing constructive feedback to support learning.

The development-oriented factor emphasizes the importance of professional growth and skill enhancement for academics such as engaging in individual training sessions to acquire new knowledge and competencies and participating in methodological training that can be directly applied to improve educational practices.

The data-/information-oriented factor highlights the importance of integrating relevant and up-to-date information into teaching practices. This factor focuses on utilizing data effectively to enrich the learning experience and ensure the curriculum remains current. Key elements of this factor are, making a deliberate effort to introduce a significant amount of data during classes to support learning and ensuring that the information presented in classes is current and reflective of recent developments.

The basis of the measure used to examine the inclusive approach was given by the Hungary CCIV Act of 2011 on Hungarian higher education, research result from European countries (see Riddell et al., 2005; Kendall, 2007; Moroń, 2014; Zajadacz & Kołodziejaczk, 2023; Zielińska, 2022) as well as the factors discovered during the Hrabéczy (2019) interview study <https://www.mdpi.com/2227-7102/13/10/1024>. The measure comprises items which are opportunities guaranteed, allowed, and executable between class and test frameworks by academics. In the case of these items, respondents had to give a statement about whether or not they applied or apply these opportunities, or if they do not consider them acceptable. Of these items, with maximum likelihood assessment and varimax rotation we created factors (KMO=0796, $p<0.001$), the structure of these factors explain 55% of statements. Three factors separated from each other, which are demonstrated in Table 8.3.

Table 8.3: Types of inclusive teaching activity

	Differentiation in the case of student product	Differentiation in mode of testing	Preparation support
Extending the deadlines of projects and assignments	.818		
Ensuring longer preparation time during exams	.776		
Permitting alternative ways to course completion	.627		
Replacing a written test with an oral test		.849	
Replacing an oral test with a written test		.841	
Permitting the use of a language lector			.749
Permitting the use of tools that assist in writing			.719
Permitting the making of a voice recording			.491
Overlooking grammar mistakes			.413
Making teaching material available in written form			.339

3. Results

We examined whether or not ties between teaching approach and the academic clusters can be seen (Table 8.4). Teaching-focused academics are best characterized by a practice-oriented approach, followed by a reflective approach. These teaching activities are in line with the characteristics of the cluster mentioned, that is, the presentation of the results of the field, modern teaching methods and cooperation with external partners. They focus mainly on teaching and on the preparation and development of students. It was also assumed that the most characteristic features of researchers would be that their courses would be dominated by the presentation of current data and research results, as well as a high level of data processing and presentation, as this group of academics demonstrates a high level of scientific activity. However, this assumption is less supported by the data.

Table 8.4: The teaching approaches of the academic clusters (N=770, average points)

	Practice-centered	Student-centered	Reflective	Development-oriented	Data-/information-oriented
Academics with an administrative focus (n=155)	.09	.09	-.00	.06	-.21
Teaching-focused academics (n=255)	.19	-.06	.05	-.04	.01
Academic leaders (n=203)	.06	.25	.14	.22	.21
Research-focused academics (n=157)	-.49	-.30	-.27	-.28	-.09
Sign.					0.001

Following this, we scrutinized whether there were differences in the acceptance and implementation of these inclusive practices among the academic clusters. Regarding this, we found significant variation concerning differentiation of the student product and mode of testing. Table 8.5 shows that the differentiation in the student product is most pronounced for teaching-focused academics, followed by academic leaders, and least pronounced for research-focused academics. Different results are found for the differentiation in the method of accountability: while it is mostly applied by teaching-focused academics, it is also applied to a large extent by research-focused academics, and least by academics with an administrative focus.

Table 8.5: Types of inclusive teaching activities by academic clusters (N=758, average points)

	Differentiation in the case of student product	Differentiation in mode of testing
Academics with an administrative focus (n=155)	.02	–.16
Teaching-focused academics (n=255)	.06	.09
Academic leaders (n=203)	.05	–.03
Research-focused academics (n=157)	–.21	.06
Sign.	–.00	.002

The study analyzed differences across five countries (HU, UA, RO, SB, SK) concerning key educational activity. Post hoc analyses using Tukey's HSD revealed significant differences in country-level perceptions across the examined pedagogical factors. The student-oriented factor ($F(4)=4.690$, $p<0.001$) was significantly higher among academic in Romania ($M=0.268$) than other countries, while Slovakia ($M=-0.182$) scored the lowest. Reflective practices ($F(4)=3.859$, $p=0.004$) were more emphasized among academics in Romania ($M=0.231$) and Slovakia ($M=0.281$) compared to Serbia ($M=-0.176$). Development-oriented practices ($F(4)=33.744$, $p<0.001$) were notably more prevalent in Ukraine ($M=0.801$) than in Hungary ($M=-0.200$). Finally, for the data/information-oriented factor ($F(4)=12.467$, $p<0.001$) Romania ($M=0.329$) and Ukraine ($M=0.330$) formed a distinct group with higher emphasis, whereas Serbia ($M=-0.208$) and Hungary scored significantly lower ($M=-0.129$).

The tests revealed significant differences across position for the practice-centered and development-oriented factors. For the practice-centered factor $F(11)=3.087$, $p<0.001$), senior research fellows ($M=-0.593$) and research fellows ($M=-0.344$) scored significantly lower than research professors ($M=0.270$). These findings suggest that research-intensive roles are less focused on practice-based activities compared to teaching-oriented roles. Similarly, for the development-oriented factor ($F(11)=3.032$, $p<0.001$), research fellow ($M=-0.593$) and senior research fellow ($M=-0.344$) scored lower, while lecturers ($M=0.409$) and research professors ($M=0.739$) showed significantly greater emphasis on developmental practices, indicating that senior academic roles prioritize growth and innovation in education.

Post hoc analysis revealed significant differences in development-oriented approaches across academic degree ($F(4)=13.370$, $p<0.001$). Academics with CSc showed the highest development-oriented tendency ($M=0.695$), followed by the academics with DSc (M=0.222). In contrast, academics with a Ph.D./DLA (M=–0.142) and habilitated doctorates (M=–0.169) demonstrated significantly lower scores. Those without qualifications (M=0.118) were closer to the higher-qualified groups. Significant differences were also observed in data/information-oriented approaches ($F(4)=5.425$, $p<0.001$). academics with CSc exhibited the strongest focus on data and information (M= 0.413), followed by academics with DSc (M= 0.111) and Ph.D./DLA (M=0.029). Conversely, individuals without academic degree (M=–0.175) or habilitated doctorates (M=–0.072) scored significantly lower.

There are significant differences in practice-centered approaches between discipline ($F(3)=22.146$, $p<0.001$). Social sciences, economics and arts exhibited the most practice-centered approaches (M=0.15 and 0.30), while health and STEM fields were less practice-centered (M=–2.52 and –2.25). Significant differences were observed in student-centered orientation ($F(3)=3.146$, $p<0.025$). Social sciences (M=0.09) were more student-focused compared to health (M=–1.44). Fields also differed significantly in development orientation ($F(3)=17.514$, $p<0.05$). Arts (M= 1.94) and health (M=0.09) were more development-oriented, contrasting with STEM (M=–3.98) and social sciences, economics (M=–1.00). Data/information-oriented differences were significant across disciplines ($F(3)=3.915$, $p < 0.05$). Social sciences and economics (M=0.22) and arts (M=0.01) prioritized data/information more than STEM (M=–0.76) and health (M=–0.69).

We also analyzed how the use of inclusive practices is distributed by academic degree, position and discipline. We did not find any significant difference in the presence of an academic degree. Regarding the position of the academics, it can be said that the differences are manifested along the differentiation in the case of student output. The professors and associate professors are more likely to use this form or inclusive practices than assistant lecturers and below ($p=0.037$). According to disciplines, a significant difference is also seen in the case of differentiation in the case of student output and assessment. In the case of differentiation in the student output, it can be said that this type of inclusive practice is used by academics in the fields of humanities and arts in the highest proportion, while it is least characteristic of academics in the fields of medicine and health sciences ($p<0.001$). They are also the least likely to differentiate in the method of assessment and are most likely to be used by academics of STEAM and agricultural science disciplines ($p=0.008$).

With the involvement of the above-mentioned factors and with the help of linear regression analysis, we examined if significant ties could be detected. During the course of the regression analysis, we applied the „enter" method, the model significance value being $p=0.005$. Based on the data of Table 8.6, it is clear that student-centeredness, and support of student preparation notably go hand in hand with workplace well-being.

Table 8.6: Interrelations between educational activity and well-being (N=720)

	Unstandardized coefficients		Standardized coefficients		
	B	Std. Error	Beta	t	Sign.
Constant	59.766	.697		85.753	0.000
Practice-centered	0.848	0.791	0.040	1.071	0.284
Student-centered	2.457	0.812	0.114	3.024	0.003
Reflective	0.018	0.834	0.001	0.022	0.983
Development-oriented	1.278	0.798	0.060	1.602	0.110
Data-/information-oriented	−0.765	0.840	−0.034	−0.910	0.363
Differentiation in the case of student product	0.027	0.714	0.001	0.037	0.970
Differentiation in mode of testing	0.746	0.698	0.039	1.069	0.286
Preparation support	1.566	0.695	0.084	2.253	0.025

4. Discussion

In the first part of the analysis, based on Kálmán (2021) we examined the academics' teaching approaches in such a way that the indicated activities show how much they characterize their academic work. In five cases the listed activities received a value higher than four, which means that these activities are typical of academics' work to a great extent. Of the activities, the linking together of theory and practice, the introduction of current data, competency development, the application of varied methods, and the initiation of conversation were most frequent. Taking into consideration labor market demands, development of inter-student cooperation, and the introduction of much data in class were partially characteristic of academic work.

From teacher competencies, mainly the evaluation of student and their own activity, that is, reflection was at the forefront. What was less characteristic of respondents was the participation in methodological training, helping students catch up, and aiding students with special educational needs. In our results, the occurrence of a sort of migration from teacher-centered, theory-centric practice to a learning-centered, student-centric approach can be seen creeping up, therefore, activities that studies found critical are ever-increasingly coming to center stage (Kovács, 2016). Behind the low measure of helping students with special educational needs could be the fact that, based on previous research results, only a small percentage of academics knows how to teach such students (Kocsis & Hrabéczy, 2023).

From the statements regarding teaching approaches and teacher competencies, we formed factors with which we strove to paint as colorful a picture about teacher activity as possible, and to test our hypotheses. The practice-centered approach comprises in itself the use of varied methods, student competency development and active involvement, consideration of students' prior knowledge and interest in the class, and, besides all this, fulfilling labor market expectations also gains pre-eminence. The approach below covers the areas which can serve as an answer to the expectations affecting higher education, such as guaranteeing an active learning-teaching environment, and competency development springing from labor market demands. In the case of the second, that is, the student-centered factor, there is significant student aid and mentoring, consideration of their opinions, along with development of the course.

The above activities are especially important during academics' work, after all, many studies on dropout have called attention to the fact that (Kovács et al., 2019) academics can function as a protective factor against dropout. For, they can offer relevant and immediate help to students who are unsure and stuck in their studies. Furthermore, these studies highlighted, one of dropout's predictors is disillusion with the course, and disappointment, thus, it is crucial to continuously improve on courses, to popularize them and to build upon student feedback. Similarly needed and key areas are an academic staff's own practice, student evaluation and feedback, which appear in the third, reflective factor. These items regarding development and training, as well as data-/information-oriented activities, form a separate factor.

We supposed that, of teaching-focused academics, student-centered, practice-oriented teaching was most typical since among them care for teaching is dominant. While for the researchers these traits are forced into the background, they drive toward information transmission (Nairz-Wirth & Feldmann, 2019). The teaching-focused academics are most characterized by the practice-centered approach, and reflectivity. These academics activities are in harmony with the mentioned cluster's characteristics, according to which the introduction of the specialty results, the modern teaching methods and the cooperation with external partners are typical of them. Most likely, they focus on preparing and improving academics and students.

We further surmised that introducing current data and research results in class would be dominant among those things characteristic of research-focused academics, the processing and introducing of large amounts of data. After all, this academic group testifies of high academic activity. In contrast to our hypothesis, we experienced that the formed teaching activities are least characteristic of research-focused academics. Neither the practice-centered, reflective, nor the student-centered approach are typical of them, not even the teaching activities, which mostly adjust to their researcher profile.

What surpassed our expectations was the academic leaders' teaching activity, since it is this academic type that excels at student-centered, development-oriented, and data-/information-oriented activities. It is paramount though that their reflective and practice-centered approach must not be left out. Academic leaders, besides their teaching, researching, and academic work also engage in institutional and faculty-level leadership tasks. Thus, we presumed, next to this great a load and number of tasks, any factors would be less typical of them. For such activities ended up in the first three factors that require more time and energy, constant monitoring, and, for this reason, we did not assume that that would be typical of the academic leaders with the widest array of jobs to do. If we take into consideration, however, that academic leaders participate in institution and department decision-making, and they clearly understand the institutions' goals and challenges, we will see them take the first step in pushing forward education and teaching. This step forward could be taking students' opinions into consideration in the interest of improving a course, forming more practice-centered courses in the interest of satisfying the employer and student needs, or doing the same in the interest of continuously improving upon their own knowledge.

The next part of the analysis, based on 2011 Nftv & Hrabéczy (2019), we, through the work of academics, examined where inclusive teaching practice could be found among academics and in what ratios. We asked academics, of the inclusive teaching opportunities found in Table 8.5 which ones they would use or have they used in the course of their teaching activities. With the help of these items, we created factors, thus making it possible to check to what extent preparation support, as well as differentiation of student product and mode of testing are typical of some of the academic types. The academic types were compared by the factors' means, among which significant variation can be seen in the differentiation of student product and mode of testing. In this regard, we supposed that the appearance of inclusive practice is most characteristic of teaching-focused academics (Heubeck & Latimer, 2002; Ryan, 2005). Based on the data in Table 8.6, we can see that both types of differentiation are typical of teaching-focused academics, being applied least of all by the research-focused academics and the academic leaders. Thus, our assumption was correct. These results are in harmony with academics' teaching approaches and activities. Based on these, teaching-focused academics focus most on student development and preparation, one dimension of this could be present in their teaching activities as well as the differentiation toward non-traditional students. According to the results of previous studies and academics' own admissions, some non-traditional student groups are looked on favorably (Debrand & Salzberg, 2005; Murray et al., 2008; Salzberg et al., 2002). Meanwhile, other studies, the institution culture, and the quality and quantity of teacher-student interactions all say the opposite (Heubeck & Latimer, 2002; Hrabéczy, 2019). Our study results add to the previous ones, according to which, alongside the previously discovered factors, the academic profile also produces variations in the inclusive approach.

Our findings highlight substantial cross-country variations in pedagogical emphases. Romania and Ukraine consistently ranked higher in student-oriented, reflective, and development-supporting practices, suggesting a stronger focus on contemporary pedagogical trends. In contrast, Hungary and Serbia exhibited lower scores in these areas, potentially reflecting differing educational priorities or systemic constraints. These findings highlight distinct patterns in the emphasis on practice-oriented and development-oriented activities across job roles in higher education. To that end, future research should investigate the cultural, institutional, and policy-related factors driving these disparities.

Professors and assistant lecturers demonstrated higher scores for both factors, reflecting their dual responsibilities in teaching and fostering student development. In contrast, research fellow and senior research fellow scored lower, potentially reflecting their primary focus on research and administrative functions. These differences underscore the need for tailored professional development programs that address the specific focus areas of various academic roles, ensuring a balanced integration of practice and development across higher education institutions. These findings highlight the influence of scientific qualifications on development-oriented pedagogical practices.

Higher qualifications (particularly the CSc and DSc) are associated with a stronger orientation toward fostering development. This trend may reflect the advanced theoretical and methodological expertise acquired during the attainment of these qualifications. The results indicate a clear relationship between higher qualifications and a data- and information-oriented approach. Academics with CSc stand out with the highest orientation, possibly due to the research-intensive nature of their training and work. Lower qualifications or the absence of formal scientific degrees correlate with a reduced emphasis on data-driven methodologies. These findings underscore the varied pedagogical emphases across disciplines in higher education. The results suggest that practice- and student-centered orientations dominate less in certain fields, like health and STEM, whereas others, such as arts and social sciences, prioritize student engagement and data-driven methodologies. Such differences may reflect the unique learning goals, professional demands, and educational traditions within these fields.

In conclusion, our analysis highlights key trends in the use of inclusive practices across different academic degrees, positions, and disciplines. While no significant differences were found based on academic degrees, academic positions revealed a notable distinction. Professors and associate professors tend to employ inclusive practices more frequently, particularly in the area of student output differentiation, compared to assistant lecturers and those in lower positions. The results also indicate significant variations across disciplines. Academics in the humanities and arts fields were more likely to implement differentiation in student output, while those in medicine and health sciences showed the least inclination toward this approach. Similarly, assessment differentiation was most common in the STEM and agricultural science fields, while it was least practiced by academics in medicine and health sciences. These findings suggest that both academic rank and disciplinary context play a critical role in the adoption of inclusive practices, which could inform future initiatives aimed at fostering inclusivity in higher education.

In closing, with the help of linear regression analysis we examined whether teaching approaches and inclusive teaching practice factors were connected to academics' well-being. About this, we assumed that of practice-centered, student-centered and reflective academics lower well-being was characteristic due to the large demand of time and energy from the above activities (Alqarni, 2021; Iyali et al., 2020; Laiho et al., 2020). To test this, during the regression analysis, using the enter method we in one step included the examined variables. Based on the data in Table 8.6, we can see that in only two cases, regarding the differentiation applied during the student-centered approach and the support of student preparation, were significant with substantial positive ties detectable. Therefore, academics who adopt a more student-centered approach and who provide more support and differentiated support for student preparation are more likely to have higher levels of well-being. In this way, our assumption was not justified. Academics who are able to devote more time and energy to preparing for lessons and responding to students' individual needs have higher levels of well-being, while academics with lower levels of well-being focus their resources on other tasks due to a lack of time and energy. We thus concluded that preparation support takes a greater degree of academics' attention and planning, than the differentiation in testing and student product does, which academics, regardless of their profile, will only be capable of, if their level of well-being is high enough.

Conclusions

Based on our results, we can see that among the academics we asked, the endeavors aimed at student development, support, and application of the varied educational methods are increasingly coming to the forefront. However, significant differences were shown between some of the teacher types. The inclusive approach toward non-traditional students was one aspect present in each teacher type, albeit present in dissimilar proportions. We could see that using varied teaching methods or taking into consideration some of the needs of higher educational actors was less characteristic of research-focused academics. The use of inclusive educational opportunities was an aspect not characteristic of any of the academic types. A fifth of respondents count as research-focused academics, which means that most likely students are taught by research-focused academics. On the contrary, previous studies support the fact that students have an ever-growing need to participate in practice-centered courses, and to acquire knowledge applicable in the labor market, or that allows them to see their own development (Kocsis & Pusztai, 2024). However, if they often come in contact with such courses that cannot be described with the above expectations. Instead that course might lead to an overall negative outlook on the course itself, resulting in disappointment, and a possible shift from an active student role to a passive one (Kovács et al., 2019). The diversification of the student society (by ability, social, cultural, and ethnic background) brought with it the need for research-focused academics, prepared to teach these students, to be able to in an inclusive way carry out their instructive duties (<https://www.mdpi.com/2227-7102/13/10/1024> Debrand & Salzberg, 2005; Kurth & Mellard, 2002; Murray et al., 2008; Salzberg et al., 2002).

Based on our results and the results of past studies, however, in regard to this, the training of academics and the formation of their approach are invaluable, though it very rarely happens at an organizational level. For this reason, we consider it critical to have tighter cooperation between academics, and greater creation of a community of practice, where they would have opportunity for the genesis of educational innovation and the transfer of knowledge/experience, to assist one another. It may also be an important factor in harmonizing course thematics, since academics of some classes have differing approaches, or belong to different academic types. However, by harmonizing the classes, it would be possible to overcome the problem of having either the theoretical knowledge transmission approach or the practice-centered approach dominant all through the course, instead having all (classical knowledge transmission, competency development, participation in field training, and the learning of academic research) appear equally and stably across the course. Furthermore, our results call attention to the importance of academics' well-being, which is critical to the institute's effectiveness. After all, the academics who are characterized by a high degree of well-being apply the student-centered approach more often, making them more practical, varied in their teaching serving student development better. The mentioned teaching approach promotes student course satisfaction, their later placement in the labor market, and their adjustment to labor market expectations.

Acknowledgment

This publication was supported by the project "Investigating the role of sport and physical activity for a healthy and safe society in the individual and social sustainability of work ability and quality of work and life (multidisciplinary research umbrella program)" and by the János Bolyai Research Scholarship of the Hungarian Academy of Sciences.

References

Akram, M. (2019). Psychological Wellbeing of University Teachers in Pakistan. *Journal of Education and Educational Development, 6*(2), 235–253. <https://doi.org/10.22555/joeed.v6i2.2473>

Alpár, D., Barnaföldi, G. G., Dékány, É., Kubinyi, E., Máté, Á., Munkácsy, B., Neumann, E., Solymosi, K., & Toldi G. (2018). Fiatal kutatók Magyarországon. Felmérés a 45 év alatti kutatók helyzetéről, karrierterveiről, nehézségeiről [Young Researchers in Hungary]. Young Researchers Academy.

Alqarni, N. A. (2021). Well-being and the Perception of Stress among EFL University Teachers in Saudi Arabia. Journal of Language and Education, 7(3), 8–22. <https://doi.org/10.17323/jle.2021.11494>

Amaral, A. (2008). The Emergence of Neo-Liberalism and the Alteration of Evaluation Systems' Objectives. In J. Audy, & M. Costa (Eds.), *Innovation and Quality in the University* (pp. 529–581). Retrived from <https://ebooks.pucrs.br/edipucrs/acessolivre/livros/inovacaoequalidade.pdf#page=530>

Aziz, F., Akhtar, M. S., & Rauf, M. (2014). Relationship Between Teachers' Competencies and Motivation at Higher Education Level in Pakistan. *Pakistan Annual Research Journal, 50*, 163–174.

Bakker, A. B., & Demerouti, E. (2014). Job demands-resources theory. In P. Y. Chen, & C. Cooper (Eds.), *Work and Wellbeing: Wellbeing: A complete reference guide*, vol. III. (pp. 1–28). John Wiley & Sons.

Bell, A. S., Rajendran, D., & Theiler, S. (2012). Job stress, wellbeing, work-life balance and work-life conflict among Australian academics. *E-Journal of Applied Psychology, 8*(1), 25–37. <https://doi.org/10.7790/ejap.v8i1.320>

Berényi, L., & Deutsch, N. (2018). Effective teaching methods in business higher education: a students' perspective. *International Journal of Education and Information Technologies, 12*, 37–45.

Brewster, L., Jones, E., Priestley, M., Wilbraham, S. J., Spanner, L., & Hughes, G. (2022). Look after the staff and they would look after the students' cultures of wellbeing and mental health in the university setting. *Journal of Further and Higher Education, 46*(4), 548–560. <https://doi.org/10.1080/0309877X.2021.1986473>

Castro, C. M., & Levy, D. (2001). Four Functions in Higher Education. *International Higher Education, 23*, 5–6. <https://doi.org/10.6017/ihe.2001.23.6594>

Chard, G., & Couch, R. (1998). Access to higher education for the disabled student: a building survey at the University of Liverpool. *Disability & Society, 13*(4), 603–623.

Cordoni, B. K. (1982). Services for college dyslexics. In R. N Malatesha, & P. G. Aaron (Eds.), *Neuropsychology of developmental dyslexia and acquired alexia and treatment. Perspectives in neurolinguistics* (pp. 435–448). Academic Press.

Cross, P. K. (1987). The Changing Role of Higher Education in the United States. *Higher Education Research & Development, 6*(2), 99–108. <https://doi.org/10.1080/0729436870060202>

Cunningham, S. (2013). Teaching a Diverse Student Body—A Proposed Tool for Lecturers to Self-Evaluate Their Approach to Inclusive Teaching. *Practice and Evidence of the Scholarship of Teaching and Learning in Higher Education, 8*(1), 3–27.

Dabney-Fekete, I. (2020). *Nemzetköziesedő tudomány—A felsőoktatásban dolgozó oktatók nemzetközi aktivitása* [Internationalisation of science—International activity of higher education staff]. CHERD-H.

Dabney-Fekete, I., Dusa, Á. R., & Pallay, K. (2024). Oktatók nemzetközi aktivitása és annak gátjai Közép-Kelet-Európában [The International Activities of Academics and Their Barriers in Central and Eastern Europe]. In K. Kovács, & K. Pallay (Eds.), *Oktatók a Kárpát-medencei felsőoktatásban*. CHERD-H. 165–182.

Debrand, C., & Salzberg, C. (2005). A validated curriculum to provide training to faculty regarding students with disabilities in higher education. *The Journal of Postsecondary Education and Disability, 18*(1), 49–61.

Elliott, G. (2017). Introduction to the special issue on "Learning for Work." *Research in Post-Compulsory Education, 22*(1),1–6.

Enslin, P., & Hedge, N. (2024). Decolonizing higher education: the university in the new age of Empire. *Journal of Philosophy of Education, 58*(2–3), 227–241.

Finstad, K. (2010). Response interpolation and scale sensitivity: evidence against 5-point scales. *Journal of Usability Studies, 5*(3), 104–110.

Fitzgerald, T. (2012). Tracing the fault lines. In T. Fitzgerald, J. White, & M. H. Gunter (Eds.), *Hard Labour? Academic Work and the Changing Landscape of Higher Education* (pp. 1–22). Emerald Group.

Gawrycka, M., Kujawska, J., & Tomczak, M. T. (2021). Self-assessment of competencies of students and graduates participating in didactic projects—Case study. International Review of Economics Education, 36, 100204. <https://doi.org/10.1016/j.iree.2020.100204>

Gill, R. (2018). Building employability skills for higher education students: An Australian example. *Journal of Teaching and Learning for Graduate Employability, 9*(1), 84–92. <https://doi.org/10.21153/jtlge2018vol9no1art739>

Hadjikakou, K., & Hartas, D. (2008). Higher education provision for students with disabilities in Cyprus. *Higher Education, 55*(1), 103–119.

Han, J., Yin, H., Wang, J., & Zhang, J. (2020). Job demands and resources as antecedents of university teachers' exhaustion, engagement and job satisfaction. *Educational Psychology, 40*, 318–335.

Harrison, D. F. (2017). *The Role of Higher Education in the Changing World of Work*. Retrieved from <https://er.educause.edu/articles/2017/10/the-role-of-higher-education-in-the-changing-world-of-work>

Heubeck, B., & Latimer, S. (2002). Ability and achievement characteristics of Australian university students with self-reported specific learning disabilities. *Higher Education Research and Development, 21*(3), 273–287.

Hill, J. L. (1996). Speaking out: Perceptions of students with disabilities regarding the adequacy of services and willingness of faculty to make accommodations. *Journal of Postsecondary Education and Disability, 12*(1), 22–43.

Holloway, S. (2001). The Experience of Higher Education from the Perspective of Disabled Students. *Disability & Society, 16*(4), 597–615.

Horváthová, A., Hrnčiar, M., & Rievajová, E. (2022). Changes in the skills of the workforce for future development of the labour market in the Slovak Republic. *Entrepreneurship and Sustainability Issues 9*(4), 212–224. <https://doi.org/10.9770/jesi.2022.9.4(11)>

Hoy, C., & Gregg, N. (1986). Learning disabled students: An emerging population on college campuses. *Journal of College Admissions, 112*, 10–14.

Hrabéczy, A. (2019). Discovering factors influencing study success of students with disabilities and learning difficulties in an interview study. *Acta Medicinae et Sociologica, 10*(28), 31–44.

Hurtado, S. (2007). The Study of College Impact. In Gumport, P. J. (Eds.), *Sociology of Higher Education: Contributions and their Contexts* (pp. 94–113). Johns Hopkins University Press.

Iyaji, T. O., Eyam, S. O., & Agashi, V. A. (2020). An Assessment of Some Stress Factors in Academic Profession and Their Health Implications Among Academics in Tertiary Institutions in Cross River State Nigeria. *International Journal of Innovative Research and Advanced Studies, 7*, 53–59.

Jin, J., Mercer, S., Babic, S., & Mairitsch, A. (2021). "You just appreciate every little kindness": Chinese language teachers' wellbeing in the UK. *System, 96*, 102400. <https://doi.org/10.1016/j.system.2020.102400>

Kalivoda, K. S., & Higbee, J. L. (1998). Influencing faculty attitudes toward accommodating students with disabilities: A theoretical approach. *The Learning Assistance Review, 3*(2), 12–25.

Kálmán, O. (2013). Tanulástámogatás a felsőoktatásban [Learning Support in Higher Education]. *Felsőoktatási Műhely, 2*, 15–22.

Kálmán, O. (2019). A felsőoktatás oktatóinak szakmai fejlődése: az oktatói identitás alakulása és a tanulás módjai [University teachers' professional development: their identity development and ways of learning]. *Neveléstudomány: Oktatás Kutatás Innováció, 25*(1), 74–97. <http://doi.org/10.21549/NTNY.25.2019.1.6>

Kálmán, O. (2021). Tanulásközpontú felsőoktatás [Learning-centered higher education]. ELTE PPK, L'Harmattan Kiadó.

Karlovicz, J. (2013). Akadályozott hallgatók a felsőoktatásban [Students with Disabilities in Higher Education]. *Iskolakultúra, 23*(10). 52–60.

Kendall, L. (2017). Supporting students with disabilities within a UK university: Lecturer perspectives. *Innovations in Education and Teaching International, 55*(6), 694–703. doi:10.1080/ 14703297.2017.1299630.

Kinman, G. (2014). Doing More with Less? Work and Wellbeing in Academics. *Somatechnics, 4*(2), 219–235. <http://dx.doi.org/10.3366/soma.2014.0129>

Kivinen, O., & Nurmi, J. (2003). Unifying Higher Education for Different Kinds of Europeans. Higher Education and Work: A comparison of ten countries. *Comparative Education, 39*(1), 83–103.

Kocsis, Zs., & Hrabéczy, A. (2023). Felsőoktatási kihívások és az oktatói jóllét összefüggései egy kvalitatív kutatás tükrében [Thee Relationship between the Pedagogical Challenges of Higher Education and the Well-being of University

Instructors: A qualitative exploratory study]. *Neveléstudomány: Oktatás Kutatás Innováció, 11*(3), 46–64. <http://doi.org/10.21549/NTNY.42.2023.3.3>

Kocsis, Zs., & Pusztai, G. (2024). "Where soft skills are (not) developing…" A study of graduates' skills and the role of university in preparing students for the labor market in Hungary. *Journal of Teaching and Learning for Graduate Employability, 15*(1), 409–429. <https://doi.org/10.21153/jtlge2024vol15no1art1826>

Kovács, I. (2016). *Country Background Report Hungary, prepared for the HE Innovate Hungary country review* [Unpublished report submitted to the OECD].

Kovács, K., Ceglédi, T., Csók, C., Demeter-Karászi, Zs., Dusa, Á. R., Fényes, H., Hrabéczy, A., Kocsis, Zs., Kovács, K. E., Markos, V., Máté-Szabó, B., Németh, D. K., Pallay, K., Pusztai, G., Szigeti, F., Tóth, D. A., & Váradi, J. (2019). *Lemorzsolódott hallgatók* [Dropped out students]. CHERD-H.

Kovács, K., & Pallay, K. (2024). *Oktatók a Kárpát-medencei felsőoktatásban. Munkajellemzők, jóllét és eredményesség* [Academics in the Higher Education of the Carpathian Basin.Work Characteristics, Well-being and Performance]. CHERD-Hungary.

Kováts, G., & Temesi, J. (2018). *A magyar felsőoktatás egy évtizede 2008–2017* [Hungarian higher education in a decade: 2008–2017]. Budapest Corvinus Egyetem Nemzetközi Felsőoktatási Kutatások Központja.

Kurth, N., & Mellard, D. (2006). Student perceptions of the accommodation process in postsecondary education. *The Journal of Postsecondary Education and Disability, 19*(1), 71–84.

Laiho, A., Jauhiainen, A., & Jauhiainen, A. (2022) Being a teacher in a managerial university: academic teacher identity. *Teaching in Higher Education, 27*(2), 249–266. <http://doi.org/10.1080/13562517.2020.1716711>

Langørgen, E., & Magnus, E. (2018). We Are Just Ordinary People Working Hard to Reach Our Goals! Disabled Students' Participation in Norwegian Higher Education. *Disability & Society, 33*(4), 598–617. <http://doi.org/10.1080/09687599.2018.1436041>.

Lankveld, T., Schoonenboom, J., Volman, M., Croiset, G., & Beishuizen, J. (2017). Developing a teacher identity in the university context: a systematic review of the literature. *Higher Education Research & Development, 36*(2), 325–342. <http://doi.org/10.1080/07294360.2016.1208154>

Lexis, L., Thomas, J., Taylor, C. J., Church, J. E., & Julien, B. L. (2021). Informational interviews help undergraduate students at the mid-point of non-specialist STEM degrees confirm their career aspiration. *Journal of Teaching and Learning for Graduate Employability, 12*(2), 299–315. <https://doi.org/10.21153/jtlge2021vol12no2art1318>

Lewis, S. G. (2017). *The changing role of higher education*. Retrieved from <https://www.iiep.unesco.org/en/changing-role-higher-education>

MacIntyre, P. D., Ross, J., Talbot, K., Mercer, S., Gregersen, T., & Banga, C. A. (2019). Stressors, personality and wellbeing among language teachers. *System, 82*, 26–38. <https://doi.org/10.1016/j.system.2019.02.013>

Malik, N. A. A., Björkqvist, K., & Österman, K. (2017). Factors associated with occupational stress among university teachers in Pakistan and Finland. *Journal of Educational, Health and Community Psychology, 6*(2), 1–14. <http://dx.doi.org/10.12928/jehcp.v6i2.7047>

Martins, H. M., Borges, M. L., & Gonçalves, T. (2017). Attitudes towards inclusion in higher education in a Portuguese university. *International Journal of Inclusive Education, 22*(5), 527–542. <http://doi.org/10.1080/13603116.2017.1377299>

Moriña, A. (2018). Learning from experience: training for faculty members on disability. *Perspectives: Policy and Practice in Higher Education, 23*(2–3). 86–92. <http://doi.org/10.1080/13603108.2018.1534759>

Moroń, D. (2014). The higher education of people with disabilities in Poland. In E. Misterska (Ed.), *EDUKACJA DLA BEZPIECZEŃSTWA* (pp. 215–228). Retrived from: <https://www.academia.edu/download/38531739/pasja_gisw.pdf#page=215>

Murray, C., Flannery, B., & Wren, C. (2008). University staff members' attitudes and knowledge about learning disabilities and disability support services. *The Journal of Postsecondary Education and Disability, 21*(2), 73–90.

Nairz-Wirth, E., & Feldmann, K. (2019) Teacher professionalism in a double field structure. British Journal of Sociology of Education, 40(6), 795–808. <http://doi.org/10.1080/01425692.2019.1597681>

Neave, G. (2012). The Evaluative State, Institutional Autonomy and Re-engineering Higher Education in Western Europe. Springer.

Nelson, R., & Lignugaris-Kraft, B. (1989). Postsecondary education for students with learning disabilities. *Exceptional Children, 56*, 246–265.

Ödalen, J., Brommesson, D., Erlingsson, G. Ó., Schaffer, J. K., & Fogelgren, M. (2019). Teaching university teachers to become better teachers: the effects of pedagogical training courses at six Swedish universities. *Higher Education Research & Development, 38*(2), 339–353. <http://doi.org/10.1080/07294360.2018.1512955>

Pleschová, G. (2024). Bringing educational development to Central and Eastern Europe: reflections on twenty years of supporting teachers. *International Journal for Academic Development, 29*(2), 219–224. <http://doi.org/10.1080/1360144X.2024.2352728>

Poláková, M., Suleimanová, J., Madzík, P., Copuš, L., Molnárová, I., & Polednová, J. (2023.) Soft skills and their importance in the labour market under the conditions of Industry 5.0. *Heliyon, 9*(8), e18670. <http://doi.org/10.1016/j.heliyon.2023.e18670>

Pusztai, G., Fényes, H., & Kovács K. (2022). Factors Influencing the Chance of Dropout or Being at Risk of Dropout in Higher Education. *Education Sciences, 12*(11), 804.

Pusztai, G., Fekete, I., Dusa, Á. R., & Varga, E. (2016). Knowledge Brokers in the Heart of Europe. *Hungarian Educational Research Journal, 6*(1). 60–75.

Reindal, S. M. (1995). Some problems encountered by disabled students at the University of Oslo—whose responsibility? *European Journal of Special Needs, 10*(3), 227–241.

Riddell, S., Tinklin, T., & Wilson, A. (2005). *Disabled Students in Higher Education. Perspectives on widening access and changing policy.* Routledge

Robinson, A. (1986). *Access to higher education for learning disabled students. Disabilities and Gifted Education.* (ERIC Document Reproduction Service No. ED355750).

Rotidi, G., Collins, J. B., Karalis, T., & Lavidas, K. (2017). Using the Teaching Perspectives Inventory (TPI) to examine the relationship between teaching perspectives and disciplines in higher education, *Journal of Further and Higher Education, 41*(5), 611–624. <https://doi.org/10.1080/0309877X.2016.1159289>

Ryan, J. (2005). Uni is a serious thing, why are you here if you've got learning difficulties? Access and exclusion in higher education. *Melbourne Studies in Education, 46*(1), 45–62.

Salzberg, C., Peterson, L., Debrand, C., Blair, R., Carsey, A., & Johnson, A. (2002). Opinions of disability service directors on faculty training: The need, content, issues, formats, media, and activities. *Journal of Postsecondary Education and Disability, 15*(2), 101–114.

Seligman, M. E. P. (2011). *Flourish: A visionary new understanding of happiness and well-being.* Atria Books.

Sicoli, M. L. C. (1985). College students with LD: Support systems and programs. *Journal of Reading, Writing, and Learning Disabilities International, 1*, 59–62.

Smith, C. M., & Sodano, T. M. (2011). Integrating lecture capture as a teaching strategy to improve student presentation skills through self-assessment. *Active Learning in Higher Education, 12*(3), 151–162. <https://doi.org/10.1177/1469787411415082>

Stalcup, R. J., & Freeman, M. A. (1980). Serving the learning disabled student in the community college. *Community College Frontiers, 8*, 36–38.

Strichart, S. S., & Mangrum, C. T. (1986). College for the learning-disabled student: A new opportunity. *Journal of Reading, Writing, and Learning Disabilities International, 2*, 251–266.

Teichler, U. (2011). International Dimensions of Higher Education and Graduate Employment. In U. Teichler, (Ed.), The Flexible Professional in the Knowledge Society: New Challenges for Higher Education (pp. 177–197). Springer.

Tinklin, T., & Hall, J. (1999). Getting round obstacles: students with disabilities' experiences in higher education in Scotland. *Studies in Higher Education, 24*(2), 183–194.

Trautwein, C. (2018) Academics' identity development as teachers. *Teaching in Higher Education, 23*(8), 995–1010. DOI: 10.1080/13562517.2018.1449739

Vogel, S. A. (1983). On developing LD college programs. *Journal of Learning Disabilities, 15*, 518–528.

Walsh, J. (2018). The Transformation of Higher Education. In Walsh, J. (Ed.), *Higher Education in Ireland, 1922–2016. Politics, Policy and Power—A History of Higher Education in the Irish State* (pp. 233–327). Palgrave Macmillan. <https://doi.org/10.1057/978-1-137-44673-2_7>

Warr, P. (1992). Age and occupational well-being. *Psychology and Aging, 7*, 37–45.

Winefield, H. R., Boyd. C., & Winefield, A. H. (2014). Work-Family Conflict and Well-Being in University Employees. *The Journal of Psychology, 148*(6), 683–697. <https://doi.org/10.1080/00223980.2013.822343>

Zajadacz, A., & Kołodziejczak, A. (2023). Studying at Higher Education Institutions in Poland as Seen by Students with Disabilities in the Context of the Geographical Model of Disability. *Quaestiones Geographicae, 42*(4), 81–89.

Zielińska, M. (2022). The Policy of Supporting Students with Disabilities At Higher Education Institutions in Poland—The Example of the University of Wrocław University and Wrocław University of Technology. *Polish Political Science Review, 10*(1), 97–113.

9. International Mobility and Its Impediments for Academics

Ilona Dóra Dabney-Fekete, Ágnes Réka Dusa & Katalin Pallay

ABSTRACT

The international activity and mobility of academics have long been overlooked, often considered the sole responsibility of the academics themselves. This neglect stemmed from the larger focus on student mobility and university internationalization strategies prioritizing students. However, the mobility of academic staff is increasingly recognized as essential for internationalization. It is complex and can be examined from various perspectives, including duration, goals, and institutional attitudes, as well as its effects on academics, students, colleagues, institutions, and the economy. Our research focused on the restrictive factors affecting higher education academics' participation in teaching and research programs abroad. We explored differences between those who engage in mobility and those who do not, considering fields of study and various demographic factors such as age, family status, and financial situation. We also assessed previously identified barriers, including foreign language proficiency, workplace integration, institutional support, and work-life balance. Using the CEETHE 2023 database, we analyzed the mobility of 853 university and college academic staff members from Hungary, Romania, Serbia, Slovakia, and Ukraine, reducing our sample to 821 after data cleaning. In spring 2023, we distributed surveys online to selected institutions, focusing on two disadvantaged regions in Hungary and minority Hungarian universities across borders. Our findings showed significant variations in academics' mobility across fields of study, with fewer medical and healthcare academic staff participating internationally. Demographics, particularly age and gender, also played a crucial role, with older Slovakian and Romanian men being the most active. Mobile academics scored higher in foreign language proficiency compared to their immobile peers. Strong workplace relationships facilitated access to information about international opportunities, though mobile academics reported lower satisfaction with co-worker support. The analysis highlighted several dilemmas and questions, offering insights that could lead to a more effective internationalization strategy for universities. Understanding these challenges is essential for developing operational internationalization planning.

Keywords: international mobility, internationalization, academics, Central and Eastern Europe

Introduction

Recently, the examination of the international mobility and activity of higher educational academics has been at the center of research attention. According to the European Commission's 2007 survey, for every academic staff trip abroad, from the EU countries surveyed, an average of 16 student trips took place annually (European Commission, 2007). Thus, it comes as no surprise that the larger group to get more attention in previous years was the student mobility group. The reason that looking into higher education employees has been placed on the back burner, says Teichler (2011), is that universities' internationalization strategies are student mobility-focused, the organization and support is mainly directed toward this group, while academic staff mobility is "a given," something that is organized, coordinated, and in a lot of cases also sponsored by the academic staff themselves.

Considering that one of the key parts of internationalization in higher education is academics' activity abroad, examining them is not only unavoidable, but absolutely necessary. When it comes to ranking institutions internationally, this is highlighted as a quality indicator. This ranking, though problematic at times, does help in building out international cooperation, giving ground for defining quality (Ghulam, 2022), and in forming economic productivity. This is the reason why we aim our study at scrutinizing international higher education academic staff mobility.

The goal of the study is, with the secondary analysis of the Central and Eastern European Teachers in Higher Education (CEETHE 2023, N=821) database, to examine the factors that obstruct university academics from their teaching- and research-oriented mobility abroad. This question is actual because, though internationalization is the flagship area of higher education and many studies prove that academic staff mobility has a positive effect on student mobility, still, the scrutiny of factors that promote or prevent academic staff mobility falls far behind the examination of student mobility, or the analysis of the condition of foreign students studying at institutions from different aspects (like studying difficulties, cultural adaptations, language learning, etc.). Our study, therefore, focuses on university academic staff members, as well as the impediments and supporting forces in their international mobility. The results may serve as indicators and guides for universities and policy makers as to how academics could be assisted more suitably in the process of internationalization.

1. The International Activity of Academics As One of Internationalization's Highlighted Fields

1.1. Academics Caught in the Crossfire of Their Roles

In the past three decades higher education in the countries of Central and Eastern Europe experienced significant and remarkable changes. These transitions took place on several different levels. Expansion, during which an increase in the number of students could be observed, restructured and reoriented the tasks and duties of academic staff in higher education as well. As a result, the body of these professionals in the academic field cannot be looked at and depicted as uniform but rather diverse (Kwiek, 2022).

At the start of the 2000s, Altbach (2002) still wrote about how professors must fulfill a three-prong role—traditional teacher and researcher roles with administrative duties tacked on—one always being more dominant than the other two.

Kwiek's examinations (2016) and his views support the notion that the research arm is most critical and an academic staff seeking to fill this role must keep all others in the background. The best researchers were once teachers who left their teaching roles having fully extracted the experience from it. Höhle and Teichler (2013) propose that studies can take on an international form, still education will remain the intimate work of universities. We, however, think that can also play into many academics desiring to place more emphasis on the researcher side of their profession, and multitudes of teachers already teaching in higher education lacking proper teacher training. For this reason, many might feel that they are not ready to educate, left in many cases without experiencing success. The administrative task is seen by many academic staff members as a burden, this burden serving as one of the roots of a conflict of roles. In Kozma's view (2004), the scholar slowly shifts emphasis from career to administration, considering that academic work is measured with administrational tools. However, this can mean the opportunities, modes for progress on the academic path are controlled by other norms. This way, the academic staff member can form an opinion of his academic performance based on, for example, how liked he or she is among students. The dominant role in the professor's self-image can also influence their effectiveness (Pallay et al., 2024).

It is clear, though, today this three-way method gives only a simplified picture. For, we are required to see in only 20 years' time the new challenges and problems that higher educational institutions face. Carrying out tasks in the professional world are a burden for academics (Perger, 2016), in the same way that they are active in doing profit-related and economics tasks as service providers lacking inner motivation (Pusztai, 2015). A critical part of this is "self-management." Thus, academics today do not have to fulfill their traditional roles, but they do need to be prepared to develop as a manager, organizer, grant writer, budget adjuster—all tasks of administration (Dabney-Fekete, 2020).

In this arena defined by roles, tasks, and obligations, academics must continue to fulfill the international activity expectations placed upon them. Thus, the question of motivation almost certainly comes up. What is more, another question arises as to what extent the academic staff member views this as a mandatory task necessary for moving up the ladder (or for keeping the job). So, how the professor would like to and is able to become connected to the process of internationalization is an essential element here.

1.2. Academics Taking on Roles in Internationalization

Internationalization and its connected processes are often made equal to globalization, although internationalization can also be understood as an answer to globalization (Knight, 2013; Knight–de Wit, 2018). This means a mostly conscious building of networks in the course of which attempts are made to apply the international academic results in academic life at the national level. Moreover, simultaneously, they strive to introduce and popularize domestic academic performance in the international arena (Dabney-Fekete, 2020). After all, internationalization in higher education can be named as one of the important sources of professional knowledge (Greek-Jonsmoen, 2021). Kwiek (2019) also emphasizes that higher education has become exceedingly stratified, and among the three main classifying factors that academic professionals can follow, one of them is the extent to which a researcher is connected to international academic co-operations. For the academic staff members, participating in these processes is mandatory, for, in this their professional advancement of academic performance is rooted, and, in many cases, their income depends on it as well.

Academics' international activity, their entering the international academic bloodstream can take many forms—through conference participation, foreign language publication, guest teaching, academic networks and co-operations, grant and exchange programs, and shared research. In this study, we considered mobility a highlighted role. Though clarification or explanation of this is needed since the pandemic, participating in conferences appeared as one of the most plausible opportunities for mobility. Although, the online format is now available too—even after the pandemic's decline.

Academic staff mobility differs much from student mobility, being more significantly complex (Teichler, 2011). Thus, defining it proves difficult, being approachable from multiple angles—duration, purpose, motivation, connection to the institution. Its effect on the individual, however, and thereby on the colleagues and students, an academic staff member's own institution and teaching, and on the world economy is indisputable. In a 2014 study, where they examined almost 5000 answers from academics participating in the Erasmus program, how academic staff mobility affects a teacher's participation in his immediate and surrounding environment. The result: the majority of respondents viewed the experience positively (Brandenburg, 2014). In total, 86% of those asked responded that mobility first and foremost helps cooperation with international partners, and 85% of them stated that it has an advantageous effect on competency development. 93% of respondents saw that intercultural, social, and interpersonal skills developed during mobility, 81% of them saying that the quality of teacher work improved (Brandenburg, 2014).

1.3. The Possible Reasons for the Backlog of International Mobility

We can see that higher education institutions are ever more consciously moving in the direction of internationalization, and based on other studies, the individual too holds this to be important. In contrast, academics have had to juggle their previously mentioned institutional and academic tasks. On top of this, handling the hardships and problems of private life, and marriage prove strenuous when added to work. These things all projected that they cannot in every case match internationalization expectations. Multiple studies looked in the factors which are seen by academics as their biggest obstacle (Viszt, 2004; Teichler, 2011; European Commission, 2015; Borm, 2020; Dabney-Fekete, 2020; Horváth et al., 2020; Malota & Gyulavári, 2022). In the tests, mostly the same eight-ten motives appear, independent of where they carried out the research.

For instance, Viszt (2004) examined Hungarian researchers, and he concluded that the primary reason for not going abroad mentioned by those working in the above university departments was lack of proper skills. Following this, family reasons and weakness of international connections appeared. Language knowledge, however, was not present, only when talking about those working at private research sites. The effect came as a surprise, for, in many tests (Teichler, 2011; European Commission, 2015; Borm, 2020; Dabney-Fekete, 2020; Horváth et al., 2020; Malota & Gyulavári, 2022), they clearly mark language knowledge as a negatively determining factor. Questions of finance also appear as explanatory factors of why academics remain at home rather than being internationally active—lack of funds, or budget support can mean problems for many, especially those who travel for conferences (Dabney-Fekete, 2020).

Part of the reasoning points to workplace climate, and weak institutional trust, while lack of information or communication in the institute, being overburdened along with lack of time and timing difficulties can also prove to be challenges. Many of the asked subjects highlighted that their own institution gets little support, and that they are not able/ do not want to find others to substitute their classes for these periods of travel (European Commission, 2015, Horváth et al., 2020; Dabney-Fekete, 2020). Though in internationalization processes, many times participation for the academic staff member is compulsory, the process of popularizing the mission at home is not without its issues (Szolár, 2009; Hőrich, 2014). As a result, so many authors and researchers mention lack of motivation among academics (Teichler, 2011; European Commission, 2015; Dabney-Fekete, 2020; Borm, 2020), who also fear for their jobs (Dabney-Fekete, 2020). The other group of restrictive factors surround planning the outbound trip, the professors feeling overburdened with the administrative and legal planning of it all like, getting visas, as well as planning and execution of the trip (Teichler, 2011; European Commission, 2015; Horváth et al., 2020).

Based on earlier examinations (Viszt, 2004; Kyvik & Larsen, 1997; Pusztai & Szabó, 2008; Smeby & Trondal, 2005; Dabney-Fekete, 2020) it can be said that regarding the backlog of academics' mobility not only the obstacles appearing on the individuals' level should be mentioned, but also the limitations and barriers deriving from the characteristics of certain disciplines could be traced. It is assumed that "hard" disciplines like economics or medical studies, could be more easily made international, since the country of the researcher has little effect on the results of the examinations. Contrary to that, "soft" disciplines, due to their strong social and cultural embeddedness, are less "translatable" (Kwiek, 2019; Kyvik & Larsen, 1997; Dabney-Fekete, 2020; Smeby & Trondal, 2005).

1.4. Hypotheses

In our study we wanted to know what the form and degree of intensity is of academics' international activity as regards the institutions in Central-Eastern Europe, more particularly to get answers to many mobility related questions. Thus, we set up three hypotheses, and, through them, tried to find reasons for international mobility and its drawbacks.

H1. There will be significant variation among academics participating in international mobility based on field of study.

H2. Demographics heavily influence mobility, factors like, (1) gender—women are less mobile, (2) age—younger ones took part in mobility less, (3) marital status—married couples were less likely to be active internationally, (4) children—those with children participated less, (5) financial standing—those on worse monetary footing were mobile to a lesser extent, (6) country of origin—academic staff members from EU member states more often took part than those from non-EU countries.

H3. The effect of the restrictive factors will be detectable in the special literature, in this way, academic staff members with poorer language proficiency will be less internationally active, as well as those who are less embedded at their workplace (because necessary information does not reach them), or professors who do not feel supported by the institution or by their colleagues, those who are burned out, or feel that their work and private life are out of balance.

2. Methodology

In our study, we used the full database of the Central and Eastern European Teachers in Higher Education (CEETHE 2023), in this way—though due to variation in the items it was limited—we could compare the mobility of academics working in the universities of five countries. In our sample, therefore, 853

Hungarian, Romanian, Serbian, Slovakian, and Ukrainian academics responded. After data cleansing that number dropped to 821.

The higher educational institutions examined were, on the one hand, from the Southern Transdanubia Region (with the University of Pécs as a representative), and the Northern Great Plains Region (with the University of Debrecen, the Debrecen Reformed Theological University, and the University of Nyíregyháza). These regions are considered to be in a less advantageous situation. On the other hand cross-border institutions were examined: the Oradea State University, the Sapientia Hungarian University of Transylvania, the Emanuel University, the Partium Christian University, and the Babeş-Bolyai University and their satellite branches in Romania, the University of Novi Sad in Serbia, the University of Trnava, the J. Selye University, and the University of Prešov in Slovakia, the Uzhhorod National University, and the Ferenc Rákóczi II Transcarpathian Hungarian College of Higher Education in Ukraine. The special value of the research was that although these were mostly minority Hungarian universities and colleges, the questionnaires were distributed in the countries' official languages as well, so that all academics could be included. Another peculiarity was that all together 62 replies came from war-torn territories in Ukraine. The composition of the answers was as follows: we received the most responses from Hungary, 61.8% (514 people), then after a huge gap come Ukraine with 14.1% (115) and Romania with 13.8% (113) replies, dropping astern Serbia with 4.9% (40) and Slovakia with 4.4% (36). The limitation of the analysis could be detected in that the sample size was low in certain countries, thus the generalization of the results could not come into play.

Our fundamental question was, what sort of differences appear between a participant in academic staff mobility, and one who does not participate. We viewed those who answered in the affirmative to the question: "did you participate or not in the academic staff mobility program?" as mobile ones, and those who answered in the negative as immobile. It is important to draw attention to the fact that the question did not have a time constraint, in other words, not only did it apply to the last five or ten years, but the entire career. This will have an important role in the analysis of the data.

As explanatory variables we examined the demographic background variables (age, gender, country of origin), as well as the disciplines, the ranks and academic degrees. Furthermore, within the boundaries that were drawn by the database, we studied whether the factors that are usually mentioned by special literature as inhibiting obstacles for academic mobility, show significant connection to academics' (im)mobility. Examining these factors we created indices. During our research we used the chi-square test, and variance analysis.

3. Results

During our examination, we found that only 40.6% of the entire sample (N=821) took part in academic staff mobility. This is substantially less than the 69% that Horváth et al. (2020) concluded in their research. Comparing men and women, we see that among men the ratio of professors who during their career took part in some sort of mobility is significantly higher. In our examination 42.2% of respondent men and 37% of women taught or carried out research abroad (p=0.02). On the other side of the coin 51.6% of all those participating in mobility in our sample are women, and 48.4% are men.

The average age of mobile respondents was 47.72, while that of immobile ones was 45.04 (p=0.000) in the database.

Substantial variation was seen according to country (p=0.000). Here, however, we again seek to call attention to variation of items by country. In Table 9.1 it is clear to see that 77.8% of Slovakian, and nearly 60% of Romanian respondents took part in mobility programs. Compared to this, the ratio of Serbian and Ukrainian mobile academics is low.

Table 9.1: The ratios of academic staff mobility by country (N= 804)

	HU	UA	RO	SB	SK	Total
Yes, I participated in international mobility	35.6%	31.8%	59.5%	41.0%	77.8%	40.5%
No, I have not	64.4%	68.2%	40.5%	59.0%	22.2%	59.5%
N	508	110	111	39	36	804

*The underlined values indicate that the number of people in that cell of the table is much higher than would have been expected in the case of random ordering.

According to the academic field, it is observable (see Table 9.2) that the ratios of mobile and immobile respondents are most even in humanities and arts departments—the ratio of those taking part in any kind of academic staff mobility being 48.4%. An earlier study at a Hungarian university (Dabney-Fekete, 2020) showed that relatively few academic staff members from the humanities field had low levels of international activity. From STEMA[1]

1 STEMA is an acronym that stands for Science, Technology, Engineering, Math, and Agriculture.

courses, 46.4% of the respondents were mobile, and in social sciences and economics fields this number was also below 50%, precisely 49.3%. Employee mobility in medical courses, however, is strikingly low, with only 20.4% (p=0.000).

Table 9.2: Ratios of teaching and research mobility by academic field (N=800)

	Humanities	STEM	Medicine	Social science and economics
Yes, I participated in international mobility	48.4%	46.4%	20.4%	49.3%
No, I have not	51.6%	53.6%	79.6%	50.7%
N	258	181	225	136

When the academics giving their answers based on the positions that they currently hold at the higher educational institutions, significant differences stood out among respondents (p=0.000): as position rises, so too does the ratio of active participants in international mobility (Table 9.3).

Table 9.3: Ratios of academic staff mobility by position (N=800)

	Assistant lecturer	Assistant professor	Associate professor	University/ college professor	Other (senior academic staff, research fellow, etc.)
Yes, I participated in international mobility	17.0%	43.5%	53.0%	56.4%	18.4%
No, I have not	83.0%	56.5%	47.0%	43.6%	81.6%
N	88	239	215	117	141

*The underlined values indicate that the number of people in that cell of the table is much higher than would have been expected in the case of random ordering.

In our study, we wanted to examine how position and mobility are related, and whether they differ in the five countries under scrutiny, thus we also included the country variable in the crosstab analysis. We can see that only in the Hungarian (p=0.00) and Romanian (p=0.018) samples remained considerable connections between position and mobility; therefore, we share only these two countries' detailed results (see Table 9.4).

Table 9.4: Ratios of academic staff mobility according to position—the Hungarian and Romanian subsample (N=615)

		Assistant lecturer	Assistant professor	Associate professor	University/ college professor	Other (senior academics, research fellow, etc.)
Hungarian respondents (504 persons)	Yes	13.4%	36.8%	54.7%	54.3%	16.2%
	No	86.6%	63.2%	45.3%	45.7%	83.8%
	N	67	133	117	70	117
Romanian respondents (111 persons)	Yes	0.0%	54.8%	64.3%	91.7%	60.0%
	No	100.0%	45.2%	35.7%	8.3%	40.0%
	N	4	62	28	12	5

*The underlined values indicate that the number of people in that cell of the table is much higher than would have been expected in the case of random ordering.

In our examination, we checked to what extent the presence of academic degree influences international activity (p=0.000). Based on our results, we determined that there is a clear relationship between academic degree and international mobility. From Table 9.5 it is evident that academics with a Ph.D. and habilitation are the most mobile.

Table 9.5: Ratio of academic staff mobility according to academic degree (N=803)

	Without academic degree	Ph.D./ DLA	CSc	Habilitation	DSc
Yes, I participated in international mobility	17.2%	47.4%	23.9%	58.6%	37.1%
No, I have not	82.8%	52.6%	76.1%	41.4%	62.9%
N	169	359	46	104	89

*The underlined values indicate that the number of people in that cell of the table is much higher than would have been expected in the case of random ordering.

We have also examined its connections with the academics types (see Table 9.6). It seems that among the academics with an administrative focus and the research-focused academics the ratio of immobile is higher, while the teaching-focused academics and the academic leaders are more mobile (p=0.000).

Table 9.6: Ratio of academic staff mobility according to types of academics (N=806)

	Academics with an administrative focus	Teaching-focused academics	Academic leaders	Research-focused academics
Yes, I participated in international mobility	29.3%	47.4%	46.0%	33.1%
No, I have not	70.7%	52.6%	54.0%	66.9%
N	157	268	215	166

*The underlined values indicate that the number of people in that cell of the table is much higher than would have been expected in the case of random ordering.

For us to better understand the reasons for participation in academic staff mobility, or for the non-attendance thereof, we created a separate index and examined which one may have an impact on the existence or absence of international activity. Founded upon previous studies (Dabney-Fekete, 2020; Medgyes-Kaplan, 2015; Vossensteyn et al., 2010; Orr 2008), we assumed that in most cases, as a part of international activity, mobility frequently is absent because the academic staff member judges his/her own foreign language skill level to be such that he/she would not be able to stand up and give a lecture at a conference, or even work as a member of a research group. Though the research itself did not directly ask about the reasons for staying home, we could still measure academic foreign language knowledge. We considered it to be present whenever the respondents published in a foreign language, took part in an international study, when they presented research findings at a conference, or held courses for international students in English. We combined all of these in one index, in the ***academic foreign language knowledge indicator***. Teaching foreign students and holding lectures at a conference were included in the index with double the weight, since, in our opinion, these assume a higher level of language knowledge than for instance publishing, where the professor can request the help of a translator. Based on our results, it is obvious that there is a connection between academic foreign language knowledge, and international activity. The constructed foreign language knowledge index's average, in the case of academics who engaged in mobility, was significantly higher ($p=0.000$)(23.97) than the average of academics who did not shoulder teaching or researching abroad (21.08).

The other reason for weaker international activity that we supposed is the extra costs accompanying mobility that burden the individual. However, the results of our test did not support this. We could use two questions to examine the connections of financial standing with mobility. The following questions were asked: one, regarding relative financial standing, "How do you find your financial standing compared to the average families living in the country?," and two, on the subjective capital indicator, "How is your financial standing currently?" We could not show substantial ties between respondents' financial standing and the lack of involvement in mobility. We did consider it interesting that Dabney-Fekete's (2020) north-eastern Hungary study, specifically regarding the absence of travel to conferences, named monetary burdens as the number one reason.

We also assumed that the holding power of the family along with the lack of foreign language directly plays the role of a restrictive factor, since, for instance the Viszt survey (2004) that was conducted among Hungarian researchers, undercovers that family reasons come in third and second place for researchers in academic institutes and university departments. Also, in Dabney-Fekete's study (2020), family duties and obligations appear as highly important hindering aspects in the case of the measured forms of international activity, particularly in connection with scholarships, guest teaching and research trips. For these are the forms of mobility that at conferences, for example, take up far greater amounts of time. On the contrary, in our study, we found that weaker international activity is not explained by the retentive power of the family.

We also wanted to know how the institute support appears in our sample, since in the special literature too, many hold the lack of it to be a retentive factor (Szolár, 2009; Hőrich, 2014; Dusa, 2017; Dabney-Fekete, 2020)—first, the absence of financial support, and second, the recognition of the mission and the substitutions due to mobility are mentioned most often. Kwiek (2016), however, clearly shows in his study that the individual's motivation carries far more weight than the support coming from the institute. In order to examine this question, we formed two indices. In the ***institutional support index***, we included the following items: (1) the institution keeps the employees' interests front and center, (2) the institution holds competition with rivals (other institutions) to be important, (3) innovation-orientedness is characteristic of the institution, and (4) flexibility and individual responsibility is typical of the institution. We assumed, after all, all of these were factors that can strengthen academic staff mobility and create institutional culture. In another index we included the questions to direct colleagues and superiors: (1) Are you happy with the level of support from the department/institute/faculty head?, (2) Are you happy with the level of support from colleagues?, (3) Do they respect your efforts?, (4) Does performance define who is promoted at the department/ institute/ faculty? Respondents could evaluate the items on a 5-point Likert scale; thus, the index minimum could be 4, and its maximum 20. In our study, we found that the institutional support index was not significant regarding mobility. The combined indices of colleagues and superiors, however, showed that it was significantly tied to mobility. Surprisingly, those who were more content with the level of support from colleagues and superiors did not take part in academic staff mobility. The average of the index for support from mobile colleagues was lower (13.16) than that of the immobile ones (13.84). In connection with this, we also looked at how much chance they see that they will be fired in the following year—here, however, we could not find significant relationship.

We wanted to cover whether for academics the inadequate flow of information at their workplace can be considered a restraining element of mobility or not. We measured this by creating ***an index with questions about their relationship with colleagues***. In the index, we used the following question block's items: How often did it occur in the last semester that ... you spoke about academic questions with your colleagues?; ... you helped a colleague prepare their doctoral or habilitation thesis, grant application?; ... you spoke about educational questions with your colleagues?; you spoke about other topics than university work with your colleagues?; ... you agreed to meet your colleague outside of work?; ... your colleague spoke with you about his/her future plans?; ... you worked together with your colleague in a research group, as a co-author?; ... you worked on an online workspace with your colleague? The respondents could answer on a four-point scale; thus, the index maximum was 32, and the minimum 8. We assumed based on Pusztai (2011) that those who converse more with their colleagues (that is, are better embedded, more types of information reaches them), are more mobile. In our study, it clearly rounded out: the average of academics participating in mobility was higher (22.41 in contrast with the 21.03-point average of immobile academics), that is they are more embedded in the life of the department/ institute, and arguably, in the case of more conversation, the probability that information regarding international activity will reach the individual is greater.

Based on the results of an earlier study (Dabney-Fekete, 2020) we counted on some of the respondents mentioning a lack of motivation as an explanation for the absence of trips abroad. Expectations and obligations of private life, workplace, and internationalization weigh heavily on academics, possibly manifesting themselves in the academics being undermotivated in the question of international mobility. Therefore, we created a ***burnout index*** and examined whether in our sample we could find connections between general workplace burnout and mobility. [1] We created the index on burnout due to work based on the following five statements: I feel emotionally exhausted because of my work.; I feel exhausted at the end of the workday.; I feel tired when I get up in the morning, and I have to face a new workday.; Working all day is very cumbersome to me.; I feel burned out from my work. The statements could be evaluated on a seven-point scale by respondents. The index maximum could be 35, and the minimum could be 5. Yet, in our study, we could not find a relationship between the two. We assumed as well that the lack of motivation may be thanks to the need for academics to fill in too many roles—we developed ***an index from work-private life*** questions, and with its help we measured this. However, we did not find any connections to the absence of mobility in this case either. We examined whether weak international activity and discontent with hours worked affect each other. We discovered no connection between them, which is not surprising since the amount of hours in most cases is not the decision of the academic staff member, but rather comes with the position, and varies from faculty to faculty. From these three indices we formed a combined indicator which examined the hardships of reconciling work with private life, from the perspective of motivation. We could not find significant ties here either. To sum it up, we can say that in the case of the academic staff members in our sample, lack of motivation truly is not an explanatory factor for the absence of mobility.

In conclusion, we would have liked to examine whether or not there is any sort of connection between participation in international mobility and teaching foreign students. We presumed, on the one hand, that the professor possessing such a level of foreign language knowledge that he/she is able to share professional content in English with students—be it lecture, seminar, practical class or lab—would be able to much more confidently integrate into one of internationalization's forms. After all, lack of language proficiency is not a restrictive factor. On the other hand, we thought that those at the forefront, regarding international activity, due to their adequate foreign language knowledge and their familiarity with being in a multicultural setting, would be far more probable to be entrusted with teaching foreign students. Our results clearly display significant ties between participation in international mobility and teaching foreign students. It is worth noticing that 65.7% of respondents admitted to not taking part in international mobility throughout their careers, in contrast, they were already drawn by the institute into instructing foreign students (see Table 9.7). It may serve as an explanation that they who are at the height of their careers have not had much opportunity to get involved in the internationalization process, but, because of their good language knowledge, there was a need for them in teaching. Perhaps it is precisely due to this that they teach in this way, since substituting them would prove difficult were they to travel away as mobile academics.

Table 9.7: The connection between education of foreign students and academic staff mobility. p=0.012 (N=772)

	Mobile	Immobile
He/she teaches foreigners	74.20%	65.70%
He/she does not teach foreigners	25.80%	34.30%
N	314	458

*The underlined values indicate that the number of people in that cell of the table is much higher than would have been expected in the case of random ordering.

That we might better understand the position of the immobile academic staff members who teach foreigners, we created four groups: 1) teaches foreigners, but is immobile, 2) teaches foreigners, and is mobile, 3) does not teach foreigners, but is mobile, and 4) does not teach foreigners and is immobile. Upon examining these four groups it was discovered that the immobile respondents who instruct foreigners are younger (p=0.001). Looking at their positions, 50% of assistant lecturers, and 41.7% of assistant professors are in this group (p=0.000). Much is also said by the fact that, by academic field, the largest ratio of those who teach foreigners but do not engage in international mobility is in the medical and healthcare field: in this group 67.9% of the medical and healthcare field, 39.2% of the STEM field, 32.1% of the social science and economic fields, and 17.9% of the humanities (p=0.000).

4. Discussion

Our study focused on the international mobility activity of academics in higher education. We examined what sort of effects of restrictive factors appear, which might make it difficult to get involved in teaching and participating in research programs abroad. For this, we used the Central and Eastern European Teachers in Higher Education (CEETHE 2023, N=821) database. For one, we were curious as to the differences between academic fields, and, for two, wanted to know something of the various demographic factors' effects (age, family status, children, financial standing, and country of origin). Aside from these, we attempted to show the effects of restrictive factors uncovered in previous studies, they are as follows: foreign language knowledge, integration into the workplace community, institutional support, effect of support from direct colleagues, workplace burnout, or balance of work and private life.

From among the demographic aspects, it was gender, age and country of origin that were significantly tied to whether or not a respondent taught or conducted research abroad, thus in these regards our second hypothesis was proven. Based on this, the older, the men, and the Slovakian and Romanian academics show higher mobility. It is interesting that though prior research called attention to the deterrent roles of family (especially of parents with children requiring more care) or poor financial standing, according to this CEETHE database, we were unable to justify this claim.

The gender ratio in our database mostly matches with data from previous studies. For instance, in the case of a study conducted at European universities (Horváth et al., 2020), of all mobile academics 42.2% were men and 57.8% women, however, no significant ties were found between gender and participating in academic staff mobility. Commissioned by the Tempus Public Foundation in 2021, in a study done among domestic academic staff (Malota & Gyulavári, 2022), the same ratios mentioned above displayed the exact opposite: here 45% of women and 55% of men were represented. Another Hungarian research also had similar results (Dabney-Fekete, 2020)—here the ratio of men was 55.2% and the ratio of women was 44.8%. As pertains to age, it is no surprise that mostly the academic staff member taking part in the mobility program are older. Since the question applied to the whole educational career, the older professors with greater chance already went abroad to teach and carry out research throughout their careers. This is closely and clearly connected to the fact that higher international activity was shown for those with higher academic positions, since academics at the peak of their career have more chances to go abroad for guest teaching, or international research collaboration (Table 9.3). This is no surprise, however, since, on one hand, for someone to have these degrees and titles, as a condition, he/she needs to complete the criteria connected to internationalization (e.g., taking part in international conferences, different international co-operations, etc.). And on the other hand, these academic degrees and titles serve as a sort of springboard which, with the completion of the right academic and internationalization indicators, can help in moving up to the next level—after Ph.D., habilitation; after habilitation, DSc. At the same time, for young academic staff members and researchers, due precisely to moving up the ranking ladder, it would be important to gain international professional experience. In previous studies (Dabney-Fekete, 2020), we found examples of this that some universities' financing systems and modes strongly influenced the type of international activity based on position: in some institutions colleagues in higher positions are those who get a large part of the support set aside for attending conferences. In this way, either younger assistant lecturers and assistant professors are left out of mobility, or—though they possess less international professional experience—it is precisely they who are forced to choose guest teaching that requires longer absence but better foreign language proficiency.

It was interesting to see that usually of those with a Candidate of Sciences degree (a scientific qualification that existed before the Ph.D. was introduced) in our sample, it is characteristic that they are less mobile. After WWII, the academic degree system patterned after the Soviet was, from the end of the 1990s, in Central and Eastern European countries officially replaced by the Ph.D. as seen in the Anglo-Saxon model. By law, CSc was supposed to be equal to Ph.D., and in the case of dr. univ. there was a possibility to have it recognized in a higher level. Nevertheless, it appears that there were those who did not wish to go further, after receiving their candidate degrees, to relinquish the opportunities for advancement provided by the new system. For us though, it was astonishing that participation in mobility of professors with DScs was low. After all, in their case, the question rightly arises, how did they successfully evade the powerful waves of internationalization in higher education over the past decades and still acquire such high academic degrees?

Besides gender and age, the country of origin also played a significant role in whether the professor is internationally active or not. Due to the low Romanian sample size, comparing the assistant and associate professor positions is relevant, and in these cases it can be seen that Romanian respondents have more experience in mobility. Based on results of previous studies (Dabney-Fekete, 2020) we surmised that the Romanian academics' stronger international activity might be in connection with confidence due to having the appropriate level of foreign language proficiency regarding international cooperation and activity. After all, these colleagues from childhood are used to communicating in multiple languages on a daily basis. In the case of minorities living in Romania, learning at least two languages (the one spoken at home and the official language of the state) is self-explanatory, and for the majority of society, due to the grammatical structure and vocabulary of the Romanian language, learning other European languages becomes relatively easier. It is therefore not strange to this society to have the multicultural environment and the presence of multiple languages in everyday life, which, when it comes to international mobility, carries great weight.

The ratio of participating in international mobility in Serbia and Ukraine is low compared to that of Slovakia and Romania. This can be explained by the fact that two countries are EU member states. Thus, the opportunities and mobility programs offered by the EU are either more restricted or are missing all together. Another explanation could also be that during the time of the survey, war persisted/persists in Ukraine, drastically decreasing the amount of academics available for the research. Serbia suffered war in the '90s, which might have strongly restricted the movement of older professors. In contrast, Hungary's very low participation (all together only 35.6% of the respondents took part in mobility programs) cannot be explained. Therefore, we can assume that willingness to participate in mobility is connected to which country the given professor is the citizen of, after all, mobility capital is certainly stronger in countries where knowing multiple languages is part of everyday life.

Based on previous research (Viszt, 2004; Dabney-Fekete, 2020) we considered that for the academics family would be another blocking factor. However, our results did not show any significant connection with weaker international mobility. Since this is contrary to previous research, we assumed that perhaps that the reason we could not find any connections was because in the survey we asked respondents about the mobility throughout their entire careers rather than just the last 5 or 10 years. Thus, in the sample many professors can be found whose children are no longer minors, and as a consequence their lack of international activity cannot be explained away with the family factor. We tested if the same was true of those under 45 years of age who were more likely to have small children. However, we experienced in their case as well that duty to family did have an effect on international mobility.

Our results confirmed the first hypothesis, namely that stark differences appear also among academic fields in the mobility of academics: similar to student mobility, the academics of the medical and healthcare majors also take part in teaching and researching projects and grants abroad in smaller ratios. Thus, it is no surprise, because, specifically in Hungarian higher education, the greatest number of foreign students have for the longest time studied these majors in these faculties. What is more, the field itself is "hard," so as a result, it is more easily translatable into English, and its fundamental language of Latin, the basis for medical terminology, is the internationally recognized mediator language in this case. However, due to the rigidity of the training structure and the physician's duty of these respondents, along with the pressure to attend international conferences and to publish internationally as well, they are hardly able to take advantage of any other opportunities for mobility (guest teaching, and guest researching).

The same differences based on academic disciplines can be seen in a study as well (Dabney-Fekete, 2020), where those from the medical field who are never mobile is slightly less than double the amount coming from the humanities. (Reciprocally the study also highlights, those who take part in international activity are incredibly active.) This reflects the mobility data on medical students. According to Debrecen data from a 2013 Eurostudent survey, though medical and pharmaceutical students would like to study abroad (43.2% stated their wish to), only 4.9% actually followed through on this intent. Of those in healthcare fields, however, neither the desire to study abroad (15.2% would study abroad), nor the actualized mobility (2.9% followed through and went abroad for study) are typical (Dusa, 2020). As found in the results of the 2023 Education at a Glance survey, medical and healthcare students make up the third largest ratio of foreign students of the 25 EU member states (In total, foreign students comprise only 19%, 22% of business, administration, and legal majors, and 29% of STEM majors). However, this applies to diploma mobility, not short international courses, or Erasmus+ programs (OECD, 2023: 260). The mobility backlog of students studying medicine can be explained by the rigid structure of their training, which hampers not only learning abroad, but also carries with it the risk of dropout (Pusztai et al., 2022).

In our view, this extent of academics' lagging behind in mobility activities can be due to the fact that in this field, if there is any at all, the mobility that exists is weak. One reason for this might be that today the number of healthcare conferences that are not specialized or focused on a specific area is quite scant (internationally as well). It is because of this that employees in healthcare mostly only annually attend one or two conferences specific to their field. Also, the structure of the medical training is less flexible, academics are simultaneously practicing doctors and researchers too. Despite all this, it still was astonishing that precisely these fields have the least mobile academic staff members, for, based on earlier studies (Smeby & Trondal, 2005; Kyvik & Larsen, 1997; Pusztai & Szabó, 2008; Viszt, 2004), we can conclude that because healthcare, a "hard" field, is easier to internationalize and "translate," more academic staff members will have higher levels of international activity.

In our research we presumed that one of the factors that hinders academics from going abroad for academic reasons is the not-sufficient foreign language knowledge. With the special index we created we could measure it, which contained such items as publishing in a foreign language or attending international conferences. We found that the point value of mobile academics was significantly higher in this index than that of immobile ones. Still, this could be mutual: the mobile academics are perhaps braver to publish internationally or to cooperate in research projects with foreign colleagues with whom they became acquainted on previous trips.

Embedding into the institutional climate, and relationships with colleagues help much in getting information, thus, it is no shock that we could find ties between mobility and the level to which relationships were maintained with colleagues: the value of the created index was drastically higher among mobile academic staff members, so it seems that they speak more with their colleagues, meaning that relevant information (even about international opportunities) reaches them sooner. This is somewhat contradicted by the fact that it is the immobile respondents, not the mobile ones, who are more content with the level of support they receive from their immediate colleagues. We could not, however, show the effect of support from the higher education institution, the upset balance of work and private life, or the effect of workplace burnout. Thus, regarding our hypothesis as pertains to the restrictive factors only the presuppositions concerning foreign language proficiency and workplace embeddedness were proven.

Conclusions

As a result of our findings, we can disclose that important discoveries and conclusions were made in relation to the international mobility of higher educational academics. First of all, indeed, there is an unequivocal difference between the particular disciplines regarding international mobility. Somewhat less than half of the respondents from social sciences and economic, as well as STEM fields were mobile, which can be considered unsatisfactory, but still twice as much as that of the health sciences. Significant difference was also detected with respect to the respondents' gender, age and the country they are from. Based on our findings, men and older people tend to be more mobile, and academics from Romania and Slovakia are also more likely to participate in this particular form of internationalization. A better and more refined level of English language knowledge was also characteristic of the internationally mobile group—it was not clear though whether the more excellent level was due to the exposure of foreign culture through traveling and participating in international activities and events, or whether it was quite the other way round.

The analysis of the data highlighted several dilemmas and raised numerous questions in connection with the international mobility of higher educational academics. These could serve as stepping stones for better understanding the problem and thus develop a more realistic and pragmatic internationalization strategy of universities for their academic staff. Grasping and being conscious of the obstacles and impediments could actually lead to a more effective, operational internationalization planning procedure. An essential finding of the research was that international activities occur way more in a supportive environment, among colleagues who have a good relationship and talk often with each other. In such an atmosphere academically important information is passed down and circulated.

References

Altbach, P. (2002). *The Decline of the Guru: The Academic Profession in developing and Middle-Income Countries*. Chestnut Hill, Boston College.

Borm, J. (2020). *Making Mobility the Norm-NORM. IO1 desk research report*. Retrived from <https://projects.uni-foundation.eu/norm/wp-content/uploads/sites/8/2023/02/IO1_NORM_Desk-Reserach-Report.pdf>

Brandenburg, U. (2014). *The Erasmus Impact Study*. Publications Office of the European Union. <https://doi.org/10.2766/75468>

Dabney-Fekete, I. D. (2020). *Nemzetköziesedő tudomány. A felsőoktatásban dolgozó oktatók nemzetközi aktivitása*. [Internationalising science. International activity of instructors in higher education]. CHERD-H.

Dusa, Á. R. (2017). Külföldi tanulás és munka határhelyzetben. Partiumi hallgatók részvétele a nemzetközi hallgatói mobilitásban. [Studying and working abroad in a cross-border situation. Participation of students from Partium in international student mobility]. In K. Bartha, & B. Balogh (Eds.), *Oktatás határhelyzetben* (pp. 116–123). Partium Kiadó.

Dusa Á. R. (2020). *Hallgatók nemzetközi mobilitása a XXI. század elején*. [International student mobility in the early twenty-first century]. Debrecen University Press.

European Commission. (2007). *Key Data on Higher Education in Europe*. Office for Official Publications of the European Communities.

European Commission. (2015). *The European Higher Education Area in 2015: Bologna Process Implementation Report*. Publications Office of the European Union. <https://doi.org/10.2797/128576>

Ghulam, A. M. (2022). A General Perspective about Institutional Rankings, Ranking Framework, Benefits Rankings and Ranking Methodological Flaws and Best Approach for Being A World Class Institution. *International Journal of Educational Research Review,* 7(3), 157–165. <https://doi.org/10.24331/ijere.1067952>

Greek, M., & Jonsmoen, K. M. (2021). Transnational academic mobility in universities: the impact on a departmental and an interpersonal level. *Higher Education, 81*, 591–606.

Horváth, L., Hangyál, Zs., Kasza, G., & Czirfusz, D. (2020). *Teach with Erasmus+ Research Report*. ELTE Eötvös Loránd University Department of Erasmus+ and International Programs.

Höhle, E. & Teichler U. (2013). The Teaching Function of the Academic Profession. In U. Teichler, & Höhle, E. (Eds.), *The Work Situation of the Academic Profession in Europe: Findings of a Survey in Twelve Countries*. (pp. 79–108). Springer.

Hőrich B. (2014). Az intézmények és oktatók mint mobilitási klíma. [Institutions and academic staff as a mobility climate] In Zs. Veroszta (Ed.), *A mozgás tere. A magyar felsőoktatás és a nemzetközi mobilitási folyamatok. Campus Hungary tanulmánykötet* (pp. 189–210). Balassi Intézet.

Knight, J. (2013). The changing landscape of higher education internationalisation—for better or worse? *Perspectives: Policy and Practice in Higher Education, 17*(3), 84–90. <https://doi.org/10.1080/13603108.2012.753957>

Knight, J., & de Wit, H. (2018). Internationalization of Higher Education: Past and Future. *International Higher Education, 95*, 2–4. <https://doi.org/10.6017/ihe.2018.95.10715>

Kozma T. (2004). *Kié az egyetem? [Who owns the university?]* Új Mandátum.

Kwiek, M. (2016). The European research elite: a cross-national study of highly productive academics in 11 countries. *Higher Education, 71*(3). 379–397. <https://doi.org/10.1007/s10734-015-9910-x>

Kwiek, M. (2019). Social stratification in Higher Education: What it means at the micro-level of the individual academic scientist. *Higher Education Quarterly, 73*(4), 419–444. <https://doi.org/10.1111/hequ.12221>

Kwiek, M. (2022). Global Vertical Stratification of Institutions and the Academic Profession: The Role of Research in Future High Participation Environments. In Klemenčič, M. (ed.), *From Actors to Reforms in European Higher Education. Higher Education Dynamics*, vol. 58 (pp 299–312). Springer. <https://doi.org/10.1007/978-3-031-09400-2_21>

Kyvik, S., & Larsen, I. M. (1997). The Exchange of Knowledge: A Small Country in the International Research Community. *Science Communication, 18*(3), 238–264. <https://doi.org/10.1177/1075547097018003004>

Malota, E., & Gyulavári, T. (2022). *Nemzetközi mobilitás a felsőoktatásban: Az oktatói/kutatói mobilitás elősegítő és akadályozó tényezői, motivációi és hatásai: Kutatási gyorsjelentés. [International mobility in higher education: facilitators and barriers, motivations and impacts of lecturer/researcher mobility. Research Report].* Tempus Közalapítvány.

Medgyes, P., & Kaplan, R. B. (2015). A magyar kutatók idegennyelv-tudása. [Foreign language skills of Hungarian researchers] In P. Medgyes (Ed.), *Töprengések a nyelvtanításról* (pp. 65–77). Eötvös Kiadó.

OECD. (2023). *Education at a Glance 2023: OECD Indicators*. OECD Publishing. <https://doi.org/10.1787/e13bef63-en>

Orr, D. (2008). *Social and Economic Conditions of Student Life in Europe*. W. Bertelsmann Verlag.

Pallay, K., Pusztai, G., Demeter-Karászi, Zs., & Marincsák, R. (2024). Az eredményesség és a teljesítményértékelés percepciói a kárpát-medencei magyar felsőoktatásában [Perceptions of effectiveness and performance evaluation in Hungarian higher education in the Carpathian Basin]. In K. Kovács & K. Pallay (Eds.), *Oktatók a Kárpát-medencei felsőoktatásban. Munkajellemzők, jóllét és eredményesség* (pp. 151–164). CHERD-H.

Perger, M. (2016). „Mi a siker titka?" A tanítással kapcsolatos nézetek és tanítási módszerek vizsgálata a BME mérnökképzéseinek legjobb oktatói körében. ["What is the secret of success?" A survey of teaching beliefs and teaching methods among the best lecturers of BME engineering courses] *Opus et Educatio: Munka és nevelés 3*(5), 527–555. DOI: 10.3311/ope.127

Pusztai, G. (2015). Pathways to Success in Higher Education. Rethinking the Social Capital Theory in the Light of Institutional Diversity. Peter Lang Edition.

Pusztai, G., & Szabó, P. Cs. (2008). The Bologna Process as a Trojan Horse: Restructuring Higher Education in Hungary. *European Education 40*(2), 85–102. <https://doi.org/10.2753/EUE1056-4934400205>

Pusztai, G., Demeter-Karászi, Zs., Alter, E., Marincsák, R., & Dabney-Fekete, I. D. (2022). Administrative data analysis of student attrition in Hungarian medical training. *BMC Medical Education 22*, 317. <https://doi.org/10.1186/s12909-022-03276-z>

Smeby, J. C., & Trondal, J. (2005). Globalisation or europeanisation? International contact among university staff. *Higher Education, 49*, 449–466. <https://doi.org/10.1007/s10734-004-2826-5>

Szolár, É. (2009). Az európai felsőoktatás átalakulása és a Bologna-folyamat céljai. [The transformation of European higher education and the objectives of the Bologna Process] *Iskolakultúra, 19*(9), 95–119. <https://www.iskolakultura.hu/index.php/iskolakultura/article/view/20896>

Teichler, U. (2011). Academic staff mobility. In U. Teichler, I. Ferencz & B. Wächter (Eds.), *Mapping Mobility in European Higher Education. Volume I: Overview and Trends* (pp. 111–146). European Commission.

Viszt, E. (2004). A kutatók nemzetközi mobilitása. [International mobility of researchers] *Magyar Tudomány, 110*(8), 886–899.

Vossensteyn, H., Beerkens, M., Cremonini, L., Huisman, J., Souto-Otero, M., Bresancon, B., Focken, N., Leurs, B., McCoshan, A., Mozuraityte, N., Pimentel Bótas, P. C., & de Wit, H. (2010). *Improving participation in the Erasmus programme. Final report to the European Parliament*. European Parliament.

10. Research Productivity and Workplace Stress Among Academics

Klára Kovács, Marianna Moravecz & Gabriella Hideg

ABSTRACT
In our study, the influencing factors of research productivity was examined among academics in five higher education institutions in CEE. Our main research question was which work-related stressors and resources reduce or contribute to their research productivity. The theoretical background of our research is based on the theory of job demands and resources (JD-R), which helps to explain and understand the relationship between job characteristics and employee productivity. For our research we used the CEETHE 2023 database (N=821). The data were collected from higher education institutions in two disadvantaged regions of Hungary, while for institutions across the border in Slovakia, Ukraine, Romania and Serbia, we targeted Hungarian minority institutions. Our results suggested that the most productive groups were older people, men in higher positions, those with an academic degree, those working in social and economic sciences, and senior academics. Stress caused by performance appraisal emerged as a negative factor for productivity.

Keywords: research productivity, JD-R theory, job demands and resources

Introduction

In this study, the factors influencing the research productivity of academics were examined in five Central and Eastern European countries (in Hungary, Slovakia, Ukraine, Romania and Serbia, which countries belong to the broader concept of the CEE region according to the interpretation of the OECD and the EU). Two main groups of work-related outcomes (well-being and productivity) have been identified. Productivity is nothing more than the behavior of the employee through which he/she contributes to the achievement of institutional goals (Utami & Vioreza, 2021). In this research, research productivity means workplace performance which the academics contribute to the effectiveness of higher education institutions, mainly measured in an international context (by publications in high-ranking journals, international conference presentations, participation in researches, receiving awards, grants etc.) or on individual level (highly motivated, satisfied academic staff) (Bland et al., 2005; Chen et al., 2006). In this competitive environment, there is an increasing emphasis on the research success of institutions, which is translated at the level of the academic staff into high requirements for publication and participation in research projects. From the perspective of academics, of the trinity of faculty roles—teaching, research and administrative duties—research dominates, while the other two remain in the background to research (Kwiek, 2016), confirming the relevance of applying the concept of research productivity we have adopted. Furthermore, research seems to be the single most stratifying factor in Higher Education at the level of the individual academic based on a comparative study among academics in 11 countries (Kwiek, 2019).

Our main question is, what are the challenges faced by the region's academics in their work, and what are the resources at the institutional and individual levels that contribute to their productivity? To investigate this issue, the job demands and resources (JD-R) theory (Bakker & Demerouti, 2014) was used as a theoretical framework. The JD-R theory is a theoretical framework that helps to explain and understand the relationships between job characteristics and employee performance and well-being. It classifies job characteristics into two categories that are negatively correlated: (negative) job demands and job-related resources, which have a direct impact on employees' stress levels, motivation, health problems and a range of organizational outcomes (Bakker & Demerouti, 2014; Szigeti & Kovács, 2022; Mudrak et al., 2018).

Previous studies have mainly examined psychological sources of stress and resources from a psychological perspective and have shown their relationship with work performance, psychological well-being and burnout (Alquarni, 2021; Han et al., 2020a; Iyaji et al., 2020). In this exploratory study, their relationship with productivity is investigated from a higher education research perspective. The validity of JD-R theory and workplace stressors has been extensively researched by academics worldwide (see Alqarni, 2021; Aziz & Quraishi, 2017; Bell et al., 2012; Fetherston et al., 2021; Han et al., 2020a; Iyaji et al., 2020; Kinman et al., 2006), but these have primarily addressed stress and resources in relation to well-being, job performance, job satisfaction, etc., and most of the research has examined linear relationships rather than using a complex theory or model (Mudrak et al., 2018). In our previous study, a similar model was used to examine the mediating role of work engagement and work exhaustion to examine the associations between job demands and resources and physical activity as an individual coping strategy with well-being. In the present analysis, these relationships have been further explored, and the model has been developed to examine these factors in relation to work performance (research productivity), complemented by additional influencing factors identified in the literature (working hours, job insecurity).

1. The Changing Higher Education Context and Its Influence on the Productivity of Academics in CEE

In the project of Changing Academic Profession in 2006, a study of academics in 19 countries worldwide was carried out, which did not include CEE countries, but the European continuation of the research, "The Academic Profession in Europe-Responses to Societal Challenges" (EUROAC), included Poland and Romania from the region in 2007–2011. The comparative studies have reached similar conclusions: although the academic profession is subject to increasing expectations and pressures, these expectations do not constrain how academics perceive their situation and how they act. Of course, they have to respond to these challenges, but they have room for maneuver in how they interpret and respond to them (Höhle & Teichler, 2013). The most important (negative) predictor of job satisfaction in almost all countries was administrative processes (Bentley et al., 2013). As a follow-up to CAP, the Academic Profession in the Knowledge-Based Society (APIKS) research was conducted in 18 countries (CEE countries were not included) between 2019 and 2021 (Aarrevaara et al.). One of the main messages of this volume is that although the academic profession appears similar in many respects across the countries studied, when examined in depth, there are very large differences even when answering a simple question such as who can be considered a researcher in a given country (Jung et al., 2021).

As a result of the advance of managerialism (Kováts, 2023), various performance evaluation systems have been developed to assess the work of academic staff. A longitudinal study of British, Dutch and Swedish academics found that in all three countries, performance evaluation itself does not really affect academics' productivity, with Swedish respondents considering it merely an administrative practice, while Dutch academics doubt the validity of outcomes due to the distance manner of evaluation. British academics accept and understand the importance of performance evaluation for the effectiveness of the institution, to ensure fairness, transparency and better teaching quality, but they also doubt that it has any connection with teaching quality and its improvement. Three factors underlie this doubt: first, the scope of evaluation remains limited; second, the disadvantages of performance measurement; third, the most important aspects are immeasurable (Teelken, 2018), as academics also mentioned in our and other previous qualitative researches (Kovács et al., 2024; Kwiek & Antonowicz, 2015).

The CEE countries have followed this process with a slight delay, with effectiveness below the average of Western European counterparts (Goncharuk & Cirella, 2022), but the process of managerialism has also emerged in the 2010s. In Ukraine and Romania, specific performance evaluation systems have been developed to assess the work of academics, while in Hungary, all but five universities have been converted to private (foundation) status, and a portion of academics' salaries is determined by the results of a newly developed performance evaluation system (Rodrigues Pimenta et al., 2021). As in Bosnia, the Czech Republic, like other Eastern European countries, has entered the arena of international competition with an underfunded higher education system, and thus there is increasing pressure on academics to increase their productivity in order to meet indicators of international competition. Although the pressure to publish, grant-based funding, performance measurement and other reforms to increase institutional effectiveness are seen by academics as necessary, they are also seen as important to maintain their autonomy and influence in universities (Mudrak et al., 2006). Given the emergence and growing role of performance evaluation in academia, our research also examines the performance of academics based on quantifiable evaluation indicators, primarily related to academic research work. Indeed, these measurement tools tend to place a strong emphasis on this dimension of academics' work.

High workload and other sources of stress such as lack of institutional role clarity, lack of managerial support, interpersonal, role and work-family conflicts, and low student motivation are sources of job stress (job demands) that negatively affect employees' well-being, job satisfaction and performance (Anastasiou & Papakonstantinou, 2014; Bell et al., 2012; Fetherston et al., 2021; Iyaji et al., 2020; Kinman et al., 2006) Physiological and psychological stress are important predictors of job performance (Ismail et al., 2015), but it should be noted that some forms of stress—if managed and prevented in individuals and organizations (eustress)—increase performance, while distress due to workload, for example, decreases it, so the type of stress is a determinant beyond its amount (Usoro & Etuk, 2016).

However, perceptions of stressors and coping strategies vary by employee gender, age, position, years of teaching, job title and type of higher education institution (Akram, 2019; Anastasiou & Papakonstantinou, 2014; Bell et al., 2012; Faisal et al., 2019; Kinman, 2014; Malik et al., 2017; Mudrak et al., 2018). Men are more resilient to work stress than women, who are more likely to experience work-life conflict (Bell et al., 2012; Chukwuemeka et al., 2023; Malik et al., 2017; Mudrak et al., 2018).

A comparative study conducted across ten countries found that higher academic rank increased publication productivity in two countries (Australia and the U.K.) (Teodorescu, 2000). However, a study on Polish academics' international publication performance and career paths revealed that high-ranking academics in the top 10 percent achieved their positions due to outstanding publication performance and had already exhibited very high productivity earlier in their careers compared to colleagues in similar positions (Kwiek & Roszka, 2024). Abramo et al. (2014) examined the publication productivity of all Italian universities over a five-year period and highlighted the exceptional productivity of researchers in natural sciences, life sciences, and mathematics. The unique research styles, processes, and techniques of different disciplines lead to significant differences in research performance both within and across disciplines (Wood, 1990). Analyzing research performance between academic ranks, Abramo et al. (2011) argued full professors publish more than associate professors, who publish more than assistant professor, but there also significant differences by disciplines. Authors emphasize, if higher academic rank is associated with greater research performance, evaluation methods should better differentiate individual scientists by rank and create performance rankings within these categories, alongside overall rankings.

According to JD-R theory, institutional resources contribute to work outcomes as intrinsic and extrinsic motivators. Among Indonesian academics, job satisfaction has a direct positive effect on productivity (Utami & Vioreza, 2021), while among Czech academics, influence over work and supervisor support as resources are positively associated with work engagement and job satisfaction. Work engagement was the most important predictor of well-being, while job demands (such as quantitative demands, work-life conflicts and job insecurity) were only associated with stress (Mudrak et al.). Work-life balance and its loss are a much-studied issue in academic work. Successfully maintaining a harmonious balance between the two is a source of strength and has a positive impact on job satisfaction (Saeed & Farooqi, 2014), contributes to optimal performance (Guest, 2002), and is also associated with higher satisfaction with family life and life in general (Sirgy & Lee, 2018). At the same time, work-life conflict has a negative impact on the well-being of academic staff (Bell et al., 2012).

Based on the previous theories and research findings, the following hypotheses were formulated:

1. Notable variations in productivity based on gender, age, country, position, and scientific field
2. Job Demands diminish academics' productivity, while available Job Resources enhance it

2. Methodology

2.1. Data and Sample

To answer the research questions, the CEETHE 2023 database was used (N=821). The data sampled higher education institutions in two disadvantaged regions of Hungary, the North Great Plain Region (University of Debrecen, Debrecen Reformed Theological University and University of Nyíregyháza) and the South Transdanubian Region (University of Pécs), while in the case of cross-border institutions in Slovakia, Ukraine, Romania and Serbia Hungarian minority institutions were targeted, but the survey was still sent in the majority language.

Based on the experience of the focus group interviews conducted prior to the quantitative research, the academics' tasks were listed, and respondents were asked to rate on a scale of 1 to 4 the extent to which they considered the given tasks to be part of their job. On the basis of the responses, we first performed a factor analysis and then a cluster analysis, separating out four different types of academics: teaching-focused academics (33.4%), academics with an administrative focus (19.7%), research-focused academics (20.3%) and academic leaders (26.6%).

2.2. Variables and Analysis

As the emergence and advance of managerialism in higher education in the region under study in recent years has led to an increasing role for the evaluation of academic performance, including the quantification of academic productivity, the academic performance of academics in this research was also measured on the basis of self-report. They were asked how many different publications, conference presentations, grant applications and leadership positions they had held the previous four years. This period was chosen because this is the time span assessed in the evaluation of academic performance in Hungary and Ukraine, and these indicators related to scientific research dominate. Although self-reporting may be biased and there may be a problem of inaccurate recall, as the questionnaire was self-administered, it was accurately documented in their performance appraisal and CV and could be used as a guide to help them tick the correct response category. The response options were numerical intervals that allowed respondents to rate their own performance on a category from 0 to 100. The nine-item scale was found to be reliable (Cronbach's α=.825) and principal component analysis was used to produce a composite performance indicator (KMO=.802, $p<0.001$, explained variance 62.561%), which was converted to a 0–100-point scale. Here, 0 represented the lowest level of productivity and 100 the highest (M=22.66, SD=15.59).

Based on the work of Kinman et al. (2006), the stress and resources at work and their perceptions were also examined (Chronbach α=.869, maximum likelihood method, varimax rotation, KMO=.856, p=000, explained variance 53.045%). Factor analysis identified three sources of stress and one resource: workload, performance appraisal and diversity of teacher roles as sources of stress and management support as a resource. These factors were complemented by good working conditions (5-item, Chronbach α=.739, KMO=.753, p=000, explained variance 50.510%), peer support (4-item, Chronbach α=.867, KMO=.827, p=000, explained variance 71.610%), and development opportunities (5-item, Chronbach α=.832, KMO=.808, p=000, explained variance 60.101%) as resources (Malik et al., 2017). In addition, other factors influencing productivity and well-being that could also serve as stressors and resources were examined. Since the main objective of this study was to uncover the hardships associated with work, Hayman's (2005) dimensions of work-life conflict, when work interferes with private life, were examined (6-item Chronbach α=.948, KMO=905, p=000, explained variance 79.545).

Among the factors influencing research productivity, the area of emotional exhaustion at work (5 items Chronbach α=.911, KMO=.852, p=000, explained variance 73.894%) and work engagement using the Ulrecht Work Engagement-9 scales (9 items, Chronbach α=.931, KMO=.900, p=000, explained variance 65.441%) were investigated (Han et al., 2020). Workplace bullying was measured using the Malik et al. (2017) completed scale (7 items, Chronbach α=.873, KMO=.890, p=000, explained variance 59.590%). Each main component was formed into a scale from 0 to 100, where 0 indicated that the main component was not at all characteristic of the respondent, and 100 that it was completely typical of the respondent. Workload, performance appraisal, diversity of teacher roles, work-life conflict, emotional exhaustion, bullying at work, working hours per week, and job insecurity are considered as job demands, while management support and work engagement are considered as job resources.

The demographic background variables examined were age, gender and country of origin, and the work characteristics were academic degree, job position, managerial position, academic discipline and type of academics. Analyses were carried out using the SPSS 29 program, using the Kruskal-Wallis test, the Mann-Whitney test and linear regression, and checking normality with the Kolgomorov-Smirnov test.

3. Results

Almost half of the respondents had no books published in their mother tongue/national language or in an international language, 44.5% had 1–5 books published in their mother tongue and 21.5% in English or another foreign language. For articles published in the mother tongue/national language, 30.1% published 1–5, and almost 10% 21–40. More than 100 articles were published in a foreign language by 44, while 14.5%, 21–40 published articles in a foreign language in the last four years. Of these, 37.5% had published 1–5 articles in Q1-Q2, and 36.3% had published none. Again, six respondents chose one of more than 100 possible answers, which was not rejected because in certain scientific fields (medicine, natural sciences) it is typical for research to be conducted in large rooms and for a very high number of authors to write articles. The majority of respondents had presented 6–10 or 11–20 papers at national conferences (~19%), with about 11% presenting none. A fifth of respondents had not presented at an international conference, 36.4% had presented 1–5 papers. Approximately one-third were not members of a national research group, and more than half were members of an international research group; nationally, 51.3% were members or leaders of at least one research groups, and internationally, 40.7% were members (Figure 10.1).

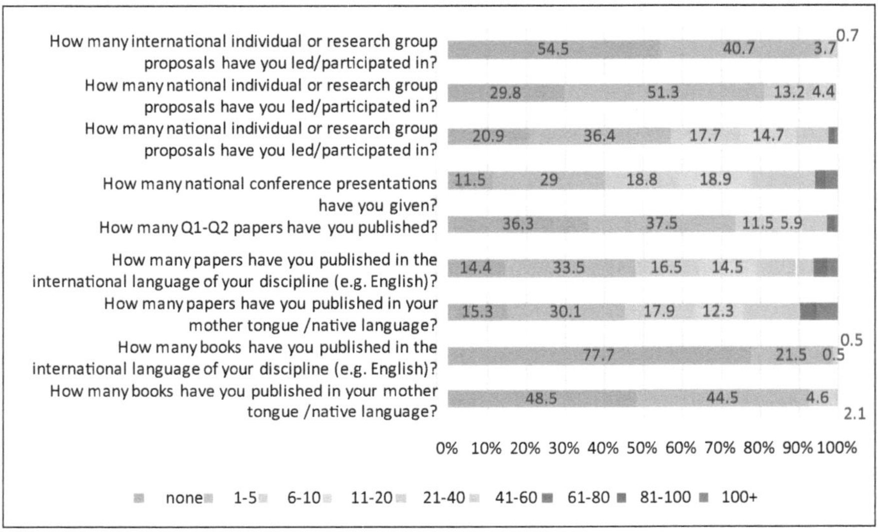

Figure 10.1: Research productivity of academics over the past four years based on self-report. *Source*: CEETHE 2023.

3.1. Relationships Between Demographic, Work Characteristics and Research Productivity

Significant differences were found for all variables except country (p<0.001). Results show that males (M=25.84, SD=17.96) than females (M=20.08, SD=12.84), researchers in social and economic sciences (M=25.32, SD=15.18), with DSc. degree (M=40, SD=22.95), those working at least as associate professors (MR=485.75) and academic leaders (M=28.8, SD=13.41) or in leader position (M=28.91, SD=17.17) have the highest research productivity. Performance also increases with age and is highest among the oldest (M=37.78, SD=26.99). The lowest performance is found among the youngest age group (M=11.58, SD=8.71) and among academics with an administrative focus (M=14, SD=11.39) and academics in the scientific fields of arts and humanities (M=20.96, SD=13.23).

When examining workplace stress sources and resources, the only factor that is unsurprisingly significantly related to research productivity is performance evaluation: academics with above-average levels of this stressor perform worse (M=21.2, SD=14.61). As working hours increase, with academics work more than 60 hours per week scoring the highest performance (M=38.37, SD=21.51), while those working 51–55 (M=26.47, SD=17.71), 56–60 hours per week scored about the same (M=25.78, SD=16). Academics working 36–40 hours per week scoring the lowest (18.19, SD=12.83). Job security is associated with higher performance, with those who think there is no chance at all of being made redundant scoring the highest (MR=25.38, SD=16.72), while those who think there is a chance of being made redundant scored the lowest (M=20.19, SD=15.19) (Table 10.1).

Table 10.1: Correlations of workplace stressors with research productivity (means, SD)

		Mean	SD	Mann-Whitney U/Kruskal-Wallis H	N	sig.
performance evaluation	below the average	24.59	16.68	57155	720	0.008
	above the average	21.2	14.61			
number of working hours per week	36–40	18.19	12.83	55.107	753	<0.001
	41–45	20.2	12.84			
	46–50	23.02	14.75			
	51–55	26.46	17.71			
	56–60	25.78	16			
	>60	38.37	21.51			
job insecurity	No chance at all	25.38	16.72	8.385	636	0.039
	Not really a chance	22.4	15.01			
	There is a chance	20.19	15.19			
	There is a very high chance	21.34	8.1			

Source: CEETHE 2023.

3.2. Predictor Factors of Research Productivity

Linear regressions were used to examine the predictors of the principal component of research productivity. Multicollinearity was checked in all regressions, and the values of VIF and tolerance showed in all cases that there was no multicollinearity between the explanatory variables. Our model for research productivity is significant ($F(36,485=8.7$, $p<0.001$), with explanatory power $R2= 0.347$. Among job-related stress and resources, only performance evaluation is negatively related to productivity ($\beta=-0.148$). Age ($\beta=0.239$), Ph.D. ($\beta=0.142$), at least associate professor position ($\beta=0.172$), belonging to teaching-focused ($\beta=0.234$), academic leader ($\beta=0.222$) or research-focused ($\beta=0.171$) group increases performance. Working too few hours, less than 40 hours, decreases performance ($\beta=-0.132$), while working too many hours (more than 60, $\beta=0.126$) increases productivity.

4. Discussion

The academic profession faces significant challenges worldwide (Altbach, 2005) and has never been as unstructured and competitive as it is today. Competition for positions and resources is intense, and within this race, academics' scientific performance plays a particularly crucial role (Kwiek, 2019; Kwiek & Antonowicz, 2015). This study focused on assessing the factors that impact research productivity among academics in five CEE countries. Work-related characteristics, workplace stress sources and resources, and demographic factors were examined. The JD-R theory served as the theoretical foundation for this research, allowing for the exploration of the influence of work-related stressors and resources on well-being and research productivity. Our model included various predictors, such as demographic factors, work-related factors, stressors, resources, and well-being, because establishing causality can be challenging. For instance, well-being is in a positive relationship with higher levels of productivity. However, success at work and excellence in performance may also contribute to higher levels of well-being.

Initially, it was hypothesized that there would be notable disparities in productivity based on gender, age, country, job title, and discipline. Our hypothesis was supported, as older individuals, men in higher positions, those with academic degrees, and individuals in the social and economic sciences and senior academic groups displayed higher levels of productivity. Age, position, and academic degree were closely intertwined but also individually contributed to increased research productivity as in previous researches of Blend et al. (2005) and Teodorescu (2000). This can be attributed to the routine nature of a research career and the demands placed on early-stage academic careers, such as teaching, course preparation, and other teaching-related responsibilities (e.g., mentoring and talent management), which require significant time and energy. Similar challenges have been reported by young academics in the Czech Republic and France (Goncharuk & Cirella, 2022; Mudrak et al., 2018), and our previous interview research also highlighted the difficulties faced by young academics in juggling multiple roles, particularly teaching which hardly allows them to do other academic work

(Kovács et al., 2024). Numerous researchers in the region have shed light on the disadvantages faced by women in academia (Engler, 2015; Engler, 2020). Not only do women experience vertical segregation, meaning that they are underrepresented in high-status positions, but they also face horizontal segregation, resulting in their underrepresentation in STEM fields where notable high-level international research and achievements occur. Additionally, the interruption in their academic careers due to motherhood negatively affects them, particularly. Our analysis reveals that female researchers are disproportionately concentrated in the humanities and arts (Fényes, 2018), which, according to our findings, have the lowest productivity. The high productivity of senior academics can be attributed to their advancement in higher education, which is primarily based on academic performance rather than managerial skills (Mudrak et al., 2018; Gebregergis et al., 2023). Thus, their ranking is primarily a result of their increased teaching productivity. However, as Porter and Umbach (2001) demonstrate that workload impact is not uniform across all academic staff. Individual characteristics, such as discipline, rank, and tenure status, interact with institutional expectations, resulting in different productivity.

In our investigation of the impact of job demands and resources on research productivity in relation to JD-R theory, a second research question was posed. The second hypothesis suggested that there would be a negative correlation between job demands and a positive correlation between resources and well-being and research productivity. However, our findings only partially supported this hypothesis, as it was discovered that only the stress caused by performance evaluation had a negative effect. At the same time, other stressors and resources did not show a significant relationship with productivity. These results are in line with Teelken's (2018) longitudinal study on academics in the U.K., the Netherlands, and Sweden, which emphasized that while evaluating the work of academics may be important for monitoring institutional effectiveness, it does not contribute to their performance. Previous research (Usoro & Etuk, 2016) has shown that anxiety surrounding performance evaluation leads to decreased productivity. It is worth noting that this relationship can also be reversed. Academics who experience greater stress from performance assessments—whether due to concerns about academic freedom or the perceived pressure to meet publication requirements—tend to have lower performance levels. In contrast, high-performing academics view the evaluation system as fairer, with clear and measurable criteria guiding each stage of their careers. This dual nature of performance assessment has been highlighted in the work of Kwiek & Antonowicz (2015) as well as in our previous interview research (Kovács et al., 2024; Pusztai et al., 2025). However, for such a system to be effective, it must be transparent, clear, and fair, ensuring that favoritism and informal relationships do not influence evaluations.

Well-being was not directly linked to research productivity; however, an indirect connection emerged through working hours (Kovács et al., 2025). Specifically, working fewer than 40 hours per week reduced productivity, while longer working hours—unsurprisingly—enhanced it. Nevertheless, when examining factors influencing well-being, it became evident that working between 50 and 60 hours per week negatively impacted it. This suggests that while excessive working hours may boost performance, they also harm the well-being of academics (Kovács et al., 2025). Overworking can lead to exhaustion and conflicts in personal life, ultimately undermining academic well-being. Thus, although no direct relationship was identified between well-being and performance, an indirect link existed through extended working hours.

Another key finding was that while higher academic ranks correlated with increased productivity, they also had implications for well-being. Leader academics tended to experience more negative emotions, such as stress, anxiety, and sadness, potentially due to work-related pressures.

Our results highlight that those who dedicate a larger portion of their work to research achieve the highest research productivity (research-focused academics and leaders), meaning they tend to be the most successful. At the same time, it is also evident that research productivity itself has led to significant stratification within the academic society. Only those who consciously invest more time and energy—particularly in international scientific work—can reach the ranks of the most successful academics. The way academics allocate their time and energy to research plays a crucial role in shaping their research productivity, as well as in balancing their teaching and administrative responsibilities. Kwiek's (2019) micro-level study of academic scientists reveals that, across Europe, top-performing academics form a relatively homogeneous group, whose high research output is driven by similar structural factors. Notably, the top 10% of academics are responsible for 50% of high-quality research publications. To be part of this elite group, academics must devote significantly more time to research than the average, requiring both a substantial commitment to research activities and a strong research-oriented mindset.

However, this often creates tensions between time dedicated to research and time allocated to other professional duties. The extent to which academics can meet these expectations is influenced by both individual choices and institutional strategies. An ideal work environment in this context is one where institutional priorities—such as an emphasis on research—align with individual ambitions, like publishing in high-impact journals. As Kwiek (2019) emphasizes, it is particularly important for early-career academics to recognize that European academic institutions operate in a competitive landscape at both national and international levels, where rankings and resource allocation are heavily influenced by scientific performance. As a result, research output often becomes the primary determinant of career progression.

Conclusions

The key message from our study is that performance appraisal pressure is decreasing and negatively affecting research productivity. It is essential to make the process, purpose, results, format and consequences of performance evaluation transparent and constantly review it with the participation of academics so that they can understand and experience its significance with as little pressure as possible. This can reduce the negative impact on productivity.

Another important message from our research, particularly for managers of small units, is that while long working hours help increase productivity, they have serious long-term negative consequences for employee well-being. They can worsen academic well-being and increase the occurrence of negative emotions such as fatigue, depression, melancholy, and sadness, ultimately leading to exhaustion and burnout. Institutional leaders need to ask themselves: what is more important? To produce more high-impact publications in a short time and with a heavy workload, thereby increasing the efficiency and competitiveness of the institution, or to work in the long term with academics who feel good about their work, who love their job, who are satisfied, committed and motivated?

Acknowledgment

This publication was supported by the project “Investigating the role of sport and physical activity for a healthy and safe society in the individual and social sustainability of work ability and quality of work and life (multidisciplinary research umbrella program)” and by the János Bolyai Research Scholarship of the Hungarian Academy of Sciences.

References

Aarrevaara, T., Finkelstein, M., Jones, G. A., & Jung, J. (2021). The Academic Profession in the Knowledge-Based Society (APIKS): Evolution of a Major Comparative Research Project. In T. Aarrevaara, M. Finkelstein, G. A. Jones, & J. Jung (Eds.), *Universities in the Knowledge Society: The Nexus of National*

Systems of Innovation and Higher Education (pp. 49–64). Springer International Publishing. <https://doi.org/10.1007/978-3-030-76579-8_4>

Abramo, G., D'Angelo, C. A., & Di Costa, F. (2011). Research productivity: Are higher academic ranks more productive than lower ones? *Scientometrics*, 88, 915–928. <https://doi.org/10.1007/s11192-011-0426-6>

Abramo, G., D'Angelo, C. A., & Di Costa, F. (2014). Variability of research performance across disciplines within universities in non-competitive higher education systems. *Scientometrics*, 98, 777–795. <https://doi.org/10.1007/s11192-013-1088-3>

Akram, M. (2019). Psychological Wellbeing of University Teachers in Pakistan. Journal of Education and Educational Development, 6(2), 235–253.Altbach, P. (2005). Academic challenges: The American professoriate in comparative perspective. In Welch, A. (Ed.), *The professoriate: Profile of a profession* (pp. 147–165). Springer Netherlands.

Alqarni, N. A. (2021). Well-being and the Perception of Stress among EFL University Teachers in Saudi Arabia. *Journal of Language & Education Volume*, 7(3), 8–22. <https://doi.org/10.17323/jle.2021.11494>

Anastasiou, S., & Papakonstantinou, G. (2014). Factors affecting job satisfaction, stress and work performance of secondary education teachers in Epirus, NW Greece. *International Journal of Management in Education*, 8(1), 37–53. <https://doi.org/10.1504/IJMIE.2014.058750>

Aziz, F., & Quraishi, U. (2017). Empowerment and mental health of university teachers: A case from Pakistan. *Pakistan Journal of Social and Clinical Psychology, 15*(2), 23–28.

Bakker, A. B., & Demerouti, E. (2014). Job demands-resources theory. In P. Y. Chen, & C. Cooper (Eds.), *Work and Wellbeing: Wellbeing: A complete reference guide*, vol. III. (pp. 1–28). John Wiley & Sons, Ltd. <https://www.isonderhouden.nl/doc/pdf/arnoldbakker/articles/articles_arnold_bakker_344.pdf>

Bakker, A. B., Demerouti, E., Oerlemans, W., & Sonnentag, S. (2013). Workaholism and daily recovery: A day reconstruction study of leisure activities. *Journal of Organizational Behavior, 34*(1), 87–107. <https://doi.org/10.1002/job.1796>

Bell, A. S., Rajendran, D., & Theiler, S. (2012). Job stress, wellbeing, work-life balance and work-life conflict among Australian academics. *E-Journal of Applied Psychology*, 8(1), 25–37. <https://doi.org/10.7790/ejap.v8i1.320>

Bentley, P. J., Coates, H., Dobson, I. R., Goedegebuure, L., & Meek, V. L. (2013). Academic Job Satisfaction from an International Comparative Perspective: Factors Associated with Satisfaction Across 12 Countries. In P. J. Bentley, H. Coates, I. R. Dobson, L. Goedegebuure, & V. L. Meek (Eds.), *Job Satisfaction around the Academic World* (pp. 239–262). Springer Netherlands. <https://doi.org/10.1007/978-94-007-5434-8_13>

Bland, C. J., Center, B. A., Finstad, D. A., Risbey, K. R., & Staples, J. G. (2005). A theoretical, practical, predictive model of faculty and department research productivity. *Academic Medicine, 80*(3), 225–237.

Chen, Y., Gupta, A., & Hoshower, L. B. (2006). Factors that motivate business faculty to conduct research: An expectancy theory analysis. *Journal of Education for Business, 81*(4), 179–189.

Chukwuemeka, U. M., Okonkwo, U. P., Njoku, C. J., Igwe, S. E., Oyewumi, T. J., & Ugwuanyi, D. C. (2023). Work-related stress, quality of life, and coping mechanism among lecturers in a Tertiary Educational Institution in Anambra State, Nigeria. *BMC Psychology, 11*, 73. <https://doi.org/10.1186/s40359-023-01114-5>

Engler, Á. (2015). The effect of student's commitment on career. In G. Pusztai, & T. Ceglédi (Eds.), *Professional Calling in Higher Education: Challenges of Teacher Education in the Carpathian Basin* (pp. 165–175). Új Mandátum.

Engler, Á. (2020). *Career Path and Family Life*. Editorial Verbum.

Faisal, F., Noor, N., & Khair, A. (2019). Causes and Consequences of Workplace Stress among Pakistan University Teachers. *Bulletin of Education and Research, 41*(3), 45–60.

Fényes H. (2018). Mennyit ér egy tudományos fokozat—különös tekintettel a tudományos eredményesség és előmenetel nemi különbségeire [How Much Is a Scientific Degree Worth?—With Special Regard to Gender Differences in Scientific Productivity and Career Advancement]. *Szociológiai Szemle, 28*(1), 60–82.

Fetherston, C., Fetherston, A., Batt, S., Sully, M., & Wei, R. (2021). Wellbeing and work-life merge in Australian and UK academics. *Studies in Higher Education, 46*(12), 2774–2788. <https://doi.org/10.1080/03075079.2020.1828326>

Gebregergis, W. T., Kovács, K. E., & Csukonyi, Cs. (2023). Fostering Psychological Wellbeing and Student Engagement in Higher Education Students through Positive Psychological Capital: The Mediating Role of Academic Stress. *Journal of Positive Psychology and Wellbeing, 7*(4), 14–33.

Gillespie, N. A., Walsh, M., Winefield, A. H., Dua, J., & Stough, C. (2001). Occupational stress in universities: Staff perceptions of the causes, consequences and moderators of stress. *Work & Stress, 15*(1), 53–72.

Goncharuk, A. G., & Cirella, G. T. (2022). Effectiveness of academic institutional models in Europe: University instructor perception case research from Bosnia and Herzegovina and France. *International Journal of Educational Management, 36(5)*, 836–853.

Guest, D. E. (2002). Perspectives on the Study of Work-life Balance. *Social Science Information*, *41*(2), 255–279. <https://doi.org/10.1177/0539018402041002005>

Han, J., Yin, H., & Wang, J. (2020). Examining the Relationships Between Job Characteristics, Emotional Regulation and University Teachers' Well-Being: The Mediation of Emotional Regulation. *Frontiers in Psychology*, *11*, 1727. <https://doi.org/10.3389/fpsyg.2020.01727>

Han, J., Yin, H., Wang, J., & Zhang, J. (2020). Job demands and resources as antecedents of university teachers' exhaustion, engagement and job satisfaction. *Educational Psychology*, *40*(3), 318–335. <https://doi.org/10.1080/01443410.2019.1674249>

Höhle, E. A., & Teichler, U. (2013). The Academic Profession in the Light of Comparative Surveys. In B. M. Kehm, & U. Teichler (Eds.), *The academic profession in Europe: New tasks and new challenges*, vol. 5, (pp. 23–38). Springer. <https://www.academia.edu/download/76812256/978-94-007-4614-5_3.pdf>

Ismail, A., Saudin, N., Ismail, Y., Samah, A. J. A., Bakar, R. A., & Aminudin, N. N. (2015). Effect of Workplace Stress on Job Performance. *Economic Review: Journal of Economics and Business*, *13*(1), 45–57.

Iyaji, T. O., Eyam, S. O., & Agashi, V. A. (2020). An Assessment Of Some Stress Factors In Academic Profession And Their Health Implications Among Academics In Tertiary Institutions In Cross River State Nigeria. *International Journal of Innovative Research and Advanced Studies*, 7(12), 53–59.

Jung, J., Jones, G. A., Finkelstein, M., & Aarrevaara, T. (2021). Comparing Systems of Research and Innovation: Shifting Contexts for Higher Education and the Academic Profession. In T. Aarrevaara, M. Finkelstein, G. A. Jones, & J. Jung (Eds.), *Universities in the Knowledge Society: The Nexus of National Systems of Innovation and Higher Education* (pp. 415–428). Springer International Publishing. <https://doi.org/10.1007/978-3-030-76579-8_23>

Kinman, G. (2014). Doing More with Less? Work and Wellbeing in Academics. *Somatechnics*, *4*(2), 219–235. <https://doi.org/10.3366/soma.2014.0129>

Kinman, G., Jones, F., & Kinman, R. (2006). The Well-being of the UK Academy, 1998–2004. *Quality in Higher Education*, *12*(1), 15–27. <https://doi.org/10.1080/13538320600685081>

Kovács, K., Dobay, B., Halasi, S., Pinczés, T., & Tódor, I. (2024). Demands, resources and institutional factors in the work of academic staff in Central and Eastern Europe: Results of a qualitative research among university teachers in five countries. *Frontiers in Education*, *8*, 1326515. <https://www.frontiersin.org/articles/10.3389/feduc.2023.1326515>

Kovács, K. (2025). Influencing factors of workplace outcomes among teachers of higher education institutions in five Central and Eastern European countries. Social Sciences & Humanities Open (under review).

Kováts, G. (2023). University Governance Reform in an Illiberal Democracy. Public Interest Trusts in Hungary. In Broucker, B., Milsom, C., Calleja, J. & M. O'Hara (Eds.), *Accelerating the Future of Higher Education* (pp. 186–204). Brill

Kwiek, M. (2016). The European research elite: a cross-national study of highly productive academics in 11 countries. *Higher Education, 71*(3). 379–397. <https://doi.org/10.1007/s10734-015-9910-x>

Kwiek, M. (2019). Social stratification in Higher Education: What it means at the micro-level of the individual academic scientist. *Higher Education Quarterly, 73*(4), 419-444. <https://doi.org/10.1111/hequ.12221>

Kwiek, M., & Roszka, W. (2024). Are Scientists Changing their Research Productivity Classes When They Move Up the Academic Ladder? *Innovative Higher Education*, 1–39. <https://doi.org/10.1007/s10755-024-09735-3>

Malik, N. A. A., Björkqvist, K., & Österman, K. (2017). Factors associated with occupational stress among university teachers in Pakistan and Finland. *Journal of Educational, Health and Community Psychology*, *6*(2), 1–14.

Mudrak, J., Zabrodska, K., Kveton, P., Jelinek, M., Blatny, M., Solcova, I., & Machovcova, K. (2018). Occupational well-being among university faculty: A job demands-resources model. *Research in Higher Education*, *59*, 325–348. <https://doi.org/10.1007/s11162-017-9467-x>

Porter, S. R., & Umbach, P. D. (2001). Analyzing faculty workload data using multilevel modeling. *Research in Higher Education, 42*(2), 171-196. <https://doi.org/10.1023/A:1026573503271>

Pusztai, G., Demeter-Karászi Zs., & Pallay, K. (2025). Performance assessment: A new dimension of institutional culture. In Pusztai, G. & Kovács, K. (Eds.), *Well-Being of Academic Staff in Rapidly Changing Higher Education: A Focus on Central and Eastern Europe.* (pp.). Peter Lang.

Rodrigues Pimenta, C. L., Rónay, Z., & Németh, A. (2021). Centralisation and Decentralisation in Higher Education: A Comparative Study of Hungary and Germany. *Pedagogy*, *93*(8), 1119–1135.

Saeed, K., & Farooqi, Y. A. (2014). Examining the relationship between work life balance, job stress and job satisfaction among university teachers (A case of University of Gujrat). *International Journal of Multidisciplinary Sciences and Engineering*, *5*(6), 9–15.

Sirgy, M. J., & Lee, D.-J. (2018). Work-Life Balance: An Integrative Review. *Applied Research in Quality of Life*, *13*(1), 229–254. <https://doi.org/10.1007/s11482-017-9509-8>

Teelken, C. (2018). Teaching assessment and perceived quality of teaching: A longitudinal study among academics in three European countries. *European Journal of Higher Education*, *8*(4), 382–399. <https://doi.org/10.1080/21568235.2018.1490661>

Teodorescu, D. (2000). Correlates of faculty publication productivity: A cross-national analysis. *Higher Education*, *39*(2), 201–222. <https://doi.org/10.1023/A:1003901018634>

Usoro, A. A., & Etuk, G. R. (2016). Workload related stress and job effectiveness of university lecturers in Cross River and Akwa Ibom States, Nigeria. *Asian Journal of Social Sciences and Management Studies*, *3*(1), 34–41.

Utami, P. P., & Vioreza, N. (2021). Teacher Work Productivity in Senior High School. *International Journal of Instruction*, *14*(1), 599–614.

Wood, F. (1990). Factors influencing research performance of university academic staff. *Higher Education*, *19*, 81–100. <https://doi.org/10.1007/BF00142025>

11. Work-Life Conflicts: A Dual Functionality Approach on Career of Academics

Emese Beáta Berei, Ágnes Engler & Klára Kovács

ABSTRACT
Maintaining a harmonious balance between work and personal life (WLB) is a source of strength, it also contributes to optimal professional performance, is associated with higher satisfaction with family life or life in general. At the same time, work-life conflict (WLC) has a negative impact on career of workers which has a large personal, family, institutional and social influence. From now on, the WLC or WLB is much more examined as a predictor of employees' wellbeing or other workplace outcomes as job (in)satisfaction. It is much less clear which factors influence these phenomena and the social evaluation of the balance or confrontation, especially in Central and Eastern Europe. In this study we proposed a holistic view of work-life conflicts, as a clash of human resources and how they are allocated, as a disfunction in both professional and private life at micro and mezzo environments, and we presented a cross-national analysis of academics' WLC. Our main question was three-prong: 1. How do academics balance between professional and personal life? 2. How can we predict conflicts? 3. How can a social evaluation of the conflicts be conducted? As independent factors, we used: age, gender, parenthood, country, working hours, academic job title, emotional exhaustion and social support at work to predict work-life conflicts. The novelty of this study is the social evaluation of the phenomenon: the conceptualization of WLC as a dysfunction at different levels of society. We adopt the dual functionality approach for different social environments: at micro, mezzo, or macro levels. For the quantitative analysis, the sample of academics from five Central and Eastern European countries (Romania, Slovakia, Serbia, Ukraine and Hungary) were used (CEETHE 2023 database, N=821). The complex questionnaire included the measures of WLC score based on Hayman (2005). Statistical analyses performed by using SPSS 29 included ANOVA tests, principal component and factor analysis, and, finally, a multistep linear regression. Results show that more than a third (37%) of academics ignore their personal needs, and a third (33%) perceive that they sacrifice their private life because of work. More than a third of them had difficulty balancing between work and private life (39%), were dissatisfied with the time spent outside the workplace (39%), and nearly half of them (42%) reported missing out on personal activities in their private life due to work. The linear stepwise regression model shows that emotional exhaustion long working hours, less academic job title (low academic positions), the decrease in social supports provided by the institution (at mezzo level) and gender (at micro level) are the significant predictors of WLC. This paper contributes to the work of higher education policy makers on social evaluation of institutional and employee functionality, seeking a better work-life balance in the career of academics.

Keywords: work-life conflict, social evaluation, dual functionality, higher education institutions, academics' career, Central and Eastern European countries

Introduction

In our previous research we examined the sustainability of academic career (Berei et al., 2024) and we highlighted the imbalance between professional and family environments, and the need for its evaluation in academic work. Work-life conflict has a negative impact on academics' well-being (Bell et al., 2012) but it is much less clear, which factors influence its process and social evaluation. In this paper, we intend to analyze the work-life conflict as a struggle among academics in Hungary, Slovakia, Serbia, Romania and Ukraine to allocate human resources to two different areas. Academics is an occupational category responsible for training people at higher levels in college and universities, working worldwide. Hayman (2005) deemed the conflict of work with the private or family sphere (the dimension examined herein WLC). Work-family (WFC) or WLC is generally discussed from two perspectives: work interference in family, and family interference in work (Allen et al., 2000). Work-life or work-family conflict refers to tension between these two important environments (Premeaux, 2007). In this perspective, WLC occurs when energy, time, or duty demands of works collides with family or personal life. Work-family conflict is a specific form of work-life conflict (Kossek & Lee, 2017). From the perspective of interpersonal conflicts, the WLCs are studied as human confrontation, followed by emotional exhaustion, cynicism, and burnout (Boamah et al., 2022). Organizational interventions are necessary for managing staff anxiety. Participants in these interventions, coming from public, private and non-profit institutions, propose rearrangement of the job sphere the changing of organizational culture, the encouragement of participative management, the introduction of work-life balance policies, as well as improvement of organizational communication (Bhui et al., 2016).

Work-life balance and its loss are a much-studied issue in academic work. The subject has been approached so far from the psychological and organizational management perspective including academics' ability to balance work and personal life and overcome such conflict (Bell et al., 2012; Dorenkamp & Süß, 2017; Johnson et al., 2019). Increased stress levels among employees can also cause institutes within a university to work less efficiently, while tired, discouraged, and undermotivated employees can also have a negative impact on the whole university/college as an organization (Bell et al., 2012). Successfully maintaining a harmonious balance between the two is therefore a source of strength. It also has a positive impact on job satisfaction (Saeed & Farooqi, 2014), contributes to optimal performance (Guest, 2002), and is associated with higher satisfaction with family life and life in general (Sirgy & Lee, 2018). Males had a lower score of the WLC than females (Bell et al., 2012; Mudrak et al., 2018; Chukwuemeka et al., 2023). Studies among females in higher education unanimously concluded they have serious difficulties in reconciling work and family responsibilities (Misra et al., 2012; O'Laughlin & Bischoff, 2005; Paksi et al., 2016). The dilemmas relating to personal life and/or career are most noticeable in the careers of women academics and researchers. If childcare is part of private life, it must be synchronized with work, and still further efforts will be needed to find a balance for both. For researchers, men and women, working in dangerous environments (laboratories), it is necessary to adapt work-to-family plans, starting with the child planning stage (Paksiand et al., 2022).

This study aims to explore the most important individual and institutional factors, which can affect WLC. Our research questions were as follows: 1. How do academics balance professional and personal life? 2. How can one predict conflicts? 3. How can a person socially evaluate conflicts?

1. The Concept of Social Functionality and Work-Life Conflicts

As for the theoretical background to answer our research questions the concept of social functionality was used. It is rooted in functionalism theory, which views society as a collection of functional micro or mezzo units forming a unitary, functional macro system (Conerly et al., 2021). The concept is currently used in the humanities and social sciences as regards the functionalities and capabilities of vulnerable people. It also addresses the social, medical, and mental health evaluation of individuals, families, and organizations (Sen, 1985; Keltner & Kring, 1998; Greller & Richtermeyer, 2006; Kotwal et al., 2016; Keating et al., 2019; Iamtrakul & Chayphong, 2022; Santana et al. 2022; Giusti et al. 2023; Silva et al. 2023). It pertains to a person's interactions with their environment and their ability to fulfill roles in various circumstances, such as work, social activities, family, and other relationships (Anttila, 2015) with a holistic overview (Pratt et al., 1969). In our study the concept of social functionality refers to the way in which academics in Central and Eastern Europe are able to function (or not) in their families (typically as parents/partners) and at work. The factors herein are explored.

In our study we designed a general strategy of analyses which scrutinizes the work-life conflict as a conflict in the functionality of humans (Fig. 11.1). Its aim is to integrate simultaneously the values, abilities, roles, interactions and social behavior as dual functionalities of individuals at different levels: in private (micro level) and professional environments (national and international institutions, organizations, projects, programs at mezzo or macro levels). At different levels, individuals use different personal and professional abilities, they are involved in different roles and actions, but these are interconnected as a whole. The novelty of this study is the conceptualization of WLC as a disfunction at different level of the society, taking into account the human values, subjective perceptions and twin roles of human resources in private life and in their professions.

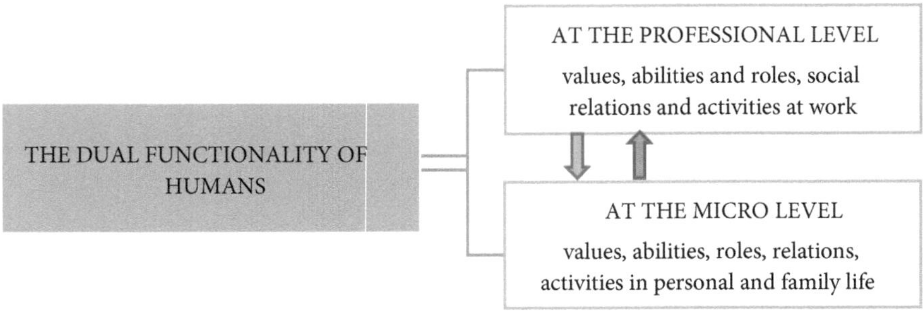

Figure 11.1: The dual functionality of humans at the personal and professional levels (Authors' design).

A global report of the International Labour Organization (ILO, 2022) studying the WLB of employers around the world, connected this phenomenon with working hours. The report made differences between short (part-time), standard, and long hours of work. "Standard" work means 40 hours/week, while up to 48 hours/week pertained to "long hours." 48 hours per week was fixed as the international standard for long working hours. The patterns differ based on where the workers are employed and whether they are full-time, part-time, self-employed, or other such working status: "Globally, 31.1 percent of employees regularly work more than 48 hours per week, but the proportion is much higher for self-employed workers, at 44.4 percent" (ILO, 2022, p. 15). In the education sector, globally 25.5% of the academics work more than 48 hours per week. During the Covid pandemic, in Eastern Europe, nearly 5% of the employees worked more than 48 hours (ILO, 2022).

A cross-national meta-analysis of WLC in 58 countries with different geographical and individual cultural values show a significant difference in WLC scores depending on the geographical region (Allen et al., 2020). In the US, 70% of workers perceived conflict between their work and personal life (Nicholes & Swanberg, 2018). Johnson et al. (2019) in their study conducted in the U.K., compared university and non-university human resources (n=652). The results of the study revealed some discrepancies between human resources who work in the academic and non-academic environments. Thus, academics reported a higher level of professional overload and a lower score in work-life balance values, while having a better organizational climate (working conditions, collegial relationships, remuneration).

In Europe the WLC subject has been researched for 20 years (McGinnity, 2021), but there is little research that has been conducted in former communist countries and also more particularly among academic human resources (junior and senior academics, professors, assistant lecturers, master teachers, researchers) in Central and Eastern Europe. Whatever was published (Dorenkamp & Süß, 2017; Johnson et al., 2019) assessed academics from Western European countries, in different environments at mezzo and macro levels and at the micro level with different personal values, relations, activities.

As a result, the aim of this empirical research was to socially evaluate the work-life conflicts as it affects dual functionality of academics, specifically how their personal and family life at the micro level is affected by their profession on the mezzo level. What is more, we seek to measure the WLC score and examine the causes that predict the conflict, to get better career guidance, and to improve institutional social and higher educational policy.

2. Methods, Samples and Instrument

The quantitative cross-border data collection was conducted by the Center of Higher Education Research and Development at Debrecen University, Hungary in 2023. The questionnaire was developed based on qualitative research focus group interviews with 41 academics in Hungary, Slovakia, Ukraine, Romania, and Serbia. The overall objective of the data collection was to explore the difficulties related to the work of academic human resources and their personal and professional well-being (Kovács et al., 2024).

In our international quantitative study, a sample of N=821 academics (13.8% from Romania, 4.4% from Slovakia, 4.9% from Serbia, 14.1% from Ukraine, and 61.8% from Hungary) was included, 80% of which came from three EU states (Romania, Slovakia, and Hungary), and 20% from non-EU countries (Serbia and Ukraine). The complex questionnaire examined the professional and social background of the academics and measured the work-life balance/conflict based on Hayman (2005).

43.7% of academics were men, 56.3% were women, the average age was 46 (SD=10.71) and the average number of years in higher education was 17 (SD=11 years). Of the respondents, 78.6% had a scientific degree, and 59% were employed in the institutional academic role as an assistant professor or in a lower position. 27.9% specialized in medical/health sciences, 32.4% in humanities/pedagogy/languages/art sciences, 16.7% in social/economic sciences, and 23% in STEM and Agriculture sciences. The majority of respondents, 68.5%, were married, and 72.4% had children. About 47.6% reported having a relatively good financial standing, 38.4% average, and 14% poor, compared to families in their environment.

The complex questionnaire included the measures of work-life conflict score based on Hayman (2005). This dimension explores how academics' personal lives are affected by work, how work causes difficulties in their personal lives, to what extent they neglect personal activities because of work, how satisfied they are with the time spent outside the professional sphere, and how well they can stabilize the relationship between work and personal life (6-item Cronbach α=0.948, KMO=0.905, p=000, explained variance 79.545%). The measuring scale is 5: 1—never, 2—probably not, 3—undecided, 4—probably yes, 5—totally yes.

Among the factors influencing WLC, we peered into the area of emotional exhaustion at work with 5 items: I feel emotionally exhausted from my work; I feel exhausted at the end of the working day; I feel tired when I wake up in the morning and have to face another day at work; Working all day is very demanding for me; My work makes me feel burned out (Cronbach α=0.911, KMO=0.852, p=000, explained variance 73.894%). The measuring scale was 7: 1—never, 2—a few times a year/less often, 3—monthly/less often, 4—a few times a month times, 5—weekly, 6—several times a week, 7—every day (Han et al., 2020).

The social support in work was measured with 4 items: I am satisfied with the level of support I get from the head of my department/institute/faculty; I am satisfied with the level of support I get from my colleagues; there is a full understanding between staff/head of the department and academics; and My efforts are appreciated (Cronbach's α =0.867). The measuring scale was 5: 1—never, 2—probably not, 3—undecided, 4—probably yes, 5—totally yes. Factorial analyses were performed on principal components, resulting in one factor from the 4 variables (KMO=0.827 and p=0.000 with 71.61% explanations), and the factor was named "social institutional supports"—SIS factor. The statistical values of the main components are given in Table 11.1.

Table 11.1: The statistical values of the main components of work-related factors

The work factors of academics	Cronbach α	Mean	SD	N
Work-life conflicts (WLC)	0.948	46.76	27.87	806
Emotional exhaustion at work (EEW)	0.911	45.76	25.38	798
Social institutional support (SIS)	0.867	60.46	24.29	807

Source: CEETHE 2023.

As explanatory factors, we included country, age, gender, having children or not, and job-related characteristics such as job title (assistant professor or less; associate professor and above positions), and working hours per week. Statistical analyses performed by using SPSS 29 included ANOVA tests, principal component and factor analysis and finally a multistep linear regression (Pallant, 2020).

3. Results

3.1. The Work-Life Balance of Academic Human Resources. Their Work-Life Conflict Score

The subjective dimensions of the work-life balance/conflict dimension explore how academics' personal lives are influenced by work, how personal lives are made problematic because of work, how much personal activities are ignored because of work, the level of satisfaction of academics with time spent away from work, and their ability to harmonize work and personal life ((6-item Cronbach $\alpha=0.948$, KMO=0.905, p=000, explained variance 79.545%). The measuring scale is 5: 1—never, 2—probably not, 3—undecided, 4—probably yes, 5—totally yes.). For half of the academics (49%), work does not cause difficulties in their personal life, and for more than a third (38%), it's not hard to balance and separate the two environments (Table 11.2). However, more than a third (37%) of academics ignore their personal needs because of work, and a third (33%) perceive that they sacrifice their private life because of work. Statistical data show that more than a third of them had difficulty balancing between work and private life (39%), were dissatisfied with the time spent outside the workplace (39%), and nearly half of them reported missing personal activities in their personal life because of work (42%).

Factorial analyses were performed on principal components (Table 11.2), resulting in one factor (KMO=0.905, p=0.000, 79.545% explanations), named WLC factor (Cronbach $\alpha=0.948$; Mean=46.76; SD=27.76; N=806).

Table 11.2: Perception of the work-life conflict (%) and the principal component factor scores

	1—never	2	3	4	5—totally	N	WLC factor
My personal life is compromised because of work	18	26	27	19	10	819	0.89
Work causes difficulties in my personal life	20	29	25	18	7	819	0.89
My personal needs are neglected for work	17	23	23	27	10	819	0.91
I push my private life to the background for work	17	24	26	23	10	813	0.90
Personal activities are missing because work	14	19	25	27	15	819	0.91
I find it difficult to balance work with a life separate from work	15	23	23	26	13	817	0.86
I am dissatisfied with the amount of time allocated to activities outside the workplace	15	23	23	24	15	818	-

Source: CEETHE 2023.

Next, we investigated the WLC score of academics, using ANOVA test to compare means of WLC scores, depending on demographic, family and academic aspects (Table 11.3). Analyzing the effect of demographic variables, significant differences were found regarding gender (F=8.9 and p=0.003) and age (F=8.7 and p=0.003). The mean WLC score of female academics (M=49 and SD=28) was significantly higher than that of males (M=43 and SD=28). The mean WLC score of academics under 40 (M=51 and SD=28) was significantly higher than that of those aged 41 or older (M=45 and SD=27).

Analyzing family characteristics, significant differences were found between academics in the role of parenthood (having children) and academics without children (F=13.8 and p=0.000). The mean WLC score of academics who do not have children (M=52 and SD=26) was significantly higher than those who do (M=44 and SD=28). Though the mean WLC scores based on the country or region in which they work were different, they were not significant.

Significant differences were identified also between the mean WLC score of academic position (F=7.2 and p=0.007). The mean WLC score of university human resources in the position of, assistant professor or lower positions (M=49 and SD=27.7) was significantly higher than that of those in more advanced positions (associate professor or other high positions) (M=43.6 and SD=27.9). Significant differences between WLC scores were identified pertaining to working hours (F=38.3 and p=0.000). For academics working more than the standard of 40 hours (M=36.6 and SD=27.8), it was significantly higher than that of those who work short or standard hours (M=50.2 and SD=27).

Table 11.3: Differences in the WLC factor by the demographic, family, and professional factors (means on 0–100 points scale)

		WLC factor score	Mean	SD	F	p	N
Working time/ week	41 h or up	50.2	46.7	27.9	38.3	0.000	595
	36–40 h	36.6					207
Gender	Male	43.3	46.6	27.9	8.9	0.003	346
	Female	49.3					443
Institutional academic role	Associate professor or higher	43.6	46.8	27.9	7.2	0.007	332
	Assistant professor or lower	49					474
Countries	non-EU	43.8	46.7	27.9	2.1	0.147	152
	EU	47.4					652

		WLC factor score	Mean	SD	F	p	N
Age	18–40	51	46.7	27.9	8.7	0.003	250
	41 or up	44.7					532
Parenthood role	no children	52.4	46.3	27.7	13.8	0.000	209
	yes children	44					552

Source: CEETHE 2023.

The ANOVA test concluded that the effect of working hours (F=38.3), the role of parenthood (F=13.8) and gender (F=8.9) were the most significant variables (p=0.000). Minimal or standard hour workers, academic parents and males had the lowest score of WLC by a significant margin. Females, academics younger than 40 years, employed as assistant professors or lower, had the highest score of WLC by far (Table 11.3).

3.2. Predictors of the Work-Life Conflicts Between the Two, Personal and Professional Environments

Next, we applied multiple linear stepwise regression to establish causalities between WLC factors and other variables, in which the dependent variable was the WLC factor. Moreover, potential conflict predictors were introduced in 5 blocks: (1) emotionally exhaustion at work and working time, (2) social institutional support, (3) gender and the job title, (4) the region, the age, and the parenthood role of academic human resources. Adjusted R-square for the blocks was: (1) 0.494, (2) 0.502, (3) 0.521, (4) 0.520. The model was significant (F=96.2 and p=0.000). The Levene's interferential statistic used to test the homogeneity of variances was not significant in every case accepted.

A significant relationship was found for five explanatory variables (Table 11.4): emotional exhaustion at work factor (Beta=0.57, p=0.000, CI: 0.565–0.69), working time/week (Beta=0.25, p=0.000, CI: 3.574–5.541), social support (Beta=–0.119, p=0.000, CI: –4.863 to –1.769), gender (Beta=0.106, p=0.000, CI: 2.926–8.913), job title (Beta=0.069, p=0.021, CI: 0.596–7.271). The best predictor of WLC was the emotional exhaustion at work. According to Cohen and Cohen (1983), strength of correlation guidelines, there was a large correlation between these two variables. If negative emotions connected to work increase, WLC also grows. In addition, there were small but significant positive WLC ties to working hours, gender, and institutional academic roles. There was a negative but small connection between WLC and social support, meaning, if institutional support increases, WLC decreases.

Table 11.4: Multiple stepwise regression analyses. Prediction of WLC

Explanatory variables	B	Beta	P	T	CI	
Emotionally exhaustion at work factor	0.627	0.57	0.000	19.7	0.565	0.69
Working time/week	4.557	0.25	0.000	9.1	3.574	5.541
Social institutional support factor	-3.316	-0.119	0.000	-4.2	-4.863	-1.769
Gender (0—male, 1—female)	5.92	0.106	0.000	3.88	2.926	8.913
Job title (0—associate professor or higher, 1—assistant professor or lower)	3.9	0.069	0.021	2.3	0.596	7.271
EU or other countries (0—other, 1—EU)	-1.83	-0.026	0.132	-0.9	-	-
Age (0-18 to 40, 1-41+)	-0.975	-0.017	0.481	-0.5	-	-
Parenthood role (0—no children, 1—yes children)	-1.673	-0.027	0.357	-0.96	-	-

Source: CEETHE 2023.

4. Discussion

In our study we proposed an empirical analysis of academic career of human resources from Central–Eastern European (3 EU and 2 non-EU) countries from the dual perspective of the professional career and personal—family life and to identify the differences in WLC scores by demographic, family and working factors. Finally, we distinguished some predictors of WLC and social environments, where these can change.

Our results indicated, the WLC mean of academics from EU countries (Ro-mania, Slovakia and Hungary) was higher than from non-EU countries (Serbia, Ukraine), but the differences were not significant. Different Central–Eastern European regions had variations on WLC score of academics, but it was not relevant. The homogeneity of experiences is due to traditional values, norms, roles at the micro level of people living in these countries and the shared historical experiences at the mezzo and macro levels.

In our analyses we found only a quarter of all samples to be minimalist or standard in terms of working hours, the majority tend to work longer. Males and Hungarians significantly tend to work longer than others. The effect of working hours had a linear, weak but significant effect on WLC score according to our research. If the hours of work increase, the WLC score rises also, similar to previous researches (Golden et al., 2011; Cicek & Gezici, 2018). Qualitative research conducted in Finland found that families with two earning adults preferred 30-hour work weeks (Tammelin, 2009). An empirical study on a representative sample in the U.K. analyzed the working time of the employees and concluded, overtime or long hours were associated with higher frequency of negative emotions. The human resources working part-time hours or irregular periods had a better WLC scores. Multinominal regression statistical test demonstrates long hour works weekly or daily in full-time job predicted not just the higher fatigue of employees, but, at the same time, their conflict between work and personal life was higher (Golden et al., 2011).

The differences depending on gender was significant, similar to previous researches (Bell et al., 2012; Mudrak et al., 2018; Chukwuemeka et al., 2023). The WLC of females was higher than of males. This is due to inequalities stemming from traditional roles, as a result of which women still have a higher proportion of domestic and family responsibilities than men (they spend more time on housework, are more likely to stay at home with their little children, they are out of the labor market and spend more time caring for children, etc.), which reinforcing the traditional gender roles among examined academics (Fényes et al., 2020). As a result of these factors, females work—life conflict score is higher even if in recent years an increasing proportion of men/fathers have also been involved in household tasks and caring for children (Sztáray & Drjenovszky, 2021). At the same time, modern father roles and associated behaviors (e.g., greater involvement in childrearing or housework) are still less common in Central and Eastern Europe, where people are more traditional than in Western European countries and have traditional values at the micro level. In the region, men's family-maintaining and existential tasks are characteristics (more responsibilities at work and higher salaries), which provides them fewer opportunities to join to family life (Fényes et al., 2020).

During the Covid isolation lifestyle, empirical analyses indicate a significant increase in the WLC mean score of females and mothers (Frank et al., 2021; Backhaus et al., 2023). Our results didn't support the increase in WLC scores of parents: academic parents had significantly lower WLC scores than those without children. This may be because the number of children is strongly correlated with age and job title. As our results above have shown, younger academics with lower academic rank work more and find it more difficult to reconcile (much) work and private life.

The mean WLC score of younger academics was significantly higher than that of those aged 41 or older. Across the lifespan, previous research (Huffman et al., 2013) found the same results: young employees had a significant higher score of the WLC, than older employees. Raiu (2021) analyzing the literature on the characteristics of employees from different generations, he highlighted that those who belong to the Y or Z generation (under 40 years old), need a high independency and flexibility at work, they are not willing to sacrifice for the company, the balance between work and personal life is very important for them. A research career is very strictly routine, and by the fact that at the beginning of an academic career, more time and energy are required from academics for teaching and for the many other an academic staff may undertake (mentoring, talent management, class and schedule preparation, etc.). In our previous interview study, young academics found, at the outset of their careers, it was difficult to cope with multiple roles, especially teaching. They often, in addition to their teaching profession, had the additional burden of doing Ph.D. studies or writing their doctoral thesis. Fulfilling the role of an academic staff hardly allowed them to do other academic work (Kovács et al., 2024).

Nearly a third (31%) of academics feel emotionally exhausted weekly or even daily, and 20% feel several times a week or even every day burned out because of their work. But it is a much more important result that the emotional exhaustion in work is the biggest negative predictor of WLC. If an academic staff is tired, burned out, sees his or her work as meaningless and even works too much, compliance with the indicators of various performance evaluation systems, the underestimation of teaching work and related sub-fields compared to academic performance, or the lack of knowledge of clear institutional goals, expectations and tasks are all job demands in our interview research among academics in the region (Kovács et al., 2024), which contributes significantly to a more difficult work-life balance. A study among Australian academics (Bell et al., 2012) analyzed the emotional involvement of academics in work: job threat stress and job pressure stress together explained 61% (R2 adj = 0.60) of the variance in work-life conflict score. On our study negative emotions at work with other variables (working time, social institutional support, gender and the institutional academic role) explained 52% of the WLC variance.

An important protective factor of WLC is the social institutional support. Peer support, such as fostering a community of colleagues and students, can have a positive impact on academics' well-being and on WLC according to our results. A positive network of relationships between academics and supportive attitudes from students can help manage stress (Vigoda-Gadot & Talmud, 2010). Since the 1970s, discourse has pointed to the fact that peer (social) support acts only as a resistance factor; however, some have argued that its absence can be a source of stress (Thoits, 1985). If an academic's work is supported, valued and appreciated in their institution, and if they are recognized by their leaders and colleagues, it helps them to find a work-life balance. In this way, they feel that their work is not in vain and that they do not have to work day and night, even at the expense of their personal life, in order to be appreciated. Another dimension of peer support is the informal relationships with colleagues with whom you can share problems (whether work or personal) and from whom you can ask for help and advice to solve them.

5. A Social Evaluation Model of Factors Contributing to the WLC Phenomenon

Finally, we give answer to the question: which social environments (the micro, mezzo, or macro levels) are involved in these disfunctions (Fig. 11.2)? The working time and the fatigue contribute to the conflicts between work and personal life, and we can extend these as a general profile of an academic worker perceiving conflict at micro and professional level, but these factors can cause disfunctions at different environments. Gender's effect on increasing the WLC, which is a micro characteristic of human resources and is connected with the identifications of other family roles and responsibilities at the micro level (how affect family or personal life the work of academics), was not achieved in this study. Institutional position and social support at the workplace belong to the institutional and macro environments. Examining workplace stress, Salami's (2011) study investigated how peer support can mitigate the negative effects of workplace stress. These results support the view that environmental and personal factors have a strong influence on workplace stress. Good working relationships between lectures and a sense of belonging to the workplace community can be a source of strength. Colleagues can help solve problems and provide mentoring and support (Thoits, 1985).

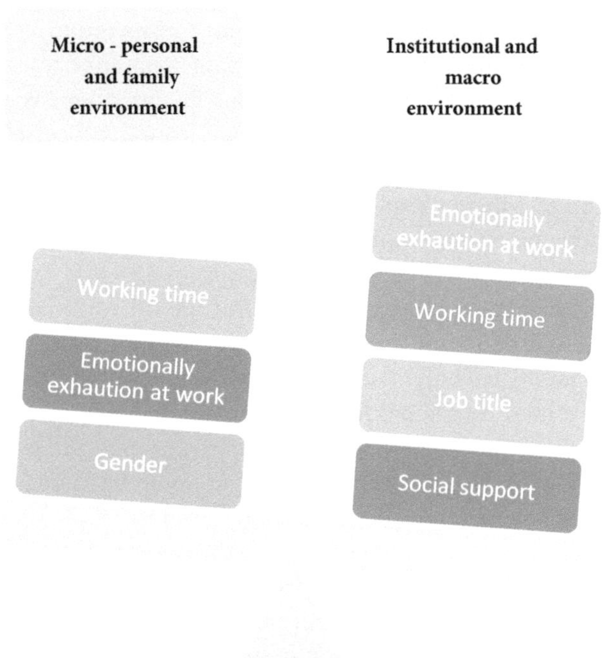

Figure 11.2: Different social environments implication on work-life imbalance (Authors' design).

The limitation of the study is that we did not cover all factors and causes of WLC and all universities, and all human resource populations from Romania, Slovakia, Hungary, Ukraine and Serbia. The study subjects were mostly Hungarian nationalities academics, and the results cannot be extent or generalized to these countries. We know that working hours are connected to workloads, specialization and work responsibilities, but here we did not introduce these dimensions. In our study we make a comparison just in regard to the academic position. One source of WLC is human values, regarding whether work interfaces with family at the level of values attainment (Perrewé et al., 1999). In addition, it would be important the social evaluation of the personal, family and professional values, and the connection or the fit of them. According to previous researches (Premeaux et al., 2007; Dorenkamp & Ruhle, 2019), WLC are related to different professional roles, responsibilities and actions connected with the workload and specialization also, so in the next study we will analyze these correlations.

Conclusions

In our study we proposed a holistic view of work-life conflict as a conflict in dual functionality of humans at different (micro and mezzo/macro) level of the society, integrating professional and personal values, abilities, roles, interactions and social behavior, as a whole. The dimension analyzed here was when work affected the personal or family life of academics from five Central and Eastern European countries. The novelty of this study is the conceptualization of the WLC as a disfunction at different level of the society, taking into account the human values, subjective perceptions and dual roles of human resources in private life and in their professions.

General organizational policy recommendation was formulated in the ILO report with the aim of decent work in the area of working time: promote health and safety; be "family-friendly" and improve workers' work-life balance; promote gender equality; increase the productivity and sustainability of enterprises; and offer workers a degree of choice and influence over their hours of work (ILO 2022, p. 148). Our results lead us in the same direction: would be useful at professional levels, for higher education institutional managers, leaders of departments, faculty or rectors creating an equitable environment at mezzo levels, offering social counseling, mentoring and support for their employers and for social policy makers, creating norms and legislation, human and family-friendly programs at macro level in Central and Eastern European countries.

One of the most important findings of our research is that, in principle, micro-private life functions do not play a role in WLC, as the number of children is not a factor, while the quantity and quality of work is the main cause of these conflicts. Our findings highlight that dual functionality for junior academics is rather a multifaceted functionality related to work. The diversity of the work and the extra workload this entails make the situation particularly difficult for young academics. Teaching, research, mentoring and organizational tasks, as well as their own research and doctoral studies, are a major challenge for them. In relation to dual functionality theory, the primary cause of WLC is the acquisition of values and the need to cope with these different roles and their associated expectations. It would be important to develop mentoring and counseling programs, especially for junior or early-career academics, to help them with professional socialization, coping effectively with different tasks, as well as the support of the supervisor in doctoral research.

Our findings raise awareness of the importance of social evaluation of WLC factors, the social and mental health counseling services also for higher education human resources, including the provision of programs and opportunities to support the development of academics' practical knowledge and skills in the area of time management, with a particular focus on female academics. Other social and psychological factors may be at the root of work-life conflicts, and the involvement of professionals is needed to identify and address these. It is important that such services are provided within an institutional framework. One such good practice is the services for university employees and their family members, provided by the Mental Health Center of the University of Debrecen.

Another suggestion is to provide training for higher education managers and leaders to learn effective tools for recognizing and managing burnout (e.g., supervision), so that they can recognize in time when their staff are overworked, exhausted, having personal conflicts, and how to reduce work-related stress. They also contribute to the development of their leadership skills, since, as Mudrak et al. (2008) argued in their study, the majority of university leaders are promoted to leadership positions on the basis of their academic performance rather than their management skills. The above suggestions could be used to reduce work-life conflict at the individual and institutional levels and to effectively achieve a work-life balance that contributes to academics' enjoyment of their work, which in turn contributes to their well-being and productivity. After all, only happy, well-balanced academics can teach satisfied students and carry out effective academic work.

Acknowledgments

This publication was supported by the project "Investigating the role of sport and physical activity for a healthy and safe society in the individual and social sustainability of work ability and quality of work and life (multidisciplinary research umbrella program)" and by the János Bolyai Research Scholarship of the Hungarian Academy of Sciences.

References

Allen, T. D., French, K. A., Dumani, S., & Shockley, K. M. (2020). A cross-national meta-analytic examination of predictors and outcomes associated with work-family conflict. *The Journal of Applied Psychology*, *105*(6), 539–576. <https://doi.org/10.1037/apl0000442>

Allen, T. D., Herst, D. E., Bruck, C. S., & Sutton, M. (2000). Consequences associated with work-to-family conflict: a review and agenda for future research. *Journal of Occupational Health Psychology*, *5*(2), 278–308. <https://doi.org/10.1037//1076-8998.5.2.278>

Anttila, T., Oinas, T., Tammelin, M. & Nätti, J. (2015). Working-Time Regimes and Work-life Balance in Europe. *European Sociological Review*, 31(6), 713–724, <https://doi.org/10.1093/esr/jcv070>

Arieli, S., Sagiv, L., & Roccas, S. (2020). Values at work: The impact of personal values in organisations. *Applied Psychology: An International Review*, *69*(2), 230–275. <https://doi.org/10.1111/apps.12181>

Backhaus, I., Hoven, H., Bambra, C., Oksanen, T., Rigó, M., di Tecco, C., … & Dragano, N. (2023). Changes in work-related stressors before and during the COVID-19 pandemic: differences by gender and parental status. International Archives of Occupational and Environmental Health, 96(3), 421–431. <https://doi.org/10.1007/s00420-022-01933-w>

Bell, A. S., Rajendran, D., & Theiler, S. (2012). Job stress, wellbeing, work-life balance and work-life conflict among Australian academics. *E-Journal of Applied Psychology*, *8*(1), 25–37. <https://doi.org/10.7790/ejap.v8i1.320>

Bettini, E., Gilmour, A. F., Williams, T. O., & Billingsley, B. (2020). Predicting Special and General Educators' Intent to Continue Teaching Using Conservation of Resources Theory. *Exceptional Children*, 86(3), 310–329. <https://doi.org/10.1177/0014402919870464>

Bhui, K., Dinos, S., Galant-Miecznikowska, M., de Jongh, B., & Stansfeld, S. (2016). Perceptions of work stress cause and effective interventions in employees working in public, private and non-governmental organisations:

a qualitative study. *BJPsych bulletin*, *40*(6), 318–325. <https://doi.org/10.1192/pb.bp.115.050823>

Boamah, S. A., Hamadi, H. Y., Havaei, F., Smith, H., & Webb, F. (2022). Striking a Balance between Work and Play: The Effects of Work-life Interference and Burnout on Faculty Turnover Intentions and Career Satisfaction. *International Journal of Environmental Research and Public Health*, *19*(2), 809. <https://doi.org/10.3390/ijerph19020809>

Carlson, D. S., & Kacmar, K. M. (2000). Work-family conflict in the organization: Do life role values make a difference? *Journal of Management*, *26*(5), 1031–1054. <https://doi.org/10.1016/S0149-2063(00)00067-2>

Chukwuemeka, U. M., Okonkwo, U. P., Njoku, C. J., Igwe, S. E., Oyewumi, T. J., & Ugwuanyi, D. C. (2023). Work-related stress, quality of life, and coping mechanism among lecturers in a Tertiary Educational Institution in Anambra State, Nigeria. *BMC psychology*, *11*(1), 73. <https://doi.org/10.1186/s40359-023-01114-5>

Cicek, I., & Gezici, A. (2018). The role of working hours on work-life conflict. *PressAcademia Procedia* (PAP), 7(73), 376–380. <http://doi.org/10.17261/Pressacademia.2018.920>

Clark Blickenstaff, J. (2005). Women and science careers: leaky pipeline or gender filter? *Gender and Education*, *17*(4), 369–386. <https://doi.org/10.1080/09540250500145072>

Cohen, P., Cohen, P., West, S. G., & Aiken, L. S. (1983). *Applied Multiple Regression/Correlation Analysis for the Behavioral Sciences* (2nd ed.). Psychology Press. <https://doi.org/10.4324/9781410606266>

Conerly, T. R., Holmes, K., & Tamang, A. L. (2021). *Introduction to Sociology* 3e. OpenStax <https://openstax.org/books/introduction-sociology-3e/pages/1-3-theoretical-perspectives-in-sociology>

Dorenkamp, I., & Süß, S. (2017). Work-life conflict among young academics: antecedents and gender effects. *European Journal of Higher Education*, 7(4), 402–423. <https://doi.org/10.1080/21568235.2017.1304824>

Engler, Á. (2013). Students with Small Children in Higher Education. *Journal of Social Research & Policy*, 4(1), 109–120.

Fényes, H. (2014). Gender Role Attitudes among Higher Education Students in a Borderland Central-Eastern European Region called "Partium." *Center for Educational Policy Studies Journal*, *4*(2), 49–70. <https://doi.org/10.26529/cepsj.203>

Finkel, S. K., Olswang, S. G., & She, N. (2017). Childbirth, Tenure, and Promotion for Women Faculty. *The Review of Higher Education*, *17*, 259–270. <https://doi.org/10.1353/RHE.1994.0016>

Frank, E., Zhao, Z., Fang, Y., Rotenstein, L. S., Sen, S., & Guille, C. (2021). Experiences of Work-Family Conflict and Mental Health Symptoms by Gender Among Physician Parents During the COVID-19 Pandemic. *JAMA Network Open*, *4*(11), e2134315. <https://doi.org/10.1001/jamanetworkopen.2021.3431>

Giusti, L., Mammarella, S., Del Vecchio, S., Salza, A., Casacchia, M., & Roncone, R. (2023). Deepening Depression in Women Balancing Work-Life Responsibilities and Caregiving during the COVID-19 Pandemic: Findings from Gender-Specific Face-to-Face Street Interviews Conducted in Italy. *Behavioral Sciences*, *13*(11), 892. <https://doi.org/10.3390/bs13110892>

Golden, L., Wiens-Tuers, B., Lambert, S. J., & Henly, J. R. (2011). Working time in the employment relationship: Working time, perceived control and work-life balance. In K. Townsend, & A. Wilkinson (Eds.), *Research Handbook on the Future of Work and Employment Relations* (pp. 188–211). Edward Elgar Publishing Ltd.

Greller, M. M., & Richtermeyer, S. B. (2006). Changes in social support for professional development and retirement preparation as a function of age. *Human Relations*, *59*(9), 1213–1234.

Guest, D. E. (2002). Perspectives on the Study of Work-life Balance. *Social Science Information*, *41*(2), 255–279. <https://doi.org/10.1177/0539018402041002005>

Han, J., Yin, H., Wang, J., & Zhang, J. (2020). Job demands and resources as antecedents of university teachers' exhaustion, engagement and job satisfaction. *Educational Psychology*, *40*(3), 318–335. <https://doi.org/10.1080/01443410.2019.1674249>

Hayman, J. (2005). Psychometric Assessment of an Instrument Designed to Measure Work Life Balance. *Research and Practice in Human Resource Management*, *13*(1), 85–91. <http://hdl.handle.net/20.500.11937/46385>

Huffman, A., Culbertson, S. S., Henning, J. B., & Goh, A. (2013). Work-family conflict across the lifespan. *Journal of Managerial Psychology*, *28*(7–8), 761–780. <https://doi.org/10.1108/JMP-07-2013-0220>

Iamtrakul, P., & Chayphong, S. (2022). Exploring the Influencing Factors on Living Alone and Social Isolation among Older Adults in Rural Areas of Thailand. *International Journal of Environmental Research and Public Health*, *19*(21), 14572. <https://doi.org/10.3390/ijerph192114572>

International Labour Organization—ILO (2022): Working Time and Work-life Balance Around the World. Geneva: International Labour Office. ISBN: Web PDF: 9789220378915.

Johnson, S. J., Willis, S. M., & Evans, J. (2019). An examination of stressors, strain, and resilience in academic and non-academic U.K. university job roles. *International Journal of Stress Management, 26*(2), 162–172. <https://doi.org/10.1037/str0000096>

Keating, L. E., Becker, S., McCabe, K., Whattam, J., Garrick, L., Frey, B. N., Sassi, R. B., & McKinnon, M. C. (2019). Impact of a structured, group-based running programme on clinical, cognitive and social function in youth and adults with complex mood disorders: a 12-week pilot study. *BMJ Open Sport & Exercise Medicine, 5*(1), e000521. <https://doi.org/10.1136/bmjsem-2019-000521>

Keltner, D., & Kring, A. M. (1998). Emotion, Social Function, and Psychopathology. *Review of General Psychology, 2*, 320–342. <https://doi.org/10.1037/1089-2680.2.3.320>

Kossek, E., & Lee, K. (2017). Work-Family Conflict and Work-life Conflict. *Oxford Research Encyclopedia of Business and Management.* Retrieved from <https://oxfordre.com/business/view/10.1093/acrefore/9780190224851.001.0001/acrefore-9780190224851-e-52>

Kotwal, A. A., Kim, J., Waite, L. J., & Dale, W. (2016). Social Function and Cognitive Status: Results from a US Nationally Representative Survey of Older Adults. *Journal of General Internal Medicine, 31*, 854–862. <https://doi.org/10.1007/s11606-016-3696-0>

Kovács, K., Dobay, B., Halasi, S., Pinczés, T., & Tódor, I. (2024). Demands, resources and institutional factors in the work of academic staff in Central and Eastern Europe: results of qualitative research among university teachers in five countries. *Frontiers in Education, 8*, 1326515. <https://doi.org/10.3389/feduc.2023.1326515>

McGinnity, F. (2021). Work-life Conflict in Europe. In F. Maggino (ed.), *Encyclopedia of Quality of Life and Well-Being Research* (pp. 1–6). Springer. <https://doi.org/10.1007/978-3-319-69909-7_3727-2>

Miller, J. E., & Hollenshead, C. (2005). Gender, family, and flexibility: why they're important in the academic workplace. *Change, 37*(6), 58–62.

Misra, J., Lundquist, J. H., & Templer, A. (2012), Gender, Work Time, and Care Responsibilities Among Faculty. *Sociological Forum, 27*, 300–323. <https://doi.org/10.1111/j.1573-7861.2012.01319.x>

Mudrak, J., Zabrodska, K., Kveton, P. et al. (2018). Occupational Well-being Among University Faculty: A Job Demands-Resources Model. *Research in Higher Education, 59*, 325–348. <https://doi.org/10.1007/s11162-017-9467-x>

Nichols, H. M., & Swanberg, J. E. (2018). Measuring Work-Life Conflict Among Low-Wage Workers. *Journal of the Society for Social Work and Research, 9*(3), 473–497. <https://www.journals.uchicago.edu/doi/full/10.1086/697254>

O'Laughlin, E. M., & Bischoff, L. G. (2005). Balancing Parenthood and Academia: Work/Family Stress as Influenced by Gender and Tenure Status. *Journal of Family Issues*, *26*(1), 79–106. <https://doi.org/10.1177/0192513X04265942>

Paksi, V., Nagy, B., & Király, G. (2016). The timing of motherhood while earning a Ph.D. in engineering. *International Journal of Doctoral Studies, 11*, 285–304. <https://doi.org/10.28945/3544>

Paksi, V., Nagy, B., & Tardos, K. (2022). Perception of Barriers to Motherhood: Female Ph.D. Students' Changing Family Plans in the STEM Fields. *Social Inclusion, 10*(3), 149–159. <https://doi.org/10.17645/si.v10i3.5250>

Pallant, J. (2020). SPSS Survival Manual: A step-by-step guide to data analysis using IBM SPSS (7th ed.). Routledge. <https://doi.org/10.4324/9781003117452>

Perrewé, P. L., Hochwarter, W. A., & Kiewitz, C. (1999). Value attainment: an explanation for the negative effects of work-family conflict on job and life satisfaction. *Journal of occupational health psychology*, *4*(4), 318–326. <https://doi.org/10.1037//1076-8998.4.4.318>

Posner, B. Z. (2010). Another Look at the Impact of Personal and Organizational Values Congruency. *Journal of Business Ethics*, *97*(4), 535–541. <http://www.jstor.org/stable/40929512.>

Pratt, C. C. (1969). *The Task of Gestalt Psychology*. Princeton University Press.

Premeaux, S. F., Adkins, C. L., & Mossholder, K. W. (2007). Balancing work and family: A field study of multi-dimensional, multi-role work-family conflict. *Journal of Organizational Behavior, 28*(6), 705–727. <https://doi.org/10.1002/job.439>

Pusztai, G., & Márkus, Zs. (2019). Paradox of Assimilation among Indigenous Higher Education Students in Four Central European Countries. *Diaspora, Indigenous, and Minority Education*, *13*(4), 201–16. <https://doi.org/10.1080/15595692.2019.1623193.>

Raiu, S.-L. (2021). Generaţiile X, Y şi Z pe piaţa muncii. Caracteristici specifice, strategii de implicare în învăţarea activă şi abordări ale relaţiei managerilor cu angajaţii. *Sociologie Românească*, *19*(2), 89–121. <https://doi.org/10.33788/sr.19.2.4>

Riemenschnieder, A., & Harper, K. V. (1990). Women in academia: guilty or not guilty? conflict between caregiving and employment. *Initiatives* 2, 27–35.

Saeed, K., & Farooqi, Y. A. (2014). Examining the relationship between work life balance, job stress and job satisfaction among university teachers (A case of University of Gujrat). *International Journal of Multidisciplinary Sciences and Engineering*, *5*(6), 9–15.

Salami, S. O. (2011). Job Stress and Burnout among Lecturers: Personality and Social Support as Moderators. *Asian Social Science*, *7*(5), 110–121. <https://doi.org/10.5539/ass.v7n5p110>

Santana, E., Silva, R., Bernardo, J., Loureiro, R., Gil, I., Mestre, T., & Reis, L. (2022). Social Representations of Violence among Brazilian Older People with Functional Dependence. *Journal of Ageing and Longevity*, *2*(3), 228–239. <https://doi.org/10.3390/jal2030019>

Santana-Monagas, E., Putwain, D. W., Núñez, J. L., Loro, J. F., & Léon, J. (2021). Do teachers' engaging messages predict motivation to learn and performance? *Revista de Psicodidáctica*, *27*(1), 86–95. <https://doi.org/10.1016/j.psicoe.2021.11.001>

Sen, A. (1985). *Commodities and Capabilities*. United Nations Development Programme, Human Developmen tReport 2006–08. United Nations.

Shockley, K. M., Shen, W., DeNunzio, M. M., Arvan, M. L., & Knudsen, E. A. (2017) Disentangling the Relationship Between Gender and Work-Family Conflict: An Integration of Theoretical Perspectives Using Meta-Analytic Methods. *Journal of Applied Psychology*, *102*(12), 1601–1635 <http://dx.doi.org/10.1037/apl0000246>

Silva, A. L. S. E., Ottaviani, A. C., Orlandi, F. S., Inouye, K., Zazzetta, M. S., Pavarini, S. C. I., & Santos-Orlandi, A. A. D. (2023). Social support perceived by elderly people in social vulnerability according to family functionality: a cross-sectional study. *Revista da Escola de Enfermagem da U S P*, *57*, e20220475. <https://doi.org/10.1590/1980-220X-REEUSP-2022-0475en>

Sirgy, M. J., & Lee, D. J. (2018). Work-life Balance: An Integrative Review. *Applied Research in Quality of Life*, *13*(1), 229–254. <https://doi.org/10.1007/s11482-017-9509-8>

Stinson, J., Wolfe, R. & Spaulding, W. (2022). Social Connectedness in Schizotypy: The Role of Cognitive and Affective Empathy. *Behavioral Sciences*, *12*(8), 253. <https://doi.org/10.3390/bs12080253>

Sztáray Kézdy, É. & Drjenovszky, Z. (2021). Hungarian Stay-at-Home Fathers: A New Alternative for Family Wellbeing. *Social Sciences*, *10*(6), 197. <https://doi.org/10.3390/socsci10060197>

Tammelin, M. (2009). *Working time and family time: experiences of the work and family interface among dual-earning couples in Finland* (No. 355). Academic Dissertation. University of Jyväskylä. <https://jyx.jyu.fi/bitstream/handle/123456789/19730/9789513935160.pdf?seq>

Thoits, P. A. (1985). Social Support and Psychological Well-Being: Theoretical Possibilities. In I. G. Sarason, & B. R. Sarason (Eds.), Social Support: Theory,

Research and Applications (pp. 51–72). NATO ASI Series, vol 24. Springer. <https://doi.org/10.1007/978-94-009-5115-0_4>

Vigoda-Gadot, E., & Talmud, I. (2010). Organizational politics and job outcomes: The moderating effect of trust and social support. *Journal of Applied Social Psychology, 40*(11), 2829–2861. <https://doi.org/10.1111/j.1559-1816.2010.00683.x>

Vveinhardt, J. (2017). *Congruence of Personal and Organizational Values—How to Deal with?* InTech. <http://doi:10.5772/intechopen.72213>

Warr, P. (1992). Age and occupational well-being. *Psychology and Aging,* 7(1), 37–45. <https://doi.org/10.1037/0882-7974.7.1.37>

12. The Cultural Involvement Patterns of Academics

Edina Márkus, Judit Herczegh & Márta Miklósi

ABSTRACT
The issue of cultural and leisure activities in general has often been raised recently in the context of well-being, with a number of researchers analyzing data from the 2007 Eurobarometer survey and finding that cultural consumption is strongly influenced by whether social mobility is lower or higher in a given country (Hek & Kraaykamp, 2013). Most studies generally examine cultural consumption; there needs to be detailed knowledge of the cultural consumption habits and attitudes toward the culture of the academics, as this is a gap area. We wanted to investigate the cultural habits, online and offline cultural consumption of academics in Central and Eastern European higher education institutions, assuming that they are more active in this area than the rest of society due to their higher education. The present study is based on a questionnaire survey and sent online to all academics of the institutions in spring 2023; the questions in the questionnaire were related to the frequency of consumption of programs and attitudes toward culture in different cultural sectors and institutions, similar to other research on the subject. The results of our research are related to the findings of Šebová and Révészová (2020), thus, two of their four clusters are very similar to our cluster. They highlighted similar characteristics of citizens belonging to this cluster even though they analyzed Eurobarometer survey data for the whole population, and we analyzed it for a more highly qualified population. Regarding the attitude of the respondents toward culture, it can be stated that the attitude is almost identical; there are no significant differences in the comparison of cultural clusters either; this may be due to similar levels of education, socio-economic status, and time use.

Keywords: higher education, academics, cultural consumption, attitudes toward culture

Introduction

In the framework of the project TKP2021-EGA-20, in collaboration with the Sports Economy Research Group, the national economic rationale of regular physical activity in Hungary for a sustainable and safe environment, we are investigating the factors influencing the health, well-being, and performance of academics in Central and Eastern European higher education institutions. In the context of well-being, the issue of cultural and leisure activities has been frequently raised recently, with several works investigating cultural consumption, participation, and subjective well-being (Boyce-Tillman, 2016; Bertacchini, 2021; Francourt & Finn, 2020). Therefore, we also considered it essential to explore the cultural consumption habits (frequency of visits to programs of specific cultural sectors and institutions) and attitudes toward the culture of the academics. Consumption is mainly passive, while participation implies a more active activity. In our research, we focused on consumption habits.

To explore the cultural consumption of academics, we cannot ignore current trends in higher education. Global, neoliberal social and educational policies have changed working conditions and work culture in universities. Enrollments have increased and the demands on efficiency have also risen (Jauhiainen et al., 2019). Currently, the trend in universities is toward professorial activism and managerialism (Laasch, 2017). The demands on efficiency have grown, and academic life has become accelerated and homogenized, including through measurable progress (e.g., annual reviews), rigorous publication standards, time-consuming management meetings and standardization of research assessment (Laasch, 2017). Berg and Seeber (2016) argue that these developments threaten the social role of professors and universities to collectively create deep, diverse and critical knowledge, and that they have less free time due to a heavier workload. In addition to the issue of efficiency, there are several issues that arise for academics in higher education, such as the dilemma of teaching versus research, the challenges of academic hierarchy, and university loneliness (Jauhiainen et al., 2019).

Social organizations and groups, which are important from the socialization point of view, besides integrating the individual into society, also play an extremely important role in the transmission of the various individual-related benefits and capital. Culture and leisure are thus able to intertwine in the process of capital formation and transmission (Bourdieu, 1977; Coleman, 1990).

Educational institutions, especially universities and colleges providing higher education, can be seen as an ideal arena for building a personal network of contacts. Thus, we cannot ignore the socio-administrative and cultural patterns of the actors of these educational institutions when describing the transmission of capital (Bourdieu, 1977).

The characteristics of cultural capital are considered to be the most relevant, since they are the social resources that also contain socialization segments. About this, Bourdieu distinguishes three forms of cultural capital: the internalized, imported capital, which is the organization's durable skill, the capital that appears in the materialized state of cultural goods (material cultural capital), such as pictures, books, lexicons, tools, machines, and finally the cultural capital that appears in the institutionalized state), which confers specific properties to capital (Bourdieu, 1977).

For the purposes of our present study, the elements of cultural capital are primarily manifested in the leisure activities and the consumption choices associated with them.

Seamen's research has investigated the extent to which cultural demand is influenced by consumers' income and educational attainment. The results pointed to the important fact that the demand for culture is much higher among the highly educated than among the less educated, but that for the same educational level, there is also an increasing influence of income on cultural demand, and thus the cultural consumption of higher education graduates cannot be ignored (Seamen, 2005).

In addition to individual patterns, macro-level social influences also have an impact at the level of leisure and cultural consumption activities. In the information society, the internet as a medium is not only meant to transmit cultural values and patterns, but can also act as a community shaper, even as a creator of social tradition. Culture, knowledge and information are spreading to all areas of life. The cultural medium that is being created is becoming part of everyday life. This specific, ever-changing and grassroots online medium also has an impact on people's values within a given social context (Dessewffy, 2004).

1. The Background of Cultural Consumption in Central and Eastern Europe

In the information society, classical patterns of leisure consumption are being overwritten by new models. For example, the leisure opportunities and consumption of men and women are accompanied by gradually decreasing differences. The online presence can be understood as a new arena for cultural consumption, rather than as a supplement to traditional opportunities (Gershuny, 2000).

Freedom of choice in individual leisure is becoming more pronounced. The individual as consumer is also present in the field of culture, communication and group formation. Lifestyle, rather than class, is the dominant organizer and primary group-former of an individual's life (Castells, 1996).

The issue of cultural consumption came to the forefront in the early 2000s, becoming part of social stratification studies. This attention is due, among other things, to the work of Chan and Goldthorpe in the 2000s (Chan-Goldthorpe, 2006; 2007; 2010). Research in this period focused on the analysis of the relationship between social classes and status groups and cultural consumption and behavior. Three main theoretical approaches compete with each other on the interplay between cultural consumption, taste, cultural practices and the structure of society: the homology assumption, the individualization theory and the omnivore-univore model. The first, already classical, is Pierre Bourdieu's homology theory, the second is the postmodern theory of individualization (Beck, 2003; Giddens,1991; Bauman, 2002), and the third can be seen in some ways as a synthesis of the first two, with cultural versatility, or omnivorousness, at its heart (Peterson-Kern, 1996; Peterson, 2005).

Our research is not without precedent; cultural consumption studies among the general public are typical internationally and domestically. Most international and domestic studies attempt to create cultural consumption groups. Specifically, we could not find any such study among academics.

Hek & Kraaykamp's 2013 research analyzed data from the 2007 Eurobarometer survey, a representative survey of the cultural consumption habits of 26746 citizens in 29 European countries. In their comparative study, they investigated the relationship between social inequalities and cultural consumption patterns. They found that cultural policies and the economic situation of each Member State have a strong influence on cultural consumption patterns, revealing significant differences between citizens from poorer and richer countries. The authors also point out that the cultural consumption habits of citizens of individual European member states are significantly influenced by the fact that the degree of social mobility in a given state is lower or higher, with higher rates of cultural participation in countries with higher social mobility. The study also found that in richer member states there is less of a difference between the cultural consumption of citizens with higher education and better financial circumstances and the cultural consumption of citizens with lower education and less wealth (Hek & Kraaykamp, 2013).

If we compare the cultural consumption practices of the populations of Western European and post-socialist countries, we can discover differences in the form of cultural capital. In other words, different social development and specific national contexts have led to different cultural consumption patterns in these countries (Šebová & Révészová, 2020).

In the case of Central and Eastern European countries, research has also shown that the social, socio-economic position of parents can be considered an important variable (Kraaykamp & Nieuwbeerta, 2000; De Graaf, 1991). Post-socialist countries face similar problems in terms of cultural policy, as Vojtíšková and Lorencová point out in their work (Vojtíšková & Lorencová, 2014). Furthermore, Šebová and Révészová's 2020 study aims to analyze the relationship between cultural consumption and socio-economic characteristics of the Slovak population in Slovakia based on the Eurobarometer surveys of 2007 and 2013 (interviewing 1000 Slovak citizens). It is, therefore, based on a secondary analysis of data. As a result of their research, cluster analysis outlined four types of Slovak culture consumers, namely: 1. heritage visitors, who rarely visit cultural events, but when they do, they prefer cultural heritage sites, museums, and libraries; 2. inactive group, who rarely visit cultural events, but when they do, they visit sites of historical importance. 3. omnivores: They often attend cultural events organized for intellectuals in the field of high cultures, such as theater, concerts, ballet performances, museums, and galleries. 4. popular culture lovers: less open to high culture programs, do not attend an opera, do not attend a ballet performance, go to the theater or a gallery less often, prefer to go to the cinema or concerts of popular music (Šebová & Révészová, 2020).

Grześkowiak compared Eurobarometer data from 2007 and 2013, looking in detail at the cultural consumption of Poles. Grześkowiak created three clusters based on the results: Cluster 1: cultural consumers who go to the theater and opera and who also enjoy ballet and dance performances; Cluster 2: audiences who attend concerts of popular music, historical sites, museums, and galleries. Cluster 3: visiting public libraries, watching cultural programs on TV/listening to the radio, and reading books (Grześkowiak, 2016).

As can be seen, cultural research approaches culture mainly from the institutional culture perspective—theater performances, exhibitions, visits to museums, libraries, classical music concerts, etc., and also examines consumer types in terms of genre choices (Piekarska-Duraj, 2020; Tomšic, 2016). Typification, as Pavluska notes, is a specific analytical and exploratory activity because it does not investigate the frequency with which certain sociodemographic groups participate in certain cultural events and programs, but rather how cultural consumer patterns—clusters—emerge based on the 'cooccurrence' or 'non-cooccurrence' of certain cultural activities and the intensity of these activities (Pavluska, 2016).

In the domestic arena, this type-making activity has been observed for decades. In her 2016 paper, Pavluska summarized the results of extensive comprehensive studies on culture /MTA Institute of Sociology/ National Cultural Status Survey (Vitányi, 1997), KSH's Lifestyle and Time Balance Survey (KSH, 2000), and subsequent comprehensive domestic culture surveys (Bukodi, 2005; Hunyadi, 2005; Antalóczy et al., 2010) / (Table 12.1). These types can be grouped into four broad categories: high culture-oriented, cultural omnivores, entertainment seekers, and passive.

Table 12.1: Cultural consumer/leisure types in Hungary from the mid-1980s to the mid-2010s

Mid-1980s	Mid-1990s	Millennium	2003	2008	2013
Autonomous—culture-oriented (15%)	Autonomous—culture-oriented (15%)	High culture-oriented (8%)	Consolidated, traditional culture seekers (9%)	Cultural elite (10.1%)	Diverse traditional culture seekers (13.7%)
Open—accumulative (24%)	Young, entertainment-oriented (24%)	Cultural omnivores (18%)	Young omnivores (7%)	Omnivores (8.6%)	Traditional culture selectors (10.7%)
Clingy—recreational (26%)	Homebody—reader (15%)	Recreation/ entertainment-oriented (23%)	One-sided fun, movie-going-party (14%)	Light entertainers (13.8%)	Culturally diverse (11.9%)
Passive (35%)	Passive—other (17%)	Passive (28%)	One-sided fun, culture house goers (10%),	Culturally interested (20.5%)	Light entertainment seekers (16.8%)
	Passive—homebodies, not reading (26%)	Not culturally engaged/ isolated (23%)	Homebodies, reading (17%)	Culturally passive (47.1%)	Going to mass events, one-way fun (15.2%)
			Passive, uncultured, dull (43%)		Culturally passive (31.6%)

Source: Pavluska 2016, p. 442.

2. Methodological Background

The questionnaire on which this study was based was translated into English, Serbian, Slovak, Ukrainian, and Romanian and sent online to all the academics of the institutions 2–3 times in spring 2023, with the permission of the respective HEI heads, to ensure probability sampling. In Hungary, we surveyed higher education institutions in two disadvantaged regions, the North Great Plain Region and the South Transdanubian Region (University of Debrecen (n=356), University of Debrecen Reformed Theology (n=7), University of Nyíregyháza (n=14) and University of Pécs (n=104)), while in the case of institutions beyond the border, we mainly targeted minority Hungarian institutions. However, we also sent the questionnaire to all academics in the majority language. The institutions surveyed in Serbia were the University of Novi Sad and the Technical College of Subotica (n=39). In Slovakia, the J. Selye University (n=26), the University of Prešov (Prešov), and the University of Trnava (Trnava) (n=8 from each of the two institutions) were asked, and, in Romania, the Christian University of Partium (n=11), Oradea State University (n=35), Emanuel University (n=14), Sapientia University of Transylvania (n=35) and Babeş-Bolyai University (n=11) (and their external campuses) were queried. In Ukraine, the questionnaire was completed by the Ferenc Rákóczi II Transcarpathian Hungarian College (n=31) and the National University of Uzhhorod (n=20), as well as by faculty members (n=62) working in institutions who teach at universities in the war zone or its immediate vicinity, so their answers provided us with valuable information about their specific situation. 48 respondents did not provide the name of the institution where they work.

The main question of the research was which factors influence the well-being of academics. Along this set of questions, our working group aimed to investigate the attitude of higher education students in the Carpathian Basin toward culture, their cultural consumption habits and the relationship between cultural consumption and well-being of students.

We believe that participation in academia, high qualifications imply higher levels of consumption of cultural sectors, higher frequency or interconnection of several sectors in consumption, more diversified patterns of consumption, lower levels of participation barriers.

The questions in the questionnaire focused on the frequency of consumption of programs of specific cultural sectors and institutions, reading habits, and agreement with attitudes toward culture, and we tried to identify possible reasons for not visiting cultural spaces. Similar to other research on this topic (Roberts, 1999; Peterson, 2005; Katz-Gerro, 2011; Yaish & Katz-Gerro, 2012; Grześkowiak, 2016; Pavluska et al., 2018; Šebová & Révészová, 2020).

This study mainly compares each question with cultural clusters formed with regard to the respondents' consumption frequency. We are interested in the extent to which respondent groups belonging to different cultural clusters behave differently as cultural consumers and hold different views on culture.

Based on the types of cultural and recreational venues and the frequency of their use, four clusters were identified from 679 respondents. We have integrated off-site cultural institutions into the training of clusters, as well as online visits to these institutions, such as ballet performances, balls, jazz concerts, festivals, literary days, major and widespread music concerts, and the like. cinema, film, museum, art gallery, monument, house of culture, folk and world music, library, opera, operetta, theater and entertainment venues and their online forms were the variables and frequency attributes associated with visits. Respondents had seven response options in frequency of visits per year (none, once, twice, three times, four times, five times, or more than five times). The four clusters were culturally versatile, elite consumers (7.1%), culturally open (29.9%), culturally open, online (9.9%), and culturally passive (53.1%). We have compared the cultural clusters we have developed with the types of academics we have created in our research (Table 12.2).

Table 12.2: Frequency of academics' use of cultural and leisure activities by cluster

		Clusters of academic types						
		Teaching-focused academics	Academics with an admin-istrative focus	Research-focused academics	Academic leaders	Total	Chi-square	p
Culturally open	N	76	41	40	46	203		
	%	33.3	31.1	28	26.1	29.9		
Culturally passive	N	115	62	86	98	361		
	%	50.4	47	60.1	55.7	53.1		
Culturally open online	N	18	15	12	22	67		
	%	7.9	11.4	8.4	12.5	9.9		
Culturally versatile, elite consumer	N	19	14	5	14	48	13.423	0.144
	%	8.4	10.6	3.5	5.7	7.1		
Total	N	228	132	143	132	679		
	%	100	100	100	100	100		

Source: CEETHE 2023 database N=679.

3. Results

As the data in Table 12.3 shows, the most popular cultural consumption activities among tertiary students are popular culture consumption venues, i.e., attending festivals, music concerts, films, cinemas, and nightclubs. These activities are, however, complemented by classical cultural consumption activities such as theater, classical music, and library visits.

Table 12.3: Frequency of use of cultural and leisure activities (%)

	None	At least once	Two times	Three times	Four times	Five times	More than five times	N
Ballet	66.5	17.7	7.7	3.5	1.1	0.9	2.7	809
Ballet online	82.8	8.4	3.1	2.5	1.0	0.4	1.9	807
Ball	69.7	18.9	6.2	3.3	1.2	0.1	0.5	806
Jazz concert	77.5	12.7	4.1	2.4	1.1	0.9	1.4	803
Jazz concert online	86.7	5.4	3.1	2.5	0.5	0.5	1.4	803
Festival	42.6	32.9	12.8	5.8	2.4	1.5	2.0	805
Literary Days	65.9	16.5	7.4	4.0	2.0	0.9	3.3	806
Literary Days Online	80.1	9.2	4.2	2.7	0.9	0.7	2.1	805
Classical Music Concert	52.1	17.5	10.4	6.3	3.8	2.0	7.8	806
Classical music concert online	71.3	11.4	4.8	3.5	1.1	1.4	6.5	799
Popular music Concert	46.8	21	12.3	8.7	2.7	1.5	6.8	803
Popular music concert online	77.8	8.4	3.0	3.4	1.8	1.1	4.5	797
Cinema	32.8	17.7	14.2	12.6	5.6	4.7	12.4	804
Film online	10.3	6.4	4.4	4.8	2.5	3.3	68.5	800
Museum/ picture gallery	24.9	23	14.5	11.5	4.5	5.1	16.4	799
Museum/ picture gallery online	74.8	9.9	41	3.4	2.0	1.0	4.8	798
Monuments	17.3	15.9	15.4	13.3	4.4	5.7	27.9	803
Cultural center	47.9	17.5	10.6	7.1	2.9	2.4	11.7	802
Folk music/world music	68.4	15.7	6.0	3.7	1.7	1.1	3.4	805
Folk music/world music online	82.8	5.9	3.0	3.2	1.5	0.9	2.7	802
Library	41.9	11.3	9.8	6.7	3.5	3.5	23.3	804
Library online	60.5	5.9	3.5	4.2	1.4	2.3	22.3	794
Opera	78.9	11.3	5.0	1.6	0.9	0.4	1.9	802
Opera online	87.6	4.6	2.5	1.6	1.0	0.9	1.8	798
Operetta/Hungarian song	86.8	7.0	3.1	1.2	0.4	0.2	1.2	802
Operetta/Hungarian song online	91.9	3.3	1.5	0.9	0.9	0.4	1.3	798
Theater	52.2	14.0	11.1	7.4	3.5	2.1	9.7	801
Theater online	69.4	8.2	4.8	3.7	2.9	1.3	9.6	788
Entertainment site/night club	35.1	13.8	7.0	8.2	4.7	3.5	27.7	805

Source: CEETHE 2023 database.

In the analysis, we found that of the cultural activities related to online space, watching a film is the only one with a very high frequency, with 68.5% of respondents choosing this form of cultural consumption more than five times a year.

In contrast to online film watching, online museum visits, theater-, opera-, ballet-, operetta-, and jazz concert visits, over 65% of respondents have indicated a lack of participation in the classic digital platforms for cultural consumption activities. In the cases of online library, theater and classical music concerts, we found a low number of participants with a high frequency of visits: 22.3% of respondents visited an online library more than five times, 9.6% attended an online theater performance and 6.5% attended an online classical music concert.

In terms of cultural activities in physical space, we found that classical cultural activities identified as high culture consumption, such as classical music, opera, and ballet, are attended with less frequency, similar to modern culture consumption or elements of popular culture, such as going to the cinema, cinema, popular music, entertainment site or nightclubs. The value of those who chose the other category is not shown in our graph due to their low proportion, but the textual responses are interesting for interpretation. Circus performances, social gatherings, scientific presentations, and sacred and sporting events were mentioned as cultural activities. These activities highlight that even highly qualified respondents with a scientific background combine forms of activity related to sports, hobbies, and religious and community life with cultural consumption elements.

The participation activity of each cluster group in the cultural sectors shows very different patterns, as demonstrated in Table 12.4. Those belonging to the culturally open, online cluster prefer the present and online forms of watching films online, visiting libraries, and also visiting monuments, historical sites, and places of interest. At the same time, other cultural activities could be more active. The culturally open is similar to the previous group. However, the activities of this group include cinema and online film viewing, library visits, visits to monuments, historical sites, and places of interest, and visits to concerts and entertainment venues. For the group of culturally versatile, elite consumers, high values are observed for several cultural activities, with higher averages for visiting cultural centers, community centers, classical music concerts, and attending literary days and theater, in addition to the frequent activities of the previous groups. Both attendance and online activity are high, whether for classical music, film, visiting museums, galleries, libraries, or the theater. Finally, a significant group, 53.1% of respondents, are culturally passive, with those in this group generally inactive in cultural activities other than online film watching.

Table 12.4: Cluster groups (cluster weights 1–7) and averages of visits to cultural and leisure activities (N=679) based on the frequency of cultural and leisure activities of the academics

	Culturally open	Culturally passive	Culturally open online	Culturally versatile, elite consumer
a ballet or other dance performance	1.96	1.32	1.56	3.12
ballet or other dance performance online	1.16	1.13	2.46	2.98
at a ball	1.60	1.31	1.36	2.27
at a jazz concert	1.59	1.20	1.42	2.72
at a jazz concert online	1.05	1.11	2.27	2.48
at a festival	2.45	1.52	1.95	4.20
literary days, reading evenings	1.99	1.22	1.80	4.60
literary days, reading evenings online	1.27	1.09	2.12	3.77
classical music concert	2.62	1.55	3.29	4.23
classical music concerts online	1.35	1.18	5.01	3.68
popular music concerts	3.08	1.62	1.91	4.48
popular music concerts online	1.27	1.22	3.71	3.60
watched a film in a cinema	4.03	2.26	2.55	5.29
watched a movie online	6.43	4.93	6.57	6.85
in a museum or art gallery	4.58	2.01	3.98	6.17
in museum or gallery online	1.29	1.25	3.18	3.98
visiting monuments, historical sites, places of interest	5.51	2.63	4.49	6.23
in a cultural center or community center	3.14	1.63	2.55	6.00
folk music, world music concerts	1.79	1.25	1.61	4.15
folk music, world music concerts online	1.17	1.12	2.46	3.31
in a public library	4.73	1.92	3.33	5.94
in a public library online	3.11	1.94	4.55	4.48
at an opera performance	1.48	1.15	1.69	2.73
at an opera performance online	1.08	1.04	2.54	2.31
at an operetta or Hungarian song performance	1.27	1.07	1.22	2.39
at an operetta or Hungarian song performance online	1.03	1.03	1.94	2.04
at a theater, stand-up comedy performance	3.24	1.66	1.67	4.85
theater, stand-up comedy performance online	1.89	1.47	3.55	4.29
in a nightclub (e.g., disco, music club, café)	5.31	2.57	2.84	4.91

Source: CEETHE 2023 database.

Table 12.4, therefore, compares the averages of the consumption frequency of each off-site and online cultural arena /respondents who could choose from seven options for the frequency of visit per year (none, once, once, twice, three times, four times, five times, more than five times)/ with the cluster types. The frequency averages in the table, which are linked to each cultural scene, show a clear consumption pattern in the four cluster groups.

Most of the research on the subject reveals differences in cultural consumption by gender, age, education, and type of settlement. We have also reviewed these variables concerning the different cultural cluster respondent groups. In our case, education is irrelevant as we have a highly educated respondent group. In terms of gender, women tend to be the most active, according to the surveys. Regarding settlement type, they show higher activity toward larger settlements, which may be related to the diversity of supply. Our data also show no deviation from trends in these areas, but we did find a divergence concerning age.

The data in Table 12.5 compare age groups and cultural clusters. Let us take the responses for each age group as a percentage and look at the cluster proportions within each age group. We see that activity increases with age, with a higher proportion of culturally open and culturally versatile, elite consumers in older age groups and a lower proportion of passive cluster members. This is the reverse in the case of the Eurobarometer's secondary analysis, where cultural consumption activity decreases with age. The 16–29 age group is much more active in the EU member states and, on average, in the EU (European Commission, 2007; Pavluska, 2014; Márkus et al., 2023). The Eurobarometer survey covers the whole population, while our survey covers the population of higher education students. It could be explained that time pressure is not an issue for older respondents, to the extent that raising children and building a career at an older age is not as important as it is for younger respondents.

Table 12.5: Respondents by age group and cultural cluster (N=660)

Age group / cultural cluster	Culturally open	Culturally passive	Culturally open online	Culturally versatile, elite consumer	Total
–35 years N	37	69	3	4	113
% within age group	32.7	61.1	2.7**	3.5	100
36-55 years N	139	236	25	31	431
% within age group	32.3	54.8	5.8**	7.2	100
36-55 years N	22	49	37	8	116
% within age group	19.0**	42.2**	31.9*	6.9	100

*The adjusted residuals are more significant than two.
**The adjusted residuals are less than -2.

One of the foundations of classical literacy and cultural capital is reading activity in one's life. The presence of recreational reading was examined for Central and Eastern European graduates, assuming they have a higher share of this activity than the overall social average, as reflected in the number of books read annually across countries. Regarding the frequency of leisure reading per 12 months, the highest number of readers in the database (340 people in total) is found among those who read between 1 and 5 books per year. This is followed by a camp of readers of 6-10 books per year with 119 people. 107 people read between 11 and 20 books per year. Based on the responses received, an intensive reader stratum of 165 people emerged in the database; they had read more than 11 books in the last 12 months. The number of people who have yet to read a book in the last 12 months was 54 (Table 12.6).

Table 12.6: Distribution of academics by number of books read in the last year (%, persons)

	Percentage of academics (%)	Number of academics
0	9.3	54
1-5 books	50.3	340
6-10 books	18.3	119
11-20 books	14.2	107
21-50 books	6.2	46
more than 51 books	1.7	12
total	100	678

Source: CEETHE 2023 database (N=678).

Compared to the results of typological studies in Hungary, among academics, we also find a group of traditional high culture-oriented, cultural "omnivores" and passive types, so there is an apparent similarity. However, the proportions show a different picture. Despite higher levels of education, the respondent group we surveyed had a much higher proportion of passive types than in previous national surveys. For this reason, we also compared clusters by reading frequency. The questionnaire asked how many books had been read in the last 12 months. This was an attempt to see whether people of the passive type might be reading, so the type of home reader in previous studies (the mid-1990s and the 2003 study, see Table 12.1) might appear as a subtype of passive. To investigate this, we focused on the non or light readers group. Compared to the cluster types, we find that there is no such subtype; passives have a very high non-response rate to the question of reading and a very high number of no or few readers (Table 12.7).

Table 12.7: Comparison of cultural clusters with the number of non- or light readers

	Lack of response	0 book	1 book	2 books	3 books	4 books	books
Culturally open	33	5	12	13	16	11	30
Culturally passive	79	40	36	42	36	16	34
Culturally open online	12	1	3	5	5	4	9
Culturally versatile, elite consumer	10	0	0	1	1	0	3

Source: CEETHE 2023 database P=0.000**.

We also asked respondents about their attitudes toward culture. We measured agreement with attitudinal statements about culture (attitudes toward culture, different aspects of cultural participation) on a scale of 1 to 5 (strongly disagree–strongly agree). For the ten statements we formulated, we used the findings published in Pavluska et al.'s (2018) research questionnaire.

The averages of the responses to each question are shown in Figure 12.1 Based on the averages, the two statements that elicited the most significant agreement among respondents were "A cultural program is good if it makes you think if it is memorable" and "A cultural program is good if it is light, entertaining, relaxing." The least agreed responses were "For me, cultural activities are mainly a question of money" and "My cultural activities are increasingly linked to the internet."

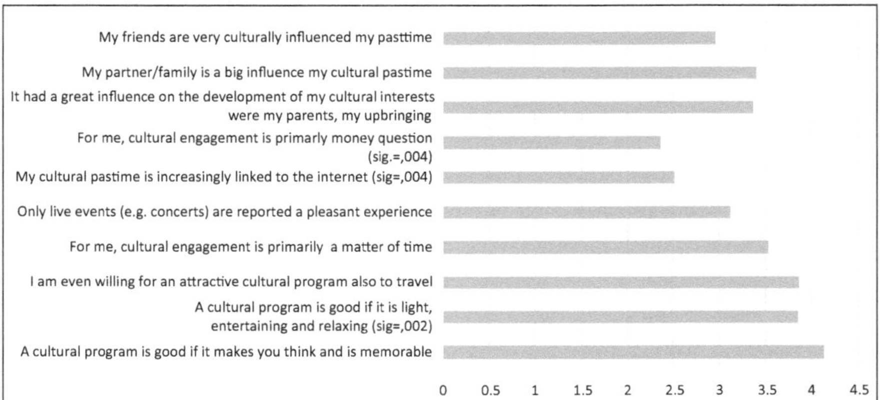

Figure 12.1: Attitudes toward culture by average of responses to attitude questions (N=757–764).

Source: CEETHE 2023.

Attitudinal questions were examined from the perspective of cultural clusters. This shows that there are no significant differences. However, some statements confirm the specificity of the clusters. For example, the mean scores for the question "I am willing to travel for an attractive cultural program" are higher among the culturally open and culturally versatile elite consumers. Thus, their activity toward culture was reflected in their response, not only in the frequency of visits that constituted the cluster. Alternatively, for example, "Only live events are an experience for me" and "My cultural pastime is increasingly linked to the internet." confirm the willingness of the cluster of the culturally open, online active to consume culture online (Table 12.8).

Table 12.8: Means of attitude statements on attitudes toward culture by cultural cluster (1–5 scale)

	Culturally open	Culturally passive	Culturally open online	Culturally versatile, elite consumer
A cultural program is good if it makes you think and remember.	4.14	4.03	4.23	4.29
A cultural program is good if it is light, entertaining, and relaxing.	3.91	3.93	3.54	3.89
I am willing to travel for an attractive cultural program.	4.09	3.69	3.83	4.23
For me, a cultural activity is a question of time.	3.50	3.53	3.43	3.52
Only live events (e.g., concerts) are an experience for me.	3.35	3.01	2.61	3.21
My cultural pastime is increasingly linked to the internet.	2.16	2.34	3.02	2.43
For me, cultural activity is primarily a question of money.	2.36	2.34	2.26	2.33
My parents and my upbringing had a significant influence on the development of my cultural interests.	3.35	3.29	3.36	3.35
My partner/family has a significant influence on my cultural activities.	3.58	3.31	3.32	3.53
My friends have a significant influence on my cultural activities.	3.12	2.87	2.91	3.04

Pavluska and colleagues (2018) found significant differences in attitudinal questions by gender, age, type of settlement, and education level in their 2018 study. We found no significant associations among these variables among our respondents. The high level of education among higher education respondents is evident, but no differences emerged along the differences for the other variables. In principle, higher education institutions are typically located in larger cities with cultural facilities, so the type of municipality is not a determinant; respondents can access facilities if needed. The average scores for the culturally passive cluster on the attitude questions show no difference compared to the other clusters, so their attitude is no different; they differ from the other respondents in the frequency of participation. The reasons for non-participation were also addressed (the question on this issue was: For what reason were the trainers not present or more often not present at the listed cultural programs (either in person or online) in the last year?), in which case, regardless of cluster type, lack of interest and lack of time were the primary.

Summary

The findings of our research are related to that of Šebová and Révészová's research (Šebová & Révészová 2020, 9-10). The researchers in Slovakia 2020 study aims to analyze the relationship between cultural consumption and socio-economic characteristics in Slovakia based on the Eurobarometer surveys of 2007 and 2013 (interviewing 1,000 Slovak citizens). Thus, their work is based on a data secondary analysis. As a result of their research, cluster analysis outlined four types of Slovak culture consumers, namely: 1. heritage visitors, who rarely visit cultural events, but when they do, they prefer cultural heritage sites, museums, and libraries; 2. inactive group, who rarely visit cultural events, but when they do, they visit sites of historical importance. This group is also present in our cluster, which is called culturally passive, and its characteristics are very similar to this group. 3. omnivores: They often attend cultural events organized for intellectuals in the field of high cultures, such as theater, concerts, ballet performances, museums, and galleries. Our research shows a cluster similar to this one and can be paralleled with our cluster of culturally diverse, elite consumers. 4. famous genre lovers: less open to high culture programs, not going to the opera, not going to a ballet performance, less likely to go to the theater or gallery, more likely to go to the cinema or concerts of popular music. Thus, two of Šebová and Révészová's four clusters are very similar to our cluster, they highlighted similar characteristics of citizens belonging to this cluster even though they analyzed Eurobarometer survey data for the whole population and we analyzed a more highly qualified population in our research (Šebová & Révészová, 2020).

We also found similarities with Grześkowiak's results. As presented in the literature section, Grześkowiak created three clusters based on the results: cluster 1: culture consumers who go to the theater and opera and who also like ballet and dance performances; cluster 2: audiences attending popular music concerts, historical sites, museums, and galleries. Cluster 3: people who visit public libraries, watch cultural programs on television/listen to the radio, and read books (Grześkowiak, 2016). Although Grześkowiak did not name his clusters, it can be concluded that the emerging groups are similar to our clusters. Grześkowiak's cluster 1 parallels our culturally versatile, elite-consuming cluster, while cluster 2 is similar to the culturally open cluster. This cluster includes cultural activities that require leaving their homes, making them the most time-consuming and cost-consuming. Cluster 3 contains the most accessible and cheapest cultural activities, such as reading books, visiting libraries, watching television, and listening to the radio (Grześkowiak, 2016), this is similar to our culturally open online cluster.

Regarding the attitude of the respondents toward culture and culture, it can be stated that the attitude is almost identical; there are no significant differences in the comparison of cultural clusters either. This may be due to similar levels of education, socio-economic status, and time use. The cultural consumption of academics can also be a model for students, as several of the studies we have been involved in have found that higher qualifications increase the frequency of cultural consumption.

References

Antalóczy, T., Füstös, L. & Hankiss, E. (2010). Magyarország kulturális térképe. (Cultural map of Hungary.) In T. Antalóczy, L. Füstös, & E. Hankiss (Eds.), *Mire jó a kultúra? Jelentés a magyar kultúra állapotáról No. 2.* (*What it's good for culture? Report on the state of Hungarian culture No. 2)* (pp. 13-52). Magna Produkció.

Bauman, Z. (2002). *Society Under Siege*. Polity Press.

Beck, U. (2003). *A kockázattársadalom. Út egy másik modernitásba.* (Risk Society). Századvég Kiadó.

Berg, M., & Seeber, B. K. (2016). *The Slow Professor: Challenging the Culture of Speed in the Academy.* University of Toronto Press.

Bertacchini, E., Bolognesi, V. Venturini, A., & Zotti, R. (2021). *The Happy Cultural Omnivore? Exploring the Relationship between Cultural Consumption Patterns and Subjective Well-Being.* Bonn, IZA—Institute of Labor Economics.

Bourdieu, P. (1977). *Reproduction in Education. Society and Culture.* Sage Publishing.

Boyce-Tillman, J. (2016). *Experiencing Music—Restoring the Spiritual: Music as Well-being.* Peter Lang.

Bukodi, E. (2005). *A „puha" rétegződés: Életvitel* (The "soft" stratification: lifestyle). TÁRKI.

Castells, M. (1996). *The Rise of the Network Society. The Information Age: Economy, Society and Culture*, Vol. I. Blackwell.

Coleman, J. S. (1990). *Foundations of Social Theory*. Oxford University Press.

Chan, T. W., & Goldthorpe, J. H. (2006). *Class and status: The conceptual distinction and its empirical relevance.* Sociology Working Papers 2006–03. Department of Sociology, University of Oxford.

Chan, T., W. & Goldhorpe, J. H. (2007). Social stratification and cultural consumption: Music in England. *European Sociological Review, 23*(1), 1–19.

Chan, T. W., & Goldthorpe, J. H. (2010). Social status and cultural consumption. In T. W. Chan (Ed.), *Social status and cultural consumption* (pp. 1-27). University of Oxford.

Dessewffy, T. (2004). *Bevezetés a jelenbe* (Introduction to the present). Nemzeti Tankönyvkiadó.

European Commission (2007). *European Cultural Values. Special Eurobarometer 278.* Retrived form <https://data.europa.eu/data/datasets/s477_67_1_ebs278?locale=en 2023.12.19. 18.00h>

Fancourt, D., & Finn, S. (2020). *What is the evidence on the role of the arts in improving health and well-being? A scoping review.* World Health Organization.

Gershuny, J. (2000). *Changing Times: Work and Leisure in Post-industrial Societies.* Oxford: Oxford University Press.

Giddens, A. (1991). Modernity and Self-Identity: Self and Society in the Late Modern Age. Polity Press.

De Graaf, N. D. (1991). Distinction by Consumption in Czechoslovakia, Hungary and the Netherlands. European Sociological Review, 7(3), 267–90.

Grześkowiak, A. (2016). Assessment of Participation in Cultural Activities in Poland by Selected Multivariate Methods. *European Journal of Social Sciences Education and Research, 3*(1), 18-26.

Hek, M., & Kraaykamp, G. (2013). Cultural consumption across countries: A multi-level analysis of social inequality in highbrow culture in Europe. *Poetics, 41*(4), 323-341.

Hunyadi, Zs. (2005). *Találkozások a kultúrával 7. Kulturálódási és szabadidő eltöltési* szokások, életmód csoportok (Encounters with culture 7. Culture and leisure habits, lifestyle groups). Magyar Művelődési Intézet–MTA Szociológiai Kutatóintézet.

Jauhiainen, A., Jauhiainen, A., & Laiho, A. (2009). The dilemmas of the "efficiency university" policy and the everyday life of university teachers. *Teaching in Higher Education, 14*(4), 417–428. <https://doi.org/10.1080/13562510903050186>

Katz-Gerro, T. (2011). Cross-National Cultural Consumption Research: Inspirations and Disillusions. *Kölner Zeitschrift für Soziologie und Sozial psychologie, 51*(Special issue), 339–360.

Kraaykamp, G., & Noieuwbeerta, P. (2000). Parental Background and Lifestyle Differentiation in Eastern Europe: Social, Political, and Cultural Intergenerational Transmission in Five Former Socialist Societies. *Social Science Research, 29*(1), 92–122.

KSH (2000). *Életmód—időmérlegfelvétel 1999/2000.* (Lifestyle-time balance survey 1999/2000.) Központi Statisztikai Hivatal.

Laasch, O. (2017). The slow professor: challenging the culture of speed in the academy. Maggie Berg and Barbara K. Seeber. *Academy of Management Learning and Education, 16*(4), 624–626.

Márkus, E., Miklósi, M., & Herczegh, J. (2023). Kulturális részvétel az Európai Unióban, különös tekintettel a visegrádi országokra. (Cultural participation in the European Union, in particular in the Visegrád countries). *Kulturális Szemle 1*, 7-16.

Pavluska, V. (2014). *Kultúramarketing. Elméleti alapok, gyakorlati megfontolások* (Cultural marketing. Theoretical foundations, practical considerations). Budapest Akadémiai Kiadó.

Pavluska, V. (2016). Milyen kultúrafogyasztók a magyarok?—A hazai kultúrafogyasztás átfogó mintázatai. (What kind of cultural consumers are Hungarians?—Comprehensive patterns of domestic cultural consumption) In A. Fehér, V. Á. Kiss, M. Soós, & Z. Szakály (Eds.), *Hitelesség és értékorientáció a marketingben.* (Authenticity and value orientation in marketing) (pp. 435-445). University of Debrecen, Faculty of Economics.

Pavluska, V., Jakopánecz, E. & Törőcsik, M. (2018). *Kultúra—a magyar lakosság kultúrával kapcsolatos beállítódása és követett magatartása generációs szemléletű vizsgálattal—országosan reprezentatív személyes (n=2001) és online megkérdezés (n=1038) eredményei.* (Culture—attitudes and behaviors of the Hungarian population toward culture through a generational approach—results of a nationally representative face-to-face (n=2001) and online survey (n=1038). PTE KTK.

Peterson, R. A. (2005). Problems in Comparative Research: The Example of Omnivorousness. *Poetics, 33*(5–6), 257–282.

Peterson, R. A., & Kern, R. M. (1996). Changing Highbrow Taste: From Snob to Omnivore. *American Sociological Review, 61*(5). 900–907.

Piekarska-Duraj, Ł. (2020). *The Invisible Hand of Europe: The Museum as a Civilizing Tool.* Studies in European Integration, State and Society, Volume 10. Peter Lang Group.

Roberts, K. (1999). Leisure in Contemporary Society. CABI Publication.

Seaman, B. A. (2005). *Attendance and public participation in the performing arts: A review of the empirical literature.* Andrew Young School of Policy Studies Research Paper Series. SSRN Retrived from: <https://papers.ssrn.com/sol3/papers.cfm?abstract_id=895099>

Šebová, M., & Révészová, Z. (2020). Unveiling Trends in Cultural Participation: The Case of Slovakia. *Social Sciences 9*(19), 1-14.

Tomšic, M. (2016). *Elites in the New Democracies.* Peter Lang Group. Retrieved from <https://www.perlego.com/book/2943087/elites-in-the-new-democracies-pdf>

Vitányi, I. (1997). *A magyar társadalom kulturális állapota. Az 1996-os vizsgálat zárójelentése.* (The cultural status of Hungarian society. Final report of the 1996 investigation). Maecenas.

Vojtíšková, K., & Lorencová, R. (2014). Public funding of culture in the Czech Republic since the fall of the iron curtain: Contemporary dilemmas. *International Journal of Cultural Policy, 21*(5), 529–53.

Yaish, M. & Katz-Gerro, T. (2012). Disentangling „Cultural Capital": The Consequences of Cultural and Economic Resources for Taste and Participation. *European Sociological Review, 28*(2), 169–185.

13. What Have We Learned About the Well-Being and Performance of Academics in EU Border Region Countries?

Klára Kovács & Ilona Dabney-Fekete

In the Introduction of this book, we examined in detail how global, international, educational policy, and organizational changes—as well as emerging new demands and expectations—have transformed the work and working conditions of academics over recent decades. Global trends in higher education (such as expansion and internationalization), along with national policy expectations aimed at increasing the competitiveness of higher education institutions and the competition for students, excellence, and resources, have made what was once a predictable and stable academic career increasingly uncertain and fragmented. This has resulted in significant diversification, stratification, and disparities among academics, despite the fact that certain career milestones are considered standardized across almost all of Europe (Kwiek & Antonowicz, 2015).

At the same time, we observe that there are significant differences among academics at similar career stages, particularly between high- and low-performing senior and junior academics, as well as across various academic disciplines. These differences are primarily shaped by institutional type, institutional goals and expectations, and research productivity (Kwiek & Roszka, 2024).

The introduction of various performance evaluation systems has further intensified competition—not only for resources but also for securing academic positions, as the stagnation of available positions coincides with an increasing number of aspiring academics. The "do-or-die" approach has not only heightened competition but has also led to high levels of frustration, uncertainty, tension, interpersonal conflicts, and distrust among academics and between academics and institutional leadership (Westerheijden, 2007). These tensions manifest significantly in differences in academic performance, attitudes toward work, and perceptions of expectations and available resources. Academics who criticize the introduction of performance evaluation systems and managerialism argue that these developments erode academic freedom and autonomy, reducing academic work to a mere commodity. However, those who have embraced and integrated these changes into their professional identities view them as providing a transparent career pathway within higher education institutions, based on clear, quantifiable criteria (Kwiek & Antonowicz, 2015).

Our interview-based research conducted in five countries (N=41) also revealed this dual nature of performance evaluation: while it makes differences in individual academic contributions and achievements more measurable, it also poses a threat to academic autonomy and weakens interpersonal relationships among colleagues. This, in turn, creates a highly competitive climate both within and between smaller academic units and significantly shapes, or even alters, the culture of higher education institutions. Furthermore, the validity of performance measurement is often called into question, as evaluation processes are not always transparent and fail to account for certain non-measurable aspects of academic work (Kovács et al., 2024; Pusztai et al., 2025).

Based on attitudes toward performance evaluation and institutional responses, we identified four distinct types of institutional cultures:

Supportive institutional cultures—These define their strength through unity, and their effectiveness is demonstrated through excellence in teaching, research, and administration.

Cohesive micro-communities—Academics within these communities share a common understanding of effectiveness and place equal importance on teaching, research, and administrative tasks, but their focus remains within their own micro-community rather than at the institutional level.

Lonely crowd institutional culture—Here, teaching plays a central role in defining effectiveness, but academics in this culture often feel isolated and left to their own devices.

Egocentric monumental institutional culture—Academics in this category prioritize individual interests, place little emphasis on teaching, take on administrative roles in exchange for remuneration, and prefer research activities (Pusztai et al., 2025).

The international trends described above have fundamentally reshaped the working conditions, opportunities, and status of academics across Europe, creating specific intra- and interpersonal challenges that have a significant impact on their well-being and performance. Our study sought to explore these macro and organizational characteristics in relation to the well-being and performance of academics in five CEE countries—Hungary, Slovakia, Romania, Serbia, and Ukraine. This region has a unique context, shaped by a shared post-socialist legacy and a delayed yet parallel adaptation of global higher education trends, primarily influenced by developments in the U.S.A., East Asia, and Western Europe. However, these changes have unfolded differently in this region due to distinct cultural norms and practices (Mudrak et al., 2018), as well as the enduring influence of post-communist traditions (Goncharuk & Cirella, 2022).

Despite this, research on the well-being and performance of academics in the CEE region remains significantly underrepresented (Mudrak et al., 2018), and—with the exception of Romania—these countries have largely been excluded from previous international studies (CAP, EUROAC, APICS).

The above findings highlight that the characteristics of academic work have been at the center of scholarly discourse for several years, yet CEE higher education institutions have often been overlooked in such discussions. Our research aimed to fill this gap by conducting an extensive investigation into the working conditions, job-related stressors and resources, work-life conflicts, emotional well-being, research productivity, teaching methods, and cultural engagement of academics (N=821) of higher education institutions in Hungary, Romania, Slovakia, Serbia, and Ukraine.

In terms of well-being, beyond the traditional examination of positive and negative emotions, our research incorporated specific factors influencing academic life, such as perceptions of workplace culture, assessments of academic development opportunities, job-related stressors and resources, work-life conflicts, and cultural involvement as a source of intellectual stimulation and recreation. Additionally, we explored two key areas of professional fulfillment: international mobility and research productivity.

In our summary study, we present the key empirical findings of our research across three dimensions: by country, by job title, and by academic types. Based on insights gathered from focus group interviews conducted prior to the quantitative research, we asked respondents to what extent they considered certain tasks as part of their job. Based on their answers, we identified four distinct academic types:

Teaching-focused academics (33.4%)—These academics value teaching-related activities, including course material development, experimentation with new teaching methods, and academic research, in equal measure.

Academics with an administrative focus (19.7%)—For this group, teaching is less important than for others, but it remains a more integral part of their work than academic research. They also place a high value on collaboration with colleagues in teaching and are characterized by a strong involvement in administrative tasks.

Research-focused academics (20.3%)—Similar to teaching-focused academics, this group places high value on academic research activities, particularly international publishing and research output. However, teaching plays a lesser role in their professional activities. Like the first group, they also consider leadership and administrative responsibilities as characteristic of their role.

Academic leaders (26.6%)—This group places equal emphasis on teaching and research but is primarily defined by leadership responsibilities within the university, which are the most critical aspects of their work.

To fully understand the situation, job characteristics, well-being, and performance of academics in each country, it is essential to interpret our findings within the broader context of national higher education policies. For this reason, we conducted a macro-statistical analysis of higher education policies in the five studied countries, examining the educational policy processes of recent decades that have significantly shaped the working conditions of academics and researchers in these institutions.

1. Higher Education in the Studied Countries: Challenges and Trends

Following the political transition, the higher education systems of the examined countries had to contend with post-Soviet traditions, remnants of which are still present in the academic sphere today—albeit to varying degrees, and in different segments. Nevertheless, global trends (such as the expansion and internationalization of higher education) eventually made their way into every post-socialist country, albeit with some delay.

A common feature of the region is that, after a phase of dynamic expansion, student numbers have now entered a stagnation phase, prompting state initiatives aimed at reducing or redistributing the costs of higher education. One approach has been the promotion of private institutions, another has been the reduction of the proportion of state-funded students, and a third is recruitment-restrictive higher education policy, which has led to the lowest rates of young graduates within the EU (38% in Slovakia, 29% in Hungary, and 23% in Romania).[1] Cost-saving measures in higher education have also resulted in relatively low student-to-academic staff ratios in this region.

Additionally, in a European comparison, the region is characterized by some of the lowest academic salaries, precarious career paths, rigid and hierarchical institutional structures, a lack of transparency in grant evaluation processes, limited access to international exchange opportunities, and the implicit discrimination against women in academic careers (Drennan et al., 2020; Gould, 2006; Kwiek & Antonowicz, 2015). These factors significantly hinder talented young researchers from choosing a career in academia.

1 <https://ec.europa.eu/eurostat/web/products-eurostat-news/-/ddn-20220524-2>.

In the countries of the region, the attractiveness of the academic profession has declined, leading to a decreasing number of academic staff and an aging workforce. This is further exacerbated by insufficient funding compared to international standards and other sectors, inadequate social status and recognition—particularly in the case of assistant lecturers—and increasing pressure on academics to secure funding through their performance to maintain international competitiveness.

After the political transition, the most significant challenges for higher education in the region included demographic decline combined with emigration, as well as the internationalization that gained momentum due to the Bologna Process. At the same time, the student-to-academic staff ratio decreased compared to previous years, and the number of newly established private higher education institutions increased. These institutions are characterized by specialized programs, smaller class sizes, and flexible schedules, alongside the already mentioned lower student-to-academic staff ratios. Another key factor shaping academic work is the increasing stringency of academic qualification requirements and performance criteria for academic positions, likely influenced by political direction, which is closely linked to academic qualification procedures and expectations for the quality of higher education (Hanesová et al., 2025; Kovács & Papp, 2025; Polónyi, 2024; Tódor, 2025).

In Ukraine, higher education has been shaped not only by the post-Soviet transition but also by economic, political, social, and historical processes such as the Euromaidan protests and the 2022 Russian-Ukrainian conflict. Due to the massive emigration caused by the war, many higher education institutions have faced operational uncertainty, and a significant proportion of students and academics have continued their studies and work in neighboring CEE countries, primarily in Slovakia and Poland. Thus, the impact of the war on (higher) education extends far beyond national borders. Salaries for Ukrainian academics remain significantly lower than those of their counterparts in the EU and even in the Visegrád Four countries. However, academic expectations have increasingly aligned with European higher education trends, including higher performance expectations, compliance with accreditation regulations, requirements for specific programs and subjects taught, and the introduction of performance assessments (Pallay, 2025).

1.1. Academic Well-Being and Health Behaviors

According to the results of our cross-country questionnaire survey, Slovakian and Ukrainian academics report the lowest levels of well-being, while Romanian academics report the highest. Controlling for all other variables, being from Romania was a positive predictor of well-being (Kovács et al., 2024b). This may be linked to the higher average subjective well-being of the Romanian population in a regional comparison, as indicated by the World Happiness Report, where Romania ranks 24th globally, with only the Czech Republic ranking higher within the region (Helliwell et al., 2023). Conversely, the well-being of Ukrainian respondents was significantly impacted by the difficulties caused by the war in both work and everyday life. Partially aligning with these well-being results, Slovakian and Serbian academics reported feeling the healthiest, whereas Ukrainian academics reported feeling the least healthy (Kovács & Michelini, 2025).

In terms of physical activity, Serbian and Slovakian academics were the liveliest, followed by Hungarians, while Ukrainians and Romanians drew up the rear. However, Ukrainians were the most frequent users of university sports facilities in the past year (30.4%), whereas Romanians were the least frequent users (12.4%) (Kovács & Michelini, 2025). Investigating the role of physical activity is crucial, as our results indicate that academics who engage in moderate or high levels of physical activity (at least 150 minutes of moderate exercise per week) report significantly higher well-being. Regular physical activity significantly reduces perceptions of stressors such as work-life conflicts, workload, and the diversity of academic roles, thereby indirectly contributing to higher academic well-being (Kovács et al., 2025a).

1.2. Workplace Stress and Institutional Support

Academics in Serbia and Hungary had the lowest agreement that opportunities for promotion exist. Serbians, Romanians, and Slovakians reported high dissatisfaction with training and development opportunities. Respondents in Ukraine described the lowest agreement on manageable workloads, while Hungarians presented the lowest satisfaction with the annual performance appraisal process. Academics in Hungary and Romania received high ratings for colleague support. Hungarians, Serbians, and Slovakians had high levels of concern regarding the deteriorating situation of academics. Academics from Ukraine, Romania, and Serbia rated their institutional infrastructure as adequate. Romanians and Slovakians reported burdensome levels of administrative work. Serbian academics generally agreed that they had sufficient time for class preparation. Interestingly, Ukrainian respondents were the most satisfied with their working conditions, career progression opportunities, development opportunities, and social support within their institutions. There were no significant differences between countries in satisfaction with salaries. In all countries, most academics were not satisfied with the salaries provided by their higher education institutions. This question elicited the highest level of dissatisfaction, regardless of the country of origin (Kovács et al., 2025b).

1.3. International Mobility and Academic Productivity

Significant differences were found in participation in international mobility programs: Romanian and Slovakian academics were the most mobile, while Hungarian and Ukrainian academics were the least mobile (Dabney-Fekete et al., 2025). For Ukraine, this may be attributed to its non-EU status, the fact that respondents completed the survey not only near the border but also from within the country, and, naturally, the war, which has made border crossings significantly more difficult, especially for men.

The higher mobility of Romanian and Slovakian academics could be explained by the large proportion of Hungarian-speaking academics in minority institutions, who often choose Hungarian institutions due to the shared language. Additionally, many Romanian-speaking respondents live in border regions where higher education institutions are within a relatively short distance, facilitating travel.

Despite differences in mobility, no significant differences in academic productivity were found between the studied countries, suggesting that academics in the region perform at similar levels overall (Kovács et al., 2025c).

1.4. Senior vs. Junior Academics

Significant differences were observed between junior and senior academics. Associate professors reported higher levels of well-being than assistant professors or those in lower positions (Kovács et al., 2025a). Daily smoking was more common among assistant professors or lower-ranked academics (13.5%), whereas non-smokers were more prevalent among associate professors or higher-ranked academics (84.4%) (Kovács & Michelini, 2025).

Junior academics worked more hours per week, struggled more with work-life balance, and had lower research productivity (Kovács et al., 2025c). Senior academics worked fewer hours, coped better with work-life balance, received more institutional and peer support, rated their working conditions more positively, and performed better in research (Berei et al., 2025; Kovács et al., 2025b).

A significant proportion of senior academics had participated in international mobility programs, compared to only one-third of early-career academics (Dabney-Fekete et al., 2025).

2. Characteristics of Academic Clusters in Central and Eastern Europe

Our research has provided a detailed and comprehensive picture of four distinct types of academics in the CEE region, based on their working conditions, well-being, and performance indicators.

Academic leaders achieved the highest productivity scores. Despite being the most overburdened, they remain the most effective. This may be attributed to their ability to delegate certain monotonous and time-consuming administrative tasks, which are not recognized as academic performance, to others—primarily to the group we identified as academics with an administrative focus.

They excel in publishing, participating in international conferences, and engaging in international research projects. They are also the most open to internationalization (including international research projects and academic mobility). However, the heavy workload and long working hours associated with these activities significantly reduce their well-being (Kovács et al., 2025c; Dabney et al., 2025), despite their general tendency to report feeling optimistic, cheerful, and enthusiastic. Their greatest source of stress is excessive administrative work.

A higher proportion of academic leaders report that their work does not cause conflicts in their personal lives, even though they work the longest hours (Berei et al., 2025). They perceive their institutions as stable and innovation-oriented. They are the most satisfied with their salaries and firmly believe that career development opportunities are available to all academics. They also believe that there is a high level of agreement between academics and university leadership and that promotions are based entirely on performance. Furthermore, they are convinced that the annual performance evaluation process fairly reflects their achievements. However, these views differ significantly from those of other academic groups. Academic leaders report the highest levels of perceived social support. They are the least likely to consider leaving academia or to feel at risk of dismissal in the near future. Consequently, they are also the most satisfied with their working conditions (Kovács et al., 2025b; Pallay et al., 2024).

Academic leaders excel in most areas of teaching and quickly adapt to institutional and student needs. Their teaching approaches are predominantly student-oriented, development-focused, and data-driven. They also believe that institutions clearly define the framework and expectations for inclusion. They are the most aware of students from underrepresented groups and consider special allowances for these students both necessary and acceptable. They primarily implement differentiation strategies for student assessment, especially when teaching non-traditional students (Hrabéczy & Kocsis, 2025).

In terms of cultural consumption, they tend to be more passive (Márkus et al., 2025).

For *teaching-focused academics*, teaching plays a central role, but they also demonstrate outstanding performance in research. They feel the least burdened by their multiple responsibilities and are satisfied with the level of support they receive from colleagues. However, they are more dissatisfied with performance evaluations, as most believe that too much emphasis is placed on assessment, which threatens their professional independence (Kovács et al., 2025a).

A significant proportion of this group struggles to balance work and personal life, and many report that work negatively impacts their private life. They rarely feel calm, but they generally display enthusiasm, cheerfulness, and optimism. They are the most likely to believe that their institution prioritizes the interests of its employees. They frequently discuss teaching-related issues with colleagues and demonstrate a high level of collaboration in research and publishing activities (Pallay et al., 2025).

Their teaching practices are highly practice-oriented and reflective, with a strong focus on providing up-to-date information and data during lessons. A high proportion of them are aware of students from underrepresented groups and find special allowances for these students more acceptable and necessary (Hrabéczy & Kocsis, 2025). This group has the highest proportion of academics actively engaged in cultural consumption (Márkus et al., 2025).

Research-focused academics primarily concentrate on domestic and international publishing. They are not motivated to establish interinstitutional networks, as institutional competition dominates this area. They are also the most pessimistic about leaving academia or being dismissed within the next three years (similar to teaching-focused academics) (Pallay et al., 2024).

They question the fairness of performance evaluations and promotions, but interestingly, the evaluation process itself does not cause them significant stress. They believe that there is little agreement between academics and leadership, and they perceive weak institutional support. They are the least satisfied with their working conditions and the level of social support within their institution, reporting the lowest levels of job satisfaction (Kovács et al., 2025b). They frequently experience exhaustion at the end of the workday, and few feel energized on a daily basis. A high proportion of them struggle to balance work and personal life, and many report that work negatively impacts their private lives (Pallay et al., 2024).

The group of *academics with an administrative focus* has the highest proportion of academics who do not yet hold a doctoral degree. Their work has the least impact on their private lives, but they express the most uncertainty regarding job satisfaction. They exhibit low levels of collaboration with colleagues in most areas, including discussions on educational and research topics, joint projects, and providing assistance to peers (Pallay et al., 2024). Their teaching practices are practice-oriented and student-centered (Hrabéczy & Kocsis, 2025).

They are significantly overrepresented among those who feel excessive pressure regarding publishing and grant writing. For them, performance evaluations represent the greatest source of stress, and they do not perceive their workplace as stable. They are the least satisfied with promotion and career development opportunities (Kovács et al., 2025b), partly because they achieve the lowest research performance. It would be beneficial to develop supportive career development programs for this group, involving senior academics, to enhance their research effectiveness alongside their teaching and administrative responsibilities.

Academics with an administrative focus were also found to be the most open to cultural consumption (Márkus et al., 2025).

3. How Can the Well-Being and Performance of Academics in Central and Eastern Europe Be Improved? Recommendations for Higher Education Leaders and Policymakers

Overall, our findings highlight that academic well-being and effective performance require both financial support and greater recognition of teaching and administrative work, which should also be reflected in performance evaluation systems. Institutions should offer diverse support to enhance the research careers and publication activities of committed academics.

Key challenges include work-life conflicts, excessive workloads, intense publication pressure linked to performance evaluations, and lack of transparent institutional goals and expectations. These pose significant stressors and challenges for academics. Therefore, institutions should provide programs to support academic career development, time management skills, and mental well-being, particularly for researchers. It is also crucial for academics to fully understand the purpose, structure, and consequences of performance evaluation systems and to have a voice in institutional decision-making processes to ensure their interests are represented.

Significant differences exist between senior and research-focused academics in terms of perceptions of academic work, recognition, satisfaction, and institutional and peer support. This highlights the urgent need for dialogue and engagement between different academic groups and university leadership.

Acknowledgments

This publication was supported by the project "Investigating the role of sport and physical activity for a healthy and safe society in the individual and social sustainability of work ability and quality of work and life (multidisciplinary research umbrella program)" and by the János Bolyai Research Scholarship of the Hungarian Academy of Sciences.

References

Buda, A., & Kovács, K. (2024). The digital aspects of the wellbeing of university teachers. *Frontiers in Education*, *9*, 1406141. <https://doi.org/10.3389/feduc.2024.1406141>

Berei, E.B., Engler Á., & Kovács, K. (2025). Work-Life Conflicts: A Dual Functionality Approach on Career of Academics. In G. Pusztai, & K. Kovács (Eds.), *Well-Being of Academic Staff in Rapidly Changing Higher Education: A Focus on Central and Eastern Europe* (pp. 305–326). Peter Lang.

Dabney-Fekete, I. D., Dusa Á. R., & Pallay, K. (2025). International Mobility and Its Impediments for Academics. In G. Pusztai, & K. Kovács (Eds.), *Well-Being of Academic Staff in Rapidly Changing Higher Education: A Focus on Central and Eastern Europe* (pp. 243–285). Peter Lang.

Drennan, J., Clarke, M., Hyde, A., & Politis, Y. (2020). Academic identity in higher education. In P. N. Teixeira, & J. Ch. Shin (Eds.), *The international encyclopedia of higher education systems and institutions* (pp. 35-40). Springer Netherlands.

Goncharuk, A. G., & Cirella, G. T. (2022). Effectiveness of academic institutional models in Europe: University instructor perception case research from Bosnia and Herzegovina and France. *International Journal of Educational Management, 36(5)*, 836-853.

Gould, E. (2006). Professor or Knowledge Worker? The Politics of Defining Faculty Work. *Higher Education in Europe*, 31(3), 241–249. <https://doi.org/10.1080/03797720601058690>

Hanesová, D., Lovňanová, L., & Zólyomiová, P. (2025). Higher Education Academics in Slovakia. In G. Pusztai, & K. Kovács (Eds.), *Well-Being of Academic Staff in Rapidly Changing Higher Education: A Focus on Central and Eastern Europe* (pp. 71–103). Peter Lang.

Helliwell, J. F., Huang, H., Norton, M., Goff, L., & Wang, S. (2023). World happiness, trust and social connections in times of crisis. In *World Happiness Report* (11th ed., Chapter 2). Sustainable Development Solutions Network. URL: <https://worldhappiness.report/ed/2023/world-happiness-trust-and-social-connections-in-times-of-crisis/> (24.06.2024)

Hrabéczy A. & Kocsis, Zs. (2025). (Inclusive) teaching practice and well-being among higher education academics in Central and Eastern Europe. In G. Pusztai, & K. Kovács (Eds.), *Well-Being of Academic Staff in Rapidly Changing Higher Education: A Focus on Central and Eastern Europe* (pp. 231–261). Peter Lang.

Kwiek, M., & Antonowicz, D. (2015). The Changing Paths in Academic Careers in European Universities: Minor Steps and Major Milestones. In T. Fumasoli, G. Goastellec, & B. M. Kehm (Eds.), *Academic Work and Careers in Europe:*

Trends, Challenges, Perspectives (pp. 41–68). Springer International Publishing. <https://doi.org/10.1007/978-3-319-10720-2_3>

Kwiek, M., & Roszka, W. (2024). Are Scientists Changing their Research Productivity Classes When They Move Up the Academic Ladder? *Innovative Higher Education*. <https://doi.org/10.1007/s10755-024-09735-3>

Kovács, E. & Papp, Z. (2025). Characteristics of the Higher Education System and Academic Staff in Serbia. In G. Pusztai, & K. Kovács (Eds.), *Well-Being of Academic Staff in Rapidly Changing Higher Education: A Focus on Central and Eastern Europe* (pp. 145–176). Peter Lang.

Kovács, K., Dobay, B., Halasi, S., Pinczés, T., & Tódor, I. (2024). Demands, resources and institutional factors in the work of academic staff in Central and Eastern Europe: Results of a qualitative research among university teachers in five countries. *Frontiers in Education*, *8*, 1326515. <https://www.frontiersin.org/articles/10.3389/feduc.2023.1326515>

Kovács, K. & Michelini, E. (2025). Physical Activity and Workplace Stress: Influences on Health Perception Among Academics in Central and Eastern Europe. *Central European Journal of Education Research, 6*(2), 1–13. <https://doi.org/10.37441/cejer/2024/6/2/15252>

Kovács, K., Borbély, Sz., Dobay, B., Halasi, Sz., Vajda, I. & Hideg, G. (2025a). Factors Influencing the Well-being of Central and Eastern European Teachers: the role of physical activity and the sources of stress and resources in the workplace. *BMC Public Health*, *25*(1), 1–12, 3001. <https://doi.org/10.1186/s12889-025-24241-7>

Kovács, K., Bălţătescu, S., Bíró, É, & Tódor I. (2025b). Interrelation between job-stress sources, resources and work engagement among Central and Eastern European academics. *Quality in Higher Education*, *31*(1), 88–107. <https://doi.org/10.1080/13538322.2025.2516907>

Kovács K., Moravecz, M. & Hideg-Fehér G. (2025c). Research Productivity, workplace stress sources and resources among academics. In G. Pusztai, & K. Kovács (Eds.), *Well-Being of Academic Staff in Rapidly Changing Higher Education: A Focus on Central and Eastern Europe* (pp. 287–304). Peter Lang.

Márkus, E. Miklósi, M., Herczegh, J., & Nagy, N. (2024). Közép-kelet-európai felsőoktatók kultúrához való viszonya, kulturális fogyasztási szokásai. [Central and Eastern European higher educational instructors' relation to culture, and their cultural consumption habits] In K. Kovács, & K. Pallay (Eds.), *Oktatók a Kárpát-medencei felsőoktatásban* [Academics in the Higher Education of the Carpathian Basin] (pp. 82-96). CHERD-H.

Márkus, E., Herczegh J., & Miklósi, M. (2025). The Cultural Involvement Patterns of Academics. In G. Pusztai, & K. Kovács, (Eds.), *Well-Being of Academic Staff in Rapidly Changing Higher Education: A Focus on Central and Eastern Europe* (pp. 327–346). Peter Lang.

Mudrak, J., Zabrodska, K., Kveton, P., Jelinek, M., Blatny, M., Solcova, I., & Machovcova, K. (2018). Occupational well-being among university faculty: A job demands-resources model. *Research in Higher Education*, *59*, 325–348. <https://doi.org/10.1007/s11162-017-9467-x>

Pallay, K. (2025). Challenges in Higher Education and for Academics in Ukraine. In G. Pusztai, & K. Kovács (Eds.), *Well-Being of Academic Staff in Rapidly Changing Higher Education: A Focus on Central and Eastern Europe* (pp. 177–204). Peter Lang.

Pallay, K., Buda, A., Berei, E. B., Demeter-Karászi, Z., Herczegh, J., Hideg-Fehér, G., Hrabéczy, A., Kocsis, Z., Márkus, E., Pusztai, G., Takács-Miklósi, M., Tódor, I. & Kovács, K. (2024). *Felsőoktatók a Kárpát-medencében* [Academics in the Carpathian Basin]. CHERD-H.

Polónyi, I. (2024). Lecturers in higher education—The Hungarian case. Hungarian Educational Research Journal. <https://doi.org/10.1556/063.2024.00309>

Pusztai, G., Demeter-Karászi Zs., & Pallay, K. (2025). Performance assessment: A new dimension of institutional culture. In G. Pusztai, & K. Kovács (Eds.), *Well-Being of Academic Staff in Rapidly Changing Higher Education: A Focus on Central and Eastern Europe* (pp. 207–230). Peter Lang.

Tódor, I. (2025). Academics in the Romanian Higher Education Context. In G. Pusztai, & K. Kovács (Eds.), *Well-Being of Academic Staff in Rapidly Changing Higher Education: A Focus on Central and Eastern Europe* (pp. 105–144). Peter Lang.

Westerheijden, D. F. (2007). States and Europe and Quality of Higher Education. In D. F. Westerheijden, B. Stensaker, & M. J. Rosa (Eds.), *Quality Assurance In Higher Education: Trends in Regulation, Translation and Transformation* (pp. 73–95). Springer Netherlands. <https://doi.org/10.1007/978-1-4020-6012-0_3>

Notes on Contributors

Emese Beáta Berei Ph.D., Social Work Education, Emanuel University of Oradea, Romania

Ilona Dóra Dabney-Fekete Ph.D., Assistant Professor, Institute of Educational Studies and Cultural Management, University of Debrecen, Hungary

Zsuzsanna Demeter-Karászi Ph.D., Assistant Lecturer, Institute of Educational Studies and Cultural Management, University of Debrecen, Hungary

Ágnes Réka Dusa Ph.D., Senior Researcher, Center for Higher Education Research and Development Hungary, University of Debrecen, Hungary

Ágnes Engler Ph.D. habil. DSc, Full Professor, Institute of Educational Studies and Cultural Management, University of Debrecen, Hungary

Dana Hanesová Ph.D. PaedDr, Full Professor, Department of Pedagogy and Andragogy, Matej Bel University, Slovakia.

Judit Herczegh Ph.D., Assistant Professor, Institute of Educational Studies and Cultural Management, University of Debrecen, Hungary

Anett Hrabéczy Ph.D., Assistant Lecturer, Institute of Educational Studies and Cultural Management, University of Debrecen, Hungary

Zsófia Kocsis Ph.D., Assistant Lecturer, Institute of Educational Studies and Cultural Management, University of Debrecen, Hungary

Elvira Kovács Ph.D., Associate Professor, University of Novi Sad, Hungarian Language Teacher Training Faculty, Serbia

Klára Kovács Ph.D. habil, Associate Professor, Institute of Educational Studies and Cultural Management, University of Debrecen, Hungary

Edina Márkus Ph.D. habil., Assistant Professor, Institute of Educational Studies and Cultural Management, University of Debrecen, Hungary

Márta Miklósi Ph.D., Assistant Professor, Institute of Educational Studies and Cultural Management, University of Debrecen, Hungary

Katalin Pallay Ph.D., College Associate Professor, Ferenc Rákóczi II Transcarpathian Hungarian University, Ukraine

Zoltán Papp Ph.D., Assistant Professor, University of Novi Sad, Hungarian Language Teacher Training Faculty, Serbia; University of Dunaújváros, Institute of Computer Engineering, Hungary

István Polónyi Ph.D. habil., Research Professor, The John Wesley Theological College, Hungary

Gabriella Pusztai Ph.D. habil. DSc, Full Professor, Institute of Educational Studies and Cultural Management, University of Debrecen, Hungary

Lenka Rovňanová Ph.D. PaedDr, Associate Professor, Department of Pedagogy and Andragogy, Matej Bel University, Slovakia

Imre Tódor Ph.D., Assistant Professor, Sapientia Hungarian University of Transylvania, Teacher Training Institute, Romania

Patrícia Zólyomiová Ph.D. PhDr, Assistant Professor, Department of Pedagogy and Andragogy, Matej Bel University, Slovakia

Index

A

Academic autonomy 19, 30, 58
Academic career 18, 29, 127
Academic identity 18, 20, 30
Academic profession 17–21, 30, 131
Academic rank 127–129
Academic staff 17–21, 60–70, 117–130
Academic stress 30, 295
Accreditation 73, 75, 79
Age distribution 83–85, 124–126
Altbach, P. 17, 131
Applied research 19, 27
Arimoto, A. 17, 38
Associate professor 79, 127
Audit society 19, 30
Autonomy 19, 58

B

Bachelor's programs 74, 116
Bologna Process 26, 73, 107
Brain drain 28, 91, 131
Branković, J. 38
Britton, J. 131
Burnout 31, 131

C

Career advancement 127
Career path 127
CEETHE 2023 34
Civil service 59
Clarke, M. 20
Collegiality 20
Cultural consumption 327–341
Cummings, W. 38
Curaj, A. 106–131
Curriculum reform 26, 88

D

Daizen, T. 38
David, R. 131
Deca, L. 106–131
Digitalization 26, 130
Doctoral education 65–66, 116
Doctoral students 65–66, 116
Dolga, L. 131
Drennan, J. 20
Dual functionality 305–317

E

Educational change 17, 114
Educational policy 17, 26, 114
Educational reform 26, 130
Ehrenberg, R. 60
Emigration 28, 130
Enders, J. 17–21, 38
Entrepreneurial university 19, 27
EU integration 26, 107
EUROAC 17
European Higher Education Area 26, 74
Evaluation systems 19, 75
Expansion 17, 26

F

Faculty workload 60, 83
Female academics 54, 85, 124
Focus group interviews 33
Foundation-based institutions 47
Fumasoli, T. 17
Functional diversity 18
Funding models 19, 93

G

Gender gap 85, 124
Geven, K. 131
Gibbs, S. 31
Globalization 17, 130
Goastellec, G. 17, 38
Gould, E. 30
Governance reforms 58
Government expenditure 93–95

H

Habilitation 55
Hargittai, I. 22

Harper, S. 126
Higher education institutions (HEIs) – throughout
Höhle, E. A. 17–21
Hyde, A. 19–20

I
Inclusive teaching 231–248
Institutional autonomy 58
Institutional culture 207–225
International mobility 263–277

J
Janik, A. 22
Jayman, M. 31
Jencks, C. 18
Job satisfaction 17, 30

K
Knowledge economy 19
Kozma, T. 26, 131
Kwiek, M. 17–21, 131

L
Leadership roles 35
Lecturer 79, 127
Lee, J. J. 38
Levy, D. 26, 131
Lifelong learning 26
Loveday, V. 31

M
Magyari, L. 107
Managerialism 19, 30
Master's programs 74, 116
Minority education 107
Mobility programs 91–93
Moraru, L. 30
Multilingual institutions 111
Musselin, C. 19, 131

N
National Accreditation Committee 55
Neave, G. 20
Nicholls, H. 31

O
OECD indicators 83–85
Online learning 26

P
Partium Christian University 107
Performance appraisal 207
Performance evaluation 207
Performance-based funding 29
Performance-based funding 29
Petríková, D. 131
Ph.D. programs 65–66
Post-socialist legacy 22, 26
Privatization 26, 107
Probst, C. 20
Professional development 80
Professors 127
Public vs. private HEIs 47, 117
Publication productivity 287–305

Q
Quality assurance 73, 75
Quantitative survey 33
Questionnaire design 33

R
Regional disparities 111, 121
Research funding 28, 65
Research productivity 287–305
Research-focused academics 35
Roszka, W. 17
Ryan, J. 256

S
Salat, L. 107
Santa, R. 131
Sapientia Hungarian University 107
Scientific qualification 55
Scott, P. 131
Seligman, M. 31
Social prestige 30
Sociodemographic indicators 124
Speed and acceleration 30
State funding 19, 93
STEM fields 48

Student-academic ratio 81, 117
Survey methodology 33
Szabó, P. C. 26

T
Teaching-focused academics 35
Teichler, U. 17–21, 38
Tertiary education 65
Theodoulides, L. 131
Tinto, V. 18
Tonk, J. 107
Transversal competencies 88
Trow, M. 26
Trow's model 26

U
University governance 58
Usachov, V. 201
Utilization of development tools 29

V
Van der Kaap, H. 20
Vančo, M. 131
Váradyová, T. 131
Vertical stratification 17
Visegrád countries 71–104
Vlachou, A. 131
Vostal, F. 30

W
Well-being – throughout
(esp. 17–21, 207–248, 295–317)
Wittgenstein's Vienna 22
Work-life balance 305–317
Workplace stress 287–305
World Bank data 83–85

Y
Yudkevich, M. 126

Z
Zacharová, J. 131
Zaťková, T. Š. 131
Zólyomiová, Patrícia 231

Higher Education Research and Policy (HERP)

Edited by Marek Kwiek

Vol. 1 Marek Kwiek / Andrzej Kurkiewicz (eds.): The Modernisation of European Universities. Cross-National Academic Perspectives. 2012.

Vol. 2 Marek Kwiek / Peter Maassen (Eds.): National Higher Education Reforms in a European Context. Comparative Reflections on Poland and Norway. 2012.

Vol. 3 Marek Kwiek: Knowledge Production in European Universities. States, Markets, and Academic Entrepreneurialism. 2013.

Vol. 4 Pavel Zgaga / Ulrich Teichler / John Brennan (eds.): The Globalisation Challenge for European Higher Education. Convergence and Diversity, Centres and Peripheries. Second Revised Edition. 2016.

Vol. 5 Jelena Branković / Maja Kovačević / Peter Maassen / Bjørn Stensaker / Martina Vukasović (eds.): The Re-Institutionalization of Higher Education in the Western Balkans. The Interplay between European Ideas, Domestic Policies, and Institutional Practices. 2014.

Vol. 6 Hamish Coates (ed.): Higher Education Learning Outcomes Assessment. International Perspectives. 2014.

Vol. 7 Gabriella Pusztai: Pathways to Success in Higher Education. Rethinking the Social Capital Theory in the Light of Institutional Diversity. 2015.

Vol. 8 Pavel Zgaga / Ulrich Teichler / Hans G. Schuetze / Andrä Wolter (eds.): Higher Education Reform: Looking Back – Looking Forward. 2016. 2nd Revised Edition. 2019.

Vol. 9 Ahoud Al-Asfour: Higher Education Privatization in Kuwait. A Study in the Processes of Policy Production. 2019.

Vol. 10 Marta Kowalczuk-Walędziak: Building a Research-Rich Teaching Profession. The Promises and Challenges of Doctoral Studies as a Form of Teacher Professional Development. 2021.

Vol. 11 Gabriella Pusztai / Klára Kovács (eds.): Well-Being of Academic Staff in Rapidly Changing Higher Education: A Focus on Central and Eastern Europe. 2026.

www.peterlang.com

www.ingramcontent.com/pod-product-compliance
Ingram Content Group UK Ltd.
Pitfield, Milton Keynes, MK11 3LW, UK
UKHW041830100926
8556IPUK00002B/104

9 783631 939680